T5-ARJ-299

Research in Criminology

Series Editors
Alfred Blumstein
David P. Farrington

Research in Criminology

Ross Homel

Policing and Punishing the Drinking Driver

A Study of General and Specific Deterrence

With 16 Illustrations

Springer-Verlag
New York Berlin Heidelberg
London Paris Tokyo

363. /25
H76 /p

Ross Homel
School of Behavioural Sciences, Macquarie University, Sydney, New South Wales
2109, Australia

Series Editors
Alfred Blumstein
School of Urban and Public Affairs, Carnegie-Mellon University, Pittsburgh,
Pennsylvania 15213, USA

David P. Farrington
Institute of Criminology, University of Cambridge, Cambridge CB3 9DT, England

Library of Congress Cataloging-in-Publication Data
Homel, Ross.
  Policing and punishing the drinking driver: a study of general and specific deterrence/Ross
  Homel.
    p. cm.—(Research in criminology)
  Bibliography: p.
  1. Drunk driving—Prevention. 2. Drunk driving—Australia—New
South Wales—Prevention. 3. Punishment in crime deterrence.
4. Punishment in crime deterrence—Australia—New South Wales.
5. Random breath testing—Australia—New South Wales. I. Title.
II. Series.
HE5620.D7H66 1988
363.1'2558—dc19

© 1988 by Springer-Verlag New York Inc.
All rights reserved. This work may not be translated or copied in whole or in part without the
written permission of the publisher (Springer-Verlag, 175 Fifth Avenue, New York, NY
10010, USA), except for brief excerpts in connection with reviews or scholarly analysis. Use
in connection with any form of information storage and retrieval, electronic adaptation,
computer software, or by similar or dissimilar methodology now known or hereafter
developed is forbidden.
The use of general descriptive names, trade names, trademarks, etc. in this publication, even
if the former are not especially identified, is not to be taken as a sign that such names, as
understood by the Trade Marks and Merchandise Marks Act, may accordingly be used freely
by anyone.

Typeset by Asco Trade Typesetting Ltd., Hong Kong.
Printed and bound by R.R. Donnelley and Sons, Harrisonburg, Virginia.
Printed in the United States of America.

9 8 7 6 5 4 3 2 1

ISBN 0-387-96715-X Springer-Verlag New York Berlin Heidelberg
ISBN 3-540-96715-X Springer-Verlag Berlin Heidelberg New York

To Lance

University Libraries
Carnegie Mellon University
Pittsburgh, Pennsylvania 15213

Preface

At one level this book is about the impact of specific drinking-driving countermeasures (random breath testing and punishments imposed by courts on convicted offenders) in a particular place (New South Wales, Australia) at two particular times (1983 and 1972). At another level, however, the research reported herein is concerned with general questions of *deterrence*, with the impact of the criminal justice system on the perceptions and behaviors of a broad cross-section of the population. In contrast to much of the research in the drink-drive field, the research questions are concerned with the psychological and sociological processes whereby behavior is altered in the short term as the result of a massive legal intervention or the routine imposition of legal punishments.

The main significance of the research probably lies, therefore, not in the detailed empirical findings for New South Wales (important as I believe these are), but in the construction of a theoretical framework and research design that allow the casual chains linking legal punishments with short-term behavior changes to be identified and the critical links to be quantified. It is my hope that another researcher could take this theoretical model and research design and apply them, with appropriate modifications, to the effects of, for example, a sudden, publicized change in the law in their own jurisdiction. However, it is unlikely that the kind of research described in this book will be carried out every time something like random breath testing (RBT) is introduced. For one thing it is expensive, since it entails (ideally) longitudinal surveys, and for another it may be seen by some pragmatic officials as unnecessarily complex and theoretical. In many instances traffic crash statistics, which are routinely collected and, therefore, do not constitute a major research cost, will provide data sufficient to enlighten all the important policy decisions. Nevertheless, for those in the field who have wondered just how law enforcement influences the perceptions and behaviors of the target population, or who have struggled with the design of a publicity campaign designed with the intention to reduce alcohol-related traffic accidents, there may be a few leads in this book and some ideas for future research.

Much of the material contained in this book has appeared previously only in technical report format. The research results are the product of about 10 years of work and reflect in part the requirements of a PhD which somehow got done along the way. The book bears the marks of the thesis, since it has a monograph structure with a tight focus on the issue of deterrence and its ramifications. Following Australian practice, but in contrast to common American usage, I have avoided the terms "drunk-driver" and "drunken driver," preferring instead "drinking driver" or "drink-driver" (together with "drink-drive" and "drink-driving"). The reasons for this preference, which relate to the ways in which the problem is perceived and socially constructed, are explained in Chapter 1. Moreover, as a matter of style, I have adopted the policy of using the masculine form when referring to the drinking driver. This is not due to any antifeminist bias (quite the contrary), but to the fact that (at least in Australia) about 85% of drinking drivers on the road are men, and 95% of all convicted offenders are men. The use of the masculine form serves as a reminder that drink-driving, like most other social problems, can be blamed mainly on males.

The studies were supported financially by the NSW Drug and Alcohol Authority, by Australian National Opinion Polls (ANOP), and by the Federal Office of Road Safety, Australian Department of Transport. I would like to thank Bruce Flaherty of the Authority and Carol Boughton of the Federal Office of Road Safety (FORS) for their encouragement. Obviously, however, the opinions and conclusions expressed in this book are my own and do not necessarily reflect those of the FORS or the Drug and Alcohol Authority. Special thanks are also due to Les Winton of ANOP, who donated resources to cover the shortfall in funds for the first RBT survey. Without Les' support and expert advice, the study could never have been undertaken. Needless to say, the questionnaires and research design are entirely my responsibility.

Apart from the funding agencies, I have been greatly assisted in the research by a large number of people too numerous to thank individually. The advice and criticism of Jeanette Lawrence, Laurence Ross, and Jacqui Goodnow in particular have been invaluable in helping me to get my thinking straight. Andrew Schachtel, June Crawford, Dale Berger, and Peter Homel greatly assisted by proofreading and commenting on versions of the manuscript. Kathie Smith provided valuable advice and assistance in the preparation of diagrams. Paul Ward originally suggested to me the idea of using canonical correlation methods in an analysis of sentencing. I acknowledge with gratitude his contribution to the development of the index of perceived penalty severity in Chapter 7.

The RBT advertisement in Figure 4.1 is reprinted by the kind permission of John Bevins Pty. Limited and the NSW Department of Motor Transport. Extensive material from a report by the author on random breath testing in New South Wales has been reused in this book by permission of the FORS and Macquarie University. The questionnaires in the Appendix are reproduced with the kind permission of ANOP.

Finally, I owe an enormous debt to my families, both nuclear and extended. My wife Beverley suffered nobly through the completion of a project that seemed simple to start with, but became (as she predicted) a marathon to complete. My children, who were really too young to understand, also suffered many weeks without Daddy as the manuscript was typed and revised many times.

I have dedicated this work to my nephew, who died on his motorcycle as this book was being born.

New South Wales, Australia   Ross Homel

Contents

Introduction

This book is concerned with the impact of the criminal justice system on the behavior of drinking drivers and potential drinking drivers. Specifically, the book is about *deterrence*.

Deterrence is at the heart of the criminal law (Morris, cited in Zimring and Hawkins, 1973), and the criminal law is the primary tool for road accident prevention. The theory of deterrence through criminal law enforcement has determined the major system of public responsibility for road safety in the United States and in countries with a similar cultural heritage, like Australia (Gusfield, 1981b). The major objective of this study is to test the claims for the deterrent effectiveness of two aspects of the criminal justice system by investigating the processes whereby deterrence may take place. The aspects of the criminal justice system which are the focus of attention are, first, the enforcement of drink-drive law by police using what is known in Australia as random breath testing (RBT), and second, the punishments routinely imposed by magistrates (judges) on convicted drinking drivers. The theoretical focus is *the process of deterrence*—the ways in which RBT or punishments succeed or do not succeed in influencing the drinking and driving behaviors of motorists. This book contains the results of two empirical studies, one concerned with *general deterrence* (how RBT in New South Wales deters potential offenders), and one concerned with *marginal specific deterrence* (the study of whether heavy penalties imposed on convicted offenders in New South Wales are better deterrents than light penalties).

Deterring the Drinking Driver

The Value of Studying Drinking and Driving

The research in many ways is the result of an attempt to follow the agenda set by Zimring and Hawkins (1973) and by Andenaes (1974) in their pioneering studies of deterrence. Zimring and Hawkins suggest four criteria for determining research priorities in the field of crime control: the social importance of the problem to be studied, the social benefits that could flow from correct hypotheses about the deterrence process, the amenability of the issue to reliable assessment, and the significance of the issue to deterrence theory as a whole. They assert that the problem of the drink-driver "scores close to the top on all four of our criteria for according research priority" (p. 345). That there has not been more research of the type described in this book is perhaps due to the common perception of drinking and driving as "junk crime"—routine and ordinary (Ross, 1984a, p. 24). Moreover, as Ross observes, the strongly applied focus of much of the literature and its relative inaccessibility in the form of narrowly circulated government reports may have encouraged the gatekeepers of the sociological literature to overlook it or to dismiss it as of no theoretical consequence.

Apart from the social and theoretical importance of the problem, one of the chief advantages of drink-driving over other offenses as a vehicle for research is the ready availability of data. The incidence of the offense is validly and cheaply indexed by publicly available accident statistics. Extensive statistics on police and court enforcement practices are frequently collected as a matter of routine practice and are made available free of the restrictions which sometimes attend the release of information on more serious offenses. Likewise in surveys, respondents will probably be more willing to discuss their drinking and driving practices than, for example, their recent attempts to burgle neighboring houses or to injure their spouse in a domestic brawl.

A further very significant advantage of studying drinking and driving is that sudden, publicized changes in law enforcement methods occur from time to time, making it possible to use quasi-experimental techniques to evaluate the impact of the change (Ross & McCleary, 1983). Random breath testing in New South Wales was introduced in this way. However, the design of the present study differs from the designs commonly employed in quasi-experimental research, in that the emphasis is on the social and psychological *processes* involved in deterrence, rather than on an analysis of fluctuations in crash statistics.

Deficiencies in Previous Research on the Deterrence of the Drinking Driver

There are a number of deficiencies in existing research on the deterrence of drink-driving. Although often of very high quality, the research on the general deterrent impact of innovations in drink-drive law and its enforcement has generally not attempted to trace the assumed causal chain linking objective legal activities with drink-driving behavior. In other words, the process of deterrence has not been examined explicitly, and deterrent effects have been inferred from variations in crash statistics. For example, it has often been argued without direct evidence that declines in traffic crash rates coincident with changes in the law have been caused by increases in subjective arrest probabilities (Ross, 1982). A specific objective of the present study is to remedy this defect by measuring perceived arrest certainty, and relating it to other elements in the assumed causal chain.

The research on the specific deterrent effects of penalties has likewise failed to pay sufficient attention to perceptual variables, since the perceived severities of the punishments inflicted on convicted offenders have seldom been measured. This omission is surprising, given that perceived severity is at the heart of the concept of specific deterrence (Brody, 1976; Gibbs, 1979). Consequently, a major objective of the penalties research reported in Chapters 7 and 8 was to develop a measure of perceived severity of penalties among convicted offenders. However, unlike the study of RBT, which is based on interviews with motorists, the penalties study was restricted to official statistics, so the measure of perceived penalty severity is indirect.

A further deficiency of the literature on penalties is that effects have usually been analyzed as if all offenders were the same. Although the need to investigate the possibility of differential deterrability has often been recognized (Brody, 1976), in practice few researchers have tested for interactions between penalties and offender characteristics, and even fewer have attempted to interpret their results in terms of a typology of offenders. Therefore, another major objective of the research was to develop from the penalties data an offender typology which integrated the information on offender characteristics and reactions to penalties, thus laying the foundation for an understanding of why some offenders may be deterred by certain penalties while others remain relatively unaffected.

In summary, the emphasis in this book is on understanding the deterrence process. The study of the casual chain which is assumed on theoretical grounds to link police RBT activity with drink-drive behavior is one way of studying the process of general deterrence. Similarly the focus on perceived severity of penalties and the development of an offender typology are ways of improving the understanding of how offenders react to punishment and how deterrent potential may vary between offender subgroups. In these respects the studies reported in this book go beyond previous research.

The Deterrence Model

To study the deterrence process, it is necessary to develop a model of how the deterrence of the drinking driver is supposed to take place, and to make explicit the causal sequence linking law enforcement with drinking and driving behavior. Such a model, developed from the general literature on deterrence and from the drink-drive literature, is explained in general form in Chapter 2, and then applied to the RBT study (Fig. 2.2) and to the penalties study (Fig. 2.3). This model is the basis for the analyses reported in Chapter 6 (RBT) and Chapter 8 (penalties). The major purpose of the data analyses is to test the adequacy of the deterrence model as a description of the impact over a 3-year period of severe compared with less severe punishments, and its adequacy as a description of the impact of RBT within 4 months after its introduction.

A fundamental assumption of the model is that general and specific deterrence are one and the same phenomenon, and that it is appropriate to consider them together within a single theoretical framework. As Zimring and Hawkins (1973) observe, specific deterrence is really a special effort to make individuals more sensitive to general deterrence. For Walker (1979), the only difference between the two processes is that one depends on memory and the other on imagination. At the level of theory this statement is fairly accurate, but complications arise when nondeterrent properties of punishment are considered (for example, the sense of injustice). Moreover, because two different populations are involved (potential offenders and those who have been convicted and punished), studies of general and marginal specific deterrence require rather different research designs. Nevertheless, in outlining a model of the deterrence process, it seems appropriate to encompass both phenomena within the same general framework.

If drink-drivers, whether convicted or not, stop committing the offense because they fear legal punishments, they may be said to have been deterred. This phenomenon is often referred to as *simple deterrence*, to distinguish it from more subtle and long-term effects of legal sanctions (Ross, 1982). Simple deterrence is the focus of the present research. Nevertheless, the studies of Gusfield (1981a, 1981b) and Norström (1981) remind us of the broad social context within which drink-drive laws operate and of the many ways in which law enforcement may affect drink-drive behavior in the short term. A very real possibility is that legal innovations like RBT may make it easier for some people to resist peer pressure to drink, thereby reducing the level of drinking and driving by a mechanism other than fear of punishment. This possibility is allowed for in the model and is tested in the RBT study.

Many other subtle variations in the model are considered, particularly with respect to the effects of sociodemographic variables such as age, sex, and alcohol consumption. However, the model does not specify in any detail the ways groups may differ in the extent to which they are deterrable. There is simply not enough known about the causes of drink-driving or the composition of the drink-drive population to allow such theoretical specification. The typology of offenders, developed from the data of the penalties study, is designed to facilitate theoretical developments of this kind.

A Summary of the Research Objectives

The major objectives of the study are:

1. to assess the evidence for the general deterrent effectiveness of RBT in New South Wales, and the evidence for the marginal specific deterrent effectiveness of penalties imposed on convicted offenders, by developing from the literature a general model of the deterrence process and testing it against the data; and

2. to develop from the penalties data a typology which identifies the kinds of convicted offenders for whom legal punishments may be expected to have greater or lesser deterrent effects.

The study addresses three weak points in the literature on the deterrence of the drinking driver:

1. the failure to study in detail the nature of the causal mechanisms linking police enforcement of drink-drive law with drinking and driving behaviors;

2. the failure to focus on the severity of penalties as perceived by offenders experiencing the punishment; and

3. the failure to develop a typology of the convicted drinking driver adequate as a framework for the study of specific deterrent effects.

The Research Designs

Although addressed to the same fundamental question (do people reduce or curtail their drinking and driving in response to the perceived risk and fear of legal punishments?), the different populations referred to in the general deterrence hypothesis and in the marginal specific deterrence hypothesis necessitate rather different research designs.

The RBT study is based on interviews with randomly selected residents of New South Wales. The study was conducted in two stages. The first stage (February 1983) involved a sample of 400 Sydney residents, and was conducted 10 weeks after the introduction of RBT (December 17, 1982). The second stage (April 1983) involved 200 Sydney residents and 400 residents in other parts of New South Wales, and was conducted 6 weeks after the first stage. In addition, in the second stage 185 drinking license holders from the first stage were re-interviewed, making the study longitudinal, and towns and cities outside Sydney were selected so as to ensure maximum variation in intensity of enforcement of RBT over the Easter period. Interviews in both surveys included questions on perceptions of sanctions, exposure to RBT, and behavioral responses to RBT.

The study of penalties reported in this book is limited to the use of data available in official records. However, a method of sampling was devised, described in detail in Chapter 7, which allowed a measure of the relative severity of the penalty. Offender/offense and penalty variables available for all 15,054 PCA (prescribed concentration of alcohol) offenders convicted in New South Wales in 1972 were entered into a canonical correlation analysis, and measures of *entitlement for punishment* and *severity of penalty* were constructed. The basic idea was that the offenders for whom the severity score was markedly higher than predicted from the entitlement score could be assumed to evaluate their penalty as being tough.

The method is based on the assumption that offenders form an idea of the penalty which they can expect, and that the severity of the expected penalty can be estimated statistically on the basis of the average behavior of all magistrates toward offenders with a given set of characteristics (blood alcohol concentration, previous convictions, and so on). Evidence for this proposition is presented in Chapters 2 and 7. Although offenders may regard a just penalty as one which has a calculable relationship with the gravity of the offense (measured, perhaps, by blood alcohol concentration), they are also aware, by and large, that magistrates take into account other aspects of the case (such as previous convictions and things like age). Therefore, the inclusion of these kinds of variables in the statistical analysis seems justified.

A sample of 1,000 offenders was selected from the population of 15,054 offenders convicted in 1972, using the framework described above, and reconvictions over 3 years for drink-drive, criminal, or traffic offenses recorded. The analysis of the relationship between penalties and reconviction rates was carried out in terms of the measure of perceived severity of penalty and also in terms of the actual penalties imposed. The marginal impact of penalties is summarized in the offender typology.

Overview of the Chapters

Chapter 1 sets the scene for the whole study. It is focused on ways of researching the interaction between the criminal justice system and the drinking driver, and on the social and cultural context of drinking and driving. An important question considered in this chapter is the identity of the drinking driver. Discussion of this question helps set the context for the deterrence analyses and for the offender typology developed in Chapter 8. This discussion also entails a consideration of the role of young men in drinking and driving, and prepares the way for an examination of whether they are more or less deterrable than other groups, a consistent subtheme of the data analyses.

Chapter 2 contains a description of the deterrence model and how it can be applied to the study of RBT and to the study of penalties imposed on convicted offenders. The model is related to the theoretical literature on deterrence, and an attempt is made to go beyond utility theory as a description of how the decision to drink and drive may take place.

Empirical research on deterrence is reviewed in Chapter 3, with particu lar emphasis being placed on drink-drive research, reconviction studies, and studies which have employed perceptual measures. The aim of the literature review is not so much to cover exhaustively all extant studies (although the coverage should be fairly complete), but rather to identify the major unanswered questions as well as the most troublesome methodological problems. A description of random breath testing as it operates in Australia, and especially in New South Wales, together with a review of the literature on the effectiveness of RBT, are reserved until Chapter 4. This chapter also contains some general information on how drink-drive law is enforced in Australia. This information should be particularly useful to non-Australian readers who wish to understand the results of the empirical research reported in this book.

Chapter 5 contains the research questions for the RBT study, as well as the research methods. It is paralleled by Chapter 7, which serves the same purpose for the penalties study. Results of the evaluation of the impact of RBT in New South Wales are reported in Chapter 6, using a model of the deterrence process developed in Chapter 2 as the framework for the analysis. Selected aspects of the study of penalties are in Chapter 8, with a particular focus on the surrogate measure of perceived penalty severity and the typology of offenders.

In Chapter 9 the implications for the deterrence model of the results of the analyses are considered and directions for future research discussed. The chapter includes a brief examination of the policy implications of the study. These policy issues are foreshadowed in Chapter 1, and bear on the principles of sentencing, police enforcement procedures, the effects of severe penalties, the appropriateness of particularly punitive measures directed at young men, and the role of publicity in enforcement. The chapter concludes with a discussion of the behavioral impact of law and the value of deterrence-based policies.

1
Drinking Drivers and the Criminal Justice System

In all developed countries, the criminal justice system is assigned a key role in the fight against drinking and driving. The problem is construed not as one of car design (constructing a crash-proof vehicle), or of the regulation of big business (reconciling profits from the sale of alcohol with public safety), or as one of the roadside environment (making it more forgiving of the inebriated motorist). Responsibility is placed squarely on the shoulders of the individual driver. If he cannot be educated or persuaded to separate drinking and driving, then reliance must be placed on the heavy hand of the law to deter, or in the case of the convicted offender, to punish and incapacitate as well. Therefore, to speak of *drink-drive countermeasures* as they currently operate is, by and large, equivalent to discussing the operation of the police, courts, licensing agencies, and prisons. This is particularly the case in Australia, which has a greater commitment to mass breath testing of motorists than almost any other Western nation.

A major purpose of this book is to report the evaluation of the effectiveness of some of the tough legal measures adopted in New South Wales to deter the drinking driver. Specifically, the focus is on the general deterrent effectiveness of random breath testing (RBT) and on the marginal specific deterrent effectiveness of severe versus lenient penalties imposed on convicted offenders. Random breath testing is a particularly important legal measure to evaluate, since it gives police power to carry out preliminary breath tests on randomly selected groups of motorists at arbitrarily selected checkpoints, regardless of whether those motorists have committed an offense.

This chapter is designed to provide a framework both for the theoretical model of the deterrence process proposed in Chapter 2, and for the data analyses in Chapters 6 and 8. In the first section of this chapter, ways of studying the interaction of drinking drivers with the police and the courts are examined briefly. The traditional approach (the approach adopted in this study) is to focus on the impact of the criminal justice system on the behavior of offenders and potential offenders. The second approach, which is usually called *interactionist*, is to focus on the definition of drinking and driving as a crime and on the way in which the problem is managed by the agents of social control (particularly police and court officials).

Some of the insights from the interactionist literature are applied to the drink-driving phenomenon in subsequent sections of this chapter. In the second section the implications for deterrence of the ambivalent status of drink-driving as a crime are explored. This is followed in the third section by an examination of what is known about the composition of the drink-driving population. The composition of the drink-driver population is of particular importance to the study of deterrence, since it is possible that not all drivers are equally deterred by legal punishments. However, the question is not simply a behavioral one—a matter of objective fact—it is also a question of definition and social control. It is argued that definitive answers to the behavioral questions are not to be had from the literature, partly because the research results reflect the shifting definitions and perspectives of competing interest groups.

Ways of Studying Drinking and Driving in the Context of the Criminal Justice System

Cohen (1973) has pointed out that in addition to the stock set of *behavioral* questions which have been the traditional focus of attention in criminology, there are a set of *definitional* questions. There are three major behavioral questions: Why did they do it? What sort of people are they? How do we stop them doing it again? All three of these questions will be considered in the present work, with particular emphasis being placed on the last one. However, the definitional questions will also receive some attention, albeit in a much less detailed and systematic manner. These questions are, in Cohen's terms:

Why does a particular rule, the infraction of which constitutes deviance, exist at all? What are the processes and procedures involved in identifying someone as deviant and applying the rule to him? What are the effects and consequences of this application, both for society and the individual? (p. 13)

Thus in the case of alcohol-related road deaths, we might ask: Why are the manufacturers of alcoholic beverages not held responsible? Why don't we have laws which require vehicle manufacturers to produce crash-proof vehicles (Ross, 1982)? Is drinking and driving really deviant in the opinions of ordinary people? Given that only a tiny minority of drinking drivers are ever apprehended, how do the police come to test and charge certain people and not others? Do all magistrates view drinking drivers as criminals, and how do they vary in their penal philosophies and sentencing behaviors? How, if at all, does affixing the label *drink-driver* to a motorist affect his self-image and his behavior?

These questions are *definitional* because they pertain to how society defines and manages the problem of drinking and driving. The focus is not only on the offenders and their behavior, but also on the activities and preoccupations of the rule-makers and the rule-enforcers, and on the interplay between the two sets of participants in the legal drama. For this reason, the approach is usually referred to as *interactionist*.

Although not addressed to the behaviors of offenders, the definitional questions are behavioral questions to the extent that they ask about the activities and motivations of legislators, police, magistrates, and others involved in the legal process. Moreover, they have a direct relevance to the questions which are focused on the behavior of offenders. For example, a knowledge of the correlates of recidivism is of limited value without a knowledge of how magistrates go about the job of sentencing. A demonstrated bias against young male offenders in the sentencing process might be contrasted with data suggesting that age and sex are unrelated to the probability of reconviction. To take a second example, the behavioral impact of police enforcement of drink-drive law cannot be assessed properly without some knowledge of what kinds of motorists are most commonly the target of suspicion. If young men are the object of a disproportionate share of police attention, a sense of being harrassed and stigmatized may amplify the very problem which such enforcement was theoretically designed to control (this is the phenomenon of *secondary deviation* referred to by labeling theorists such as Lemert, 1978).

This book contains the results of two studies of deterrence, and therefore has a behavioral focus. However, the behavioral research should be viewed as part of a broader research program concerned with the operation of the criminal justice system. A way of conceptualizing the relationship between research focused on definitional and behavioral questions is illustrated in Figure 1.1.

The study of the effects of RBT is largely a study of the effects of a particular form of police enforcement of drink-drive law. This needs to be paralleled by a study of the factors which influence the way in which a motorist comes to police attention for a screening breath test, with an emphasis on the nature of police discretion (Homel, 1983c). The study of the effects of penalties on convicted offenders needs to be paralleled by a study of the sentencing process, with an emphasis on the styles of sentencing employed by magistrates and on the offender/offense characteristics which influence magistrates with different sentencing styles (Homel, 1983b).

In Figure 1.1, the studies of apprehension and sentencing are labeled as *managerial* because they are concerned with how drink-driving is managed and controlled through the criminal justice system. Overarching all the studies is the issue of how drinking and driving is viewed in our society. This is truly a definitional question. Following Gusfield (1981b), it is proposed that behind the drink-drive legislation is the image of the *killer drunk*, the morally flawed character who has committed more than an ordinary

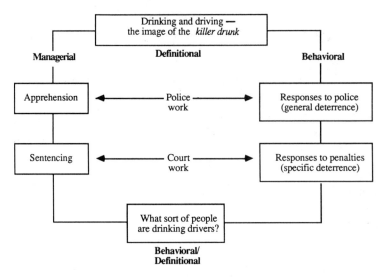

FIGURE 1.1. Representation of the relationship between studies of deterrence and studies of the operation of the police and the courts.

traffic violation. Undergirding all the studies is another general question: Who is the drinking driver? This question has generally been regarded as a behavioral one, and has inspired many offender typologies (Wilkins, 1969). A typology developed within this research tradition is presented in Chapter 8. However, some attention will also be paid to the way in which perceptions of what drinking drivers are like are determined by what the current concerns of the authorities may be. Just as the cultural forms of our society generate a particular type of accountability (the offense of drinking and driving), so the shifting balance of power between various kinds of experts leads to different answers to the question: Who?

An Interactionist Perspective

The interactionist approach to the study of crime and deviance has become popular in the last two decades, particularly through the work of sociologists who have been concerned with the effects of the criminal label on the behavior of those so labeled. Apart from the already noted interest in the agents of control and their interactions with those labeled as criminal, probably the hallmark of the interactionist approach is the concern with constructing the social reality of the criminal (Poveda & Schaffer, 1975). Interactionists are interested in the *meaning* of events for the criminal or deviant, the way in which he understands and interprets the world around him.

Most researchers working within this sociological tradition have emphasized the crucial role played by social audiences, arguing that the responses of others—and how these responses are interpreted—sharply influence an individual's actions (Goode, 1978). An audience may consist of one's peers or some group with whom one is in face-to-face interaction, but it may also consist of one's conception of society at large and of the police, courts, and prisons. Whatever the audience, there is an ongoing creation of meaning within the immediate social setting. Representing an older tradition within criminology, positivists conceptualize crime as a problem of defective individuals impelled by social or psychological forces beyond their control. In contrast to this view, by emphasizing the subtleties of the immediate social situation, interactionists see deviant behavior as the result of a dynamic and negotiable process rather than as the almost inevitable outcome of a preexisting condition.

Although it does not appear to have been often appreciated, there are at least two ways in which the deterrence model, as propounded by classical theorists such as Beccaria and elaborated by modern sociologists, bears a close affinity to the tenets of the interactionist school. It is now commonly recognized that at the heart of the deterrence process is the *perception* by an individual of the costs and rewards associated with the commission of an illegal act (Gibbs, 1975). If these costs and rewards are interpreted broadly to include such things as informal sanctions imposed by one's peers, the interactionist's emphasis on the meaning of the situation to the actor becomes rather pertinent. (The ethnographic research of Gusfield [1981a] on drink-driving in the context of bars, discussed in Chapter 2, is particularly relevant as a bridge between interactionist and deterrence research.) Second, the deterrence model is in accord with interactionism in that it has little place for fixed character traits or acquired dispositions which exert an influence independently of the social environment. Just as the interactionist emphasizes the dynamics of the immediate social setting and an active process of interpretation by the individual, so deterrence theorists see a criminal or deviant act as the outcome of a complex process of evaluation and calculation. The emphasis in both cases is on factors in the immediate setting and in the broader social environment which are interpreted and acted upon by the individual.

Of course an interactionist approach to the study of social phenomena has not been restricted to sociologists. Fifty years ago, the psychologist Lewin proposed that behavior is a function of both the person and the environment, and this interactionist approach has been the subject of considerable development by psychologists since then (e.g., Magnussen & Endler, 1977). Recently Gottfredson and Taylor (1986) investigated person-environment interactions in a study of recidivism, demonstrating that the performance of "good risk" and "bad risk" offenders after being released from jail depended on the quality of the neighborhood into which they were released. They propose a perspective on interactionism called the *prison-environment integrity model*, in which the person, the environment, and the person's behavior in that environment form a single system and influence each other reciprocally.

In the drink-drive field Vingilis and Mann (Mann & Vingilis, 1985; Vingilis, 1985; Vingilis & Mann, 1986) have drawn upon the psychological research of Mischel (1973) and others to develop what they call the "psychosocial control model" as a framework for studying drinking and driving behavior. The essence of this model is that "certain personal characteristics interacting within certain situational references lead to conditions conducive to drinking-driving crashes" (Vingilis, 1985, p. 90). Among the situational references are legal controls, but since the model emphasizes the role of cognitive processes in assimilating environmental information and initiating behavior, as well as the roles of biological and other psychological factors in interaction with influences in both the immediate environment and the larger sociocultural context, the effectiveness of legal controls clearly cannot be assessed without a good deal of additional information. The value of this model, as Vingilis and Mann (1986) point out, is not that it provides a formal theoretical model for drink-driving behavior, but that it presents a framework for analysis and "posits some psychological processes at which the interactions between person and situation that determine behavior occur" (p. 36).

Among the central objectives of the present research are to quantify some aspects of the processes of perception and evaluation which are at the heart of the deterrence model, and to measure features of the social environment—particularly peer pressure to drink and the objective credibility of the legal threat—which could have a direct influence on these processes. Although consistent with an interactionist approach (whether formulated in terms of cognitive processes or in sociological terms with an emphasis on meaning), the logic of this procedure really flows from the nature of the deterrence model itself. Without some understanding of the social contexts in which drinking and driving takes place, and the ways in which an offender or potential offender construes his situation, it is impossible to come to any definite conclusions as to whether he has been deterred by a legal threat.

Drinking and Driving as Crime

A handbook for victims of drinking drivers in the United States (Rochester Against Intoxicated Driving Foundation, 1986) begins with the declaration: "You are the victim of a terrible crime" (p. 1). It was this feeling of outrage at the senseless loss of her daughter Cari, hit while walking one morning to Sunday school, that impelled Candy Lightner to start "her own revolution against a nation of drunk drivers" in September 1980 (Plunk, 1984, p. 14). Since then, citizens' groups in the United States, the most prominent being MADD (Mothers Against Drunk Drivers), have enjoyed astonishing success in persuading legislators to enact a range of tough new laws aimed at drinking drivers. According to Plunk (1984), writing in the *MADD National Newsletter of Fall 1984*, 360 new drunk driving laws were enacted at the state level between 1981 and 1984. Snortum (1988) argues that MADD, RID (Remove Intoxicated Drivers), and other citizens' groups deserve much of the credit for the introduction of "per se limits, implied consent laws, preliminary breath testing, roadside revocations, sobriety checkpoints, and increased use of fines, license actions, and jail sanctions" (p. 59). Imprisonment for up to 3 days is now mandatory even for first offenders in 15 states, and 40 states provide for mandatory jail terms of 2 to 60 days for second offenders (Voas, 1986).

The success of these groups led to the establishment of the Presidential Commission on Drunk Driving in April 1982, whose report in November 1983 stressed (predictably) strategies directed at individual behavior change—education, treatment, publicity, and especially deterrence (Mosher, 1985). As Ross (1984b) notes, politics is very much in the hands of citizen activists and represents their point of view; their point of view is that "the drunk driver is a villain and deserves to be punished" (p. 63). Yet there is considerable evidence that this version of reality is not really shared by all sectors of the American population.

One line of evidence is that *in practice* the enforcement of drink-drive law in the United States is riddled with contradictions and loopholes. Thus Snortum (1984b) cites evidence that in some parts of the United States the odds of conviction for a person arrested for drunk driving the first time are as low as 1 in 20, and that due to plea bargaining many offenders are convicted of a lesser charge. A second line of evidence comes from cross-national surveys: despite the political ferment surrounding drunk driving and the plethora of legislation, Americans continue to drive "while slightly intoxicated" much more frequently than Norwegians (Snortum, Hauge, & Berger, 1986) and are less likely than Swedes to rate drunken driving as a serious crime (Snortum, 1984b). In addition, the level of moral agreement with the law in the United States is markedly less than in Norway (Snortum et al., 1986). All this suggests that MADD's view of the drunken driver as a dangerous criminal has not yet achieved widespread acceptance, despite evidence presented by Snortum (1988) implying that the activities of MADD and the burst of legislative activity may have effected some very recent changes in attitude among some sections of the population.

Thus there is evidence of ambivalence in American attitudes to drinking and driving. However, it should be emphasized that this ambivalence is not restricted to the United States, with its history of relatively lax drink-drive law enforcement. In a number of respects Australian enforcement is much more rigorous and public support for tough measures is higher than in the United States, yet the same kinds of contradictions are evident.

In most parts of Australia the amount of alcohol permitted in the blood of a driver, or the *blood alcohol concentration* (BAC), may not exceed .05 gm of alcohol per 100 ml of blood. This *prescribed concentration of alcohol* (PCA) is as low as would be found in any jurisdiction throughout the world, and is much lower than the level permitted in most parts of the United States, where the limit is usually .10 (Cameron, 1979). Moreover, large numbers of motorists are charged each year under the drink-drive legislation, and convictions represent about one-third of all criminal matters dealt with at magistrates' courts (excluding minor traffic offenses such as speeding and negligent driving).

Lest it be thought that, once charged, there are many points at which the accused can escape punishment, it should be noted that in a typical year in New South Wales, 98% of all positive breath analyses for which records are kept result in a court appearance for PCA, and that 99% of these court appearances result in a finding of guilt (NSW Bureau of Crime Statistics and Research, 1984). These figures stand in marked contrast to those for the United States, but are comparable with Norwegian patterns (Snortum, 1984b). In addition, the laws are enacted and enforced in an atmosphere of public approbation (although citizens' groups have mostly been absent from involvement in the legislative process, again in contrast to the United States).

Consistently, opinion polls have indicated community condemnation of drink-driving and widespread support for vigorous enforcement and severe penalties. In a national poll conducted in April 1974 (Australian Public Opinion Polls, 1974b), alcohol was the factor most frequently cited as a major cause of road deaths. In February of the same year (Australian Public Opinion Polls, 1974a), 93% of a sample of adult Australians rated drunken driving as being "very wrong," compared with 53% who rated speeding in the same way. In August 1975 (Australian Public Opinion Polls, 1975), 62% of Australians called for more severe penalties on drunken drivers, but only 30% called for RBT. By March 1979, the vote in favor of RBT had risen to 73% (Australian Public Opinion Polls, 1979), but in New South Wales in March 1984 (2 years after RBT was introduced), the approval level was a record 91.5% (Cashmore, 1985). These levels of support for RBT are much higher than in the United States (57%) and approach those of Norway (95%) (Snortum, 1988).

Thus people of all ages and both sexes in Australia seem prepared to support a policy of strict enforcement, and there seems little doubt that many view the offense in moral terms. However, these polls sit rather uneasily with other surveys which suggest that drinking and driving is a very widespread phenomenon (Freedman, Henderson, & Wood, 1973; Sloane & Huebner, 1980). Sloane and Huebner estimated that in Victoria in the period November 1978 to January 1979, 10% of the 2 million licensed drivers in the state drove with a BAC over .05. In addition, they found that about 60% of their respondents who reported drinking in the week prior to the interview did not regard drinking drivers as criminals. It is clear that many who condemn the offense in response to a survey must actually commit it fairly often—perhaps not surprising in a nation with the highest alcohol consumption in the English-speaking world.

At the level of law and its enforcement further puzzles are evident. In New South Wales drinking and driving is an offense which is listed not in the Crimes Act but in the Motor Traffic Act. Thus it appears in company not with murder, rape, and arson but with negligent driving, speeding, and crossing an unbroken center line. Moreover, Homel (1983b) has shown that when sentencing drink-drivers, magistrates do not take into account previous nontraffic criminal offenses. The evidence is that for many magistrates, and for many other legal officials, drinking and driving is viewed as not much more serious than a traffic misdemeanor.

The Symbolic Role of Law

An explanation for these apparent contradictions in the United States, and Australia, and probably in other countries as well, may be sought at the level of individual attitudes and psychological processes. For example, part of the explanation for the discrepancy between the different forms of survey data may lie in an "us and them" mentality. People either deny, to themselves and others, that they consume enough liquor to put them over the legal limit, or they consider themselves more able to hold their liquor than others (and are therefore not a danger). Thus, put into colloquial terms, "drinking and driving is wrong when the other guy does it, but it's OK for me because I know my limits." However, individual level explanations do not contribute much to an understanding of the peculiar status of drinking and driving as behavior which, when viewed from some angles, is an excusable traffic misdemeanor, but when viewed from other angles is a contemptible criminal act.

To answer this question, a broader perspective is required. The most promising ideas come from those social scientists who (with interactionists) are concerned with the culture of public problems—that is, with the relationship between shared symbols or ways of seeing and the labeling of some behaviors as deviant, criminal, or morally reprehensible. Anthropologists Douglas and Wildavsky (1982) have attempted this task for environmental dangers, arguing that "a cultural approach can make us see how community consensus relates some natural dangers to moral defects" (p. 7). A cultural theory of risk perception sees the social environment, selection principles, and perceiving subject as all one system.

Gusfield (1981b) has most effectively carried out this type of analysis for drinking and driving. According to Gusfield, behind all drink drive legislation is the image of the killer drunk, the morally flawed character who has committed more than an ordinary traffic violation. The drinking driver is a villain who threatens the lives of others through indulgence in his own pleasure, and is more open to condemnation than the motorist who occasionally lapses from proper driving conduct. Echoing Durkheim (1964), the criminal justice system through drink-drive legislation both expresses a particular system of values and helps to maintain a society against which the drinking driver appears factually and morally deviant. "The punishment of the offender is the ritual action which attests to the validity in fact and morality of the law" (p. 157).

In contrast to drink-driving, traffic offenses are clearly not regarded as criminal. As Braybrooke (1975) has pointed out, traffic offenses do not fit easily into the general criminal justice system since there is either harm without intention or intention without harm, or neither harm nor intention. Traffic offenses are ubiquitous, their perpetrators are representative of the driving population, and the offenses do not carry a stigma. They are a "folk crime" (Ross, 1960). From the legal perspective, traffic law is essentially a form of administrative activity—"the regulation of the flow of automobile traffic in a convenient and safe form" (Gusfield, 1981b, p. 123).

The fact that all motorists are potential traffic offenders has important implications for the status of traffic offenses as noncrimes. Cressey (1974) has highlighted the presence of respectable, powerful, and influential people among the population of traffic offenders, and the consequences of this for police enforcement. He argues that historically the most significant impact of the automobile's advent was the raising up of a different and more powerful population of offenders who claimed the normal prerogative of the rich and powerful: freedom from regulation. Extending his argument slightly, we may conclude that traffic offenses (maybe even serious ones like drinking and driving) are not really crimes because to label them as such would be to criminalize the behavior of the very people who make and enforce the laws.

But, insists Gusfield, while there is much that is similar in the drink-drive laws to those of other traffic offenses, drinking-driving legislation is also unlike traffic legislation and more akin to laws about crimes without victims. In drink-driving it is the behavior itself, the hostile, antisocial menace, which is singled out for greater disapproval. "The enforcement of drinking-driving legislation, from this perspective, is as much a matter of public morality as it is of public convenience and safety. The drinking-driver is a public criminal and a faulty person" (Gusfield, 1981b, p. 129).

Gusfield's emphasis on law and its enforcement as dramas for the consumption of an audience has implications which are critical for deterrence research. In effect, he has challenged the conventional notion that these performances are intended (except perhaps as an afterthought) to achieve a deterrent impact:

I find it useful to see the various parts of the legal process less as artillery weapons aimed at a target than as self-contained games, only tangentially part of a linear strategy instrumental to traffic safety. The police and the courts are attuned to the drinking-driver as criminal offender, not to the traffic analyst's knowledge and concerns . . . the firing of the cannon is as much a matter of the love of noise as of a desire to reach a target (Gusfield, 1981b, pp. 144–145).

The actual enforcement of drink-drive law blunts its cutting edge as a deterrent. As a matter of Law (the law on the books), drinking and driving is a criminal offense; as a matter of law (the world of the police, attorneys, lawbreakers, and magistrates), it is not more than a traffic violation. At the level of the routine actions of daily life, the drinking-driving event becomes part of a negotiated reality constructed through the choice, discretion, and power of the several parties interacting in the process of law. The general and abstract rules of legislation are transformed into a new, less formal set of rules, reflecting such things as organizational and time constraints and the prejudices and theories of individual law enforcement officials.

In practice the enforcement of drink-drive law is a ritual of *upgrading*. The police and the courts are sobered by a perception of drink-driving as a minor sin, no more mortal than other traffic violations. The court process is routinized and penalties are normally far below the maxima specified in legislation. The actual process of enforcement "diminishes the deviance of the drink-driver and restores him to community, slightly dented but still intact" (Gusfield, 1981b, p. 162).

It is for these reasons that the behavioral impact of law is a problematic, empirical question. The implication of Gusfield's analysis is that deterrence, at least on a lasting basis, is a most unlikely outcome.

Who is the Drinking Driver?

The Social Drinker Versus the Problem Drinker

The cultural perspective emphasizes symbols and public rituals, and helps us to see how the phenomenon of drinking and driving is translated through moral outrage at the image of the killer drunk—the hostile, antisocial menace—into specific legislation and enforcement practices. From this point of view, the procedures of law are a morality play for the consumption of an audience. However, Gusfield also argues that the structure of public problems involves a *cognitive* dimension as well as a moral dimension. "Without both a cognitive belief in alterability and a moral judgement of its character, a phenomenon is not at issue, not a problem" (Gusfield, 1981b, p. 10). Moreover, the cognitive dimension is related, in complex ways, to social organization and to arguments about who "owns" the problem of drinking and driving and who is responsible for its solution. A variety of groups and institutions "compete and struggle over ownership and disownership, the acceptance of casual theories, and the fixation of responsibility" (Gusfield, 1981b, p. 15).

In view of Gusfield's analysis, it is hardly surprising that there has been a great deal of debate about the most appropriate way of categorizing drink-drivers. Even the use of the term "drink-driver" in this book in preference to the common U.S. expression "drunk driver" conveys a hidden message, since it suggests that the problem should be seen as driving after drinking, rather than driving carried out by drunks. The distinction is not simply semantic—thinking in terms of "drunken driving" conjures up images of the pathetic but dangerous alcoholic, while "drink-driving" or "drinking and driving" widens the picture to include, potentially, just about anybody who drinks. Moreover the competing terminologies reflect not just different ways of viewing the problem, but a different mix of social and political forces. In the United States, citizens' groups have been able to set the political agenda, whereas in Australia "reform seems to tend generally to be more organizational, professional, and indeed government-based" (Room, 1984, p. 34). Thus in Australia, and probably in Scandinavia as well, road safety and alcohol experts have been more influential in determining the public face of the alcohol-driving problem, leading to "drink-driving" rather than "drunk-driving" and to a .05 limit rather than .10.

Of course simply settling on the term "drink-driving" does not solve the classification problems; if anything, by widening the picture it exacerbates them. Tomasic's (1977) review of the literature leaves the impression that there is no consensus in the field at all. Should we talk, for example, of alcoholics and nonalcoholics, dividing the latter group into "excessive" and "responsible" drinkers? Should a BAC of .15 or higher be evidence of an excessive drinking problem? Are some drink-drivers "typical criminals," while others are "typical motorists?" Raymond (1973) argues that existing evidence suggests that there are two fairly distinct types of drinking drivers. One attracts police attention and gets caught, the other drives in a responsible manner and does not get caught. Her thesis is that a particular type of driver continually comes to the attention of the authorities, regardless of the method of detection used, and this group is similar in characteristics to recognized alcoholics. This implies that all convicted drink-drivers tend to be similar to each other in that they are alcoholics or potential alcoholics, and often have a record of drink-drive, traffic, or criminal convictions.

Raymond's position is supported by McLean and Campbell (1979), whose research might be regarded as typical of its kind. These authors compared a sample of 70 drink-drivers convicted in Victoria with 39 hospitalized alcoholics and 39 university students rated as "heavy drinkers." They found that the drink-drivers and the alcoholics (or problem drinkers) had lower mean profiles on the California Psychological Inventory than did the university group, and that the differences between the drink-drivers and the problem drinkers could probably be attributed to the fact that the problem drinkers were generally older. This implies that drink-drivers are problem drinkers detected early—a useful conclusion for those offering alcohol treatment programs.

The drinking driver as a problem drinker or alcoholic is a recurring theme in the literature. Cameron (1979) has pointed out that in the United States in the 1940s, the "moderate" drinker was seen as the real menace since drivers in an advanced state of inebriation were assumed to draw attention to themselves before they caused any trouble. However, by the mid-1950s, chemical testing in Canada had revealed high BACs in many drivers who were involved in accidents or arrested, suggesting that problem drinkers were a large part of the road safety problem. It was concluded that rational appeals, including those involving the threat of punishment, were unlikely to be successful, and that the appropriate response to the problem was to initiate treatment programs. The unique importance of the small number of problem drinkers was officially recognized when the United States introduced the Alcohol Safety Action Projects (ASAPs) in the early 1970s (National Highway Traffic Safety Administration, 1979). These programs, which were implemented at the local level, emphasized both police enforcement and treatment of offenders.

The redefinition of the drinking driver as deviant problem drinker during the 1960s occurred not only in North America, but in Europe as well. One of the earliest studies in the field of traffic offenses was carried out by Willett (1971), an English sociologist who demonstrated in 1964 the link between conventional criminality and the commission of many serious traffic offenses, including drinking and driving. However, Buikhuisen (1969), a Dutch criminologist, asked whether we should think of a "criminal on the road" or a "patient on the road" (p. 6). He noted a high incidence of alcohol abuse among convicted drinking drivers, and also found them to be more neurotic, more extraverted, more impulsive, less socialized, and more likely to take risks than matched control groups of people free of traffic convictions. One consequence of this transformation of the drinking driver is that ownership of and responsibility for the drink-drive problem pass very largely from the police and the courts to the medical profession and to psychiatrists and psychologists. If the drinking driver is sick, he needs to be cured, not punished.

From his interactionist perspective, Gusfield (1976, 1981b) argues that this view of the problem is not simply a conclusion drawn from unambiguous scientific data, but is also a product of rhetoric and polemic. In discussing an article by Waller (1967), in which the author drew a strong distinction between social drinkers and problem drinkers, Gusfield draws attention to the "literary art of science" (Gusfield, 1981b, p. 83). According to Gusfield, it is not that scientific articles are works of art, but that a rhetorical component is unavoidable if the article is to have theoretical or policy relevance. By selecting certain data and by emphasizing certain relationships the scientist's interpretation involves theater: "It involves a performance and a presentation which contain an element of choice and which both enlist and generate a context, a set of meanings which give content and imagery to his data" (pp. 107–108). Thus in Waller's presentation, and indeed in most of the articles written by psychiatrists and psychologists on this topic, the social drinker is cast as a comic, but not dangerous, figure, while the problem drinker, with his lowly status and compulsive drives, is a figure of pathos, a candidate for therapy.

The selection of data and the emphasis on certain relationships are most clearly seen in the debates over the concept of alcoholism. Researchers cannot even agree on how to define or measure alcoholism or alcohol-related problems (Sanson-Fisher, Redman, & Osmond, 1986), so it is not surprising that the dominant explanation for alcoholism, which is the notion that it is an illness, has been assailed from many quarters. As Finlay (1979) argues, "the illness concept is, after all, a theory—a way of marshalling and organising data" (p. 56). Room (1981, 1983) points out that this concept, with its emphasis on the individual drinker and his problems, is now giving way to an emphasis on the consequences of drinking for the community and for the whole of society. Consistent with Gusfield's analysis, it can be argued that alcoholism is not something which exists in itself, but is rather a social creation of particular times and situations, in much the same way that drinking and driving as a public problem arises out of deeply felt values and fears that are characteristic of a particular culture. It is surely significant that historically the concept of alcoholism rose to prominence after the repeal of Prohibition, when it became convenient to locate the source of alcohol problems in the drinker rather than in the industry which produced the drinks (Wagenaar, 1983).

Unfortunately, the demise of the disease concept of alcoholism, one sign of which was the use of the term "alcohol dependence syndrome" in a recent WHO report (Room, 1981), creates a problem in reviewing the drink-drive literature, in which the term alcoholism has been used freely. Vingilis (1983), in her recent review of studies which examine the relationship between drink-driving and alcoholism, solved this problem in a pragmatic fashion by, in effect, simply accepting anyone as an alcoholic who has been labeled as such in the literature. Although the same approach will be adopted in this book, it should be remembered that alcoholism refers to the label affixed by society to an individual, not to some assumed underlying disease state.

Even accepting this simplification, Vingilis (1983) notes a number of difficulties. Often the alcoholic populations for study are drawn from various treatment facilities and cannot be regarded as representative of the total alcoholic population. In addition, the Michigan Alcoholism Screening Test (MAST), which was devised by psychiatrists Selzer and Lowenstein (cited in Vingilis, 1983) to detect alcoholism among drivers involved in "alcohol-related" collisions, will almost certainly produce a high proportion of falsely positive identifications. Vingilis comments that a first-time drink-drive offender, feeling badly about his drinking but endorsing no other question, would be classified as producing "presumptive evidence of alcoholism" (p. 303). In the light of this kind of obvious bias, Gusfield's (1981b) analysis seems particularly apt.

After reviewing about 50 studies, Vingilis (1983) comes to the conclusion that drinking drivers, drink-drive offenders, alcoholics, and collision drivers represent overlapping but not identical populations. The majority of drinking drivers (people who have driven over the limit at least once) are not alcoholics, but among the "high-risk" groups involved in collisions and/ or alcohol-related violations, the number that could be considered problem drinkers or alcoholics is considerably higher. Vingilis does support the conclusion of Raymond (1973) and others that drink-drive violations and collisions may be one of the early predictors of alcoholism.

Identifying High Risk Drinking Drivers

The National Academy of Sciences' Panel on Alternative Policies Affecting the Prevention of Alcohol Abuse and Alcoholism (1981) has drawn attention to several theoretical distinctions which are necessary if further progress is to be made in determining the nature of alcohol use and its relationship to public problems like drink-driving. One critical distinction, consistent with the abandonment of the disease concept of alcoholism, is between problems caused by episodes of drunkenness and problems caused by total consumption. To the extent that problems are linked with drunkenness, and to the extent that the large number of moderate-to-heavy (but not alcoholic) drinkers get drunk out of proportion to their consumption ("binge" drinking), a high proportion of the social problems associated with alcohol may be contributed by nonalcoholics who get drunk only occasionally. It is likely that for many young men drinking follows this binge pattern.

From this point of view, the small minority of alcoholics still cause problems out of proportion to their numbers, but the fact that drinkers with a lower consumption are so much more numerous means that most of the "problem incidents," including drink-driving, are caused by them. In other words, problem drinking is not restricted to those who may have been designated "problem drinkers" on the basis of consumption, a common practice in the literature (e.g., Selzer & Weiss, 1966). An important consequence of this argument is that although in any sample of drink-drivers alcoholics or problem drinkers will comprise a higher proportion than would be predicted from their numbers in the population, the great majority of drink-drivers will be ordinary drinkers. A further consequence is that it is necessary to look beyond measures of consumption in order to identify high risk drinking drivers.

One factor, suggested by the work of Willett (1971) and more recently by Argeriou, McCarty, and Blacker (1985), is conventional criminality. Many convicted drinking drivers have a record for nontraffic criminal offenses, and these offenders typically have a higher reconviction rate for both traffic and criminal offenses. As Wilson and Jonah (1985) observe, "impaired driving may be just one behavior which is part of a deviant behavioral syndrome typified by high-risk behaviors" (p. 531). In a discussion of predispositional factors in drinking and driving, Vingilis (1984) draws attention to the fact that drive-while-intoxicated offenders frequently have a better knowledge of the law, but are more accepting of drink-driving than other motorists. She also cautions, however, that there is really very little research directed at the identification of potentially high risk drinking drivers. "The populations most at risk from drunken driving are not as well known as those at risk from AIDS, and the drivers most responsible are not profiled as accurately as aircraft hijackers" (Haight, quoted in Vingilis, 1984, p. 28).

Given an interactionist perspective, the reasons for the difficulties in identifying high risk or other types of drinking drivers should be clear. The various subgroups do not exist in their own right just waiting to be discovered; rather, classifications are made by researchers with particular interests operating within certain theoretical traditions. Depending on one's purposes, drinking drivers may usefully be characterized as "alcoholic," "criminal," "deviant," "social drinkers," "binge drinkers," and so on. Moreover, an interactionist approach would suggest that to be most useful, any classification system should be based not only on the properties of the person, but also on the properties of the social context. There may be several high-risk person-situation combinations, and any individual may be a high-risk impaired driver under certain circumstances (Mann & Vingilis, 1985; Wilson & Jonah, 1985).

One of the most useful features of the chapter on the nature of the alcohol problem prepared by the Panel on Alternative Policies Affecting the Prevention of Alcohol Abuse and Alcoholism (1981) was the emphasis on the contexts in which drinkers do their drinking. The context may affect quantities and rates of alcohol consumption, and may also determine the risks to which drinkers are exposed due to hazards in the environment. Because they drink away from home, or because in some situations (like the pub) there may be intense pressure to drink, certain groups, such as young men, may be more prone to alcohol-related problems than others. It may be possible to moderate the risks for these groups without reducing their total consumption.

The Panel's emphasis on contexts is of great importance for the study of the relationship between youth and drinking and driving, since much of what is assumed in the literature about this relationship is based on studies of accident statistics or of convicted offenders. Both types of data are biased by factors such as time and place of drinking and the amount of driving (and hence exposure to risk), and these factors in turn are heavily influenced by the drinking contexts preferred by young men. Since young drivers have been the target of considerable drink-drive legislation in recent years, this discussion of the nature of the drink-driving population will conclude with an examination of their role in accidents and impaired driving.

The Young Driver as Drinking Driver

It is in fact quite common to hear the view expressed that drinking and driving is predominantly a youth problem. For example, Douglass (1982) has advocated substantial redirection of law enforcement efforts to younger drivers and attention to the increased risks caused by low blood alcohol levels among young people. He is particularly critical of the Alcohol Safety Action Program (ASAP) experience.

. . . for some incredible reason, the entire ASAP experience was directed at drivers with chronic drinking problems without recognizing that most young people who are crash involved are not necessarily deviant or chronic drinkers, but are certainly intoxicated and involved in acute trauma (p. 5).

However, detailed epidemiological research reveals a picture which is far more complex than these generalizations suggest. The research of the Panel (1981) illustrates how variations in drinking practices and in the contexts of drinking may be correlated with other variables which influence police enforcement and accident involvement. Other researchers have identified a wide range of factors in addition to alcohol as influences on the high number of traffic crashes involving young people. These factors include inexperience (Cameron, 1982; Clayton, 1985; Jonah, 1986; Mayhew, Warren, Simpson, & Haas, 1981; Pelz & Schuman, 1971), driving exposure (Cameron, 1982; Carlson, 1973; Mayhew et al., 1981; Pelz & Schuman, 1971; Robertson, 1981), feelings of rebellion, hostility, machismo, and alienation (Cameron, 1982; Carlson & Klein, 1970; Klein, 1972; Snow & Cunningham, 1985; Sobel & Underhill, 1976), risk-taking, including the nonuse of seat belts (Jonah, 1986; Peck 1985), drugs (McPherson, Perl, Starmer, & Homel, 1984; Whitehead & Ferrence, 1976), and peer group characteristics (Clark & Prolisko, 1979; Knapper, 1985; Nusbaumer & Zusman, 1981).

There is no doubt that alcohol is a contributing causal factor in many crashes involving young people, as it is for crashes involving older drivers. However, there is a fair body of evidence that young drivers on any given trip are less likely to drink and drive than older drivers, and that if they do drink and drive they consume less alcohol than their older counterparts (Homel, 1986; Mayhew et al., 1981). Nevertheless, small quantities of alcohol appear to have a substantially greater effect on young drivers than on older groups, and in any case they engage in impaired driving more often since their lifestyle provides them with more opportunities to combine drinking and driving (Berger & Snortum, 1985; Jonah, 1986; Mayhew et al., 1981; Mayhew, Donelson, Beirness, & Simpson, 1986). One further complication is that young drivers are not a homogeneous group. There is little doubt that men drink and drive more than women (Freedman et. al., 1973; Sloane & Huebner, 1980; Warren & Simpson, 1980). Moreover, there seem to be differences in the crash rates and levels of drinking and driving among different age groups: 16- and 17-year-old drivers are at high risk of *nonalcohol*-related crashes, but after the age of 18 (the legal age of drinking in many jurisdictions) and up to about the age 25, alcohol-related crashes become a bigger problem (Cameron, 1982; Pelz & Schuman, 1971).

This review of the epidemiological evidence highlights the way in which alcohol is frequently singled out from a vast array of other factors as a uniquely important cause of accidents involving youths. Although very few attempts have been made to *equate* the drink-drive problem with the problem of young drivers, there is a strong movement in both Australia and North America to isolate young drivers as a *high risk* group with respect to drink-driving. As a result of this movement, the legal age of drinking has been increased in many states and provinces in North America (Vingilis & De Genova, 1984), and in Australia a zero BAC requirement for drivers in their first year of driving has been introduced in several states (Kelly, 1980; South & Johnston, 1984).

Homel (1983c) has argued that one reason for this legislative attention to youth is the similarity in Western culture of the perceived attributes of the killer drunk and those of the adolescent or young man (antisocial, hedonistic, uncontrolled, frivolous, etc., [Gusfield, 1981b]). A further practical consequence of these perceived attributes is that in both Australia and in North America young men appear to be over-represented in the conviction statistics (Homel, 1983c; Vingilis, Adlaf, & Chung, 1982) because they are the target of a disproportionate amount of police attention. It is clear that if the conviction statistics are to be understood, attention must be paid to the criminal justice system, particularly the operations of the police (Carr-Hill & Stern, 1979).

Overview: Who is the Drinking Driver?

At the level of Law and political pronouncements, drinking and driving is an offense committed by individuals who are judged to be a menace to society and who are castigated for their moral dereliction. If not quite criminals in the sense of being a murderer or a rapist, drinking drivers are deemed to have committed more than an ordinary traffic violation. Those concerned with the development of scientifically objective classifications of drinking drivers are not immune to these symbols and images which motivate legislators and law enforcement officials. Thus the special attention devoted to young drivers as a high risk group is an example of how attributes of the killer drunk can be imputed to, or be more clearly seen in, certain classes of persons. Moreover, drink-driver classifications reflect in part the struggle for ownership of the problem on the part of various groups (or in the case of the liquor industry, the struggle to disown the problem). This struggle is most clearly reflected in the attempts by some members of the medical profession to label drinking drivers alcoholics rather than social drinkers, and hence to subsume the problem within the medical model.

These suggested classification systems are not necessarily wrong, and for some purposes they may be quite useful. There does seem little doubt that people who are alcoholics or problem drinkers, labeled as such through various social processes, do comprise a part of the drink-drive population, and in the case of convicted offenders probably a fairly significant part. Indeed, convicted offenders seem to consist of a variety of deviant sub-groups, including those with a serious criminal record (Argeriou, McCarty, & Blacker, 1985; Buikhuisen, 1969; Willett, 1971). However, the status of young men as exemplars of the drinking driver is much more uncertain than would be supposed from some of the recent literature. No doubt drinking drivers on the road are overwhelmingly male, and certainly the convicted drinking driver is frequently a man younger than 30 years, but there is evidence that the age and sex profile of the convicted offender may to some degree be a function of selective police practices (Homel, 1983c; Vingilis et al., 1982).

A general conclusion, supported by the kind of model of drinking behavior proposed by the Panel on Alternative Policies Affecting the Prevention of Alcohol Abuse and Alcoholism (1981), is that it would probably be a mistake to concentrate too much on the search for deviant or pathological subgroups. As Radzinowicz and Hood (1975) pointed out in a discussion of traffic offenses, criminological research has gradually freed itself from bondage to the positivist position that all criminals are inherently different from normal people. The most common view nowadays seems to be that although a small proportion of offenders may commit large numbers of serious offenses, perhaps the bulk of crime is committed by quite ordinary people in the face of particular temptations and opportunities (Clarke, 1979). This position is consistent with the interactionist perspective, and with deterrence theory.

From the point of view of deterrence, two conclusions seem warranted. First, there is no compelling evidence that more than a tiny minority of drinking drivers are so dominated by a craving for alcohol that they may be impervious to threats of punishment. Indeed, as we have seen, the very concept of such an addiction is increasingly being called into question (Room, 1983), and even if it does apply in some cases, such people will not necessarily be addicted to *driving* (Zimring & Hawkins, 1973). Second, given the little understood complexities of person-environment interactions there is no well-validated typology which can be gleaned from the general drink-drive literature and used as a basis for a theory of the differential impact of the legal threat, although many hypotheses concerning differential deterrability have been proposed (e.g., Wilson & Jonah, 1985). The most impressive typologies which have been developed relate to arrested offenders, and therefore have most direct relevance to specific deterrence. These typologies are considered further in Chapters 3, 8, and 9 in the specific deterrence context.

Summary

One objective of this chapter was to demonstrate the value of an interactionist approach to the study of the deterrence of drinking and driving. Among the hallmarks of the interactionist approach are the emphasis on the rule-makers and rule-enforcers as well as the offenders, the concern with the perspective of the offender, and the focus on the interaction between the individual and the social environment.

Although drinking and driving has been the target of an unprecedented array of legislative measures in the United States, Australia, and other countries in the past few years, drink-driving is not unambiguously a crime and in practice the enforcement of the law is a ritual of upgrading, with the arrested offender usually being spared the full weight of the law. Gusfield's (1981b) analysis of drinking and driving as a public problem contains an implicit rejection of the idea that law and its enforcement can have much of a deterrent effect on behavior. Indeed, from this perspective law enforcement is not intended to be a road safety measure as much as it is intended to be a drama for public consumption.

A significant feature of the drink-drive literature reviewed in this chapter is the conflicting evidence on the nature of the drinking driver. The drinking driver is not necessarily an alcoholic, accepting the traditional usage of that term, and it has certainly not been demonstrated beyond doubt that a policy of isolating young men as a high risk group of drinking drivers is justified. To some extent, the question of who the drinking driver "really" is is unanswerable, since the results of any analysis are partly dependent on the ideological bias of the researcher. Moreover, interactionist theory suggests that the nature and incidence of drinking and driving will depend on complex and poorly understood interactions between the person and elements of the social environment. One consequence of the confused state of the literature is that there is no ready-made typology of drink-drivers which can be used as a basis for incorporating statements about differential deterrability in a theory of the deterrence process.

In Chapter 2, a model of the deterrence process is proposed. The model is stated in general form, covering both general and specific deterrence. The emphasis is on the casual chain which is assumed to link judicial and police activity with drink-driving behavior, but with one exception no predictions about differential deterrability are made. Using this model, the impact of RBT on drinking and driving behaviors is investigated in Chapter 6 and the effects of punishments imposed on convicted offenders are investigated in Chapter 8. The problem of developing a typology is also dealt with in Chapter 8 in the context of responses to the experience of punishment. The typology is not itself part of the model, but could form the basis for developments in those aspects of the model relevant to the effects of legal punishments on convicted drinking drivers.

2
A Model of the Deterrence Process

Deterrence Theory and the Deterrence Doctrine

According to the classical doctrine of deterrence, which is generally traced to the writings of the 18th-century utilitarian philosophers Bentham and Beccaria, "The rate for a particular type of crime varies inversely with the celerity, certainty, and severity of punishments of that type of crime" (Gibbs, 1975, p. 5). Thus, it is argued that if punishment for drinking and driving in a jurisdiction is swift, sure, and tough, the rate of occurrence of the offense will be correspondingly low. From this perspective, the beauty of RBT is that it should influence the variable which historically has been regarded as the most important, namely the *certainty* of punishment. After all, if any motorist at any time can be breath-tested, the potential drink-driver, no matter how skilled he believes he is in avoiding detection when over the limit, will have cause to think twice before actually committing the offense. In the same way, it is argued, the convicted offender who has suffered a severe punishment, perhaps a long period of license disqualification or even imprisonment, will have reason to reflect at leisure on his experience and on the futility of further malefactions.

At the heart of the arguments for deterrence as a tool for social control is the belief that the behavior of human beings can be modified by making them fearful of the consequences of committing illegal acts. As Gibbs (1975) has put it: "*Deterrence* can be thought of as the omission of an act as a response to the perceived risk and fear of punishment for *contrary* behavior" (p. 2). One virtue of this definition, involving as it does perceptions, motivations, and the calculation of risks, is that it highlights the inherently psychological nature of the assumed phenomenon. More than that, however, deterrence is a psychological process which is clearly intended to take place within a broad social context. The punishments which are supposed to follow the commission of prohibited acts are prescribed by law, and offenders are apprehended and punished not in a psychological laboratory, but in the real world of human activity.

As Beyleveld (1979b) points out, a theory for predicting deterrence needs to specify the concrete social circumstances which determine specific beliefs and perceptions of sanctions and ways of processing them. Such a theory should be distinguished from statements of the deterrence *doctrine* (e.g., swift, sure, and severe punishments reduce crime), not only because the doctrine is vaguely formulated, but because it explains neither deterrence nor the offense rate. Propositions of the deterrence doctrine are in fact predictions from a "theory for predicting deterrence" (Beyleveld, 1979b, p. 216). For Beyleveld, such a theory need not specify all the details of the actual decision-making process. For example, we know very little about the calculation of personal utilities (or indeed whether deterrence occurs in this fashion at all), and elaboration of these processes requires empirical research.

In this chapter an attempt is made to specify a model which predicts a deterrent effect of RBT as implemented in New South Wales and which also predicts a deterrent impact of severe as opposed to light penalties actually imposed on offenders. The emphasis is on the social and psychological processes linking the official actions of legal agencies (RBT, the imposition of punishments) with the drinking-driving behavior of threatened or punished individuals. As indicated in the Introduction, a fundamental assumption is that general and specific deterrence are one and the same phenomenon, and that it is appropriate to consider them together within a single theoretical framework.

A distinction which is not made explicitly in the model is that between criminal *involvement* and criminal *events*. This distinction is proposed by Cornish and Clarke (1986) as a major component of what they call the "rational choice perspective" on crime:

Criminal involvement refers to the processes through which individuals choose to become initially involved in particular forms of crime, to continue, and to desist. . . . Event decisions, on the other hand, are frequently shorter processes, utilizing more circumscribed information largely relating to immediate circumstances and situations (p. 2).

They illustrate the initial involvement process for the offense of burglary, postulating that a wide range of factors such as upbringing, previous experience, and generalized needs combine with reactions to chance events (such as an urgent need for cash) to produce a readiness to commit burglary and then an actual decision to do it.

Although the distinction between involvement and the crime event makes a great deal of sense for offenses like burglary, since most individuals must overcome a number of social and psychological hurdles before embarking on a life of crime, it is rather less useful for the offense of drink-driving for which chance events and the exigencies of the immediate situation would seem to play a more leading role. As we saw in Chapter 1, drink-driving is not unambiguously a crime in public consciousness, it is an offense committed reasonably often by a large number of motorists, and many people do not feel it is a particularly bad thing to do. Consequently, an involvement model for drink-driving (distinct from an event model) would really need to focus on *persistent or high risk offending*, but as we have seen we currently lack the theoretical and analytical tools for the development of such a model. Nevertheless, the models proposed by Cornish and Clarke (1986) for initial involvement, the event, continuing involvement, and the desistance all contain elements which are of direct relevance to drink-driving. These elements include previous experience with offending and with law enforcement, conscience and moral attitudes, persuasion by friends, and the perceived costs of various forms of action when driving after drinking is contemplated.

Thus, given the nature of drinking and driving as an offense, the deterrence model proposed in this chapter is mainly a model of the event. The model is outlined in summary form in the next section, and then some basic definitions of deterrence are proposed. Following this, the assumptions of the model are examined in some detail, beginning with the notion of rationality in human decision making. Some ideas from *prospect theory* are applied to the drink-drive decision as a way of dealing with criticisms of utility theory as a description of the decision-making process. After a discussion of the nature of the evidence required to decide whether deterrence has taken place or not, the model is applied both to RBT and to the effects of punishment, and elaborated within each context.

The Model

Four key propositions undergird the model. First, individuals must be *exposed* personally to law enforcement or must receive information about law enforcement before they can be deterred. Second, neither exposure to law enforcement nor perceptions of legal sanctions have any influence on behavior apart from a process of *evaluation* whereby these experiences or cognitions are given a meaning. Third, the extent to which an individual is deterred can, in principle, be measured by questioning him. Finally, there must be an investigation of the effects of official legal activity (RBT, punishment) on *nonlegal sanctions* which inhibit or encourage drinking and driving, so that the deterrent effects of legal activity can be clearly distinguished from other effects.

Briefly stated, the model proposes that official legal activities and drink-driving are linked through exposure to law enforcement, leading to perceptions of severe and/or certain sanctions and hence to attempts to avoid committing the offense when there is a risk of driving while impaired. The classes of people to whom deterrence will be applicable are, in the case of RBT, drivers who drink (at least occasionally), and in the case of penalties, those who have been penalized. The behavior of all types of persons can be described in terms of the deterrence model, including the behavior of persons who might have highly developed consciences concerning drinking and driving and the behavior of "high risk" people such as those labeled as problem drinkers or alcoholics. However, it is recognized that a number of nonlegal sanctions may also influence behavior, often in directions contrary to that of legal sanctions.

The incorporation of nonlegal sanctions in the model highlights the importance of the physical and social environment. The individual is assumed to be subject to three, and only three, types of social control mechanisms: guilt feelings resulting from the internalization of norms, the threat of social stigma resulting from informal sanctions, and the threat of physical and/or material deprivation. One source of material deprivation is formal, legal punishments (loss of license and so on), but other sources include the costs and inconveniences involved in *not* driving after drinking (e.g., paying for a taxi home after a party and then again the next morning to pick the car up), as well as the nonlegal material costs entailed in committing the offense. Probably the major material cost which can result from drink-driving is having an accident. Fear of crashing has presumably restrained many a driver from foolhardy and illegal driving behaviors even when the direct legal threat has had negligible impact. Although for many offenses the threat of social stigma operates to discourage offending, for drinking and driving the reverse frequently occurs, with the peer group imposing informal punishments if an individual does *not* drive after drinking. Thus feelings of guilt if an individual does drink and drive (self-imposed punishment) and informal sanctions imposed by peers often operate in opposite directions.

Given this complex array of contradictory sanctions, it is proposed that when an individual who has been drinking or who plans to drink makes decisions about transportation he is faced with a *choice between losses*. If he drives after drinking, he runs the risk of getting caught or of having a crash, and may in addition feel guilty. If he avoids driving after drinking, he may be ridiculed by his friends and he will certainly have to make alternative arrangements for transportation. Thus the perceived costs associated with nonlegal sanctions enter into the individual's decision-making process together with the perceived costs of legal sanctions in a complex and possibly interactive fashion.

Perceptions and evaluations of sanctions (both legal and nonlegal) influence behavior. Legal sanctions may encourage individuals to adopt strategies to avoid drinking and driving on occasions when committing the offense is a possibility, but informal sanctions may have the opposite effect. In particular, the belief that threatened punishments would be personally unpleasant and the belief that the chances of arrest are high lead to increased attempts to avoid drink-driving. (Note that the measurement of attempts to avoid drink-driving necessarily requires some degree of reporting of motivations by the respondent, since only actions which are undertaken for a specific *reason* are of theoretical interest.) Such avoidance strategies, in turn, lead to less drinking and driving (or to drinking and driving at lower blood alcohol levels) and this results in fewer traffic crashes.

Given that informal and formal sanctions operate in opposite directions in many cases, a prediction concerning deterrence is not possible unless the effect of legal sanctions on the informal sanctions can be stipulated. In the case of both RBT and the infliction of penalties, it is proposed that the legal actions reduce peer pressure to drive after drinking by providing an exculpatory defense or legitimate excuse for actions taken to avoid the offense. In the case of those with a conviction, the more severe the punishment actually experienced, the more cogent the excuse.

To be a sociological model, perceptions must be linked in some way with the objective legal actions. It is proposed that official legal activity is relevant to the individual only inasmuch as it enters the world of his everyday experience. Laws which are passed or punishments which are imposed without the knowledge of the individual cannot affect his decision-making processes, at least until the activities of other people who affect that individual are altered. Thus *exposure* to the legal actions is the variable linking official activity with perceptions and evaluations of sanctions. The more intensive or frequent the official activity, the more intense or frequent will be the exposure of the threatened or punished population. Exposure might occur through observing or experiencing police breath testing or through knowing others exposed in this way. In addition, the experience of punishment through a conviction is a form of exposure. The model predicts that those exposed to legal sanctions in any of these ways will be fearful of the consequences of drinking and driving and will modify their behaviors accordingly. On the other hand, individuals who have broken the law with impunity, particularly those who have successfully driven over the legal limit, will not fear legal sanctions as much as those without this experience of law breaking. Thus successful drink-drive episodes are also a form of exposure to objective legal activity.

However, the relationship between exposure and fear of sanctions is not automatic. Once again, it is proposed that an individualized process of evaluation takes place. The experience of being randomly tested may have more impact on one driver than on another; the experience of a heavy fine and a long period of disqualification may be interpreted by a repeat offender as fair or at least to be expected, while the same penalty may be interpreted by a first offender as extremely tough. Similarly, a motorist with a previous conviction for drinking and driving may perceive the chances of apprehension for drink-driving at exactly the same level as a motorist without a conviction, but may because of his earlier encounter with the law respond more strongly to the legal threat. Thus different forms of exposure to legal activity, or differing constructions of the meaning of similar experiences, will lead to differing evaluations of threatened or actual legal sanctions even if there are no differences in *perceptions* of what the legal threat actually is.

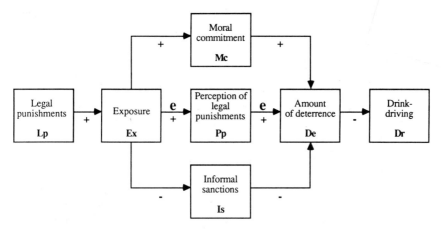

FIGURE 2.1. A model of the deterrence process.

Finally, the model incorporates a range of social and demographic variables such as alcohol consumption, age, and sex. These variables are assumed to influence all components of the model, including rates of exposure, evaluations of the meaning of exposure, perceptions and evaluations of legal sanctions, strategies to avoid drinking and driving, drink-driving behavior, and the intensity with which nonlegal sanctions apply. Although predictions concerning the nature of the effects of some of these variables can be made, the possibilities are so numerous and complex that they are better dealt with on an ad hoc basis when the major paths of the model are investigated.

The details of the model, as well as its antecedents, are examined throughout this chapter. It may assist at this point, however, if the model is represented in diagrammatic form, albeit in a greatly simplified fashion (Fig. 2.1). Since in a number of respects the model is an extension and elaboration of that proposed by Gibbs (1975), a similar form of terminology is used. The arrows denote positive and negative casual relationships, and the small e's denote the process of evaluation.

At a first step toward explanation and elaboration of the model, it will be useful to clarify further the key concept of deterrence by introducing some definitions. However, it should be recognized that there is considerable controversy in the literature about definitions, and even more argument about appropriate forms of evidence for the occurrence and effects of deterrence. Indeed, the literature fairly bristles with reviews, overviews, theoretical arguments, conceptualizations, reconceptualizations, criticisms, and rebuttals. Tittle (1980a) has referred to "an almost chaotic situation" (p. 24), claiming that "the literature is burdened with a large number of critical hypotheses and issues that remain problematic because of absent or incomplete data or because theoretical arguments and/or research findings are divergent or contradictory" (p. 24).

It is impossible, in general, to come to any definite conclusion about the offenses affected by general deterrence or the conditions under which general deterrence might operate (Anderson, 1979; Gibbs, 1979; Tittle, 1980b). Fortunately we are on stronger ground in the study of drinking and driving than in the study of other offenses, since the drink-drive researcher has a number of advantages (such as access to reliable and relatively valid measures of the extent of drink-driving) which make the field uniquely suitable as a context for deterrence research (Ross, 1973, 1982). However, since deterrence is an imprecise concept, even drink-drive research suffers from many of the evidential problems which plague research into the effects of actual or threatened punishment on other types of offenders.

It would be tedious (in fact, impossible) to present a blow-by-blow account of deterrence research as it has developed in recent years. The present chapter is focused rather on issues which are most salient to a study of the deterrence of drinking and driving. The definitions discussed below are those most relevant to the study of RBT and the study of penalty severity.

Definitions of Deterrence

A distinction is usually made between *general deterrence*, which relates to the impact of the threat of legal punishments on the public at large, and *specific deterrence*, which relates to the impact of legal punishments on those who have suffered them. However, these terms in no way do justice to the complexities inherent in the concept of deterrence. Gibbs (1975) developed a typology consisting of 16 combinations of conditions, reflecting the individual's previous experience with punishment for the crime in question and with punishment for other types of crimes, and his history of commission of crimes of the type in question or of other types. Thus, for example, *potential restrictive deterrence Type IV A* relates to a situation in which an individual has never suffered any prescribed punishment for any crime, but has previously committed the type of crime in question as well as other types of crime.

Gibbs (1975) points out that the empirical validity of the assertion "punishment deters crime" is relative to particular types of conditions. Since it would be extremely cumbersome to formulate a separate theory for each of 16 types of deterrence, it is fortunate that some simpler definitions derived from Gibbs will suffice. *Absolute deterrence* denotes instances where an individual has refrained throughout life from a particular type of criminal act at least in part because of the fear of punishment, while *restrictive deterrence* is the curtailment of or reduction in criminal activity for a period because of the fear of punishment. Since absolute deterrence pertains to individuals who have never committed the crime in question, it is likely that any deterrent effects of punishment are largely restrictive in nature. This would seem to be particularly the case for drinking and driving, where substantial proportions of the population at risk report having committed the offense at least once (Freedman, Henderson, & Wood, 1973; Job, 1985). To limit the meaning of general deterrence, Gibbs (1975) equates it with absolute and restrictive deterrence. *Specific deterrence* may be defined as the omission or curtailment of some type of criminal activity by an individual throughout a period because he has been punished for an offense and is therefore unwilling to risk being punished again. Note that this definition deals explicitly with the possibility that punishment for one type of offense (say drink-driving) deters an offender from committing other types of offenses (perhaps speeding).

A further distinction which is important when assessing the impact of penalties is between *absolute specific deterrence* and *marginal specific deterrence* (Gibbs, 1975). All studies of the correlations between penalty severity and recidivism rates deal implicitly with marginal specific deterrence, the effects of severe punishments compared with lenient ones. A more important question, however, is the effect of conviction and punishment in absolute terms. To answer this latter question, it is necessary to compare the frequency of criminal acts among individuals who have committed a crime but went unpunished with the frequency among those who have been punished for the crime. A confusing aspect of this terminology is that *absolute* is used in a sense that differs from its meaning when it applies to general deterrence.

A fundamental question arising out of the usual definitions of deterrence is the nature of sanctions, the independent variable in the equation. It has been implicitly assumed so far in the discussion that deterrence is based on the threat of state-imposed legal sanctions, and indeed much deterrence research has focused entirely on legal punishments. However, as Grasmick and Green (1980) point out, general sociological theory posits three mechanisms of social control: the threat of guilt feelings resulting from the internalization of norms (i.e., self-imposed punishment); the threat of social stigma resulting from informal sanctions imposed by peers; and the threat of physical and/or material deprivation, one source of which is formal, legal punishment. Should the term deterrence apply only to the operation of legal sanctions, thus relegating other sanctions to the status of covariates or moderating variables, or should all forms of sanctions be incorporated in a general deterrence model, as Grasmick and Green (1980) and Tittle (1980a) argue? To some extent, the decision is a matter of convenience, provided the importance of investigating the effects of all types of sanctions is recognized. In keeping with most previous uses of the term, deterrence in the present study will refer to the effects of legal sanctions, but the roles of peer pressure, internalization of norms, and nonlegal material sanctions are included as additional factors in the model (Gusfield, 1981a; Norström, 1981).

A final problem of definition is closely related to the question of sanctions. Should deterrence refer only to the effects of legal sanctions in inhibiting individual deviant impulses by the mechanism of fear (as Gibbs [1975, 1979] argues) or should other preventive mechanisms be included? Gibbs (1975) enumerates nine possible ways that punishment may prevent crime, other than through fear. These mechanisms are incapacitation (e.g., imprisonment limits opportunities to commit crime), punitive surveillance (e.g., probation and parole make the offender visible to authorities), enculturation or socialization (public knowledge of laws is furthered by punishment), reformation (the moral jolt of arrest or punishment), normative validation (legal punishments reinforce social condemnations of an act), retribution (legal punishments discourage crime victims or their families from seeking revenge), stigmatization (the anticipation of stigma may deter the typical citizen more than the punishment itself), normative insulation (incapacitating punishments like imprisonment reduce the influence of offenders on the attitudes and values of others), and, finally, habituation (people may initially conform to the law through fear or for some other reason, but eventually compliance becomes a habit). In Gibbs' (1979) view a definition of deterrence which included all possible preventive consequences of punishment would make it a "sponge concept" (p. 667), a contention vigorously disputed by Tittle (1980a). In this study we will once again opt for simplicity of terminology, using the term deterrence to refer to the mechanism of fear. This definitional restriction does not, of course, entail turning a blind eye to the operation of other mechanisms, but it is consistent with a desire to develop a research design focused on a small number of manageable questions which are clearly central to deterrence research.

In summary, "deterrence" in this book will refer to *the effects of legal sanctions on behavior through the mechanism of fear of legal punishments.* This is what Ross (1982) calls *simple deterrence,* to distinguish it from other possible effects of law, particularly the long-term educative or habit forming effects (Andenaes, 1977). A confusing aspect of the drink-driving literature is that simple deterrence is often used when general deterrence (as used in this book) is meant, and general deterrence is used when general prevention (as used by Andenaes, 1974, 1977) is meant (e.g., Snortum, Hauge, & Berger, 1986). The terminology adopted in this book is more or less consistent with that of Andenaes and Gibbs: general deterrence is reserved for the fear component of law, and general prevention for the (usually) long-term educative or habit-forming effects.

The difficulties involved in identifying and measuring the effects of non-deterrent preventive mechanisms should not be underestimated. As Gibbs (1979) has wryly noted, even the *possibility* of such effects creates horrendous evidential problems in deterrence research. For example, when considering the effects of drink-drive law and RBT, there is a very real possibility that any long term impact will not be achieved through deterrence but through normative validation (Norström, 1981; Zimring & Hawkins, 1973). However, in the words of Ross (1982), ". . . demonstration of the origins of non-legal norms in the historical exposure of a population to specific legal threats is extremely hard to accomplish by scientifically persuasive techniques" (p. 9). This problem is largely beyond the scope of this book.

Deterrence, Human Rationality, and Drinking and Driving

Utility Theory

Isaac Ehrlich (Ehrlich & Mark, 1977), an economist who has written extensively on the subject of deterrence, has referred to the "heretical" nature of the proposition that potential offenders respond to incentives (p. 293). The notion is heretical because for many years the majority of sociologists and criminologists have been committed to a positivist tradition in which criminals are seen as ill or maladjusted, and therefore rehabilitation or treatment have been the favored control policies. Positivists emphasize deterministic explanations, conceptualizing crime as a problem of maladjusted individuals, defective families, or of alienating communities (Poveda & Schaffer, 1975). Punishment as a tool for social control has, within this tradition, been regarded with repugnance (Menninger, 1968), and some have even characterized deterrence as a form of "human sacrifice" (Walker, 1979, p. 139). Moreover, functionalist sociologists, the dominant school for many years, had little time for force as a mechanism for social control, emphasizing instead internalization of norms and avoidance of social disapproval as the primary inhibitors of illegal behavior (Grasmick & Green, 1980).

As Palmer (1977) notes, the debate about the deterrence hypothesis is to some extent a debate between disciplines, with economists on the whole finding evidence in its support, and sociologists finding the opposite (especially with respect to the death penalty). In economic theory the decision to engage in crime depends on the benefits and costs associated with crime and with alternative lawful activities. Increasing the penalties for a crime or the chances of apprehension are, from the economist's viewpoint, ways of increasing the costs involved in committing the crime. An individual will commit fewer crimes if the benefits from crime decrease, the costs of crime increase, the benefits from lawful activities increase, or the costs of lawful activities decrease (Palmer, 1977). One complication of economic theory is that benefits from crime can be pecuniary or nonpecuniary, the latter referring to the enjoyment which comes directly from the criminal act itself. Clearly the benefits from drinking and driving are nonpecuniary in nature but it is not clear how these benefits can be identified, measured, or weighted.

Underlying the economic model is the idea of rational potential criminals weighing possible consequences of their actions, both positive and negative, and taking advantage of a criminal opportunity only if it is in their self interest to do so (Cook, 1980). Economists are aware, however, that individuals respond differently to equivalent criminal opportunities. They differ in their willingness to accept risks, their "honesty preference" (p. 217) or moral attachment to the law, their evaluation of the profit to be gained from a crime, and their objective circumstances, such as their skills in evading capture (Cook, 1980). Nevertheless, they argue that these kinds of variables can, in principle, be incorporated into the model of rational decision-making.

Carr-Hill and Stern (1979) have expressed in mathematical terms the basic model employed by economists and others. Referring to property crimes, they assume that a potential criminal starts off with wealth W. If he gets away with the crime he gains G, to give him wealth $W + G$, but if he is caught his loss is L, leaving him with $W - L$. However, individuals differ in the value they accord to gains and losses of a given amount, and hence it is customary to refer to the *utility* of a consequence, $U(.)$. If the probability of apprehension is p, the expected utility EU for a given individual if he commits the crime is defined as:

$$EU = (1 - p)U (W + G) + pU (W - L)$$

The rational individual maximizes his expected utility, and hence commits the crime if $EU > U (W)$. In the extreme case when capture is certain, EU reduces to $U (W - L)$ and the crime will not be committed, since the utility function is monotonic (although not linear). Conversely, if the probability of capture is zero, EU reduces to $U (W + G)$ and the rational individual would definitely commit the crime. It follows that in order to deter crime, authorities need to increase p, although the exact level required will vary from individual to individual since utility functions are unique. Alternatively, penalties (L) could be increased, or access to property could be made more costly for the criminal, reducing G. Note however that this model does not incorporate any nonpecuniary benefits, such as the utility of the act itself.

Utility theory has a long history, dating back at least to Bernoulli in the 18th century, but in more recent years attempts have been made to apply comprehensive scientific theories of both a prescriptive and descriptive nature to human behavior, especially gambling decisions (Lee, 1971). (Prescriptive theories of choice impose consistency or rationality by beginning with a set of mathematical axioms governing the behavior of hypothetical people.) For example, it is possible to replace the actual probabilities in Carr-Hill and Stern's (1979) model with subjective probabilities, a necessary step if these models are to have any value in predicting real crime behavior (in this case, we should strictly speak of *subjective* expected utility). Attempts have been made to estimate the shape of the utility function for individual subjects, but as Lee argues, this requires an enormous amount of effort for only a slight improvement on predictions of choices based on actuarial values. Indeed, the mathematical developments of utility theory, beginning with Von Neumann and Morgenstern (1953), have been rather more impressive than the applications to behavioral decision theory. Lattimore and Witte (1986) refer to a number of empirical problems with the expected utility model. These include the phenomenon of "preference reversal," in which an individual simultaneously prefers one choice but places a higher value on the other choice, "context effects," in which decisions depend on how they are represented (e.g., as insurance or gambling), and the common use of heuristic principles leading to systematic errors in assessing probabilities.

However, as Pitz and Sachs (1984) note, *EU* theory has been and continues to be productive despite its limitations, since it has yielded deeper insights and prompted more refined questions than would have been possible without it. For example, some researchers have recently carried out experiments to determine the effects of introducing a multidimensional definition of utility, incorporating such concepts as "regret" (p. 143). Pitz and Sachs consider that "the interaction of prescriptive and descriptive theory through multi-attribute formulations of decision problems promises to increase further its prescriptive value . . . as well as its descriptive power" (p. 144).

Researchers investigating the effects of legal sanctions on drinking drivers often mention utility theory without considering its implications in any explicit fashion. The studies conducted by Summers and Harris (1978, 1979) and by Shapiro and Votey (1984) are exceptions to this rule.

The main purpose of Summers and Harris' research was to provide, through an integrated conceptual framework based on utility theory, a computer simulation model to guide systematic development and evaluation of drink-drive countermeasures. The conceptual framework, and the research questions with which the study concludes, are probably the most valuable features of the report. Beginning with utility theory, Summers and Harris (1978) cite research which suggests that most people are characterized by risk avoidance. They argue that if an outcome is potentially severe, people tend not to take the risk even though the probability of the outcome might be very low. The model which they develop is very comprehensive, incorporating perceived risk as well as laws, driver trips, enforcement, adjudication, and information feedback. In the model, general deterrence operates to feed back information through various media (e.g., word-of-mouth exposure) to increase the perceived risks entailed in drink-driving. Since data were not available for the key variables such as perceived risk, values were developed empirically by iteration until simulation outputs were consistent with outputs expected from the literature. The authors concluded, among other things, that relatively small changes in perceived risk are likely to produce large changes in the number of drink-drive trips or related accidents. They also concluded that word-of-mouth feedback from drivers caught is not likely to reduce drink-driving appreciably, and that the countermeasure with greatest potential is a combination of vigorous enforcement and widespread publicity concerning this enforcement.

Shapiro and Votey (1984) developed a theoretical model based on utility theory which allowed the probability of driving after drinking to be related to the perceived utility of drinking and driving, the perceived cost (or utility) of an arrest, the actual costs (penalties) and the actual probabilities of arrest. The model incorporated a coefficient alpha which related subjective to objective arrest probabilities, and model parameters were estimated from aggregate Swedish arrest data for the period 1976–1979. However, in applying the model to aggregate data a large number of simplifications had to be introduced, including the assumptions that subjective arrest probabilities are an exponential function of actual arrest probabilities, that the only personal characteristic which affects the exponent (alpha) is number of previous arrests, and that legal costs for an individual can be replaced by the expectations of various components (such as period in jail) for a whole community. Nevertheless the analysis yielded the interesting result that an arrest reduces the probability that a person will drive while drunk, either by increasing the perceived probability of arrest or by increasing the unpleasantness of an arrest.

These studies illustrate how testable and nontrivial predictions can be generated through a rigorous application of utility theory combined with plausible assumptions about the roles of key social variables. The continuing productivity of *EU* theory, albeit in a much more complex form than that usually considered in discussions of crime, is encouraging for proponents of deterrence. Nevertheless, it is as well to take cognizance of the arguments of those who attack the whole idea of rationality in criminal decision making, especially since drinking and driving may be one of the less calculating offenses. (One of the drink-drive offenders interviewed by Petersen [1982] was asked whether he thought drinking after driving was worth the risk. He replied: "Oh, I always think about it before, but when you get to the pub and have a few drinks you never think about it till after" [p. 43].)

Objections to a Model Which Assumes Rational Decision Making

A RED HERRING

One of the earliest challenges, not only to the predictions of the deterrence doctrine but also to the rationalistic psychology upon which it was assumed to be based, came from psychologists interested in learning theory. Andenaes (1974) cites some psychological studies in which attempts were made to elucidate the problems of deterrence by reference to laboratory animal research, where there is little place for rational calculation on the part of the subject. Although some of these researchers found evidence to support the deterrence doctrine, particularly with respect to the importance of certainty of punishment, most were skeptical that legal punishments could have much impact in practice. Most psychologists have argued that legal punishments lack the properties required for effective punishment, such as swift, continuous, and repeated application (Chopra, 1969).

The great majority of deterrence theorists have rejected the claim that the predictions of the deterrence doctrine can be proved or disproved from laboratory experiments (Andenaes, 1974; Geerken & Gove, 1975; Gibbs, 1975; Zimring & Hawkins, 1973). Andenaes' summation is most eloquent and most pertinent to the approach adopted in the present study:

The application of legal punishment is the result of the violation of a *general norm* which prescribes punishment and which the offender normally will know in advance. *The whole experience derives its meaning* [italics added] from this relation between the general norm and the application of punishment in the individual case. The situation is very different from the situation of the confused rat or pigeon which is desperately trying to adapt its behavior to the incomprehensible manipulations of the psychologist (pp. 185–186).

However, despite the general consensus that legal punishments are more generalized and qualitatively different from the punishments administered by psychologists in a laboratory, attempts are still being made to bring deterrence under the umbrella of learning theory. Recently, Cavender (1979) has claimed that since criminal behavior is operant behavior, operant learning theory provides an appropriate standard for the evaluation of deterrence.

Cavender limits his evaluation to specific deterrence, comparing the operation of legal sanctions with the criteria for effective punishment developed by Azrin and Holz (cited in Cavender, 1979). These 12 criteria include principles which state that escape from punishment should be impossible, punishment should be intense, each response should be punished, and so on. Cavender concludes that legal punishments do not satisfy a single criterion, and that therefore the predictions of a specific deterrent effect of sanctions cannot be sustained. However, Cavender's argument is really based on a sleight of hand which appears to make plausible the proposition that deterrence theory and operant learning theory have enough in common to make evaluation of deterrence in terms of learning theory principles a reasonable thing to do.

The argument is heavily qualified, and Cavender finds it necessary to abandon the strict environmental determinism of Skinner in favor of a model which has some place for human interaction and reflection. Nevertheless, the 12 criteria for evaluation all appear to arise from conventional laboratory research, and in the end he contradicts himself by arguing that the introduction of legal sanctions along the lines dictated by learning theory would be socially and ethically unacceptable. That, of course, is just the point. Deterrence theorists are not concerned with the effects of electric shocks administered in a laboratory, but rather with the effects of actual legal sanctions, which are subject to the constraints of law.

To evaluate the predictions of deterrence theory, it is necessary to deal adequately with its assumptions. It is not sufficient to assert that criminal behavior is operant behavior and is therefore maintained by its consequences without also demonstrating that the alternative model of criminal behavior underlying deterrence (which in minimal form includes the idea of perception of legal sanctions and evaluation of profits and losses) is incorrect or inferior. In effect, the learning theorist who criticizes the deterrence theorist is arguing that *if* human beings were like animals in a laboratory and *if* the punishments administered were like current legal sanctions then such punishments would not be very effective in suppressing criminal behavior. This may be true, but it is of no interest.

CRIMINOLOGICAL CRITIQUES

A number of criminologists have reacted angrily to the modern emphasis in criminology on crime control and deterrence. For example, Cressey (1978) has attacked the foundations of the classical school, rejecting the notion of free will and arguing for a return to the kind of positivist criminology which sought the causes of crime, if not in individual pathology, then in "the kind of social organization characterizing modern industrialized nations" (p. 183). Fattah (1980, 1983) has gone even further than Cressey in attacking the idea of deterrence and its foundation in assumed human rationality: ". . . if deterrence does work, it is likely to affect only the rational, thoughtful, premeditated behavior of normal people under normal circumstances. The problem is, very few people will commit serious, premeditated crimes under normal circumstances!" (Fattah, 1980, p. 82). He adds, however, that "man is not a rational being, he is a rationalizing creature" (p. 83), and that the economist's view of the potential criminal is nothing more than a "legal fiction or a philosophical abstraction" (p. 80).

Other criminologists have adopted a more moderate approach, seeking a model which allows deterrence in some circumstances but which also takes into account the many complex forces which may determine behavior. Henshel and Carey (1975) suggest a conception of man as *goal-seeking but not information-seeking* (p. 57). Such a man may be influenced by legal sanctions, but only if he hears about them and only if the source of information is credible. In the model proposed by Henshel and Carey and also in the model proposed in the present study, *public knowledge* of legal sanctions is of critical importance.

Webb (1980) has proposed a 3 × 3 table for assessing the applicability of the deterrence model. The three rows of the table correspond to three population subgroups proposed by Zimring and Hawkins (1968), namely those who abide by the law because of the socialization process, those who are on the margin of crime (who will commit the crime given the opportunity), and the criminal group (who commit a given crime and have certain social, psychological, or attitudinal characteristics which set them apart from the general population). The three columns of the table correspond to three kinds of acts: instrumental (e.g., planning a bank robbery), compulsive (e.g., theft because of drug addiction), and impulsive (e.g., shoplifting as a spur-of-the-moment act). He claims that deterrence applies to only two of the nine cells of the table: instrumental acts committed by the marginal or criminal groups.

Applying Webb's table to drinking and driving, it is probably fair to say that given the widespread use of alcohol in our society, there are fairly large marginal and criminal (habitual drink-driver) groups, but it is not clear whether the behavior is instrumental, compulsive, or impulsive. In certain circumstances it could be all three, so Webb's (1980) classification system fails to clarify the status of drinking and driving as a deterrable offense. Moreover, despite its grounding in common sense, we have little evidence for the empirical validity of Webb's system.

Zimring and Hawkins (1968), from whom Webb derived one dimension of his table, were not concerned with developing a set of categories to which people could be allocated. Rather, they attempted to build a framework for analysis which took into account the fact that some people refrain from criminal activities for reasons other than fear of punishment, and that the remainder respond (if at all) to legal threats in a variety of ways and through a variety of mechanisms. This perspective has been taken into account in the development of the model proposed in this study by including nonlegal sanctions related to moral beliefs and to peer pressures.

More difficult is the other dimension of Webb's table, referring to criminal acts as instrumental, compulsive, or impulsive. Not only is it not clear how drink-drivers should be classified in terms of this dimension, it is not clear that the distinctions are useful for understanding the deterrence process. As Andenaes (1974) has pointed out, fear may be an element in behavior which is not rationally motivated. Cornish and Clarke (1986) maintain that a rational choice perspective on criminal behavior does not "exclude the operation of pathological motives acting in concert with rational means to secure 'irrational' ends" (p. vii). Many offenses (like theft committed by drug addicts) which might be classified as compulsive could just as easily be analyzed within a deterrence framework by assigning a very high value to the utility associated with the commission of the criminal act. Bennett and Wright (1984), in a study of burglary offenders, conclude that there was little evidence of compulsivity or impulsivity in the burglars' accounts of their actions. Cornish and Clarke refer to the "essentially nonpathological and commonplace nature of much criminal activity" (p. 6). Dix and Layzell (1983) suggest that most cases of drinking and driving are premeditated and that many drivers know they are over the legal limit but consider themselves perfectly capable of driving.

Nevertheless, the debate about rationality and decision making is not capable of quick or easy resolution, and deterrence theorists need to deal somehow with the argument that at least some crime is nonrational in nature and therefore not capable of control through the threat of punishment. Cook (1980) has attempted to meet this challenge. He points out that deterrence theory is concerned with making predictions about *aggregate behavior*. The accuracy of such predictions does not require that every person act predictably, only that some be capable of rational decision making. Moreover, a person whose judgment is clouded by emotion or inebriation may still be guided by his personal "standing decisions" (p. 220), which in turn may reflect concern with the threat of punishment. There is some evidence for this latter argument from the alcohol and drink-driving literature. The Panel on Alternative Policies Affecting the Prevention of Alcohol Abuse and Alcoholism (1981) cited evidence that heavy alcohol consumers are responsive in their drinking to the same economic factors as moderate drinkers (maybe they buy liquor when they are sober), and Snortum, Hauge, and Berger (1986) found that heavy drinkers in Norway were capable of exercising restraint when cast in the driving role. Thus the existence of high risk or heavy drinking groups does not preclude the possibility of a rational response by these people to costs or incentives, at least when they are not drinking.

Despite these arguments, there is a clear need for research which throws light on the ways in which decisions deviate in predictable ways from rationality. It is significant that every theorist has recognized in one way or another that deterrence is a cognitive phenomenon, and since cognitive phenomena are usually considered the province of psychologists, psychological theories are potentially of great importance in deterrence research. Cook (1980) hails Carroll's (1978) experimental research as an entering wedge to further research which applies modern cognitive psychology to the study of the effects of legal sanctions. In Carroll's (1978) model we have "the 'psychological person' who makes a few simple and concrete examinations of his or her opportunities and makes guesses that can be far short of optimal" (p. 1513). Carroll found in a series of three-outcome gambles involving crime and punishment that most subjects focus on one dimension, that different subjects focused on different dimensions, and that the expected utility model was not supported. He clearly saw his research as establishing a new paradigm for deterrence research, since he asserted that "the debate between sociologists and economists has now become a forum" (p. 1520).

Unfortunately, a search of the recent literature has not revealed the expected flood of psychological publications on deterrence, although the collection of studies edited by Cornish and Clarke (1986), organized around the theme of "the reasoning criminal," demonstrates that good progress has been made since Carroll's (1978) pioneering paper. For present purposes it will be helpful to focus (with some of the authors in *The Reasoning Criminal*) on one alternative to expected utility theory, *prospect theory*, to clarify the ways in which the decision whether or not to drink and drive may be viewed by the potential offender (Tversky & Kahneman, 1981).

Prospect Theory and the Drink-Drive Decision

Three key concepts of prospect theory will be applied to the drink-drive decision: the ideas of *framing, decision weights*, and *precommitment*. These concepts in no way exhaust the applications of prospect theory to criminal decision-making, as Lattimore and Witte (1986) make clear, but are selected for discussion here because of their usefulness in explaining drinking and driving.

FRAMING

Tversky and Kahneman (1981) distinguish two phases in the choice process: an initial phase in which acts, outcomes, and contingencies are framed, and a subsequent phase of *evaluation*. *Acts* are simply options among which one must choose (to drink and drive or to take some action which does not involve drinking and driving), *outcomes* are the consequences of these acts (e.g., getting home quickly or spending an uncomfortable night sleeping on the floor), and *contingencies* are the conditional probabilities that relate outcomes to acts (e.g., the chances of getting caught if you drink and drive). A fundamental difference between prospect and utility theory is that in prospect theory outcomes are judged relative to current "wealth" as the reference point, and outcomes are gains or losses around this point rather than final "wealth" positions (Johnson & Payne, 1986).

Tversky and Kahneman show that an important aspect of framing is whether the problem is construed as a choice between gains or as a choice between losses. For example, with 600 lives at risk, a choice (on the one hand) between the certain saving of 200 lives and a 1/3 probability of the saving of 600 lives and the 2/3 probability that no people will be saved can be contrasted with a choice between the certain death of 400 people or the 1/3 probability that no one will die and the 2/3 probability that 600 people will die. Actuarially, all alternatives entail an expected loss of 400 lives, but in the first case the choice is presented in terms of lives saved, in the second in terms of lives lost. For the first framing the majority choice is *risk averse* (people tend to opt for the certain saving of lives), but for the second framing the majority choice is *risk seeking* (people tend to shun the certain loss of lives). In the language of decision theory, this suggests that the utility or value function is S-shaped: concave for gains and convex for losses. In addition, Tversky and Kahneman (1981) and Kahneman and Tversky (1982) demonstrate that the response to losses is more extreme than the responses to gains, in that the pleasure of winning a sum of money is much less intense than the pain of losing the same sum. Thus the value function is asymmetric.

We can apply this model to the drink-drive decision. Imagine that a man has traveled by car to a party and knows that he has drunk enough alcohol to put him over the legal limit; this is his current situation or "wealth" position. Depending on his circumstances, he has a number of choices. He could simply drive home and run the risk of a crash as well as the risk of apprehension and punishment for driving with the prescribed amount of alcohol, or perhaps he could leave his car, take a bus or taxi home, and return to pick up his car the next day, or perhaps he could persuade a sober companion to drive him home, either in his or his companion's car. The precise options are not as important as the general question: How is he likely to frame the decision problem? In general, it seems highly likely that the problem will be construed as a choice between *losses*, a sure loss if he does not drive home, and a possible loss if he does. According to prospect theory, he will probably act in a risk-seeking manner; in other words, commit the offense. Prospect theorists would not deny that offenders might be influenced by calculations concerning possible losses if apprehended, but would argue that given the framing of the problem as a choice between certain and possible losses, there is in most cases a bias toward avoiding the certain loss. Moreover, as Carroll and Weaver (1986) observed for shoplifters, few offenders consider the *distal* consequences of offending, which in the case of drinking and driving are also the merely possible consequences: arrest and conviction or having an accident. The demands of the immediate situation are paramount.

Some careful thought is required to clarify the nature of the losses entailed in the choices facing the potential drink-driver. Apart from the various costs and inconveniences associated with finding alternative transport there are likely to be, as noted earlier, strong social pressures on many people to drink heavily and drive home afterwards. Gusfield (1981a), in a most interesting ethnographic study of drinking-driving in the context of bars, argues that "the failure to drive after drinking is the event that needs to be explained" (p. 160). Starting from the assumption that one's self is an object about which the human being can think and feel, he argues that actors attempt to manage the self-impression conveyed by their actions. "It is in how the individual handles the risks of drinking and driving and of drinking-driving that the self is presented and one's moral status performed" (Gusfield, 1981a, p. 160). This suggests that for many drinkers the most serious cost flowing from a decision not to drive home is to be portrayed as incompetent in one's own eyes or in the eyes of one's peers. Such a portrayal is one of the nonlegal sanctions posited by Grasmick and Green

(1980), although it is one of the more interesting aspects of drinking and driving that the sanction operates to encourage, not inhibit, law-breaking.

Given the work of Norström (1981, 1983), it is necessary to make one other entry in the ledger of possible losses: individuals who believe that drinking and driving is an immoral or antisocial act may experience strong feelings of guilt if they do drink and drive. Such self-imposed punishment is the second of Grasmick and Green's (1980) nonlegal sanctions, and to the extent that it occurs may be regarded as a *sure* loss associated with the act of drinking and driving. As noted earlier, Zimring and Hawkins (1968) have argued for the existence of a law-abiding group in the community consisting of people who have received strong moral training in their early years and who cannot commit crimes because their self-concepts will not permit them to do so. However, the model proposed in this study corresponds to a parallelogram of forces, rather than to a division of the population into those to whom deterrence applies and those to whom it does not. A person's conscience is only one force influencing behavior, competing with peer pressure and fear of punishment, although in some cases the force of conscience may be the major influence.

In summary, the decision whether or not to drink and drive seems best framed as a choice between losses. There are two kinds of certain losses associated with *not* drinking and driving: the costs and inconveniences entailed in finding alternative transport, and one's portrayal as incompetent in one's own eyes and in the eyes of one's peers. On the other side of the coin, feelings of guilt, if they occur, may be viewed as a sure loss entailed in the decision to drink and drive. In addition, some possible losses flowing from arrest and conviction or having an accident are entailed in the commission of the offense. Prospect theorists would predict that unless guilt feelings are very strong, people will generally behave in a risk-seeking manner and avoid the certain losses inherent in finding another way home. This prediction seems generally consistent with observation (Steenhuis, 1983).

DECISION WEIGHTS

In addition to the emphasis on framing, prospect theory differs from the expected utility model in its treatment of probabilities. In utility theory the utility of a less than certain outcome is weighted by its actuarial or subjective probability (p): in prospect theory the value of a less than certain outcome is multiplied by a decision weight $\pi(p)$, which is a monotonic function of p but is not a probability. Applied to drinking and driving, p is the perceived probability of arrest. The weighting function has a number of properties, which are described by Tversky and Kahneman (1981), but for present purposes the most interesting feature is that although events with a very low or zero probability are discounted altogether ($\pi(0) = 0$), moderately low probabilities are overweighted ($\pi(p) > p$).

This distinction between p and $\pi(p)$ is a very useful feature of prospect theory not found in utility theory. Applied to crime decisions, a distinction can be made between *perceptions* of arrest probabilities and the weighting or *evaluation* of those perceived probabilities. Similarly, through the value or utility function a distinction can be drawn between perceptions of sanctions and the evaluations of these sanctions (Tuck & Riley, 1986). For example, two potential offenders may agree that the chance of being randomly breath tested in the next month is quite high, but differ markedly in the weight they accord this perception in their drinking and driving decisions. Similarly, two individuals may have very similar (if inaccurate) perceptions of penalties for drinking and driving, but may evaluate this perception in different ways (Buikhuisen, 1974). It is of some importance that the sociologist Tittle (1980a), in his wide-ranging study of deterrence in a general population sample, strongly emphasized the need for the distinction between perceptions and evaluations to be drawn for sanction severity. Our analysis of prospect theory suggests that the distinction should also be drawn for the probability of arrest (see Dix & Layzell, 1983, and Bennett & Wright, 1984, for empirical support).

The properties of the decision weight discussed before suggest that under normal circumstances police enforcement has little impact on drink-drive behavior, given that the actual probability of apprehension is of the order of one in a thousand and can therefore safely be equated to zero (Ross, 1982). However, during a special campaign or police blitz, the subjective probability of apprehension may be elevated out of the "negligible" into the "moderately low" category, even if the actual chances of getting caught are still less than 1 in a 100. Following the predictions of prospect theory, the weights $\pi(p)$ attached to these probabilities will be such that the psychological threat will be exaggerated out of all proportion to the actual threat and the campaign will have more impact than would be expected from strictly actuarial calculations, at least until the subjective probabilities sink back once more into the negligible category. This pattern predicted by prospect theory is consistent with observations of the effects of enforcement campaigns in many parts of the world (Ross & LaFree, 1986).

PRECOMMITMENT

A final feature (or consequence) of prospect theory as discussed by Tversky and Kahneman (1981) is relevant to deterrence. The authors compare the dependence of preferences on frames to the dependence of perceptual appearance on perspective, and go on to show how the metaphor of changing perspective can be applied to other phenomena of choice, such as the problem of *self-control*. The idea is that just as Ulysses requested that he be bound to the mast of the ship in anticipation of the irresistible temptation of the Siren's call, so in general an individual may take action in the present to render inoperative an anticipated future preference. This phenomenon of *precommitment* ("standing decisions" in Cook's [1980] terms or "self-regulatory systems and plans" in Vingilis & Mann's [1986] interactionist model) may be particularly relevant to the drink-drive decision, and may be one of the more direct ways in which laws like RBT have an effect on behavior. That is, legal interventions may be important not so much for their effects on the balancing of losses when the decision is all but made, but for the way in which people may be encouraged to employ preventive strategies while completely sober, such as leaving the car at home or, even more drastically, giving up drinking altogether.

LIMITATIONS OF PROSPECT THEORY

These three aspects of prospect theory—framing, decision weights, and precommitment—have been included in this discussion of deterrence, since these concepts promise to yield insights into how human decisions depart from rationality (in the sense of utility theory), yet do so in a predictable fashion. However, we still seem to be a fair distance from a psychological theory of decision-making under risk which can be applied in an analytical fashion to the study of deterrence (Johnson & Payne, 1986). There are many aspects of decision-making not covered adequately by prospect theory or by any other theory, such as the use of heuristics or information processing strategies, which cause people to depart significantly from the prescriptions of formal decision theory (Pitz & Sachs, 1984). It would seem that if the notion of rationality is to be salvaged, it may have to be in the form of *limited or bounded rationality* (Johnson & Payne, 1986; Simon, 1957), substituting "the incredibly clever economic man of decision-making theory with a choosing organism of only limited knowledge and ability" (Douglas & Wildavsky, 1982, p. 77). Henshel and Carey's (1975) notion of human beings as goal-seeking but not information-seeking reflects a similar outlook.

It is important to recognize that human decisions, including those concerned with law-breaking, are made within a social environment. What appear in the laboratory to be short sighted or limited decisions may be quite functional in everyday life. Although this possibility has recently been recognized by psychologists (". . . heuristics may be adaptive mechanisms for coping with a complex, dynamic environment, not just efforts to overcome cognitive limitations" [Pitz and Sachs, 1984, p. 140]), the case has been expressed most clearly by anthropologists Douglas and Wildavsky (1982) in their study of risk and culture. As part of a critique of prospect theory and of the notion of limited rationality, they warn against an excessively individualistic theory:

We now think it is time to incorporate some sociological dimensions into the description of simplifying procedures. Humans are not isolated individuals. Their sociality should be included in the analysis of how their minds work. In risk perception, humans act less as individuals and more as social beings who have internalized social pressures and delegated their decision-making processes to institutions (pp. 79–80).

This suggests that a complete study of deterrence would be fully situated in the social world of the potential offenders, paying close attention to the "infra-structure of everyday comportment" (Douglas & Wildavsky, 1982, p. 81).

Measuring Deterrence: Gibbs' "Fundamental Problem"

One of the more interesting consequences of the attempt to find evidence for deterrence is the facility with which one is led to very complex theoretical and empirical problems. For Gibbs (1975) the fundamental problem is expressed as a paradox: regardless of whether an individual commits a crime or not, it is not evidence for deterrence. If he commits the crime, clearly he has not been deterred. However, if he does not commit the offense, the omission might be attributed to the effects of one of the nonlegal sanctions, such as feelings of guilt. At the heart of Gibbs' difficulty is his adherence to a strict positivism, which assumes that people cannot be expected to be able to give authentic accounts of the reasons for their behaviors.

Gibbs recognizes that in principle a direct measure of deterrence would solve all the evidential problems. In the case of drinking and driving, such a measure would relate directly to the relative frequency with which an individual contemplated but refrained from drink-driving because of the perceived risk of punishment. He insists, however, that such a measure cannot be derived from observations of that individual's behavior, and that ". . . it would be naive to base a purported measure of deterrence on reasons given by individuals for refraining from criminal acts (not to mention practical problems entailed in attempting to gather such data)" (p. 15). This appears to be the only point in his book where Gibbs entertains the possibility of a direct measure of deterrence based on questioning.

In taking this position Gibbs is presumably not claiming that his respondents would all be liars. Rather, the assumption is that people are forgetful, lazy, occasionally defensive of their actions and beliefs, and are always impelled by a desire to present themselves to the interviewer in as favorable a light as possible. Moreover, it is proposed that even if internal states and feelings are not simply epiphenomena, people are incapable of reliably reporting relevant features of these internal states. This means that when a question relies for its answer on memory, challenges the propriety of the interviewee's public image, or deals with feelings, motivations, and other states of mind, the responses should be treated with great caution or discounted altogether.

It follows from this perspective that the use of interviews to gather data is mostly a matter of convenience. Since it is impossible to follow a large number of people around and observe their behavior, we must rely on reports of what they say they do (or have done). Followed to its logical conclusion, the person within this philosophical tradition is reduced in status to an organism with a variety of properties which can be determined entirely by outside observers. This organism responds in measurable ways to stimuli which can also be observed and quantified. Conclusions about deterrence, which is a statement about people's internal states, are therefore (within this paradigm) necessarily based on inference.

There is no doubt that in many situations this philosophical position has its virtues, and in fact evidence in its favor may be adduced from a number of the analyses presented in this report. (It will be seen in Chapter 5 that even as simple and concrete a question as whether the respondent had been randomly tested was subject to considerable unreliability.) However, there is also no doubt that the dominance of this approach in the social sciences has led to the neglect of an obvious method for studying deterrence, which is simply asking people *why* they refrained from (or why they committed) a criminal act. After all, from a layperson's point of view, if one wished to find out why a person did or did not perform some action the simplest strategy would be to ask them for their reasons. (Q: "Why didn't you drive home from the party last night?" A: "Oh, I saw the cops out earlier and decided not to take the chance.")

There is in fact at least one paper in the literature in which this approach is adopted. Meier (1979) compared people who claimed not to have used marijuana because of fear of arrest with those who refrained from use for other reasons. As Meier (1979) reasonably points out, this approach ". . . views the detection of deterrence as an empirical question and assumes that persons who act in a conforming manner and perceive legal threats as a cause of such action to be instances of deterrence" (p. 13). It seems, however, that other researchers have not been willing to make this assumption, and even Meier, in an earlier paper (Meier & Johnson, 1977) was defensive about it.

Since Gibbs wrote his book, there have been developments in the social sciences, particularly in psychology, which have involved a recognition of and a coming to terms with the role of subjectivity (Jessor, 1981). There has also been a renewed interest in verbal reports as data, and their relationship to cognitive processes (Ericsson & Simon, 1980; Nisbett & Ross, 1980; Nisbett & Wilson, 1977; Smith & Miller, 1978). Some of the philosophical underpinnings required for the analysis of verbal reports have been provided by writers interested in developing a phenomenological or cognitive approach to psychological research. For example, Harré and Secord (1979) (in a chapter entitled "Why not ask them . . . ?") challenge the mechanistic and behaviorist model outlined above by arguing that person predicates form a bodily mental spectrum, not two or more exclusive groups. They point out that philosophers have distinguished between predicates like "150 pounds," which a person can share with a lump of rock, and predicates like "conscience struck," which seem to have application only to people, and then only on the basis of a person's categorization of his own feelings. These predicates were applied by philosophers to a person's body and mind, respectively, but then predicates like "elated" or "deterred," which presupposed an interaction between the corporeal and mental substances, could not be dealt with.

Harré and Secord propose instead that predicates of this type be dealt with by dual criteria, one concerned with the external indicators and one with the internal state. They argue that although a man may well be the best *authority* on how he is feeling or why he is acting, he is not the only one with *access to* information of this sort. In cases of dispute, if we wish to maintain the observer's point of view over against that of the person himself, a special case (such as a Freudian explanation) must be made. What Harré and Secord's argument seems to amount to in the present instance is that people's reports of their reasons for not drinking and driving may be accepted as evidence, but not uncritically and not in isolation from the more objective kinds of evidence normally considered. Putting the matter positively, the admission of evidence on which the respondent is the most privileged observer (reasons for not drinking and driving) is essential for the determination of a verdict on whether or not deterrence has been operating, since the predicate is by its nature one for which the application of both types of criteria (overt and covert) is required.

There is some empirical evidence to support the contention that, under certain circumstances, people are capable of reporting reliably on their cognitive processes, including the reasons for their actions. A review article by Nisbett and Wilson (1977), in which the authors concluded that individuals have little or no direct introspective access to higher order cognitive processes, generated considerable controversy, with critics asserting that Nisbett and Wilson's position is stated in a nonfalsifiable fashion and is based on incorrect interpretations of the experimental evidence (Smith & Miller, 1978). Ericsson and Simon (1980) argue that the inaccurate reports found by some researchers result from requesting information that was never directly heeded, thus forcing subjects to infer rather than remember their mental processes.

However, even Nisbett and Wilson conceded that although people may not be able to observe directly their cognitive processes, they will sometimes be able to report accurately about them. "Accurate reports will occur when influential stimuli are salient and are plausible causes of the responses they produce . . ." (p. 231) This implies that in the study of why a person did not commit a crime it should be established, before asking about reasons, that opportunities to commit the offense occurred in a given time period and that the person was aware of legal sanctions and understood what they meant. The issue of public knowledge of sanctions is a problem emphasized by Henshel and Carey (1975). It is possible that the apparent ineffectiveness of some legal sanctions is a product of public ignorance rather than the lack of deterrent potential.

Applying these insights to the present study, it is argued that given the widespread publicity about RBT and the high level of police enforcement in New South Wales, RBT must be regarded as a salient stimulus and one plausible explanation for the driving and drinking behaviors of the great majority of license holders who drink. This is not to say, of course, that the mere act of publicity and enforcement proves the success of RBT, but that the conditions required by Nisbett and Wilson (1977) for people to be able to report accurately on RBT as a possible cause of their actions would appear to be met.

It is concluded that Gibbs (1975) was too pessimistic in his conclusions about the impossibility of obtaining a direct measure of deterrence based on questioning respondents about the reasons for their behavior. Attempts to develop such measures are certainly not "naive," although possibly more care should be exercised in asking respondents about reasons than in asking about their experience or their behavior. It is noteworthy that several recent criminological studies are based on an analysis of how offenders think, using techniques such as interviews (Bennett & Wright, 1984) and verbal protocols (in which individuals "think aloud" while performing the behavior of interest [Carroll & Weaver, 1986]). In the study of RBT reported in this book, the main measure of deterrence is based on a question about strategies which respondents were employing *because of RBT* to avoid drinking and driving. This question does not even ask directly about reasons, but focuses instead on behaviors which the respondent claims are part of their response to RBT. Given that interviews were conducted within a few months of the introduction of RBT when there was a very high degree of public awareness, the conditions required for responses to this question to be accurate would seem to be assured.

Elaborating the Deterrence Model for Random Breath Testing

The Model in Summary

In this section the deterrence model proposed earlier in this chapter is applied in detail to the effects of random breath testing in New South Wales. The model predicts that as the police commence random testing and as the media publicity begins, people become aware of RBT and possibly experience it personally, perhaps by driving past an RBT operation. This experience or awareness is interpreted in terms of the individual's previous experiences, beliefs, and knowledge; he also forms a perception of the likelihood of being tested and, more generally, the chances of being arrested for drinking and driving. It is predicted that the more intense the exposure and the more varied it is in form, the higher the subjective probability of arrest for drinking and driving will be.

The perception of arrest certainty is in turn evaluated in terms of the individual's personal values and previous experiences, and this evaluation influences the extent to which attempts are made to avoid drink-driving on occasions when it is a possibility. The relative frequency of such attempts is a direct measure of the degree to which the individual has been deterred. It is predicted that the higher the subjective probability of arrest, and the more worrying the prospect of arrest appears to the individual, the more likely he is to be deterred and modify his drinking and/or driving. Finally, the more frequently the individual adopts strategies to avoid drinking and driving, the less often he will drive over the limit, and the less likely he will be to be involved in a serious or fatal traffic crash.

In the discussion of prospect theory, a model of decision-making was proposed in which the drink-drive decision will typically be framed as a choice between losses. If an individual drives over the limit, there are the losses entailed in getting caught or having an accident, losses which are far from certain, together with a sure loss resulting from feelings of guilt. On the other hand, if the individual does not drink and drive, there are two certain losses: the costs involved in arranging alternative transportation and (in many cases) the cost of appearing incompetent in one's own eyes or in the eyes of one's peers. This theoretical model corresponds implicitly to an additive statistical model; in particular, it is assumed that the operation of legal sanctions is not contingent on how guilty one feels or on the social stigma from not committing the offense. The possibility that this assumption should be modified is considered next.

The Effects of RBT on Nonlegal Sanctions

The model allows that legal sanctions may have an effect not only through fear of punishment, but also through effects on informal social sanctions or feelings of guilt. For example, in recent years in New South Wales efforts have been made to increase the effectiveness of the drink-drive law by depicting the drink-driver as a "slob" rather than a hero, and by emphasizing the degrading and stigmatizing aspects of arrest (Henderson & Freedman, 1976). Such an emphasis counters prevailing community attitudes to drinking and driving (which was why the campaign was run), and thereby serves to remind us that drinking and driving takes place within a social environment in which the illegal act is frequently rewarded, not punished.

The scholar who has dealt most thoroughly with this aspect of the phenomenon is Joseph Gusfield (1981a, 1981b, 1985). Reference has already been made to his ethnographic study of drinking-driving and the context of bars (Gusfield, 1981a). On the face of it, Gusfield's work is not concerned at all with deterrence, but with the context of social drinking. However, its relevance to the present topic becomes apparent when one considers how a legal innovation like RBT might affect behavior. According to Gusfield (1981a), a crucial distinction in the study of drinking patterns is not how much drinkers consume, but whether they are portrayed in their own eyes and in those of their peers as competent or incompetent drinkers. One determination of the competence of people in American (and Australian) culture is their ability to undertake ordinary risks, and so driving after drinking is part of the test of competence. There is an implicit assumption that adequate drinkers do not get caught and can avoid having an accident.

For Gusfield, what needs to be explained is why people *don't* drive after drinking, and it is here that exculpatory defenses, legitimate excuses, come into play. One exculpatory defense is the responsibility to work; another is past arrests for drink-driving. These circumstances make the avoidance of driving understandable and reasonable, and allow the image of competence of the drinker to be preserved. In view of this, it is quite reasonable to argue that RBT has achieved its (apparent) impact in New South Wales by allowing many drinkers to maintain their image of competence while reducing their level of drinking. In effect, the presence of police carrying out RBT provides a powerful exculpatory defense, since there are in principle few steps the drinker can take to avoid being pulled over. Since it could happen to anyone, there is no disgrace in not drinking or in not driving. It seems important therefore that a study of the impact of RBT should allow a test of this hypothesized effect (see Herbert, 1982).

It is not clear that RBT will have the immediate effect on moral attitudes that it would be expected to have on informal sanctions. Nor it is clear that moral attachment to the law has as much effect on behavior outside Scandinavia as Norström (1981) suggests it does in Sweden (Steenhuis, 1983; Snortum, Hauge, & Berger, 1986). Petersen (1982) notes that no one in his sample of convicted Australian offenders questioned the legitimacy of drink-drive laws, and they regarded the offense as serious because it could have led to death or injury. However, as Gusfield (1981b) has argued, the drink-driver also has another understanding of his behavior, which is linked to the world of his everyday life. He calculates the risks and knows that he can get home without mishap. He does not reject the immorality of the behavior, but operates in a different framework to that of the abstract, other-worldly logic of law. In the light of these attitudes, it is hard to see how RBT, as part of the legal reality, would immediately effect a change in beliefs about the immorality of drinking and driving. What is more likely is that as compliance with the law becomes a habit for other reasons, beliefs about the wrongness of the offense might be reinforced and might in turn have a greater influence on behavior. Some preliminary evidence for this proposition is presented by Homel, Carseldine, and Kearns (in press), based on survey data collected 4 years after the RBT law.

Interactions Between Perceptions of Legal Sanctions and Other Factors

If deterrence research has yielded few undisputed conclusions, it has been responsible for the generation and testing of a large number of hypotheses.

Most of these hypotheses relate to the conditions under which a deterrent effect may or may not be expected, and are therefore conveniently expressed as *interactions* between sanction perceptions and other factors. These postulated interactions are of three types: an interaction between perceptions of the chances of arrest and perceptions of the severity of penalties; interactions between peer group norms and/or moral attachment to the law and perceived sanctions; and interactions between a variety of demographic factors and sanction perceptions.

Perhaps the most theoretically central hypothesis is the one which predicts an interaction between perceptions of arrest certainty and of penalties. The argument is that if people do not expect to get caught, severe penalties will not be a deterrent, and conversely if the penalties are regarded as inconsequential, a perceived high likelihood of arrest will not serve as a deterrent. As Cohen (1978, p. 94) has observed, this idea is "simple, obvious, and central to the notion of deterrence," yet only a minority of studies have tested for such an interaction.

Given the conceptualization of legal and nonlegal sanctions as forces acting on the individual like vectors in a parallelogram of forces, it is appropriate to raise the possibility of interactions between legal and nonlegal sanctions. However, in the literature these possible effects tend to be discussed in terms of discrete groups of people rather than in terms of statistical interactions between variables. As Grasmick and Green (1980, 1981) and Grasmick and Appleton (1977) point out, there are two arguments in the social science literature which relegate the threat of legal sanctions to a position of secondary importance in a general theory of social control. One argument is that the threat of legal sanctions is a deterrent only for those individuals whose peers would impose informal sanctions if the person were exposed as a law violator (Zimring & Hawkins, 1973). As we have seen in the case of drinking and driving, this effect is problematic. The second argument is that the threat of legal sanctions only influences the behavior of those individuals who are not morally committed to the law (Zimring & Hawkins, 1968). For drinking and driving, the interaction corresponding to this situation is more plausible.

The arguments concerning interactions between sanction perceptions and characteristics of respondents (age, sex, and so on) are rather confusing. With one notable exception, deterrence theory itself does not generate predictions concerning different levels of deterrability in different population subgroups, but plausible arguments adducing such differential effects can be derived from other theoretical perspectives. One possibility is that some individuals labeled as deviant will become more deviant, creating a countervailing force to deterrence. If this kind of effects is more likely among certain groups, such as motorcycle gangs, then an interaction between sanction perceptions and the relevant social characteristics might be expected.

Firmer predictions of an interaction effect can be made for those who have had previous contact with the law. A particularly interesting group in any study of general deterrence consists of those who have already suffered legal punishments for the offense(s) under study or for other offenses. Deterrence theory would suggest that these people should be more sensitive or responsive to sanction threats than those who have never tangled with the law. Reconviction studies appear at first glance to contradict this prediction, since the invariable finding is that offenders penalized severely are no less likely to be reconvicted than those who received a light or nominal penalty (Homel, 1981a). However, these studies of recidivism bear only on the issue of marginal specific deterrence (one penalty compared with another); they tell us nothing about the absolute impact of arrest, conviction, and punishment.

In one study bearing on this issue, Tittle (1980a) concluded that "those who have been arrested are more deterred by their perceptions of sanctions than are those who have not been arrested" (p. 321). What he means by this is that individuals who have been arrested will be more *responsive* to the threat of further punishment—they will accord more weight to their perception of sanctions than people who have never been arrested. If supported in future research, this result is of the utmost importance, since it implies that conclusions about the ineffectiveness of penalties in the sense of absolute specific deterrence may have been wrongly drawn from the studies of marginal specific deterrence. In other words, it may not matter much (from a deterrence perspective) what one does to people once they have been caught, but the actual act of arrest and punishment may itself be a deterrent. The present study allows a test for the interaction between previous drink-drive convictions and perceptions of sanctions, and is therefore capable of shedding light on this issue for the offense of drinking and driving.

In conclusion, there are strong theoretical grounds for testing for a variety of interaction effects. The most critical interactions are those between perception of arrest certainty and perception of penalty severity, and between perceptions of sanctions and the possession of a conviction for drinking and driving. Others can be incorporated to test specific hypotheses about the effects of nonlegal sanctions or of sociodemographic variables.

The Relationship Between Actual and Perceived Legal Sanctions

The discussion of interaction effects has been concerned with the relationship between perceptions of legal punishments (Pp) and attempts to avoid drink-driving (De) or the involvement by individuals in the offense (Dr). Although this relationship has received most of the attention in the literature, with the possibility of interaction effects promising to generate much more research, several authors have stressed the importance of understanding more about the relationship between the *actual* legal punishments obtaining in a jurisdiction (Lp), and the perceptions of those punishments (Pp). Since it only makes sense to think of Lp at the aggregate level (e.g., the arrest rate in a jurisdiction, or the proportion of drink-drivers jailed), investigation of the relationship between Lp and Pp raises a critically important theoretical question: Should deterrence be conceptualized as occurring at the aggregate or at the individual level?

Although it is easy to formulate a definition of deterrence which refers to an individual's decision rather than to aggregate crime rates, it can be argued that to have social policy implications, deterrent effects should manifest themselves at the aggregate as well as at the individual level. Gibbs (1979) argues that the theoretically most appropriate units for analysis are ecological, not individual, since "objective properties of punishments are characteristics of a jurisdictional unit, not of individuals. Moreover, unless the research incorporates objective properties of punishment, it cannot be a complete test of the deterrence doctrine, nor have obvious policy implications" (p. 662). Although the majority of empirical investigations of deterrence have been conducted at the level of political units, most commentators (while accepting the force of Gibbs' argument) seem to agree that nearly all of these studies entail insuperable problems of interpretation. These problems include the impossibility of determining causal directions, the difficulty of eliminating competing explanations for observed correlations, and the reliance on crude estimates of actual sanctions rather than those perceived by the general public (Anderson, 1979; Ross & LaFree, 1986; Tittle, 1980a, 1980b).

The problem then is that it is difficult to conceptualize or measure objective legal threats at the individual level, but an individual level analysis is desirable to trace the links between perceptions of sanctions, attempts to avoid drink-driving, and drink-drive behavior. However, the problem is not insurmountable: in general, two approaches seem viable. First, there seems to be no reason why individuals selected from a variety of jurisdictional units could not be surveyed, and objective properties of punishments in each jurisdiction incorporated as one of the predictors in an individual level analysis. It is true that this variable would be constant for all individuals within a given jurisdiction, but since it would vary from area to area, there seem to be no theoretical or methodological impediments to such an analysis. Second, as proposed in the model described in this chapter, attention could be focused on respondents' *exposure* to crimes and arrests or to information about crimes and arrests. It may well be that personal experience with or observation of law enforcement has a significant impact on perceptions of legal sanctions, or that exposure to formal or informal publicity about crime and punishment has an influence. This necessitates the introduction of the variable Ex between Lp and Pp.

Both approaches to the problem have been employed in the present study. One of the many advantages of studying drinking and driving and random breath testing is that objective sanctions can be easily quantified, both through the personal exposure of individuals to random testing or to publicity about random testing, and through records of the number of random breath tests conducted in different areas of the state. However, in the general literature on deterrence there appears to be only one study in which the authors have attempted to link actual and perceived certainty of punishment at the individual level. Parker and Grasmick (1979) investigated the effects of newspaper crime stories, personal experiences with crime, and the personal experiences of one's acquaintances on arrest perceptions. They found that people's estimates of the official arrest rate for burglary were influenced by their experiences as victims, particularly by the number of arrests which they knew took place as a result of these experiences, *provided* they knew of at least one arrest. Newspaper stories did not appear to influence perceptions.

In summary, following the approach adopted by Parker and Grasmick (1979), the introduction of the exposure variable (Ex) is proposed as the natural solution to the problem of linking objective legal sanctions in an area with perceptions of those sanctions. As Henshel and Carey (1975) have emphasized, sanctioning outcomes (such as arrest rates or levels of punishment) are not typically part of the pragmatically necessary knowledge required in our society, and it cannot be assumed that because police in an area are active in breath testing motorists, this will be automatically translated into perceptions of a high chance of being arrested. The intervening variable of knowledge or exposure is what influences such perceptions. Of course, as noted previously, experience with the law either through arrest or through undetected law-breaking is also a form of exposure.

Other Influences on Perceptions of Sanctions

Tittle (1980a) has stressed the importance of shifting focus to the question of how perceptions of sanctions are formed. Indeed, he regards this issue as a top priority for future research, and speculates that objective properties of sanctions may turn out to be relatively minor elements in the formation of perceptions. In his own research he has investigated the effects of gender (Richards & Tittle, 1981) and socioeconomic status (Richards & Tittle, 1982), but as with some of the arguments about interaction effects, the grounds for investigating these variables are found outside deterrence theory. For example, Richards and Tittle (1981) suggest that differential stakes in conformity may be one explanation for the higher chances of arrest perceived by women in comparison with men. On the other hand, Finley and Grasmick (1985) found that whether a woman was "traditional" or "nontraditional" had no effect on perceptions of legal sanctions.

In the present study no explicit predictions along these lines are made, but the possible influences of a range of sociodemographic variables on perceptions of arrest certainty and penalty severity are investigated in the analysis. Part of the problem with making specific predictions is that it raises the whole issue of differential deterrability and high risk groups discussed in Chapter 1. No doubt differential deterrability does occur, but given the theoretical and empirical limitations of the drink-driving literature and the probable interaction of person and situation variables (Vingilis & Mann, 1986), such effects are best investigated empirically.

There are two concrete predictions about influences on perceptions of sanctions which can be derived from deterrence theory. It is predicted that people who have committed an offense but have escaped punishment will have lower perceptions of the chances of arrest than those who have not committed the offense. This is referred to as the *experiential effect* in the literature (Minor & Harry, 1982; Paternoster, Saltzman, Waldo, & Chiricos, 1982) and is a variation on the exposure effect discussed above, since it reflects the effects of a *lack* of exposure to the strong arm of the law. The prediction does not refer to individuals who have committed the offense and have been punished (the convicted group), since their experience is fundamentally different from that of the group who have violated the law with impunity.

One prediction for the convicted group, as argued above, is that the relationship between perceived arrest certainty and drink-drive behavior (or attempts to avoid drink-driving) is stronger than for those who never have been convicted; in other words, they are more responsive to sanction threats. Another prediction is that the experience of arrest or conviction will influence perceptions of arrest certainty or perceptions of sanction severity—in other words, arrest affects *sensitivity* to the legal threat. Unfortunately the direction of the relationship is not clear, since it is possible that the experience of arrest could, like undetected offending, lead to a lower (more realistic) estimation of arrest likelihood. However, the findings of Paternoster, Saltzman, Waldo, and Chiricos (1986) for petty theft and writing checks with insufficient funds, and of Shapiro and Votey (1984) and McLean, Clark, Dorsch, Holubowycz, and McCaul (1984) for drinking and driving, suggest that if arrest affects subjective arrest probabilities, it increases them.

Perceptions and Evaluations

The concept of responsiveness to perceptions of sanctions implies that people are not all equally affected by a given perception of legal sanctions. The theoretical importance of distinguishing perceptions from the weight attached to these perceptions has been discussed in the context of prospect theory, and is also emphasized by Vingilis and Mann (1986) in their dicussion of Mischel's theory of the cognitive processes underlying the assimilation of environmental information (they refer in this context to "subjective stimulus values" [p. 8]). Tittle (1980a) has expressed the point nicely:

Severity is not just a matter of perception, it is basically a question of subjective evaluation. It is far-fetched to imagine that individuals will have correct cognitions of the magnitude of formal sanctions, but it is even more absurd to assume they will interpret those cognitions on a common continuum of dreadfulness (p. 324).

Grasmick and Green (1980) have developed a method of questioning which avoids the complications involved in recording the details of individual perceptions of penalties, but instead goes directly to subjective evaluations. In their study, respondents were asked to imagine that they had been convicted and a punishment decided. They were asked to imagine what the penalty would be (without telling the interviewer) and to "indicate how big a problem that punishment would create for your life." This method has been employed in the present study.

Few studies have explicitly incorporated questions which distinguish perception of arrest likelihood from evaluations of that perception. That such a distinction could be useful is illustrated by the work of Dix and Layzell (1983) on interactions between motorists and the police. They demonstrate that arrest itself is an event which is evaluated and weighted, with some motorists referring to the embarrassment, shock, uncertainty, and inconvenience of being pulled over by the police. The present study of RBT probes the distinction between perceptions and evaluations in two ways: first, the process of apprehension and arrest is carefully unpacked in a series of questions so that perceived loopholes in law enforcement are identified, and second, a question is included which explicitly asks how *worried* the respondent would be about getting caught (as opposed to how *likely* he or she regards it).

A Schematic Representation of the RBT Deterrence Model

The deterrence model applied to the introduction of RBT in New South Wales is shown in Figure 2.2. This diagram provides an operationalized framework for the analysis of the RBT survey data (Chapters 5 and 6), inevitably simplified compared with the theoretical model outlined before, but incorporating as many insights as were possible in an interview study. A full description of the study design is presented in Chapter 5, but for present purposes it is sufficient to note that two waves of interviews were carried out, the first in February 1983, 10 weeks after the introduction of RBT, and the second in April 1983, 6 weeks later. In the second stage 185 motorists were reinterviewed. The diagram relates most directly to the April survey, in which more extensive data were collected, although aspects of the longitudinal component of the study are also represented in the diagram.

The elements of the basic deterrence model are police enforcement (Lp), exposure to random testing (Ex), perceptions of sanctions (Pp),

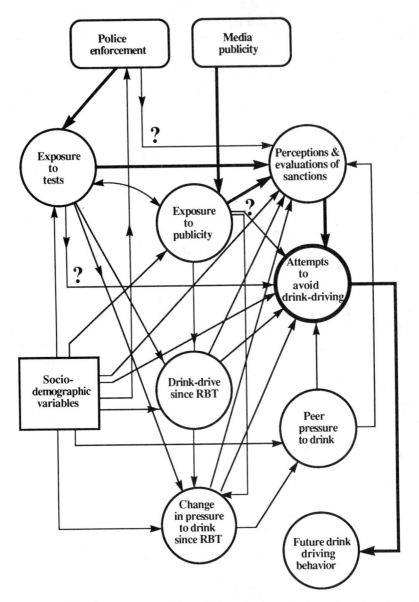

FIGURE 2.2. The deterrence model applied to the introduction of random breath testing.

attempts to avoid drink-driving (De), and future drink-driving behavior (Dr). Police enforcement and exposure to tests refer to the period between the introduction of RBT and the second-stage interviews (April 1983), while perceptions of sanctions and attempts to avoid drink-driving refer to the situation at the time of the second stage interviews. Police enforcement, which is measured by the number of random tests per 1,000 license holders carried out in each of the 10 areas sampled, is assumed to determine the likelihood that an individual will have been exposed to random testing, which in turn is assumed to influence current perceptions of arrest certainty and hence attempts to avoid drinking and driving. Although it is difficult to see how it could happen, it is also possible that the level of police enforcement could have a direct effect on perceptions of arrest certainty, perhaps through aspects of exposure not measured in the present study. Therefore this path is represented in the diagram by an arrow with a question mark. Similarly, it is possible that being exposed to random testing has a direct effect on attempts to avoid drinking and driving. Once again, this could only be because of limitations in the measures of perceptions of arrest certainty, since it is hard to imagine how exposure could affect behavior other than through such perceptions.

It is possible, of course, that any of the paths within the basic model are spurious, in the sense that they could reflect the operation of other variables. So, for example, if low status individuals are more likely to rate the chances of arrest as high and are also likely to do more driving, a positive correlation between exposure and perceptions of arrest certainty may not reflect deterrence but the effects of social class. For this reason the socio-demographic variables (age, sex, occupation, level of drinking, and so on) play an important role as covariates. They are also important in their own right, since significant associations between them and elements of the deterrence model shed light on possible differential effects of RBT in different population subgroups (hence the value of testing for interactions). Consequently, the sociodemographic variables are represented as having direct effects on all groups of variables in Figure 2.2, including the levels of police enforcement. The reason for this last mentioned path is that police may well tailor their enforcement of RBT to the social characteristics of an area, particularly the incidence of heavy drinking and the relative frequency of public as opposed to private or at-home drinking. In this connection it should be noted that the sociodemographic variables box represents both individual and aggregate level characteristics. Ideally these two levels should be distinguished, but in the interests of simplicity they have been analyzed as a single group of variables.

Deterrence researchers have frequently found that those respondents who have successfully committed an illegal act see their chances of being caught as less than do respondents who have not committed the act (the experiential effect). This possibility has been covered in the present study by including drinking and driving since the introduction of RBT as an influence on current perceptions of sanctions. Drinking and driving in the last 3 months is in turn assumed to be influenced not only by exposure to RBT and exposure to publicity (via unmeasured perceptions of arrest certainty at a time earlier than the April interview), but also by perceived changes in the social pressure to drink (and to drink and drive) brought about by RBT.

In the model, perceived change in social pressure affects all the variables which relate to the current situation: perceptions of sanctions, attempts to avoid drink-driving, and perceived pressure from drinking companions to keep drinking. This last variable (peer pressure) in turn affects both perceptions of legal sanctions and the extent to which the respondent takes steps to modify his or her travel and drinking habits. (In fact these last two paths could plausibly be argued to operate in the opposite direction as well, but for simplicity—and because peer pressure is not the main focus of the study—these possibilities are not represented in the diagram.) Perceived change in peer pressure, which in some ways is more theoretically relevant than the other peer pressure variable, is assumed to be a function of exposure to RBT (including publicity) in interaction with sociodemographic variables such as age, sex, and level of drinking.

Further elaboration of the deterrence model is necessary to take into account the effects of the formal media campaign. Unfortunately, in contrast with police enforcement it is difficult to quantify the levels and types of publicity in different areas, since a retrospective content analysis of television, radio, and newspapers is required (Cashmore, 1985). However, the exposure of individuals to these forms of publicity can be recorded, and the effects of this exposure on other elements of the model (particularly perceptions of arrest certainty and the severity of penalties) can be incorporated in the model.

Self-imposed guilt feelings occasioned by drink-driving, which may be regarded as a type of sanction additional to state-imposed penalties and peer-imposed stigma, are not represented in Figure 2.2. This is not because guilt feelings are not considered important, but because resources for the study were limited and, as argued earlier, it was not clear that RBT would have the immediate impact on moral attitudes that it would be expected to have on peer pressure. Since a choice had to be made with respect to which material to omit, the decision was made to probe moral attitudes through a question on reasons for not drinking and driving, and not to include these responses in the overall quantitative model. Further research should include questions on beliefs about drink-driving, with a view to developing a reliable measure which could be incorporated in the quantitative model.

It is important to note that Figure 2.2 is not strictly a path diagram, although careful attention has been paid to the probable causal ordering of the variables represented. Most of the variables depicted in the diagram actually represent *groups* of variables, and in some cases interaction terms are included as well. In addition, two of the boxes represent variables which are "off-stage" in the analysis: no measure of formal media publicity is included, and there is no measure of future drink-driving behavior in the main analysis, although the analysis of the longitudinal data includes such a measure.

Although not a formal path diagram, Figure 2.2 does purport to represent hypothesized causal relationships, and therefore the analyses based on it may be open to the same criticisms as path analysis (Gibbs, 1978; Kempthorne, 1978). The essential point made by the critics is that so-called causal models cannot provide a basis for inferences about causes when applied to data on the synchronic association between variables (i.e., where the values of the variables are for the same points in time). In general, it is agreed that causal relationships can only be inferred from particular *changes* in one variable and concomitant changes in another. However, it is at this point that we can take advantage of the fact that RBT constitutes, in effect, an experimental intervention of considerable magnitude. Most of the variables represented in Figure 2.2 actually measure changes in some phenomenon resulting from RBT (itself a change in the social environment). For example, the key dependent variables in Figure 2.2 are changes in drinking and travel behaviors reportedly occasioned directly by RBT. Similarly, the measures of exposure to RBT or to publicity about RBT may be regarded as measures of change, since such exposure is a new phenomenon brought about by RBT. A strong correlation between these two sets of variables would therefore constitute evidence that the intensity of RBT enforcement affected the extent of behavior change.

A second point which should be noted is that the variables in Figure 2.2 cannot really be regarded as synchronic, although they were all derived from interviews conducted at approximately the same time. Modifications to drinking and travel behaviors, as well as perceptions of sanctions and peer pressure to drink, may be regarded as pertaining to the present, while exposure, changes in peer pressure, and drink-drive behavior apply to the period between the introduction of RBT and the present. Since by definition nobody was modifying their behavior *because of RBT* before RBT was announced, the number of strategies currently being used by someone to avoid drinking and driving is simultaneously a measure of change, relative to pre-RBT behavior, *and* a measure of current behavior. The same argument can be put for perceptions of the chances of being randomly tested, but less certainly for the general measure of subjective arrest probability. It follows therefore that we are on much stronger ground for inferring causal relationships than we would be if we were using purely synchronic data. Nevertheless, the inferential base can be strengthened even further by means of the longitudinal data, which are also analyzed in Chapter 6.

Elaboration of the Deterrence Model for the Study of Penalties and Reconviction Rates

There is a superficial simplicity about the ideas underlying specific deterrence. It seems intuitively obvious that people who have actually suffered a legal penalty, particularly a severe one, will be more sensitive to the threat of punishment in the future than those who have been dealt with leniently or those for whom the threat is purely theoretical. However, deterrence theorists such as Gibbs (1975) and Zimring and Hawkins (1973) have argued that, in fact, the predictions of the deterrence doctrine at this point are rather vague, since it is not clear how threat responsiveness is supposed to change as a result of punishment. Moreover, the predictions of a deterrent effect do not take into account the possibility that punishment, through the attaching of a label to the offender, may create secondary deviance (Hart, 1979) or that punishment may do any one of a number of other things discussed by Zimring and Hawkins.

In the light of the discussion of sensitivity and responsiveness to legal sanctions, it is proposed that for a given level of arrest certainty, someone who was penalized severely will be deterred more than someone who received a light penalty. The hypothesized reason for these differential effects, as noted in the previous section, is that the experience of punishment, particularly the perception that the punishment was severe, increases the fear of the threatened penalty. For a given subjective probability of arrest, someone who has already been disqualified for 6 months will have a greater fear of a 12-months license disqualification than someone never convicted or convicted but disqualified from driving for only 2 weeks. However, even this relatively straightforward prediction may not be able to be sustained on theoretical grounds, since as noted before punishment may have effects which run counter to the operation of deterrence. The argument that the perceived fairness of the penalty may be particularly important in this respect will be discussed in the following section.

There are three main ways in which the deterrence model applied to the analysis of penalty effects differs from the model for RBT. One difference is that $Lp = Ex = Pp$ (i.e., the actual legal punishment is what is experienced by the offender, and he presumably has an accurate perception of the penalty he suffered). A second difference is that the effects of punishment on nonlegal sanctions are not specified. The prediction is made that the fact of a conviction, particularly when a severe penalty was imposed, will serve as an excuse for not drinking and driving in the future (Gusfield, 1981a), but this is not incorporated formally in the model for analysis since relevant data are mostly lacking. The final difference relates not so much to the deterrence model as to the methods used to measure illegal behavior. In the present study, as in the vast majority of similar studies, reconvictions are used as an indicator of drink-drive or other illegal behavior. In the light of the evidence cited in Chapter 1 about the biases inherent in the process of apprehension, it is necessary therefore to extend the model to include aspects of police activity.

The Experience of Punishment

It has been emphasized that perceptions of the properties of legal sanctions (e.g., the penalty received for drink-driving) are not the same as the evaluations of those perceptions. It is proposed that in the case of punishment which is actually experienced there are at least two aspects of evaluation. The first aspect involves an assessment of the *severity* of the penalty in terms of the respondent's own situation in life, and the second involves deciding how *fair* the penalty is in terms of its severity. It is proposed further that fairness has two aspects: a *justice* aspect, which relates to whether the offender believes he got what he deserved, and an *equality of treatment* aspect, which relates to whether the offender considers he was dealt with as leniently as other offenders who committed an offense of similar gravity.

A complication of the model is that the penalty imposed on the offender is actually a rather complex quantity. From the point of view of the authorities, the penalty is simply the punishment imposed by the judge or magistrate. However, Petersen's (1982, 1983) study of arrested drinking drivers suggested that during precourt procedures the motorist may undergo many experiences which he regards as unpleasant, such as abuse by the police or a period in the jail cells. The perceived unpleasantness of these experiences may be regarded as another aspect of the perceived severity of the penalty (see also Bennett & Wright, 1984). Similarly, these experiences may be assessed in terms of whether they were deserved and whether they were inflicted to the same extent on all other offenders.

This model of the experience of punishment creates some complications for predictions of a deterrent impact. Clearly penalties which are perceived as severe should, according to deterrence theory, be more effective in preventing further illegal behavior than penalties perceived as light. However, it is more than likely that penalties perceived as severe will also be perceived as unfair, and it is not obvious what the impact of perceived unfairness will be on involvement in illegal behavior. It is even arguable (Casper, 1978) that lenient but fair penalties are more effective deterrents than severe but unfair penalties. Indeed, Hart (1979) has demonstrated empirically that a sense of injustice at the imposition of a penalty can result in increased law-breaking. Since there is little in the literature to indicate when labeling or deterrent effects will predominate, it is not possible to make predictions about the effects of penalties which are as clear as the predictions concerning the effects of RBT.

The Perceived Severity of the Penalty

A number of scholars have recognized the importance of perceptions of penalty severity in the context of specific deterrence (Brody, 1979; Erickson & Gibbs, 1978; Gibbs, 1979; Wilkins, 1969; Willett, 1971, 1973). Indeed, it is a matter of common sense that a heavy fine will be experienced as a tougher penalty by an unemployed 18-year-old than by a wealthy businessman, and that disqualification will hurt a travelling salesman more than a self-employed professional who works from home. However, the use of perceptual measures in studies of specific deterrence appears to be most uncommon (a doctoral dissertation by Burgess, 1982, is a recent example of such a study).

The need to include such perceptions has been demonstrated empirically by Buikhuisen (1969). He asked 107 drink-drive offenders convicted in Holland which they would prefer: to be disqualified from driving for 6 months or to go to prison for 2 weeks. He found that 51% preferred prison, but that the preference depended strongly on the offender's need for a car and his social status. The point is that a given penalty is not equally severe to all offenders, a proposition supported by responses to a question similar to Buikhuisen's which was put to the sample of New South Wales motorists in the RBT study (Chapter 6).

The Perceived Fairness of the Penalty

The need to include perceived fairness in an analysis of specific deterrence does not appear to have been widely recognized in the literature. The study by Hart (1979) is a notable exception. Casper (1978) has also touched on the problem, in his analysis of defendant evaluations of the fairness of their treatment in three criminal courts in the United States. He notes in passing that if recidivism is to be reduced it may be necessary to think more in terms of perceived justice or fairness than in terms of stiffer penalties. There are also hints of this line of argument in the literature on traffic offenses.

Williams, Hagen, and McConnell (1984b) report that over half of a group of suspended drinking drivers in California considered their suspension as fair, but that a minority who considered the license action unfair claimed disastrous effects on their marriage and employment status. Willett (1971) cites the example of one of the English drink-drivers whom he interviewed, who had been fined £50 and disqualified for 2 years. This particular offender thought his sentence was quite unjust, since he only had a slight collision with one car, while another offender whose case had just been reported in the local paper had hit three cars and did not stop or report the accident, and yet he had been fined only a few pounds and disqualified for 3 years. "Surely my offense does not compare as closely with his as the two sentences would suggest?" he commented (p. 283).

Willett's example illustrates how offenders evaluate the fairness of their penalty by comparison with the penalties received by others. However, the precise ways in which offenders get information about what others have received, and how they arrive at an idea of what they can expect to get themselves, are rather complex. Petersen (1982) has illustrated in great detail the process of information getting for a sample of drinking drivers in Australia. In one case an offender's mother phoned a lawyer, found out the likely fine, and was advised that if it was any higher, her son should appeal. However, friends are most likely to be the source of information; as Petersen comments, it is of interest that very few offenders bothered to conceal the fact of their offense from those with whom they regularly interact. Frequently there are discussions with other defendants in the waiting room before the hearing, and these also help to provide the drink-driver with a base from which he can assess the severity of his own sentence. If the drink-driver does not have a fair idea of the penalty for his charge before his hearing, it is the Welfare Officer or the Duty Counsel rather than the police who is likely to provide the information. Petersen found that of his 66 respondents, 60% received the penalty they expected, 25% received less than they expected, 13% received more than they expected, and only 2% (1 case) did not know what to expect. Most of those not getting what they expected relied on the advice of friends or previous experience, and not on judicial personnel.

These examples illustrate how offenders arrive at a sense of how fair their penalties are through a complex process of comparison with others. As Casper (1978) emphasizes, however, a direct sense of justice is also a frequent contributor to the offender's evaluation. Central to this aspect of the process is the notion of *just deserts*, although what this means may depend on whether the offender is referring to his own experience or to the experience of others. Radzinowicz and King (1977) have expressed the essential point most clearly. There is

. . . an apparently ineradicable sense that as wages should be to work, punishment should be to crime: the more difficult or valuable the work the higher should be the pay, the worse or more damaging the crime the severer the punishment. In both fields, whatever may be argued to the contrary, there is a customary level of expectation, which changes only gradually. In a court the level is known to judges, barristers, probation officers, to all but the most naive offenders. Any sudden departure from it . . . produces a sense of shock (p. 202).

In concrete terms, the calculation by offenders of what punishment is deserved seems to be based exclusively on the seriousness of the crime, not in any way on personal characteristics, even previous record. In a survey of 331 offenders (Law Reform Commission, 1980), more than half strongly agreed with the proposition that a person's previous record plays too great a part in the sentence. The overall impression from this survey is that offenders demand a retributive approach to sentencing, based solely on the gravity of the offense. This impression is supported by the research of Morris and Giller (1977) in children's courts. These researchers found that both parents and children demand a justice approach based on offense and tariff criteria. In the case of drink-driving, BAC, and the circumstances of the offense (e.g., whether or not there was an accident) would seem from this perspective to be the critical aspects of the case.

The Fairness of the Judicial Process

Feeley (1979) has argued in a book of the same name that "the process is the punishment." Feeley spent a year studying the lower criminal court in New Haven, Connecticut, and concluded that for defendants the concrete costs of the pretrial process are of great significance, greater than the stigma attached to the conviction and greater than the formal penalty. The primary concern of most arrestees was to get out of the system as quickly as possible. Although the court studied by Feeley may have been unusual in the leniency of its formal penalties (Ryan, 1981), many of Feeley's conclusions were supported by Petersen (1982). Petersen emphasizes the frequent resentment of the police, and the way in which they are perceived to distort "the facts" of the case. For most offenders their hearing is both an expedient and impersonal affair, with neither the allocation of time (the median hearing time was 2 minutes 27 seconds) nor the exploration required to do justice to the case. Although the drink-driver might receive a penalty in keeping with his expectations, it is unusual that he will experience a sense of justice.

The Use of Randomized Designs

Although strictly a matter of method rather than theory, the issue of whether randomized designs should be employed in research into marginal specific deterrence has a direct bearing on the arguments presented above about perceived severity and perceived fairness. Randomized designs are frequently advocated as essential to disentangle the effects of offender characteristics from the properties of the punishments being compared. Since magistrates tend to impose less severe penalties on first offenders and on those who are perceived to have committed less serious offenses, and since these offenders are usually less likely to reoffend (or at least be reconvicted), it may appear that lenient penalties are a more effective deterrent than severe penalties (Gibbs, 1979; Wilkins, 1969).

Researchers such as Gibbs (1979) and Farrington (1978) have insisted that the only way this problem can be overcome is through designs in which the penalty is assigned at random to the offender. However, these arguments seem to overlook a major problem flowing from randomization, namely *the sense of injustice* which would be engendered by its use in a real court situation. It seems obvious that if penalties of varying degrees of presumptive severity were assigned at random to offenders, and if the fact of randomization were known to the offenders (which would seem essential for ethical reasons), the majority of offenders (except perhaps the few who got off extraordinarily lightly) would be outraged. Randomization violates all the principles of fairness just discussed, and would probably lead quickly to the collapse of the experiment or to complete cynicism on the part of those who were punished. To the extent that ideas of justice or fairness are an inevitable outcome of the imposition of legal punishments and are a major influence on the behavior of offenders, randomization would appear to be not only difficult in practice, but undesirable in theory.

Furthermore, even ignoring the problem of perceived injustice, randomization does not solve the problem of perceived severity. Although randomization ensures that the actual penalties are distributed on a random basis, the perceived severity of penalties is not randomized, since it depends on the characteristics and interpretations of individual offenders, and cannot be manipulated by the experimenter. If perceived severity, not actual penalty, is the important variable in a test of marginal specific deterrence, there seems little point in the use of randomization.

This last argument against the use of randomization is weakened to the extent that perceived and actual punishments are similar. It is likely that the two quantities are quite highly correlated, particularly if penalties are chosen which are vastly different in presumptive severity (e.g., conviction without penalty and imprisonment). However, this is precisely the situation in which ethical objections to randomization have greatest force.

It might be argued that traffic offenses in general and drink-driving in particular are not subject to some of the above criticisms, since punishments are really a form of administrative action, are equal in severity, and can in good conscience be randomized without the offender's knowledge. Zimring and Hawkins (1973) note that randomization has been used in a number of studies of juvenile traffic offenders, where the penalties are such things as fines, probation to attend a traffic school, or writing an essay on traffic safety. However, whatever the merits of the arguments for randomization in the traffic context (and there is no doubt that in its place it is a very powerful technique), it is clear from the description of societal reactions to drinking and driving in Chapter 1 and from the great variation in penalties imposed by judges for drink-driving that these arguments do not apply in the present case.

OVERVIEW OF THE DETERRENCE MODEL APPLIED TO THE PENALTIES STUDY

The model of the experience of punishment presented before is consistent with common-sense notions. The idea of fairness in particular is so central to lay discussions of punishment that it is extraordinary that studies of specific deterrence have not dealt with the problem from the beginning. Undoubtedly one factor inhibiting such developments has been the positivist and behaviorist approach to the study of behavior, modeled on animal experiments in the laboratory and epitomized by the attempts at randomized experiments in the fields of corrections and traffic law enforcement. In contrast to this mechanistic model, the model proposed above is informed by an interactionist emphasis on meaning and shared perspectives. Humans do not respond passively to social stimuli like arrest, conviction, and punishment, but actively interpret and guide the social situation. Moreover, meanings are constructed not by isolated individuals but by individuals in interaction with others, communicating and developing shared perspectives (Blumer, 1969).

The approach adopted in the penalties study to the measurement of perceived severity and fairness (described in detail in Chapter 7) is probably the best that can be done within the constraints imposed by official records. It needs to be recognized, however, that no matter how neat the analysis of court records, such an approach can at best yield an indirect measure of the quantities of interest. Moreover, the analysis of court records is altogether incapable of yielding information on the perceived toughness or justice of the prehearing processes. On the other hand, the approach based on the use of official statistics has the advantage that large numbers of offenders can be studied, and in particular those receiving relatively very severe or very lenient penalties can be included through careful sampling in sufficient numbers to throw light on the effects of the extreme penalties. If validated by some external criterion, such as appeal rates, this approach is a cheap and powerful method of incorporating data on perceived penalty severity in the research design.

In addition, it is unlikely that the objective penalty will bear no relationship to the perceived severity or fairness of the punishment. Casper (1978) notes that often an unfair penalty appeared simply to be a penalty which the offender did not like. It seems reasonable to assume that although 2 weeks in prison might be comparable with a 6 months disqualification, 6 months of imprisonment will be regarded as a more severe penalty than almost any other form of penalty a drinking driver is likely to receive. This means that a direct study of penalties has value, particularly if combined with an index of perceived penalty severity. A method which also includes subjective evaluations from interviews with offenders is a desirable second step if resources are available.

A Schematic Representation of the Deterrence Model Applied to the Study of Penalties and Reconviction Rates

There are at least two major problems with the use of reconvictions as a criterion for the success of a punishment or a treatment. The first problem is that the imputing of a deterrent effect to a penalty on the grounds that it is associated with lower reconviction rates must remain a pure inference. Even if it can be shown that penalties reduce or eliminate the incidence of a crime, the mechanisms involved may not be deterrence but reformation, incapacitation, stigmatization, or something else. To take one simple example, a young man may not be deterred from committing a traffic offense by having his license disqualified. However, his family may take the penalty seriously and confiscate his vehicle for the duration of the disqualification, thus reducing the opportunities for the offender to drive while disqualified or to commit some other offense.

For policy purposes, the mechanism whereby penalties prevent reoffending may not matter very much. If a certain kind of penalty can be shown to work, then that is sufficient justification for employing it within the limits set by considerations of justice. However, if reconviction data are to throw any light on the validity of the deterrence model, some evidence must be produced showing that observed correlations between penalty severity and probability of reconviction are the result of fear of sanctions rather than some other mechanism. The purpose of the measure of relative severity of penalty developed in Chapter 7 is to make inferences of a deterrent effect more plausible.

The second problem is that reconvictions are not necessarily a good indicator of reoffending. Despite the frequent claim that reconviction should be the main criterion of the failure of judicial penalties or treatment programs (e.g., Clarke & Sinclair, 1974), it is clear that what is actually meant is that *reoffending* is the crucial thing. For example, in arguing for reconviction rates as a criterion, Hood (1971) states that treatment is not given to make an offender "a better person" simply on the grounds of humanity, but because a better person is less likely to offend again. "The acid test is his ability to 'go straight'" (p. 171). The trouble is, we only usually know if an offender has or has not gone straight if he gets caught for some offense. Studies of police enforcement practices (Homel, 1983c; Kirkham & Landauer, 1985) suggest that certain kinds of offenders—notably young, unskilled, or unemployed men who drive at night in conspicuous vehicles and in a conspicuous manner—are more likely to be noticed by police.

Thus the basic problem, recognized by some reseachers (e.g., Buikhuisen, 1974, Gibbs, 1975) is not that not all offenders are caught, but that those who do get caught are unrepresentative. If apprehension and conviction were a random process, it could be argued that reconvictions are an unbiased indicator of reoffending. Since this manifestly is not the case, and since for reasons which are detailed in Chapter 7 reconvictions were the only criteria available for the study, the only possible strategy is to introduce statistical controls (including age, sex, and social status) to reduce the bias in the outcome measure. These controls also allow a more valid comparison of the effects of penalties of differing severity.

The proposed model is set out diagrammatically in Figure 2.3. Most of the variables depicted in the diagram are not explicitly included in the penalties study, but are included in the figure to show the hypothesized links between various stages of the deterrence process and the enforcement

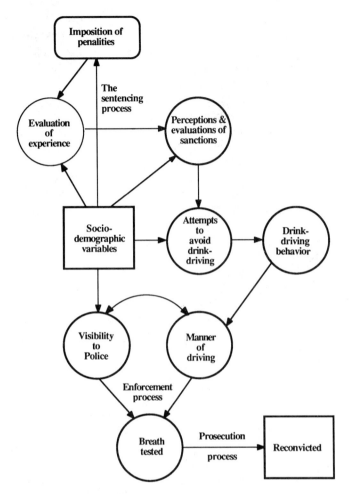

FIGURE 2.3. A model of the relationship between penalties and rates of reconviction for drinking and driving.

process. The key variables available in the analyses are penalties (measured in the form of relative severity), sociodemographic variables, and reconvictions.

It is proposed that the penalties imposed on an offender are evaluated by the offender in terms of their severity and fairness. These evaluations are influenced by the offender's personal characteristics, such as age and previous convictions. Both the evaluation of the penalties and the sociodemographic characteristics influence the offender's perceptions and evaluations of further threatened legal sanctions, which in turn influence attempts to avoid drink-driving and actual drink-driving behavior. The sociodemographic variables, particularly age, sex, and employment and social status, determine the settings in which drinking takes place and the times and frequencies of drink-driving, and these in turn have a strong bearing on the offender's visibility to the police. Actual drink-driving behavior also affects levels of visibility to police via the manner of driving. Driving while intoxicated may cause excessively slow or cautious driving as well as reckless driving or crashes, and these actions are a signal to the police that the driver may have been drinking. Once tested and found to be over the limit, the driver may or may not be convicted, depending on the jurisdiction (the probability of conviction in Australia is on the order of 98%).

The model does not explain reconvictions for offenses other than drinking and driving. Although it is likely that a very similar model would be suitable for traffic reconvictions, a criminal reconviction is probably a product of a rather different process, because both the behavior involved and the factors determining visibility to the police are different. Nevertheless, it is proposed that perceptions and evaluations of legal sanctions, as well as visibility to the police, would continue to play an important role.

Summary

The deterrence model described in this chapter specifies how legal punishments could influence drink-drive behavior through a process of exposure to enforcement, evaluation of the meaning of such exposure, calculation of arrest likelihood, and perception and evaluation of the severity of threatened penalties. Although some form of calculation is central to the deterrence model, individuals need not behave according to the prescriptions of utility theory in order to be deterred. Whatever the exact psychology of the decision-making process, the drink-drive decision involves a weighing of the legal threat, the chances of an accident, the pangs of conscience against the inconveniences entailed in alternative modes of action, and the likely loss of status in the eyes of one's peers. The drink-drive decision is normally framed as a choice between losses, so there will be a strong tendency for drinking and driving to occur on a regular basis, since the certain losses entailed in the decision not to drink and drive will offset the merely possible costs incurred in breaking the law.

The central variables in the model are open to measurement only through the disclosure by respondents of their motivations and interpretations. Individuals who are exposed to punishment or to police activity do not automatically modify their behavior. A process of evaluation takes place, whereby these experiences are interpreted and given a meaning. In addition, whether or not someone has been deterred can, in principle, be determined only through questioning him. However, in some cases reasonable inferences can be drawn from readily available data, such as the relative severity of punishment. A complication of the model in the case of specific deterrence is that the perception of a punishment as severe may be confounded with a sense of injustice.

It is predicted that compared with motorists without a conviction for drinking and driving, previously punished individuals will be more responsive, if not more sensitive, to the threat of further legal punishments. However, no other predictions are made about differential responsiveness to legal threats, although it is clearly necessary to test for the possibility of interactions between legal sanctions on the one hand and sociodemographic variables and nonlegal sanctions on the other. Through such empirical research, it may be possible to extend the model and improve its predictive power.

The general model has been applied to the introduction of RBT in New South Wales and to the effects of punishments routinely imposed on convicted offenders. In the latter case, it has been necessary to augment the model by incorporating some predictions about the ways in which reconviction rates are generated. The goodness-of-fit of the model as a description of the effects of RBT and of punishment is the subject of the empirical research reported in Chapters 5–8.

In the next chapter, the literature on the general and specific deterrence of the drinking driver is reviewed. The major purposes of the review are to investigate the evidence for deterrence and the nature of the deterrence process, using the model developed in this chapter as a framework; to identify gaps in previous deterrence research; and to identify the methodological problems which have limited the probative value of previous research.

3
The Evidence for Deterrence

In the past 15 years there has been a considerable upsurge in research on deterrence, although there are studies, particularly of recidivism, dating back 50 years or more. The literature falls into five main categories. One category, perhaps the largest, consists of the studies of the marginal specific deterrent impact of sentences imposed by courts, using recidivism as the criterion for success. The earliest and most common approach to the study of general deterrence involved the analysis of crime rates and properties of legal sanctions measured at the level of political jurisdictions. A second type of study of general deterrence, which has achieved prominence in the last decade, is based on a survey methodology and focuses on the relationship between self-reported criminality and perceptions of legal sanctions. General deterrence, particularly of driving offenders, has also been investigated through what are usually called quasi-experimental studies. These studies capitalize on sudden changes in the law and use data, such as traffic crashes, which are not subject to the evidential problems characteristic of crime statistics or survey data. A final category consists of experimental studies, which have been addressed both to specific and general deterrence.

Experimental studies are few in number and will be dealt with only in passing in this review, since most are not relevant to the deterrence of drink-drivers. Similarly, the majority of ecological/correlational studies have not been concerned with drinking and driving, and in any case they have been extensively reviewed elsewhere (Beyleveld, 1978; Blumstein, Cohen, & Nagin, 1979). In addition, the problems involved in interpreting many of these studies are so great that their capacity to shed light on the deterrence question is strictly limited (Gibbs, 1975; Ross & LaFree, 1986).

Given the objectives of this book, in this chapter most of the attention will be paid to the perceptual and reconviction research, with particular emphasis on studies of drinking and driving. Because there is a debate in the perceptual literature about the validity of conclusions concerning deterrence, it is necessary to devote some space to methodological problems generated by the survey research. Studies on the deterrence of the drinking driver will be dealt with in most detail. These studies include the research in which quasi-experimental techniques have been used to examine the effects of legal interventions on traffic crashes, as well as those which have been based on survey or other techniques. The purpose of all stages of the literature review is to assess the evidence for deterrence and its manner of operation and to identify major methodological problems.

Perceptual Research

Perhaps the most promising line of research for investigating the validity of the deterrence doctrine is that based on sample surveys, since surveys, as Tittle (1980a) and Anderson (1979) have noted, allow the perceptual and psychological factors deemed so important in the deterrence process to be thoroughly probed. In addition, surveys permit the measurement of aspects of the social environment within which people evaluate sanctions and make decisions about criminal acts. Indeed, the survey is one of the few research tools which allow the measurement, and therefore statistical control, of those features of the social environment of the respondent which might modify the nature of the deterrent process or might point to an alternative to deterrence as an explanation for correlations between perceptions of sanctions and involvement in criminal behavior.

On the whole, the survey research which has been conducted appears to support the deterrence doctrine. That is, it has been found that people with higher perceptions of the chance of arrest report fewer infractions of the law (Anderson, 1979; Grasmick, Jacobs, & McCollom, 1983; Richards & Tittle, 1982; Tittle, 1980a). A number of commentators, however, have argued that this support is the product of methodological artifacts (e.g., Minor & Harry, 1982; Paternoster, Saltzman, Waldo, & Chiricos, 1982) and that we are in fact no closer to closure on this issue than we were before the perceptual research began. Although some of these authors have since modified this pessimistic conclusion (Paternoster, Saltzman, Waldo, & Chiricos, 1986), it is certainly true that close attention must be paid to problems of method before the contribution of the perceptual research to the deterrence literature can be assessed.

Problems of Measurement and Causation

In simplest form, the deterrence surveys have four objectives: to measure perceptions of legal sanctions (the independent variables), to measure criminal behavior (the dependent variables), to establish a negative correlation between these two sets of variables, and to demonstrate that this correlation is due to deterrence and not to some other mechanism. The basic problems therefore relate to measurement and to causation.

Problems of measurement in self-report surveys of crime and delinquency have been the subject of a very large literature. Some issues specific to the design of the questionnaire used in the present study (such as the measurement of alcohol consumption) are dealt with in Chapter 5. However, as part of this overview of the results of survey research it will be valuable to touch on some of the arguments concerning the measurement of both sanction perceptions and deviant behavior. This will lead us into the problems involved in establishing causation.

HYPOTHETICAL VERSUS ACTUAL PERCEPTIONS

A particularly serious problem in the use of surveys to probe the influence of sanction perceptions on criminal behavior is that there may well be a disjunction between perceptions of sanctions in hypothetical and actual situations. Self-complete questionnaires require, by appeal to the imagination or memory of the respondent, the construction (or reconstruction) of situations in which the respondent is faced with legal or nonlegal sanctions or with the choice of whether or not to commit the offense. There is always an element of the hypothetical in such a process, since it is impossible to match the subtle variety of choices and environmental contingencies experienced by individuals in real situations through the use of standard questions. Even a completely open-response-type interview which allowed the detailed documentation of commonly occurring situations would be subject to doubts, since it is always possible that there is little relationship between, for example, a respondent's perception of the chances of arrest while sitting at home being interviewed and his perception of arrest likelihood when actually faced with a choice between legal and illegal behaviors.

In defence of surveys, Tittle (1980a) has argued:

. . . that over time people develop patterns of response to life situations so each situation is not seen as unique. . . people have habits by which they deal with problematic situations. . . Hence if a person usually responds to real life sanction threats in a particular way that person is likely to display that pattern of responding even in the contrived situations posed in an interview (p. 34).

These comments are reminiscent of the argument about standing decisions which was put forward in the last chapter as one way in which legal sanctions may deter potential offenders. The issue was particularly troublesome in Tittle's (1980a) research, since his dependent variable was the respondent's personally estimated probability of future deviance, under a hypothetical condition where there is a strong desire to commit the offense. The present study of RBT avoids the need for such a hypothetical measure by employing instead a measure based on current steps being taken to avoid drinking and driving, together with reports of past drinking and driving behavior. The assumption is that the validity and reliability of survey measures can be maximized by focusing on concrete behaviors occurring within a relatively short time period prior to the interview.

Nevertheless Tittle's defense is still relevant, since questions probing perceptions of sanctions (legal or nonlegal) necessarily entail a hypothetical element.

SELF-REPORTS OF DEVIANT BEHAVIOR

The response validity of self-reports of deviant behavior is obviously open to question. It is generally accepted that there are three conditions for successful interviewing on any topic (Cannell & Kahn, 1968): the required information must be *accessible* to the respondent, he or she must *understand* the respondent's role and the informational transaction required, and there must be the *motivation* to take the role and fulfill its requirements. Of these three conditions the most likely to be (wrongly) taken for granted is the respondent's motivation. The respondent is seen as having a need to maintain self-esteem, to be perceived by the interviewer as a worthy person who does not violate important social norms (Cannell & Kahn). Given the stringency of these conditions, it is not surprising that the general conclusion from methodological research is that most interview data is subject to substantial invalidity. In particular, prestigious behavior tends to be overreported, while deviant or even mildly socially unacceptable behavior may be subject to underreporting. Even such a widespread and acceptable practice as alcohol consumption is known to be substantially underreported (Cannell & Kahn, 1968; Pernanen, 1974).

Fortunately, it seems that the invalidity and unreliability of measures of self-reported delinquency and criminality are not quite as bad as one would imagine. Both retest and internal consistency reliability indices have been at least acceptable (Nietzel, 1979), and a number of validity checks have produced encouraging results (Hindelang, Hirschi, & Weis, 1979; Nietzel, 1979; Tittle, 1980a). A comparison of "known" criminal groups (such as incarcerated drug addicts) with "ordinary citizens" yield differences in self-reported crime in the expected direction, and checks against officially recorded crime and against the reports of informants (such as an adolescent's peer group) have in a number of studies (although not all) suggested accuracy levels on the order of 80% (Tittle, 1980a). Much of the debate about self-reports of crime has concerned the relationship between criminality and social class (Hindelang et al., 1979; Tittle, Villemez, & Smith, 1978) and in this connection Kleck (1982) has argued that lower-class respondents are more likely than middle-class respondents to give dishonest or incomplete answers. In reply, however, Tittle and co-workers (1982) argue that the opposite is more likely to be the case (since middle-class respondents have a higher stake in conformity), and that in any case the data are not available to decide with any assurance. The debate continues.

The psychological research on interviewing suggests that since respondent motivation is the key to response validity, behaviors which are only moderately deviant should be reported more accurately in surveys than involvement in serious crime. Since drinking and driving is an offense committed by a large number of people fairly often and is not in practice regarded as a particularly heinous crime (Gusfield, 1981a), it is reasonable to expect that respondent motivation to conceal drink-drive episodes would not be as great a problem as for more serious offenses. Probably the greatest threat to validity arises from the simple act of forgetting occasions of impaired driving, but fortunately there is evidence (Homel, 1986) that underreporting is not seriously biased by social factors such as age or sex. However, the research of Locander, Sudman, and Bradburn (1976) suggests that *convictions* for drink-driving will be underreported by at least 35%, even when using randomized response techniques which ensure respondent anonymity, and the degree of underreporting may well vary by social class.

In summary, the dependent variable of self-reported criminality appears from the literature to be rather more robust, in terms of validity and reliability, than might initially be expected. There are some grounds for believing that self-reports of behaviors which are viewed as only mildly deviant (such as minor acts of delinquency, smoking, and drink-driving) are more valid than reports of serious offenses, although it is likely that arrests, even for minor offenses, are substantially underreported. There is also evidence that self-reports of drink-driving are probably relatively free of bias due to social factors, particularly age and sex.

PERCEPTIONS OF LEGAL SANCTIONS

The validity of measures of perceptions of sanctions is more problematic than the validity of self-reported criminality, since there are no clear objective standards for comparison. A loose or null association between objective sanctions in a jurisdiction and perceptions of those sanctions does not bear on the validity of the perceptual measures, since we cannot be sure that the assumption in the deterrence model of a close association is in fact correct. There are however three issues related to validity which have been discussed in the literature: the desirability of distinguishing between perceptions of sanctions and the evaluation of those perceptions, the appropriateness of other-referenced measures, and the time ordering of measures of perceptions and reports of criminal behavior.

The distinction between perceptions and evaluations was discussed in Chapter 2. In the present study of RBT, one question about penalties goes straight to evaluations by asking respondents to imagine the punishment they would receive if arrested and convicted and then, "How big a problem would that punishment be in your life?" (Grasmick & Green, 1980) Moreover, the measurement of arrest certainty involves questions about each aspect of the law enforcement process, as well as a question on how worried people would be about being tested. However, apart from the research by Grasmick (Grasmick & Bryjak, 1980; Grasmick & Green,

1980) and Tittle (1980a), little attention has been paid to this problem in the perceptual literature.

In a number of research projects, respondents have been asked to estimate the probability of arrest for "people in general" or for "a person like yourself" (e.g., Anderson, Chiricos, & Waldo, 1977). However, as Grasmick and Green (1980), Tittle (1980a), and Zimring and Hawkins (1973) have argued, consistency with the utilitarian paradigm requires that perceived certainty be measured by asking a respondent to estimate the probability that he (or she) would be arrested if he (or she) committed the offense. Zimring and Hawkins cite evidence that delinquent boys may believe they possess a "magical immunity mechanism" (p. 102), since they estimate their personal chances of arrest as being lower than the general chance. Moreover, studies in which both types of measures are employed indicate that perceptions of personal risk are more powerful predictors of illegal behavior than the aggregate measures (Grasmick & Green, 1980).

By far the most controversial feature of the perceptual research is the chronological order of perceptions and involvement in illegal acts. Probably the majority of studies, particularly those conducted in the early 1970s, have been cross-sectional in design, and have therefore asked about *current* perceptions of sanctions and *past* criminal behavior (Anderson, 1979). A negative correlation between these two variables has been taken as evidence of deterrence, but it is now widely recognized that in fact such a correlation probably reflects *experience* rather than deterrence. That is, people who commit a crime and get away with it (by far the most likely outcome) come to perceive the chances of arrest as less certain than those who have not committed the offense in the period specified by the interviewer. A cross-sectional design might be satisfactory if it can be shown that perceptions are stable over time, so that current perceptions can "stand in" for the respondent's perceptual state at the beginning of the period of questioning. Unfortunately, the evidence indicates that this assumption is not correct (Minor & Harry, 1982; Paternoster et al., 1982).

Clearly what is required is that sanction perceptions be measured at the beginning of the time period over which involvement in illegal activity is recorded. However, the required design—a panel or longitudinal study in which respondents are repeatedly interviewed—is very expensive. For this reason the majority of workers have employed one or more alternative strategies. A common approach to the problem has been to ask about expected future criminal behavior (Grasmick & Green, 1980; Jensen & Stitt, 1982; Tittle, 1980a). Teevan (1976) asked about perceptions of sanctions at an earlier time. However, as Anderson (1979) and Paternoster and co-workers (1982) have pointed out, neither method deals adequately with the problem of causal order since each requires that a new and untested assumption be put in place of the assumption of perceptual stability. Significantly, Greenberg (1981) in a reanalysis of data from the cross-sectional study of Grasmick and Green (1980), argued that the correlations claimed by Grasmick and Green to be evidence of a deterrent effect could be due to experience or to the operation of extraneous factors.

The present study of RBT attempts to deal with the problem in two ways: first, measures of attempts to *avoid* drinking and driving which may be regarded as synchronic with the perceptions of sanctions are developed, and second, a longitudinal design is used to analyze the impact of sanction perceptions on drinking and driving behavior. It is worth noting, however, that longitudinal designs are subject to a number of difficulties in addition to their cost and are therefore not a perfect solution. Apart from the fact that respondents are lost from one time to the next, "if the relationship between sanctions and behavior is processual and ongoing, even a longitudinal approach will not eliminate the causal ambiguity of deterrence research" (Anderson, 1979, p. 133; Paternoster et al., 1986). Granted that longitudinal studies are probably the best design available, it is interesting to note that two of the earlier such studies (Minor & Harry, 1982; Paternoster et al., 1982) found no evidence for deterrent effects, although there was strong evidence for experiential effects, but that more recent research focused on the relationship between perceptual and behavioral *change* has provided stronger (but not unequivocal) support for deterrence (Paternoster et al., 1986).

Interaction Effects in the Deterrence Process

In Chapter 2, the possibility of interactions between sanction perceptions and other variables was discussed. Some survey research has been designed to investigate whether these interactions occur in practice. In evaluating the evidence for these hypothesized interaction effects, it should be recalled that only one of the studies cited below was based on a longitudinal design, so it is necessary to exercise some caution in interpreting the findings.

Grasmick and Bryjak (1980), using the refined measure of penalty severity described above and both prior criminal involvement and estimated future involvement as dependent variables, produce evidence for a significant interaction between perception of arrest certainty and perception of penalty severity. As Paternoster and Iovanni (1986) comment, this result is a potentially important contribution to the perceptual deterrence literature since perceived penalty severity looms large in deterrence theory but has rarely been demonstrated empirically to have an influence on behavior. However, these authors demonstrate, using longitudinal data, that Grasmick and Bryjak's strong negative correlations at high levels of arrest certainty are due to the experiential effect, and that the true deterrent effects are much smaller. Moreover, their analysis suggests that for the offenses studied (minor offenses committed by juveniles) the refined severity measure reflects the effects of informal rather than formal sanctioning. In other words, asking respondents to imagine the punishment and then to "indicate how big a problem that punishment would create for your life" confounds the effects of the legal punishment with the informal sanctions which would be imposed by parents and others. Given this appraisal of Grasmick and Bryjak's study, it is necessary to conclude that their hypothesis of an interaction between perceptions of arrest certainty and perceptions of penalty severity has not been proven.

This negative outcome is consistent with other studies. Cohen (1978), in a study of the deterrence of speeding among military personnel, found no evidence at all for such an interaction and neither did Hollinger and Clark (1983) in a study of deterrence in the workplace. (Hollinger and Clark did find a significant penalty effect, over and above the effect of perceived certainty, but the model was additive.) Tittle (1980a) found no direct evidence for the hypothesized interaction, although his analysis did suggest the existence of "thresholds" below which perceptions of certainty and severity have no effect. Earlier studies summarized by Tittle produced results as negative as those cited before.

The validity of a model which is additive in terms of the effects of legal and nonlegal sanctions has been investigated in a number of studies, none of which unfortunately was focused on drinking and driving (although Grasmick & Green [1980] used driving under the influence as one of a number of offenses from which they constructed composite scales). Grasmick and his colleagues (Grasmick & Appleton, 1977; Grasmick & Green, 1980, 1981) have concluded that there is at best only weak evidence for an interaction with threat of social disapproval, and no evidence for an interaction involving moral commitment to the law. Grasmick and Green (1980) cite five earlier studies which also support the conclusion of no interaction with variables related to peers, a conclusion also reached by Tittle (1980a). However, there is at least one study (Rankin & Wells, 1981) which did find an interaction with peer group characteristics (the number of delinquent friends possessed by an individual), although it should be noted that this study used an other-referenced measure of sanction perceptions.

The evidence concerning interactions between sanction perceptions and characteristics of respondents (age, sex, and so on) is extremely confusing. Grasmick and Milligan (1976), for example, draw on labeling theory and differential association theory to explain their finding (using an other-referenced measure of perceptions) that young drivers were less deterred from speeding offenses than older drivers. However, the finding of an age differential has by no means been unanimous. Two articles (Grasmick & Milligan, 1976; Hollinger & Clark, 1983) support the argument that the young are less deterrable than the old, but three (Jensen, Erickson, & Gibbs, 1978; Meier, 1979; Tittle, 1980a) find no differences by age. The evidence with respect to the relative deterrability of men and women is equally equivocal. In a recent review, Hollinger and Clark (1983) cite two studies which found a sex difference, one concluding that men are more deterrable, the other concluding the opposite. Hollinger and Clark themselves could find no interaction with sex, a result consistent with those of Jensen and co-workers (1978), Meier (1979), and Tittle (1980a).

Apart from age and sex, only socioeconomic status (SES) and previous arrests have received more than passing attention as characteristics of individuals which could condition the deterrence process. Grasmick and co-workers (1983) present evidence that for offenses less serious than those reported routinely by the FBI, high SES persons perceive a lower certainty of legal punishment than low SES persons and are less deterred by the threat of sanctions. They draw on what they call "radical criminology" to explain this finding, arguing that lower-class persons are "more likely to be scrutinized and therefore to be observed in violation of the law" (Chambliss, 1969, p. 86). It is interesting that among the offenses they studied was drinking and driving, although they summed over eight offenses to produce composite scales.

Probably the most important interaction suggested in the literature is that between perceptions of arrest certainty and convictions for a criminal offense (Tittle, 1980a), with the convicted group being more responsive to fear of arrest. More research is needed to confirm this interaction, which suggests the operation of absolute specific deterrence.

Determinants of Perceptions of Sanctions

The research into interaction effects is concerned with the relationship between perceptions of sanctions and involvement in illegal behavior. It appears that this relationship is not affected by nonlegal sanctions, but may be moderated in some circumstances by characteristics of individuals, such as socioeconomic status or previous arrests.

The Relationship Between Objective and Perceived Legal Sanctions

There are a few studies which have examined the stage earlier in the causal chain, namely influences on perceptions of sanctions. Consistent with his emphasis on objective properties of punishments as characteristics of a jurisdictional unit, Gibbs has carried out an aggregate-level analysis correlating objective certainty of arrest, public perception of the certainty of arrest, and official crime rates (Erickson & Gibbs, 1978). The method was rather unusual; aggregate-level studies invariably compare crime rates in different areas, usually states, but Erickson and Gibbs compared types of crime in the same jurisdiction. They did this in order to incorporate the perceptual variable, which was constructed by averaging the perceptions of arrest certainty for 10 types of crime among respondents in a survey of 1,200 Arizona residents. (Thus all correlations were computed from the data for the 10 offenses.)

They found that, as predicted by deterrence theory, there was a positive (although not strong) correlation between objective and perceived certainty of arrest and that the crime rate varied inversely with both the objective and the perceived probability of arrest. However, the relationship between the crime rate and objective certainty appeared to be mediated not by the perceptual variable but by social condemnation. While this appears to cast doubts on the validity of the deterrence model, it must be remembered that this pattern of correlations at the aggregate level does not preclude the possibility of the perceptual variable playing a mediating role at the individual level, although such a possibility does not appear to be recognized by Erickson and Gibbs.

As argued in Chapter 2, it is necessary to recognize that exposure to law enforcement intervenes between the objective legal sanctions and perceptions of them. However, this appears to have been recognized by only a few researchers, among them Parker and Grasmick (1979) and Henshel and Carey (1975). There appear to be very few studies which have been concerned at all with the crucial relationship between objective and perceived sanctions, and the way such a relationship may be mediated. Recent work by Paternoster and colleagues (1986) and by Shapiro and Votey (1984), discussed in Chapter 2, does suggest that the experience of arrest can make offenders more sensitive to the legal threat (i.e., increase their assessments of the likelihood of arrest).

OTHER INFLUENCES ON PERCEPTIONS OF SANCTIONS

A number of researchers have demonstrated that members of the public overestimate the chances of arrest for a variety of crimes (Cohen, 1978; Parker & Grasmick, 1979; Richards & Tittle, 1982). This phenomenon certainly applies to drinking and driving, especially during special enforcement campaigns (Ross, 1982), and may perhaps be explained in terms of the properties of the decision weight function discussed by Tversky and Kahneman (1981). In any case, the disjunction between real and imagined threat levels suggests the operation of factors additional to actual law enforcement in the formation of sanctions. Factors considered in the literature include age, sex, and socioeconomic status. The evidence is most consistent for socioeconomic status, with Cohen (1978), Richards and Tittle (1982), and Grasmick and co-workers (1983) all finding that lower-status respondents estimated the chances of arrest at a higher level than their higher-status counterparts. As noted above, Grasmick and co-workers (1983) suggest that low SES persons encounter more agents of social control and are more deterred from committing less serious offenses, thus explaining the higher levels of involvement in these offenses reported (at least in one study) by high-status respondents.

The roles of other factors in the perceptual process have received only perfunctory attention in the literature. Apart from Cohen (1978), there appear to be no studies which have investigated age as a predictor of sanction perceptions (Cohen found a null relationship). Richards and Tittle (1981) investigated sex differences in perceptions, and found "that women perceive systematically higher chances of arrest than do men, and that differential visibility and differential stakes in conformity seem to be the most promising accounts for these differences" (p. 1182). They argue that this finding may account for the apparent anomaly of lower violation rates reported by women, despite lower objective chances of arrest and punishment.

It should be clear from these citations that investigations of the perceptual process promise to shed considerable light on the social distribution of criminal behavior and criminal labels. Since much additional work needs to be done in this direction, the study of random breath testing reported in Chapters 5 and 6 was designed to allow a systematic investigation of the predictors of sanction perceptions and evaluations of those perceptions. Before leaving this discussion of the perceptual process, however, it should be recalled that one powerful influence on perceptions appears to be previous involvement in illegal behavior (Minor & Harry, 1982; Paternoster et al., 1982). This phenomenon was discussed before as the experiential effect, since people who learn from experience that they can commit crime and get away with it lower their perceptions of the likelihood of arrest. Minor and Harry found an interaction effect, confirmed by Paternoster and co-workers (1986), which suggests an interesting modification to this process: the experiential effect (for two offenses) was found primarily among those who initially had a high perception of risk. In other words, those with initially low estimates of risk have little to learn from experience. These findings point to involvement in illegal behavior, as well as contact (or lack of contact) with the police, as important variables in the perceptual process.

Overview of Perceptual Research

The review of the perceptual research reveals the complex nature of the problems entailed in demonstrating that perceptions of legal sanctions influence involvement in illegal behavior. Although the majority of studies have produced evidence supportive of the deterrence model, methodological problems are sufficiently serious to prevent firm conclusions. Probably the most serious problem is that of causal order: most studies have correlated current perceptions of legal sanctions with reports of past criminal activities, thereby probing experiential rather than deterrence effects. Other problems include the use of other-referenced questions and the use of indirect measures of illegal behavior (e.g., estimated likelihood of future criminality), and the failure to distinguish between perceptions and evaluations of sanctions. One strength of the research appears to be the relatively high reliability of self-reports of illegal behavior, especially when the behavior is (like drinking and driving) considered only mildly deviant.

The evidence concerning the deterrence process is also rather confused. The factors influencing perceptions and evaluations of legal sanctions are not well understood, and the relationship between objective legal actions and subjective evaluations of these actions has seldom been explored. The mediating role of exposure to law enforcement has seldom even been recognized. The research on interaction effects is consistent, on the whole, with a simple account of the deterrence process in which legal sanctions operate in the same manner for all population subgroups and at all levels of intensity of nonlegal sanctions, but much more research on a variety of offenses occurring in a diversity of social situations is required to establish this conclusion firmly.

In the next section these issues are explored further in the context of drink-drive research.

General Deterrence of the Drinking Driver

Studies of Traffic and Drink-Drive Law Enforcement

With some notable exceptions the literature on deterring the drinking driver has developed in isolation from the kind of research discussed in previous sections, and consequently it has a tendency to be atheoretical and "mission oriented" (Ross, 1982, p. 99). In particular, there is a dearth of studies dealing with *the deterrence process*, the linkages between actual law enforcement, perceptions of arrest risk, and drink-drive behavior. It should be clear by now that in order to put the deterrent impact of legal innovations beyond doubt, it is necessary to demonstrate that the perceived risk of apprehension (or maybe the perceived severity of penalties) has increased, and that this increase has had an effect on drinking and driving behaviors. Yet as Ross (1982, p. 108) has observed, few published evaluations of "Scandinavian-type legal innovations" (i.e., per se breathalyzer laws) have included a systematic study of perceptual variables.

Although much of the drink-drive literature has been isolated from the more general deterrence literature, it should not be concluded that drink-drive research is automatically inferior in quality. Indeed, as we have already noted there are several reasons why a focus on the offense of drinking and driving facilitates an examination of key questions concerning deterrence. One advantage is that in serious injury and fatal crash statistics we have relatively valid and reliable measures of the dependent variable, drinking and driving behavior, although such surrogate measures are not perfect (Noordzij, 1983). A second advantage is that sudden, publicized changes in drink-drive law enforcement have taken place in a number of jurisdictions, allowing quasi-experimental designs to be employed. For all their faults these designs are a vast improvement on the correlational analyses of ecological data which have so dominated deterrence research (Blumstein, Cohen, & Nagin, 1979). A third advantage, stressed by Ross (1982), is that in much of its domain traffic law is virtually the only mechanism of social control, so that if changes in law enforcement correspond to changes in traffic crash rates the causal mechanism may more easily be argued to be deterrence rather than the inhibiting effects of conscience or social pressure to conform. A further advantage, of direct relevance to the present study, is that because opportunities to drive while impaired present themselves relatively often to license holders who drink, it is possible to quantify the steps which these people are taking to avoid committing the offense. Thus drink-drive research allows the construction of a new kind of dependent variable which forms a further link in the hypothesized causal chain linking police enforcement with traffic crashes.

Given the importance of traffic accidents as a public problem, and given the prominence of law enforcement as a way of securing safety on the roads, it is not surprising that there is a considerable (although frequently obscure) literature devoted to an evaluation of policy activity. One stream is concerned with the general question of the efficacy of police enforcement of traffic law, but it is not focused particularly on the drink-driver (e.g., Cameron, 1977; Cameron & Sanderson, 1982; Hauer & Cooper, 1977; Rothengatter, 1982; Saunders, 1977; Shoup, 1973). The general, although not unanimous, conclusion from this type of review seems to be that enforcement does have a deterrent impact and is often effective in preventing accidents, but that different offenses require different strategies. The study reported by Buikhuisen (1974), in which he demonstrated that a police blitz resulted in a doubling of the renewal rate of worn tires, is a classic of its kind and is probably the best example in the literature of how traffic offenses facilitate controlled experimentation. Indeed, in many respects this experiment, more than any other study, furnishes us with compelling evidence that deterrence actually can be achieved in practice, although as Beyleveld (1979a) has observed it is not completely clear that the blitz and associated publicity did not achieve some of its effect through an appeal to conscience rather than through a fear of prosecution.

In a wide-ranging review of the effectiveness of police operations on the road, Cameron and Sanderson (1982) conclude that general deterrence operations aimed at "fixed offences" (like bald tires or drink-driving) appear more effective than such operations aimed at "transient offences" (like speeding). They observe for example that traditional, but visible, speed enforcement operations appear to have very localized and short-term effects, and they doubt their cost-effectiveness. In contrast, their review of data from Melbourne, Victoria, encourages them to believe that such visible enforcement aimed at drinking and driving is very cost-effective.

The differing requirements for effective police enforcement, depending on whether fixed or transient offenses are the target, illustrate the dangers of treating traffic law enforcement as a unitary phenomenon. Clearly it will be necessary to restrict attention to studies which deal only with drinking and driving, although it is also clear that the implications for deterrence research of the general literature on traffic law enforcement have never been fully investigated (Ross, 1982). However, even the literature on drink-drive countermeasures is vast, and only some of it is directly concerned with general deterrence. As Cameron (1979) has noted, the countermeasures literature falls into three broad categories, revolving around (a) public education campaigns, (b) laws and enforcement programs, and (c) rehabilitation programs. Nothing more will be said in the present review about education and rehabilitation programs, except to report the common conclusion that, on their own, they do not appear very effective (Cameron, 1979; Samuels & Lee, 1978).

Focusing on laws and enforcement programs, it is necessary to distinguish measures designed to control either drinking or driving, as opposed to those which are designed to prevent the combination of the two. As an example of the literature of the first kind, there are by now many publications reporting evaluations of the raising or lowering of the legal drinking age in North America (e.g., Vingilis & De Genova, 1984). Such publications are beyond the scope of this review despite the common finding of its impact on traffic crashes, since raising the drinking age is not a strategy which applies to the whole population and in any case the preventative mechanism is more akin to incapacitation than deterrence (although obviously deterrence could play a part in the enforcement of the drinking law). In the remainder of this section, we will focus on the literature directly relevant to the effects of legal sanctions on drink-driving behavior. The rapidly growing body of Australian publications on random breath testing is reserved for special attention in the next chapter.

THE DRINK-DRIVE LITERATURE

In the past decade, a number of books and articles have appeared in which the effectiveness of the enforcement of drink-drive law has been reviewed. These include Raymond (1973), Tomasic (1977), Cameron (1979), West and Hore (1980), Ross (1982, 1984c), Johnston (1982c), Jonah and Wilson (1983), and Snortum (1984a). The present review is based partly on an analysis of these publications and partly on an evaluation of a number of source documents which seem of special relevance to a study employing a survey methodology. Particular attention is paid to those studies in which a coherent theoretical framework has been employed.

What features should be included in any such framework? Gusfield (1985) laments the limited character of sociological and cultural studies of drinking and driving, and the lack of attention in the literature to the social environment and institutional variables. One author who has gone some distance toward incorporating a few of these factors in a quantitative model of drinking and driving in Sweden is Norström (1978, 1981, 1983). Norström's work is also of particular interest because he is one of the few researchers who has investigated the perceptual aspects of the deterrence of drinking drivers. He reports two studies of the impact of drink-drive law enforcement: one conducted at the aggregate level and one at the individual level (Norström, 1983). His aim is to contrast the potential of law enforcement to combat drink-driving with the potential of alterations to the opportunity structure underlying drinking and driving. The assumption behind this latter approach is that higher levels of alcohol consumption and more extensive use of cars produce a higher frequency of drink-driving.

Both sets of analyses lent support to the opportunity model, with alcohol consumption being a more powerful predictor than driving. However, simple deterrence received no support at all, since in both analyses both objective and subjective risk of detection were of negligible predictive value. In the individual level model the most important variable, apart from alcohol consumption, was moral attachment to the law. Norström concluded that (in Gibbs' terms) the Swedish law influenced behavior through habituation or normative validation.

There are however some problems with Norström's methods which weaken the conclusion of no simple deterrent effect. Firstly, as the author himself recognizes, not all the measures were completely satisfactory. The aggregate level analysis used as a dependent variable the percentage of license holders sentenced for drinking and driving, rather than the actual rate of drinking and driving in each region. Since police enforcement practices could differ systematically between regions, this variable is a biased indicator, despite the control for the level of urbanization of each area in the analysis. Secondly, although the author recognizes the importance to deterrence theory of linking objective and subjective risks of detection, and then linking the latter to drink-driving behavior, there are no measures in the individual level analysis of personal exposure to breath testing (Sweden introduced a form of RBT on an experimental basis in 1974 [Ihrfelt, 1978], two years before Norström collected his data). Such exposure variables, which include things like media publicity and the experience of friends as well as direct personal experience of police activity, form a crucial link between the objective levels of enforcement and subjective estimates of the risk of detection.

Perhaps the most serious methodological problem is the ambiguity of causal ordering in Norström's models. Given the arguments of Paternoster and co-workers (1982) and Minor and Harry (1982), unless perceived risk can be shown to be stable over time, the measure of risk should be obtained sometime *before* the measure of drinking and driving. Since subjective risk and drinking and driving behavior were apparently recorded at the same time, inferences concerning the meaning of any correlation (or lack of correlation) are somewhat uncertain.

Berger and Snortum (1986) have replicated Norström's causal analyses for the United States. They confirmed his major findings, particularly the negligible role of perceived arrest risk and the importance of moral attachment to the law. In addition they demonstrated that peers may influence drink-driving, a factor Norström did not consider in his models. However, some of the methodological criticisms of Norström's work can also be leveled at the U.S. replication. The authors themselves acknowledge that their test of the effects of the fear component of the law is perhaps inadequate, partly because arrest risks were estimated for generalized others rather than for oneself.

Studies of Simple Deterrence

The studies of Gusfield (1981a, 1981b), Norström (1978, 1981, 1983), and Berger and Snortum (1986) remind us of the broad social context within which drink-drive laws operate and of the many ways in which law enforcement may affect drink-drive behavior. However, the remainder of this review will focus mainly on studies concerned with what is referred to in the drink-drive literature as "simple deterrence" and in Chapter 2 as "general deterrence" (the effect of law on behavior through the mechanism of fear of legal punishments). This is a more tractable problem than general prevention and one which has received most of the attention.

THE WORK OF LAURENCE ROSS

Ross has evaluated the deterrent impact of drink-drive laws and law enforcement by drawing on published data from a number of jurisdictions around the world (e.g., Britain: Ross, 1973; Scandinavia: Ross, 1975; France: Ross, McCleary, & Epperlein, 1982). He has also published a review of the field (Ross, 1982; 1984c). As Snortum (1984a) has noted:

Ross's review (1982) is selective not only in his exclusive focus upon simple deterrence but also in his emphasis upon studies employing interrupted time series analysis as an evaluation procedure. Indeed, this methodological selectivity is quite appropriate in light of Ross's interest in drawing direct causal inferences about intervention effects (p. 137).

The review and his own research are concerned with the evidence for the behavioral impact of certain, swift, and severe punishments. Since there are practically no studies which focus on celerity (legal punishments are seldom swift), the specific cases of official interventions reviewed cover the introduction of Scandinavian-type laws, police crackdowns, and increases in the severity of the legal threat of punishment. A major purpose of both police crackdowns and per se (Scandanavian) laws is to increase the perceived risk of arrest for impaired driving.

Ross' analysis of the impact of the British Road Safety Act of 1967 best illustrates his approach (Ross, 1973, 1982). The 1967 Act brought two major changes to existing British legislation: it created an offense of driving with the prescribed concentration of alcohol (.08) and it permitted police to conduct screening breath tests in a variety of situations, including accidents. Initially the government had proposed that random breath tests be allowed, but such a principle was at that time unprecedented, even in Scandinavia, and was so strongly resisted on civil-libertarian grounds that the government withdrew this provision from the proposed law. Nevertheless the controversy generated an enormous amount of publicity and in Ross' judgment helped to achieve and maintain a perception of increased threat.

Interrupted time series analysis of accident and fatality rates, adjusted for mileage, during the period 1961 to 1970 strongly supported the claim that the Act had a deterrent effect on drinking and driving. That the change was due to the law rather than to some simultaneous historical event was indicated by the sharp drop (66%) in fatal and serious injury crashes on weekend nights (when drinking and driving is at its peak), and by the fact that there was no change in such crashes during weekday commuting hours (when alcohol is rarely involved in serious crashes). Ross (1973) presents additional data to support the deterrence interpretation (miles traveled, sales of alcohol, reported changes in drinking patterns, etc.). He goes on to point out, however, that "although evidence is strong that the Road Safety Act was initially effective, it is now equally clear that this effect dissipated within a few years" (Ross, 1973, p. 31).

This pattern of a temporary impact is characteristic of all the legal innovations reviewed by Ross (1982), except that increases in penalty severity without a corresponding increase in certainty could not be shown to have had any deterrent impact even in the short term. He points out that in fact the chances of apprehension for drinking and driving in Britain, and anywhere else, are so low as to be almost negligible. He argues that the deterrent effect of Scandinavian-type laws and enforcement campaigns is due to an exaggerated perception of the probability of arrest of violators.

Ross' emphasis on the role of exaggerated fears of arrest in causing the initial success of legal interventions is of theoretical interest, since there is some evidence from the prospect theory literature and from the simulation study of Summers and Harris (1979) that slight actual increases in arrest probability will be transformed into substantial increases in subjective probabilities. The argument also has important practical implications, since obviously the situation after a legal intervention is unstable, with the driver quickly learning that "in an unintentional and well meant fashion, his government was engaged in deception" (Ross, 1982, p. 108).

Ross' explanation for the evanescence of the deterrent effect found in all jurisdictions which have introduced sudden and publicized changes in drink-drive law or police enforcement is both plausible and well-argued, yet there is surprisingly little perceptual data available to clinch the argument. Ideally each specific innovation would have been accompanied by a series of surveys conducted both before and after the change in the law, but this design has only very recently been used (Job, 1985; Ross, 1985). In particular, the hypothesized decline in subjective arrest probabilities has never been documented. The present study of RBT contains the results of a modest attempt to fill this gap in our knowledge by comparing the perceived chances of being randomly tested on two occasions 6 weeks apart.

REACTIONS TO ROSS' RESEARCH

Because of the unique research advantages of studying traffic offenses, Ross' works (particularly the British study) are of great importance, and indeed seem generally to be regarded as cornerstones of the empirical deterrence literature (Beyleveld, 1979a; Cook, 1977; Snortum, 1984a). Nevertheless, some of Ross' methods and conclusions have generated considerable controversy, particularly his reliance on the methodology of interrupted time series and his assertion that the deterrent effectiveness of the tough Scandinavian laws is not proven ("the Scandinavian myth;" Ross, 1975, 1978).

Klette (1979) completely dismissed Ross' Scandinavian research on the grounds that the two main conditions for using the interrupted time series analysis, namely a sharp introduction of the legal change and valid measures of crashes over an extended time period surrounding the study, were and still are lacking. In a more conciliatory tone, Andenaes (1978) has presented some evidence for the deterrent effectiveness of Norwegian laws, while also arguing for the moral and educative impact of these laws. It needs to be kept in mind, however, that Ross (1975) never concluded that the Scandinavian laws did not have a deterrent effect, but simply that the case was not proven: "The effectiveness of the Swedish and Norwegian laws is shown to be a matter of speculation and introspection" (Ross, 1978, p. 58).

Probably the most persistent critics of Ross' methods and conclusions (including those concerning Scandinavia) have been econometricians Harold Votey and his colleagues (Phillips, Ray, & Votey, 1984; Votey, 1978, 1982, 1984; Votey & Shapiro, 1983). The debate between these two camps parallels, for drink-drive research, the debate between economists and sociologists in the 1970s concerning capital punishment and other aspects of deterrence (Blumstein, Cohen, & Nagin, 1979; Ehrlich & Mark, 1977). The essence of Votey's approach can best be communicated by summarizing one of his papers, which is concerned with the apparent deterioration of deterrent effects found in all the studies reviewed by Ross (Votey, 1984). He argues that the decline over time in the effects of a legal intervention, apparent in time series plots of traffic crashes, is not evidence showing that such a deterioration is actually taking place. Such a conclusion would require that all exogenous forces which could affect the number of crashes be invariant over the series, a most unlikely possibility. These forces include mileage driven and alcohol consumption (the opportunity structure investigated by Norström), as well as vehicle mix (e.g., the ratio of motor bikes to four-wheel vehicles) and resources devoted to law enforcement.

According to Votey (1984):

> . . . none of the studies cited by Ross. . . take into account the many exogenous factors influencing accident levels or even standardize for variations in enforcement intensity. . . . The threat of punishment may be deterring drunken driving, but if the population of drinkers is increasing as more persons drink, or if the average drinker consumes more, the threat may only moderate the *rise* in drinking-driving (p. 126).

Thus Votey argues that if these exogenous forces operate in the manner described, then if a legal intervention is regarded as an interrupted time series and examined simply by visual inspection, a researcher is almost certain to make a Type II error, accepting the null hypothesis of no deterrent effect when in fact there is one.

The paper by Phillips and colleagues (1984) in the same issue of *The Journal of Criminal Justice* represents an actual attempt to introduce some of the controls discussed by Votey (1984) through the development of an econometric model of highway casualties in Britain. Their statistical methods include the Box-Jenkins transfer function-intervention model, a technique close in spirit to interrupted time series, but differing in the way in which casual relations between the indicator of drinking and driving and sanctions is sorted out. They conclude that:

> . . . the British Road Safety Act of 1967 had a significant effect in reducing casualties but was a minor factor compared to vehicle traffic and rainfall. The impact it did have occurred when the law went into effect—not before, say due to publicity—and persisted (p. 113).

Underscoring this last point, they found that the effect of the law was *not* transitory, but that its effect on serious injuries was relatively small, explaining only 2 or 3% of the variance.

Cohen (1984) and Snortum (1984a), in the same issue of the journal, comment on the paper by Phillips and co-workers (1984). Cohen is very critical, arguing that ". . . the analysis suffers from sufficient methodological flaws to seriously limit confidence in the results" (Cohen, 1984, p. 150). Chief among her criticisms is that the sanction variable is inappropriately specified (the raw number of arrests was used), the intervention variable is inadequately formulated, and there are insufficient controls for other explanatory variables. Snortum is less extreme in his criticisms. Although conceding the force of Votey's argument about the need to control for contextual influences upon alcohol-impaired driving, he nevertheless regards the interrupted time series approach as the most appropriate for drawing direct causal inferences about the effects of interventions (Snortum, 1984a).

Ross himself has replied (Ross, 1982) to some of Votey's earlier criticisms of the Scandinavian research by arguing ". . . that an arbitrary selection of input variables and a variety of debatable assumptions concerning their formal status negate the elegance of the mathematical models and statistical procedures used to process them" (pp. 67–68). In a recent paper with McCleary (Ross & McCleary, 1983), he strongly defends the "time-series quasi-experiment" as the best way of cheaply controlling for typical threats to internal validity, such as history (specific events coincident with but unrelated to the intervention causing the observed change) or maturation (natural growth processes unrelated to but temporally coincident with the intervention causing the change).

It is clear that the issues raised by Votey and his colleagues are going to generate considerably more argument in the future. These researchers seem to have made a good case that the interrupted time series approach, although appropriate for determining the short-run impact of an intervention, is less useful in determining long-term effects. This is also a point emphasized by Snortum (1988), who argues that new laws may have a gradual, cumulative effect not easily detected by the quasi-experimental techniques advocated by Ross. In a review of U.S. experience, Snortum maintains that despite the apparent ineffectiveness of simple deterrence, there are two bodies of indirect evidence indicating that stable deterrence may exist. One strand of evidence comes from a comparison of Norway and the United States (Snortum et al., 1986), which demonstrates that Norwegian drivers, with their background of strict laws, good knowledge of the law, strong sanctions, and strong moral support for control efforts, are more conscientious than Americans in not driving after drinking. Another comes from the United States where between 1980 and 1985 there was an unprecedented, steady decline in the proportion of fatally injured drivers over .10, as well as a decline in impaired drivers detected through roadside surveys. This decline coincided with a period of intense legislative activity initiated as a response to pressure from MADD and other groups, but untangling specific cause-effect relationships is clearly far from simple.

One major conclusion to be drawn from the debate around Ross' work is that additional *kinds* of data need to be collected. No matter how sophisticated the statistical analyses, inferences concerning deterrence will always remain less than certain on the basis of traffic crash data alone. In particular, Ross' hypothesis that the perceived certainty of arrest declines over time after a legal intervention needs direct confirmation through surveys.

THE INTERNATIONAL RESEARCH PICTURE

Ross' 1982 review covers the great majority of good quality studies published up until that time. His more recent conclusions (Ross, 1984c, 1985) echo those of his earlier study, namely that well-publicized campaigns emphasizing the certainty of arrest have a short-term deterrent impact and that extremely severe penalties generate distortions in the criminal justice system without achieving notable safety benefits. However, in his reviews he has not emphasized survey research, so there is value in reviewing developments in a number of countries, concentrating particularly on research which probes perceptions of legal sanctions.

BRITAIN

Riley (1985) is pessimistic about the potential of the criminal justice system to further reduce the road toll. He bases this conclusion on an analysis of the British Crime Surveys of 1982 and 1984, which suggest that in the week previous to the interview one in 4 male drivers and 1 in 13 women drivers had driven over .08. He identifies several high-risk groups, including the "ignorant," those under social pressure to drink-drive, and those not fully aware of the penalties.

This pessimistic tone is reinforced by Ross' (1986) review of British deterrent measures. He notes that the implementation of the Blennerhassett Committee's recommendations in 1983 may have had a slight effect on rural casualties (the essence of the changes was the simplification of the detection and prosecution of offenders), and the package of publicized enforcement measures implemented in the "Christmas Crusade" of December 1983 definitely had a temporary impact on casualties, with a 23% reduction during the month of the "crusade." But effects beyond a year or so have not been obtained.

SCANDINAVIA

Based on the review of Ross, Klette, and McCleary (1984), it seems that in the past decade there has been a movement in the Scandinavian countries (with the exception of Norway) from an approach emphasizing severity of punishment to one emphasizing certainty of apprehension. The use of prison sentences has been reduced, with a corresponding increase in the popularity of fines and therapeutically oriented sentences. In the late 1970s and early 1980s random breath testing procedures were implemented in Finland, Denmark, Sweden, and Norway, but in all countries the "very restrained use of this technique prevents firm conclusions at this time" (p. 471). The authors do note however that Norway's experience with RBT warrants closer attention, since despite a lack of statistical significance the curve of fatalities declined by 9% on an apparently permanent basis. Analysis of drunk-driving indexes suggested that the overall liberalization in laws has been accomplished without increasing the number of impaired drivers on the road.

Recent Scandinavian research supports the value of policies emphasizing the perceived probability of detection rather than severe punishments. Åberg (1986) compared two counties in Sweden differing in the number of "routine breath tests" conducted, and found that in the county with the greater number of tests drivers had a higher perceived probability of being tested, and that the perceived probability was linearly related to the number of tests personally experienced. It is of interest that publicity concerning enforcement through the mass media did not influence perceptions.

Assum (1986) compared levels of drink-driving and alcohol-related crashes in Norway and Sweden. He observed that despite the fact that Norway imprisons drivers caught over .05 while Sweden only fines them (up to BAC levels of .15), more drink-driving actually takes place in Norway. He concluded that Sweden's better record is due to the higher actual and perceived risk of apprehension in that country, and recommends less use of prison sentences in Norway together with a greater emphasis on surveillance.

CANADA

The Canadian drinking-driving countermeasure experience is reviewed by Liban, Vingilis, and Blefgen (1987). Like the United States, Canada has lagged Australia and Scandinavia in the use of roadside breath testing, RBT, and so on. Random spot checks have been employed, although it appears that the police must still have reason to suspect alcohol use before demanding a breath test. Evaluations of these campaigns (the Alberta CHECK-STOP program, the Reduce Impaired Driving in Etobicoke program [RIDE], the Reduce Impaired Driving Everywhere [in Toronto] program, the Niagara project, and the British Columbia COUNTER-ATTACK program) all failed to reveal either a large or sustained impact on drink-driving behavior or accidents (with the possible exception of the COUNTERATTACK program). All these campaigns appeared to suffer to some extent from a lack of media support and limited public awareness. Indeed, Canadian researchers generally seem to stress the critical importance of media publicity (Cousins, 1980; Mercer, 1984, 1985). They have also conducted several analyses of perceived risk of arrest, but unfortunately have used hypothetical drink-drivers or the "average driver" rather than personal risk (Mercer, 1984; Vingilis & Salutin, 1980). Perhaps this is part of the reason why deterrent effects have generally not been found (Grasmick & Green, 1980).

NEW ZEALAND

Random stopping has been conducted in New Zealand since November 1984. The mode of operation appears to be similar to that employed in parts of the United States: roadblocks to check licenses and equipment, with the demand for a breath test if the officer has reason to believe that the driver has been drinking. Derby and Hurst (1986) review the impact of this program, and conclude that it may have had an effect in the first 3 months, when operations were most intense, but that the effects have been negligible ever since. In particular, the effect that did occur was not one of a reduction in numbers from a previous level but instead a leveling off of numbers of nighttime accidents while daytime accidents increased.

THE UNITED STATES

Trends in the United States are very difficult to evaluate because there is such a diversity of approaches in the different states. "Sobriety checkpoints" are becoming increasingly popular, but are plagued with legal and operational problems. These checkpoints are mounted by stopping all cars, or a systematic sample of cars, at designated highway locations, interviewing the drivers, and testing those individuals whose behavior generates the suspicion that they may be impaired by alcohol. When California police began checkpoints in 1984, the American Civil Liberties Union proceeded immediately to the California Supreme Court, seeking an instantaneous ban on checkpoints on constitutional ground (Smith, 1985). Within academic circles, the propriety and value of checkpoints is still hotly debated (see Ross [1988] and Christoffel [1984] for contrasting views). Moreover, because of the Constitutional and legal restrictions, the police encounter difficulties not faced by their antipodean and Scandinavian counterparts (Burns, 1985; Jones & Lund, 1986).

Although the American police are enthusiastic about checkpoints and positive results are reported (Stone, 1985), they tend to see checkpoints as having a role subsidiary to traditional enforcement techniques in contrast to Australians and Scandinavians (Smith, 1985). In any case, hard evidence that they have succeeded in reducing crashes is not currently available. Williams and Lund (1984) review the deterrent effects of checkpoints in Maryland and Delaware, and conclude that although the roadblocks are highly visible and did increase drivers' estimates of the likelihood that drunk drivers would be arrested, there was no change in drinking and driving behaviors.

The results of U.S. legal interventions not incorporating sobriety checkpoints are equally disappointing. Using interrupted time series analysis, Hilton (1984) analyzed the impact of new California legislation on fatal accidents during the first postintervention year. The California law of 1982 introduced per se provisions (at .10) and provided for tougher penalties, including mandatory jail for all repeat offenders and reduced access to plea bargaining. The evaluation showed that although alcohol-related fatalities did decline, nonalcohol-related fatalities declined by about the same amount. However, there was some indication that deterrent effects occurred for injury accidents.

Hingson and co-workers (1986) evaluated the impact of a law in Maine that was very similar to the California law, but was described by the Governor of Maine as the "toughest drunk driving law in the nation" (p. 1). They also evaluated tougher penalties in Massachusetts. The authors' conclusion was that in neither state did the measures sustain drunk driving and fatal crash reductions; indeed, in Massachusetts such effects were not even initiated. This is a very disappointing conclusion, because over the first 2 years it appeared that marked effects in Maine (a 40% reduction in single-vehicle, nighttime fatal accidents) were going to be sustained.

CONCLUSION

It is tempting to conclude from this review of the international literature on the general (or simple) deterrence of drink-driving that permanent deterrent effects are beyond the grasp of law enforcement agencies. While this conclusion is certainly warranted for British, New Zealand, and North American efforts to date, the evidence for Norway and Sweden is that random (or routine) testing is effective, although further research on the permanency of effects of random testing in Norway is required. Lest it be thought that failure is somehow inevitable for English-speaking jurisdictions, the Australian experience with random testing, reviewed in the next chapter, should be kept in mind.

On the research side, it is encouraging to see the increased attention being devoted to the study of the perceptual elements in the deterrence process. However, many of the lessons which could be learned from a study of the general sociological literature on deterrence do not appear to have penetrated the drink-drive field to any great extent. One could cite as examples the need for longitudinal surveys to chart variations in risk perceptions over time and also to unravel the direction of causality between perceptions of sanctions and driving while impaired, the desirability of personal rather than other-referenced measures of arrest risk, and the need to pay much closer attention to the assumed causal chain linking actual enforcement levels to drink-driving behavior.

Studies of Penalties and Reconvictions

Punishment Versus Treatment

Much of the research into the impact of judicial actions on the behavior of offenders has centered on various kinds of treatment programs which had a rehabilitative rather than a punitive or deterrent orientation. Of course whether these "treatments" are perceived by the offenders themselves as anything other than punishment is an open question (Brody, 1976). There is an enormous amount of literature on the effects of correctional treatment, much of which is based on recidivism as a success criterion. In a well-known review of this literature up to the early 1970s, Lipton, Martinson, and Wilks (1975) are generally believed to have concluded that nothing works. A more accurate summary of their conclusions would probably be that nothing works any better than anything else, an interpretation disputed by some (e.g., Gottfreidson, 1982).

Given the popular image of drinking drivers as problem drinkers or alcoholics, it is not surprising that there have been extensive efforts to develop rehabilitation programs as an alternative to, or a supplement for, the traditional penalties of fines, bonds, license disqualification, and prison (Tomasic, 1977). This literature has been reviewed by Mann, Leigh, Vingilis, and De Genova (1983). These authors concluded that although the effectiveness of rehabilitation programs has yet to be established, there are indications that some have had positive impacts on traffic safety measures, although the impact on recidivism is less clear. However, the authors stress the poor design and inadequate statistical procedures of many of the studies (also a feature of the general literature on rehabilitation [Gottfreidson, 1982]), and recommend not only an improvement in methods, but that attention be paid to classifications of offenders so that treatment can be matched more effectively with offender needs.

In the present review, rehabilitation schemes are examined only to the extent that they have been compared directly with traditional punishments.

The Marginal Impact of Penalties on Drink-Drivers

Apart from scattered references in the literature to the differential effects of legal threats on the behaviors of those with and without a conviction (e.g., Tittle, 1980a), there is almost no literature relevant to absolute specific deterrence. Most research has been restricted to a study of the marginal specific deterrent effects of penalties, using reconviction rates as a criterion. Reviewing the results of many of these studies, Zimring and Hawkins (1973) concluded that:

. . . those treated more leniently have lower rates of subsequent criminality than those punished more severely. But when such comparisons are controlled for differences in the offender groups other than type of punishment, the dominant feature of the results is that the overall differences between various methods of treatment are small or non-existent (p. 244).

These findings are not consistent with the deterrence doctrine; in fact, they indicate that the particular type or severity of penalty imposed is irrelevant to the subsequent behavior of the offender. More recent reviews (e.g., Brody, 1976) have yielded similar findings.

Zimring and Hawkins (1973) go on to say that the apparent lack of significance could be the result of more severe punishment producing significant positive effects in some types of offenders and significant negative effects on others that tend to balance out. This implies that the possibility of interaction effects between offender characteristics and penalties should be carefully considered in a study of specific deterrence. This issue is considered in more detail in the following sections.

Unfortunately there have been relatively few studies of the specific deterrent effect of penal sanctions on driving offenders, including drink-

drivers, although it is a topic that has attracted the attention of criminologists in a number of countries. Since the style of research varies a little
from country to country, it will be convenient to divide the available research on a geographical basis.

GERMANY

Middendorff (1968) provides a comprehensive summary of many studies
undertaken in Europe and the United States up until about 1968. One
West German study to which he refers compared the effect of a suspended
jail sentence with an actual period of imprisonment on a sample of drinking
drivers. The reconviction rates between the years 1959 and 1962 averaged
8% for both groups; there was no significant difference. However, these
figures are open to the criticism that they were not adequately controlled
for differences in regions or for variations among the drivers who received
the two types of penalties. More recently, German researchers have integrated a variety of treatment approaches with penal sanctions, with
promising results (Valverius, 1985; Barthelmess, 1986).

HOLLAND

More information is available from Holland than any other country except
the United States. In a very detailed paper, Buikhuisen (1969) described
the psychiatric and personality characteristics of many samples of convicted offenders, and also examined the impact of penalties on recidivism
rates. He reports results for the effects of five penalties on a sample of
3,875 offenders, but unfortunately he did not control for background characteristics. Nevertheless, the simple correlations suggested no relationship
between the probability of reconviction and penalty type, period of disqualification, or period of imprisonment.

Dijksterhuis (1974) evaluated the specific preventive effect of a special
prison for drunken drivers in Holland. He matched 76 drink-drivers in a
traditional prison with 76 drink-drivers from a special prison for traffic
offenders called Bankenbos. Bankenbos involved minimum supervision,
and prisoners worked in the garden or woods and were allowed to wear
their own clothes. There was some input of information about traffic problems. The traditional prison was quite different, involving strict supervision
and consisting of prisoners of all kinds. The two groups were matched individually on age, social status, and time of year of imprisonment.

Dijksterhuis found that the experimental group had a more positive
overall opinion of Bankenbos than the control group did of the traditional
prison, but that the rate of reoffending for drink-drivers, as reported in an
interview with the offenders 2 years after release, did not differ significantly
between the two groups. In fact 52.6% of the experimental group admitted
to driving under the influence, compared with 44.7% of the controls. There
was no difference in the reported frequencies of drinking and driving. Dijk-

sterhuis concluded that a more humane prison climate, however valuable in itself, does not in itself make for a clear-cut difference in terms of specific prevention. On the other hand, the study provides no support for inflicting harsh treatment on drink-drivers.

In a later study, Dijksterhuis (1975) examined the impact of a range of judicial penalties on reconviction rates for drinking and driving among a sample of 1,674 offenders. He controlled for the effects of 15 background variables, but combined all six judicial outcomes into a severity of penalty scale, preventing any conclusions about the effects of specific types of punishment. The background variables explained 13% of the variance in recidivism for drinking and driving, with previous convictions of all kinds and the age of the offender being the major predictors (young drivers and multiple offenders were more likely to be reconvicted). Controlling for these variables, there was no correlation between penalty severity and probability of reconviction.

Most recently, van der Werff (1981) examined rates of reconviction over a 6-year period for seven categories of offenders, including drink-drivers. After controls for age, sex, and penal record, she found no significant negative relationship between penalty severity (noncustodial versus custodial) and probability of reconviction, but, contrary to deterrence predictions, slight positive correlations. There was also no relationship between length of custodial sentence and reconviction rates for drink-drive offenders.

Like the Germans, the Dutch have recently developed treatment programs for incarcerated and other offenders, with promising results (Bovens, 1986). In particular, drink-drive reconviction rates for imprisoned offenders appear to be reduced by education programs (Lambregts & Soenveld, 1986).

ISRAEL

Shoham (1974) describes a study of the effect of penalties on traffic offenders in Israel. He found that there appeared to be a positive correlation between the severity of penalty for first offense and the number of subsequent offenses. Thus, for example, of those drivers who were warned on their first offense, 52.7% remained free of further convictions compared with 38.7% of those who were fined. Shoham's explanation for these puzzling findings is that severe punishments may increase the anxieties of drivers and lower their self-confidence, thus making them poorer drivers. This study has since been extended (Shoham, Geva, Markowski, & Kaplinsky, 1976; Shoham, Rahav, Markovsky, Chard, Ben-Haim, & Baruch, 1982).

The main interest of Shoham's research, despite the fact that it does not deal directly with drink-driving, is that it is an attempt to demonstrate empirically some of the negative consequences of labeling which are in his book, *The Mark of Cain* (Shoham & Rahav, 1982). However, another explanation for Shoham's finding that there is a positive correlation between recidivism and penalty severity is that he has not adequately controlled for the characteristics of offenders in his analysis.

BRITAIN

The most thorough study of the impact of the legal system on driving offenders in Britain was undertaken by Willett (1973). This was a project parallel to Hood's (1972), which studied disparities in sentencing driving offenders and the theoretical basis of sentencing as perceived by magistrates.

In Willett's study, the individuals in the sample of people convicted of relatively serious driving offenses (causing death by dangerous driving, driving under the influence, etc.) were followed up and interviewed as many as three times over a period of 2 years. Nearly three-quarters (71%) of the 181 offenders felt their sentences were unjust, especially the drunken drivers. More than one in three (36%) of those disqualified from driving admitted to having disobeyed the disqualification order, and most of them were never caught. After a 4-year period, 39% were reconvicted for some offense, whether driving or not. Twenty-seven percent committed a driving offense.

Willett found that overall about two-thirds of the offenders were relatively untouched by their sentences. There was a great distaste for disqualification, but its power rested mainly on bluff; as soon as it was realized that the disqualification order is not energetically enforced, it was reduced to the status of an irritant. On average, offenders were younger than a control sample of drivers, of lower education and occupational status, and were more likely to have had previous convictions for both driving and nondriving offenses.

Willett's study gives little encouragement to the view that heavier penalties or the use of one type of penalty (such as disqualification) rather than another will deter offenders from further offenses. Moreover, it seems that sentences are most effective in the case of law-abiding drivers, rather than the group of experienced law-breakers who tend to ignore disqualification and fines.

THE UNITED STATES

A number of studies have been conducted in the United States, mainly by government research organizations. One of the most interesting was by Blumenthal and Ross (1973), since it is one of the few examples in the literature of an attempt to use a randomization methodology with drink-drive offenders (see also Ross & Blumenthal, 1974, 1975). The researchers were concerned with the effects of a fine, conventional probation, or rehabilitative probation on drink-drivers who were first offenders. With the cooperation of the judges, it was hoped by the researchers that all the offenders in a specified month would (with few exceptions) receive one of these types of penalties.

Unfortunately, the lawyers got wind of the experiment and either introduced delaying tactics so that their client did not appear until the month when fines were to be imposed, or they argued persuasively for a penalty other than probation. Thus the advantages of a randomized experiment were lost and statistical controls had to be introduced. As far as the researchers were able to determine, the type of penalty imposed on the 500 first offenders who were sampled had no effect on subsequent drink-drive behavior or traffic safety. Those sentenced to jail rather than to one of the three prescribed treatments were also found not to differ from the balance of the group in subsequent records. Overall about 5% of the sample were reconvicted for a DUI offense within 1 year.

This study is important, not so much for its findings, which are very much the same as those obtained in other studies, but for its method. Ross and Blumenthal (1975) were well aware of the ethical problems entailed in random allocation experiments and defended their design on a number of grounds. They argued that the experiment did not involve any penalty which was not frequently imposed on first offenders, the experimental prescription went only to the quality or type of sanction, not to its quantity or amount, and the value of the possible results of the study seemed sufficient to outweigh any marginal costs to the offender. They note, however, that not all of their colleagues were convinced as to the ethics of the design.

The fundamental difficulty encountered by Ross and Blumenthal was that defendants disliked probation and the education clinics far more than they disliked fines, and this determined the actions of their lawyers. This illustrates the point that perceived severity is more important than the formal penalty, and that randomized experiments cannot be justified on the basis that all penalties being compared are equal in severity unless evidence is produced that in the eyes of offenders this is actually the case. However, if it were possible to produce this evidence there would be no grounds for expecting a deterrent effect.

Probably the most thorough research into the effects of sanctions on drink-drive offenders has been carried out in California. Hagen (1978) was able to take advantage of one of the more curious aspects of American law enforcement when he matched 1,501 multiple DUI offenders who had their licenses suspended or revoked with 1,501 multiple offenders who had their previous offenses declared unconstitutional, presumably on technical grounds. Although Hagen does not say so, it appears that all drivers were convicted, since all received a fine and/or a jail sentence (of unspecified severity). The groups were matched on county of conviction, number of prior DUI convictions, and sex.

In a 6-year follow-up, Hagen found that those disqualified had lower DUI reconviction rates and fewer traffic crashes. The effects lasted 42 months for reconvictions, and 48 months for crashes, which was longer than the 3 years which would have been the maximum disqualification period any offender would have received. However, disqualification had no effect on DUI convictions or crashes for offenders younger than 30 years, although it had an effect on the incidence of both minor and major traffic convictions across all age groups.

Hagen's sample was drawn from those offenders convicted in the first 6 months of 1970. In 1976, California adopted a new approach to the treatment of recidivist drink-drivers, with the introduction of alcohol abuse treatment programs as an alternative to license suspension. These pilot schemes were evaluated by Hagen, Williams, McConnell, and Fleming (1978), who concluded that mandatory license actions were a more effective traffic safety countermeasure than participation in the rehabilitation program.

A more extensive evaluation has since been conducted by Sadler and Perrine (1984), who used a 4-year follow-up instead of the 1 year employed by Hagen and colleagues (1978). The study by Sadler and Perrine is clearly the most rigorous evaluation published to date of the specific deterrent impact of penalties on repeat drink-drivers. Their major conclusion paralleled that of Hagen and colleagues: the recipients of license actions did far better than the participants in the rehabilitation program, the latter group having about 70% more nonalcohol related accidents and convictions than those who were disqualified. Among the license-action recipients, those who received 3-year revocations had fewer subsequent nonalcohol related accidents and convictions than those who received 12-month suspensions. This was especially true among subjects under 36 years of age. However, there were no differences between any of the groups on alcohol-related convictions and crashes. The authors concluded that although nothing seemed to have much effect on DUI recidivism, license action provides some degree of compensation for the greater traffic risk posed by the DUI offender by reducing nonalcohol-related accidents and convictions.

The constancy of DUI recidivism rates across many forms of treatment and different periods of license suspension suggests the existence of a group of nondeterrable alcoholics. However, Sadler and Perrine (1984) and Peck, Sadler, and Perrine (1985) cite a number of other American studies which suggest that license suspension can be effective in reducing DUI recidivism (see also Williams, Hagen, & McConnell, 1984a).

Although license suspension appears to be the most effective sanction for drinking drivers, there are some indications that probation may also have some positive effects, especially for nonproblem drinkers (Landrum et al., cited by Sadler & Perrine [1984]; Marsh, 1986). However, very little can be said for the positive specific deterrent properties of imprisonment. Following the success of citizens' action groups in the United States, imprisonment for up to 3 days is now mandatory even for first offenders in 17 states, and 42 states provide for mandatory jail terms of 2 to 60 days for second offenders (Voas, 1986). It is perhaps ironic that the Scandinavian countries (especially Finland) have been moving away from heavy prison terms at the same time that community groups in the United States have been so successful in getting them introduced. It is worth repeating the conclusion of Ross, Klette, and McCleary (1984), that the declining use of prison in Scandinavia has *not* been accompanied by any increase in impaired driving.

What is the U.S. evidence? Although his review did not reveal any positive specific or general deterrent impact of prison, Voas (1986) concluded that ". . . it would be a mistake to reject the use of incarceration on the basis of current evidence, if for no other reason than that the expanded use of this sanction in the United States will generate new evidence bearing on the issue." This is a not unreasonable position, since one problem with evaluating the impact of jail in the past has been the fact that those imprisoned are very different from those receiving less severe penalties. In addition, there is some preliminary evidence that for first offenders 2-day jail terms do reduce recidivism (Compton, 1986), perhaps by as much as 40% over 2 years.

Nevertheless, the Scandinavian experience, together with the great bulk of research evidence to date, strongly suggests that prison does not achieve deterrent effects and may well be counterproductive (Salzberg & Paulsrude, 1984). In addition, even if prison is shown to have some deterrent effects, are such effects any greater than those obtained through license suspension (Peck, Sadler, & Perrine, 1985)? New evidence from the United States must be evaluated carefully as it comes to hand.

AUSTRALIA

Other than the research reported in this book and by Homel (1980a, 1981a), little work on the specific deterrent effects of penalties has been conducted in Australia. Robinson (1977) in a mail survey of 1,552 disqualified drivers found that at least 36.4% drove while disqualified, with over 40% of those subjects driving on more than 20 occasions. Drivers who committed more serious offenses, many of whom were drinking drivers, were less likely to admit to driving while disqualified (30.4%). The relation between driving and length of disqualification was curvilinear, with the highest frequency of violations reported by subjects disqualified for a period of 1 or 2 months (46.2%). Subjects disqualified for less than 1 month or for 12 months or more had the lowest rate of reported violations (29.5% and 29.9% respectively).

In a review of previous research on license disqualification, Robinson (1977) concluded that the proportion of drivers who violate the sanction is between 32% and 68%, but some studies suggest that many who do drive while disqualified drive more carefully. The evidence bearing on the relationship between length of disqualification and probability of driving while disqualified appears to be contradictory. Some findings indicated that those who do drive during a period of disqualification tend to be younger and of lower status, but again the evidence is not unanimous.

In an interesting study of the driving records of 546 people descended from multiproblem families in Tasmania, Hagger and Dax (1977) documented the relationship between driving offenses and other kinds of social pathology. Although not a quantitative analysis, their discussion of the relationship between these families and the police is instructive. They ask whether the penalties for traffic offenses for these people have much meaning, since there is no stigma associated with arrest and prison may provide accommodations superior to what they are accustomed to. To the extent that drink-drivers from multiproblem families or deprived backgrounds constitute a significant percentage of convicted drink-drivers, the research by Hagger and Dax helps to inject a note of realism into the discussion of the likely effects of penalties. That drivers from multiproblem families do occur more frequently than expected on a population basis among those convicted is implied by the findings of Vinson and Homel (1975, 1976). These authors found a strong relationship between crime (including drink-driving) and other kinds of social problems, and an over-concentration of both crime and social problems in a small number of "high risk" neighborhoods (see also Michalowski, 1975).

OVERVIEW OF RECONVICTION LITERATURE

The review of literature presented before leads strongly to the conclusion that drink-drive recidivism rates are generally unaffected by type or quantity of penalty. The major exception to this conclusion is that license disqualification may be an effective deterrent, especially for nonalcohol-related motoring offenses, and longer periods of disqualification may be more effective than shorter periods. Certainly license action is to be preferred to alcohol treatment, although the positive results for treatment reported recently from Europe should be kept in mind. The evidence on probation is not clear, although there is some evidence of positive effects. Imprisonment, which is the harshest penalty available to a court, has not been shown to be a better specific deterrent than less severe penalties.

Offender Typologies

Many authors have noted the importance of matching punishment or treatment with offender characteristics. Given the generally negative findings of research into the marginal effects of penalties, such classifications seem to offer one of the few positive ways forward (Brody, 1976). However, it was argued in Chapter 1 that there are no convenient offender typologies which can inform deterrence research, and that it is not even clear what actually is the nature of the alcohol problem manifested by many offenders. Should we, for example, speak of alcoholism as a disease of the individual or should we speak of problems associated with the use of alcohol in specific social contexts? It is also necessary to keep in mind the distinction between convicted drink-drivers and drinking drivers who are never arrested, and the ways in which certain groups of offenders may be selected for arrest and conviction.

There are a few leads in the literature which may assist in the understanding of how offender characteristics can condition the deterrent impact of punishment. However, these leads point to possibly significant variables rather than to complex combinations of characteristics. For example, Hagen's (1978) finding that license disqualification was more effective for offenders over 30 years of age suggests that age should be incorporated in interaction terms with penalties. Similarly, the finding of Landrum and colleagues (cited in Sadler & Perrine, 1984) that probation and rehabilitation were more effective for nonproblem drinkers suggests some interactions involving BAC. In addition, the studies by Shoham and co-workers (1982) and Parsons (1978) of samples of motoring offenders point to recklessness and involvement in criminal violence as factors which are likely to influence responses to penalties.

There are some pointers from the criminology literature concerning effective offender typologies. One of the more ambitious attempts to build such typologies has been made by Gibbons (1975), who stresses what he calls *role careers*, which involve the attempt to specify criminal behavior patterns which describe the law-breaking life career of individual persons. According to Hood and Sparks (1970), such typologies are useful provided that they distinguish (as Gibbons does) between occasional and persistent offenders, and provided persistent offenders are further subdivided according to whether they display homogeneous or mixed careers. Applying these ideas to drink-drive offenders, we might look, for example, for the "traffic delinquent" who commits a variety of driving offenses but not criminal offenses, or for the "criminal offender" for whom drink-driving is a minor, even infrequent, episode in a multifaceted career of deviance.

Despite the hopes which have been held out for offender typologies, it would probably be a mistake to expect too much in the way of insights into the causes of drink-driving or its effective control (Arstein-Kerslake & Peck, 1985). Gibbons himself has become skeptical about the prospects for uncovering a relatively parsimonious set of criminal role-careers. Consistent with the emphasis of Chapter 1 of this book, he believes that "situational pressures" and "risk-taking processes" (p. 153) are of greater importance in understanding crime than had been recognized in criminological theorizing up until that time (1975). He concludes that classification should be focused on specific groups of offenders within certain limited correctional settings and have relatively modest goals. This is precisely the policy adopted in the construction of an offender typology reported in Chapter 8.

Summary

The literature on marginal specific deterrence is particularly easy to summarize: with the exception of license disqualification and maybe probation applied to some classes of offenders, neither type nor quantity of penalty makes any difference to the probability of reconviction. A priority for research into specific deterrence is to develop offender typologies which could provide the foundation for theoretical developments of the deterrence model to account for these results. In addition, it is possible that more powerful research designs which go beyond the use of reconvictions and probe evaluations of the experience of punishment could produce stronger evidence for marginal specific deterrent effects.

Although the perceptual research on general deterrence is deficient in a number of respects, it is superior to drink-drive research in providing a description of how the deterrence process might operate. On the other hand, the quasi-experimental drink-drive research has provided some of the clearest evidence that legal innovations can have marked deterrent effects, at least on a short-term basis. What is needed now is research which combines the best features of both traditions; that is, research which capitalizes on sudden, well-publicized changes in the law, but which goes beyond the analysis of traffic crash data by exploring directly the perceptual foundations of deterrence.

In Chapter 5 such a design applied to the introduction of RBT in New South Wales is outlined. In order to set the scene for this empirical research the next chapter contains a brief description of random breath testing in Australia, together with a summary of the evidence bearing on the effectiveness of the random testing programs implemented in different states.

4
Random Breath Testing in Australia

Random breath testing (RBT) may be viewed as a particularly vivid, yet simple application of the classical doctrine of deterrence, since it is in essence a law which enables police to administer a screening breath test even when they have no reason to believe that the driver has been drinking. Although details of operation vary between the states of Australia, RBT always involves arbitrarily selected checkpoints, usually on main roads, which are varied from day to day and from week to week and are not announced publicly prior to the RBT operation. In principle, testing can be carried out on any day of the week and at any time of day or night, but in practice RBT is concentrated in the evening hours, especially on weekends, when driving after drinking is most likely to occur. Motorists passing a checkpoint are pulled over for a breath test in a more or less haphazard manner, and in principle any driver of a car, motorcycle, or truck can be asked to take a test, regardless of age, sex, or manner of driving.

This chapter is about RBT in Australia: how it operates and the effects it has had. We begin with a brief examination of the road safety situation in Australia, making some comparisons with the United States. The patterns of alcohol use and drink-driving in Australia are then considered as a background to the examination of drink-drive laws in the various states and territories. RBT will be put in historical perspective, and it will be shown that variations between jurisdictions in both legislation and methods of enforcement make it very difficult to consider RBT as a unitary phenomenon. The RBT campaign in New South Wales will be described in some detail, since it and the Tasmanian campaigns are the best examples of their type in Australia, and possibly anywhere else in the world. The New South Wales model is particularly important in view of the evidence that the deterrent effects of RBT in that state have been permanent. The description of RBT in New South Wales will prepare the way for the evaluation which is described in Chapters 5 and 6.

in Road Safety

~ustralia is a large country, not much smaller in area than the mainland United States. In contrast to the United States, however, the total population is only about 16 million, with 85% living in urban areas of 25,000 or more. Australia is therefore among the most highly urbanized (or suburbanized) countries in the world, a fact which may have something to do with the readiness of the Australian populace, accustomed to suburban conformity, to seek legal remedies for social problems such as the road death toll. Certainly the concentration of Australians in cities and the vast land area means that many rural roads are well below world standards: of 800,000 km of road length, 90% is in rural areas, and only a quarter of that length is sealed (Johnston, 1982c).

As well as being one of the most urbanized nations in the world, Australia is one of the most motorized, with fewer than two persons per vehicle. Around 3,000 people die in road crashes each year, and as in other developed nations traffic accidents are a leading cause of death in the population up to 45 years of age. Historically Australia has had a higher death rate per 100 million vehicle kilometers traveled than the United States, although in recent years the gap between the two countries has narrowed (in 1985 the rates were 2.1 and 1.5, respectively). It is interesting to note, however, that the statistic that is of most interest to epidemiologists, fatalities per 100,000 people, reveals that there is now almost no difference between the United States and Australia (18.3 and 18.7, respectively). Obviously this is partly because Americans drive a little further each year than Australians and are therefore more at risk, but recent declines in the Australian curve suggest that countermeasures specific to Australia may have had an effect.

Why have fatality rates improved in Australia to such an extent? Jiggins (1985) suggests that several factors may be important. Over the last two decades, approaches to road safety have become more scientific, and the road user is now regarded as a fallible component of a complex system. Major programs of road upgrading have been implemented, the roadside environment has been made more forgiving of human error, and vehicle design rules have been greatly expanded in scope. As noted above, Australians were also willing quite early on to introduce and obey stringent laws which are still being argued in most other jurisdictions. For example, the state of Victoria introduced in 1961 compulsory wearing of helmets for motorcyclists, in 1966 per se laws for drinking and driving were introduced, and since 1970 vehicle occupants have been required by law to wear seat belts. Victoria was also the first state in the Commonwealth to introduce RBT, in 1976. Most other states acted soon after the Victorian initiatives.

All these factors need to be kept in mind when considering trends in fatalities, and in particular when assessing the impact of RBT. The emphasis in Australia on behavior modification through deterrence-based measures is, relatively speaking, a recent phenomenon and should not be allowed to obscure the longer-term contribution of road engineering and vehicle design standards.

Alcohol Use and Drink-Driving in Australia

It is part of the national self-image that Australians, particularly men, consume and manage larger quantities of alcohol than the inhabitants of other nations. The capacity to imbibe large quantities of beer and remain upright is a badge of honor, a sign of manhood, among many young Australians of all social backgrounds. However, as Donald Horne has noted in his famous book, *The Lucky Country*, "Australians have never been quite the nation of boozers they imagine themselves to be. . ." (Horne, 1971, p. 36). In fact Australia in 1981 ranked 12th in total absolute alcohol consumption with 10.00 liters per capita, well behind many European nations (e.g., France: 13.7, Spain: 13.0, West Germany: 12.5), but ahead of all other English-speaking countries (United States: 8.3, United Kingdom: 6.8, Canada: 9.1). There is even evidence that Australian alcohol consumption is declining relative to the rest of the world, since in 1975 Australia's relative position was 10th. Clever marketing of low alcohol beers (less than 1% by volume) may be a factor in the decline in overall levels of consumption (Jiggins, 1985).

Notwithstanding Australia's middling position in terms of total alcohol consumption, in the 50 years since the Depression per capita alcohol consumption increased by a factor or five (from 2.5 liters in 1932). In the past decade wine has more than doubled its share of the market (at the expense of beer), perhaps because as a "struggling primary industry" it does not attract government taxes. In 1983 66% of men and 41% women reported that they usually drank alcohol on one or more days of the week, while 16% of men and 8% of women reported usually drinking every day of the week (Commonwealth Department of Health, 1986). The other side of the coin, however, is that the percentage of total abstainers has risen in recent years, with the figure currently standing at around 21% of adults aged 16 to 65 years. As Room (1984) has noted: "Despite popular Australian preconceptions to the contrary, abstainers are not a negligible fraction of the population, and appear at least to be holding their own in recent years" (p. 24).

Drinking and driving has long been recognized as a problem in Australia, as the early initiatives in the state of Victoria indicate. Indeed, as Room (1984) points out, "drink-driving is the alcohol issue uppermost in politicians' minds" (p. 34). The most accurate figures on levels of drink-driving come from random roadside surveys conducted in South Australia, which suggest that prior to RBT, on any trip randomly selected over the whole week 2.6% of drivers were over .05, with peaks of around 16% on weekend evenings (McLean, Holubowycz, & Sandow, 1980). Frequent drink-drive episodes are confirmed by self-report studies (Sloane & Huebner, 1980; MacLean, Hardy, Lane, & South, 1985).

The relatively severe nature of Australian legislation on drink-driving has been noted by a number of commentators (e.g., Johnston, 1982b). Per se, or "Scandinavian-type" laws, were introduced early, so that currently fewer than 5% of drink-drive offenders are convicted on evidence other than that of a breath test. A feature of Australian legislation which is shared with the Scandinavian countries is the use of a legal limit of .05g/100ml for motorists in four jurisdictions (the limit is .08 in the remaining four states and territories). Whether the limit is .05 or .08, BACs estimated from breath analysis are permitted to be used as evidence in court; blood tests are not necessary, although one may be requested by a motorist. Despite the evidence cited in Chapter 1 that teenage drivers are not particularly likely to drink and drive, nearly all Australian jurisdictions have moved to zero or near zero BAC levels for novice drivers. In addition, in many states and territories drivers admitted to a hospital after an accident are required by law to be blood tested to determine their BAC.

Penalties were also increased during the 1970s and the early 1980s, with punishments in all jurisdictions now being tied to BAC and previous drink-drive convictions. In New South Wales in 1983 82.4% of PCA (prescribed concentration of alcohol) offenders received a fine and a period of license disqualification, the average fine being around $400 and the average disqualification period being 6 months (NSW Bureau of Crime Statistics and Research, 1985). Moreover, as noted in Chapter 1, penalties in most Australian jurisdictions are relatively certain once an offender has been apprehended. Practices such as plea or charge bargaining in drink-drive cases are very rare.

The trend in Australia to low legal BAC levels, high certainty of punishment for apprehended individuals, and tougher penalties in court perhaps conveys the impression of a relentless system of enforcement unmatched anywhere except in Scandinavia. However, as argued in Chapter 1, drink-driving is no more unambiguously a crime in Australia than it is in the United States. Thus, despite the tough legislation and severe maximum penalties, actual punishments in Australia are far from draconian and are frequently less severe than those imposed in the United States or Britain. In particular, imprisonment is a relatively uncommon penalty for drink-driving. *In New South Wales fewer than 1 PCA offender in 50 is imprisoned, a pattern that is probably also true for other states.* Moreover there are statutory provisions in many states for first offenders to be found guilty, but without the conviction being recorded. Thus each year in New South Wales around 5% of offenders, often older men of good standing in the community, are released without penalty. These patterns of moderate penalties are of some importance when considering the impact of RBT, which is aimed at increasing the perceived likelihood of arrest rather than the perceived severity of penalties.

Random Breath Testing

In July 1976 the state of Victoria introduced RBT. Since then, both territories and all but two states have followed suit: the Northern Territory in February 1980, South Australia in October 1981, the Australian Capital Territory and New South Wales in December 1982, and Tasmania in January 1983. Moreover, in Western Australia and Queensland, the two non-RBT states, roadblocks or random stopping procedures are employed, whereby motorists may be stopped at random to have their licenses and vehicles checked. If the police officer has any cause to believe that the driver has been drinking, he may require the driver to undergo a preliminary breath analysis. Random stopping has been conducted in the form of blitzes in Western Australia (Maisey & Saunders, 1981), and in Queensland (where the program is known as RID, for "reduce impaired driving") it has been supported since August 1986 by intense publicity over Christmas, so in practice RBT or something close to it operates in all parts of Australia.

However, the existence of RBT-type legislation in most parts of Australia does not mean that what actually happens in terms of enforcement is the same in all parts of the country. In fact there is considerable diversity, and so it will be convenient in reviewing the effects of RBT in Australia to classify the different laws into broad types.

The roadblock or random stopping programs in Western Australia and Queensland may be referred to as *RBT by the back door*, since the *intention* is to conduct random testing, although the legislation is not formally in place. This seems a devious way of proceeding, hence the use of the term "back door." The situation in South Australia, the Northern Territory, and the Australian Capital Territory is characterized by legislation but low levels of enforcement, and may therefore be referred to as *Clayton's RBT* after a nonalcoholic beverage advertised in Australia as "the drink you have when you're not having a drink." Although RBT in Victoria is usually enforced at a fairly low level, it is reinforced periodically by intensive blitzes in the Melbourne metropolitan area, so it may be referred to as *RBT some of the time*. Finally, New South Wales and Tasmania have opted for high levels of enforcement on a continuous basis together with extensive publicity. For this reason the Australian term *boots and all* seems an appropriate characterization, meaning to go in with "all one's strength or resources" (*The Macquarie Dictionary*, 1981).

RBT by the Back Door: Western Australia and Queensland

Roadblocks are pseudo-RBT operations inasmuch as the probability of being tested does not depend on a motorist's manner of driving. However, the final decision to test depends on police suspicion of alcohol use (e.g., smell), so there is clearly more scope for an inebriated driver to escape a preliminary breath test than in full random testing. According to the only published evaluation of the Western Australian operations (Maisey & Saunders, 1981), the Christmas/New Year campaign in 1980–1981 resulted in a reduction in nighttime casualty crashes comparable to the one obtained in Victoria using full random testing. Nevertheless the proportion of motorists killed with BAC levels over .05 remains much higher in Western Australia than in the eastern states with full RBT (Federal Office of Road Safety, 1986).

The RID program in Queensland has been surrounded by fierce political controversy (Moller & North, 1986). The only published evaluation suggests that initial effects were substantial but began to dissipate after a few months (Queensland Transport Policy Planning Unit, 1987).

RBT Some of the Time: Victoria

Victoria has been widely cited in Australia as the state which has most effectively solved its drink-driving problem through the use of RBT (so much so that its perceived success has almost taken on the status of a "Scandinavian myth"), but unfortunately the conditions under which it was introduced make evaluation extremely difficult. In the early months, random testing was conducted for only 10 hours a week, and was restricted to the Melbourne metropolitan area (RACV Consulting Services, 1983). Testing has always been at a much lower level than in New South Wales, with the total number of tests in 1982 being a mere 72,957, compared with the nearly one million tests in New South Wales in the first year (1983). Given that Victoria was the first state to introduce RBT, and given the controversial nature of the legislation, it is perhaps understandable that the authorities should have been somewhat diffident about pushing enforcement too far in the first year or two. Consistent with this reluctance to be too heavy-handed, motorists found to be over the limit in Victoria are not arrested, but charged on summons and subsequently breath analyzed at a police station. Only then, if they are found to be over .05, are they arrested.

Notwithstanding this low-key approach, the distinguishing feature of Victorian RBT has been the use of intensified periods of testing in areas selected according to a predetermined experimental design. In fact the only direct evidence that RBT has had any effect in Victoria comes from evaluations of the effects of these scientifically planned police blitzes in selected areas of Melbourne (Cameron, Strang, & Vulcan, 1980; Cameron & Strang, 1982), which is not the usual manner of its enforcement.

During a 7-week period late in 1978, Victoria police carried out each week an average of 100 hours of RBT on Thursday, Friday, and Saturday nights in one of four sectors of Melbourne. Over the period of the experiment, all four sectors were systematically blitzed. The authors reported large reductions in fatalities and serious casualty accidents at night in the areas tested, with residual effects for at least 2 weeks after testing. Unfortunately, their method of analysis involved comparing the 1978 statistics for each sector with the figures for the same period in 1977. As Darroch (1981) has pointed out, there is evidence that for the weeks of the blitz the 1977 figures were abnormally high, suggesting that the figures presented by Cameron and colleagues (1980) exaggerate the impact of the blitz. The basic problem is that threats to internal validity, such as history or regression to the mean (Ross & McCleary, 1983), cannot be controlled through the use of only one comparison year. Cameron and Strang (1982) recognized the problem, but argued that their resources were inadequate to construct and analyze a separate set of time series for each sector of Melbourne included in the experiment. As a compromise, they included the previous 2 years as controls in later analyses of the above experiment and two subsequent ones. However, this strategy was in turn criticized by Johnston (1982c), who carried out his own analysis of the proportion of drivers killed in the period 8:00 p.m. to 4:00 a.m. over a 13-year period, with equivocal results.

Ross (1982) concluded that although the evaluation was not as methodologically strong as one might like, the results reported by Cameron and Strang (1982) resemble those reached in most other studies of short-term enforcement efforts. The operative word here, however, is *enforcement*, since it is quite possible that similar blitzes without using RBT could achieve comparable effects (Homel, 1980b; Homel, 1981b). In fact this possibility has been conceded by Cameron and Strang (1982) in a discussion of the Western Australian experience with roadblocks. The study by Sykes (1984) of a police drink-drive blitz in a local area of Superior, Wisconsin, although subject to the same kinds of methodological criticisms as Cameron and co-workers (1980), also supports the argument that RBT is not a necessary ingredient of a successful short-term enforcement campaign.

Despite these problems, the argument that RBT in Victoria has in fact achieved some deterrent effect is supported by a long-term decline in the proportion of drivers in single vehicle crashes with an illegal BAC, an increase in the perceived risk of detection by police of a drinking driver whose driving is not obviously impaired, and a slight decline in self-reported levels of drinking and driving between 1978 and 1986 (RACV Consulting Services, 1983; Hutchinson, 1987; South & Stuart, 1983). Unfortunately there is no clear connection between changes in the perceived risk of detection and legal interventions such as RBT, weakening the deterrence interpretation. The evidence for a general *preventive* effect of RBT in Victoria over the past few years—that is, changes in habits or in moral attitudes to drink-driving—is also rather weak (MacLean et al., 1985).

Clayton's RBT: South Australia and the Territories

Both the Northern Territory and the Australian Capital Territory have small populations, and little is known of the effects of RBT in these jurisdictions. The best evidence is that enforcement and publicity have been at low levels, and that effects on road casualties have been small but statistically significant (Federal Office of Road Safety, 1986). More information is available for South Australia.

As Bungey and Sutton (1983) note, in many respects South Australia's experience with RBT has been unique in Australia, since it was opposed not only by specific interest groups but by one of the two major daily newspapers. Because of the publicity generated by the controversy, RBT seems to have had a greater impact shortly *before* it commenced operation than afterwards. On the other hand, an aspect of the South Australian experience which makes it very similar to that of Victoria is the low level of enforcement and the limited official publicity. Despite the controversy surrounding the law, the percentage of the population in favor of the law rose, from 55% one month before RBT, to 63% 11 months after it was implemented (Fischer & Lewis, 1983). Nevertheless these levels of support are well below those recorded in New South Wales.

Only the South Australian RBT campaign has been evaluated using one of the theoretically most attractive tools: random roadside surveys (McLean et al., 1980; McLean et al., 1984). The first such survey was run 7 months before the introduction of RBT, the second 5 months after RBT, and the third a year after that. The percentages over .08 were 2.7, 2.3, and 2.7, respectively. The reversion to pre-RBT levels was not quite as complete when the percentages of drivers with any alcohol were examined, leading McLean (1984) to conclude that initially RBT had an effect on all drinking drivers but that a year later the residual effect was concentrated among light drinkers, some of whom gave up drinking altogether when they were driving. These data are consistent with self-reports of decreased drinking and driving recorded by Fischer and Lewis (1983). McLean also reports a marked reduction in casualty accidents during the hours 10:00 p.m. to 3:00 a.m. in 1981, compared in the 2 previous years, and an increase in 1982, but not to the earlier levels. In addition, there was a reduction in the proportion of hospital casualties who had been drinking.

McLean (1984) is of the view that RBT in South Australia did have an initial, slight effect, which in itself is remarkable since in the first 18 months it operated at the lowest possible level: one unit in the metropolitan area and one in the country. Moreover there was a 40% increase, in relative terms, in the proportion of accidents on back streets between 10:00 p.m. and 3:00 a.m. on Friday and Saturday nights as drivers sought to evade the police. McLean concludes that in the first 18 months of RBT in New South Wales much more was achieved than in the first 3 years of the South Australian experiment. However, from the point of view of deterrence theory there is one other fascinating outcome reported by McLean and co-workers (1984): RBT appeared to have a disproportionately large impact on the drink-driving behavior of drivers with a previous charge of drink-driving. It seems that even an intervention as minimal as South Australia's is capable of amplifying the deterrent impact of a previous encounter with the law.

RBT Boots and All: Tasmania and New South Wales

Tasmania

Tasmania, a small island state to the south of the mainland, introduced RBT a month after New South Wales, in January 1983. In contrast to Victoria and South Australia, but in line with New South Wales, RBT has been enforced and publicized at an intense level (Madden, 1986; Sutton, Farrar, & Campbell, 1986). In 1985 more than 200,000 roadside tests were conducted out of a driving population of only 268,887! Three mobile breath analysis units are commonly transferred to at least five different sites in an 8-hour shift, and since they are equipped with breath analysis equipment as well as cooking, toilet, and electricity generating facilities, testing can proceed uninterrupted over the shift. Occasional massive operations, Victorian style, are undertaken, and only after their completion are public announcements about them made by the authorities. It is thought that by this method the public will remain convinced that RBT is not an empty threat. Since Tasmania is a small state, publicity through the electronic media is not bought by the government, but extensive (free) publicity is achieved through newspapers. In particular, a daily list of the names of convicted drink-drivers is published in the papers.

Commensurate with the intensity of enforcement, there has been a marked decline in alcohol-related casualty crashes, which appears to have been sustained since 1983. Although Tasmania's small population makes an examination of fatality data difficult, it is noteworthy that alcohol involvement in fatal crashes in the 3-year post-RBT period was 42% less than for the 6 years prior to RBT (Federal Office of Road Safety, 1986). The same figure for casualty crashes was a 29% reduction. As Sutton and colleagues (1986) noted in a comparison of Tasmania with four states in the eastern United States, the consistency and intensity of enforcement of

RBT in Tasmania renders it a much more powerful tool than in the United States, where court challenges have generally severely circumscribed police powers.

The Introduction of RBT in New South Wales

RBT was not introduced in New South Wales in a political vacuum. Other states of Australia, notably Victoria and South Australia, had already introduced RBT, and by 1982 the perceived ineffectiveness of earlier attempts in New South Wales to contain the problem of road accidents had put pressure on the New South Wales government to follow the example of these states. All opinion polls conducted since 1979 indicated majority support for RBT. As measured by the question, "Do you agree or disagree with random breath testing of drivers in New South Wales?" support in Sydney rose from 70% in March 1979 to 79% in December 1981, 80% in December 1982 (the month RBT was actually introduced), and 91% in March 1983 (Cashmore, 1985). These levels of support are considerably higher than the figure of 37% recorded in 1973 (Freedman et al., 1973), indicating a marked change in community attitudes over the decade of the 1970s. Thus by 1982 the climate of opinion was right for RBT, a fact reflected in the official government report which recommended that RBT be introduced (Staysafe, 1982).

Despite the fact that RBT was not the only legal innovation implemented on December 17, 1982, from the beginning it received the lion's share of publicity. (Other measures included increased penalties and compulsory blood tests of drivers admitted to a hospital.) Many early reactions to RBT by police, the medical profession, and the media could only be described as euphoric. The head of the New South Wales Breath Analysis Unit was quoted in the *Sydney Morning Herald* on December 29, 1982, as being "ecstatic" about the state's low road toll over Christmas, and medical spokesmen from many hospitals in and around Sydney agreed with one doctor that the quiet hospital scene over the holiday period was "just incredible." The *Sydney Morning Herald* had commented the previous day:

> The dramatic drop in the New South Wales road toll over the last fortnight, including the first few days of the Christmas holiday period, is, of course, exceedingly welcome. There can be little doubt that random breath testing is responsible. ("The 0.05 line," 1982, p. 6).

Thus very soon after its introduction, RBT was popularly seen as being a spectacular success, and this view has, by and large, persisted.

However, more cautious voices were also raised, and the fact that the government had introduced RBT for a 3-year trial period was emphasized by a number of police and politicians. Indeed, to their credit, the politicians most directly concerned with the introduction of RBT were generally rather restrained in their claims about its success. RBT was introduced in

New South Wales following a period of essentially symbolic attempts to curb drinking and driving (the introduction of heavier penalties, lowering the limit to .05, etc.), and it seems that the caution which so characterized earlier government policy carried over into official attitudes towards RBT. In announcing the new measures in a press release, the Ministers for Police and for Transport said that in the face of "mounting supportive evidence for RBT, the government has had little alternative but to agree to a trial period." This hardly indicates overwhelming enthusiasm for the new law. There were in fact good grounds for caution, since the literature on drink-drive countermeasures (reviewed in Chapter 3) generally suggests that the deterrent impact of these kinds of laws is, if anything, strictly short term. It is likely therefore that the Ministers did not wish to identify too closely with a countermeasure which might have lost popularity after a short period. Nevertheless, they did provide the resources required.

Publicity and Enforcement in New South Wales

PUBLICITY

Despite their ambivalence about RBT, or perhaps because of it, the politicians ensured that RBT was well-publicized. The early publicity was of a high professional standard and achieved a substantial impact in the target population. Nearly everyone knew about RBT and most were aware of the increase in penalties (Cashmore, 1985). More than $1 million was spent on television, radio, and print advertising over Christmas 1982 and Easter 1983. Since then, many more millions have been expended. The early publicity was organized around the slogan, "How will you go when you sit for the test, will you be under .05 or under arrest?" set to a catchy tune which ensured not only that the message got across but that it was remembered.

This slogan was particularly apt for New South Wales, since unlike Victoria or South Australia, if the breath test is positive the driver is under arrest *solely* for the purpose of obtaining a more precise breath analysis on the bus or at a police station. Should the breath analysis show a reading of .05 or higher, the driver is formally charged (at a police station) with driving with the prescribed concentration of alcohol (PCA). If the reading is under .05 the matter is stopped and the driver is released. The slogan received extensive air time on radio and television and was emblazoned along the sides of government buses. An award-winning example of the print advertising campaign is reproduced in Figure 4.1.

An important aspect of media publicity was the interest expressed spontaneously in newspapers in the form of letters, articles, editorials, and cartoons. These "unofficial aspects" of the publicity surrounding RBT have been extensively analyzed by Cashmore (1985). It is clear that interest peaked in December 1982, at the time RBT was introduced, but that other high points were recorded at holiday times, particularly Christmas. The

What happens if you're under ·05:

What happens if you're under arrest:

Fail the roadside Random Breath Test and you are arrested there and then. It is not a pleasant experience. The procedure is long and humiliating. You are treated like a criminal. Here is a summary of what you can expect.

1. You are advised to lock up your car. Obviously you are not permitted to move it. Police will do their best to assist any inconvenienced family or passengers, but are under no obligation to do so.

2. You are taken away by police car, or led to the Breathalyzer bus, for the purpose of obtaining an accurate analysis of your Blood Alcohol Concentration. Since you are in police custody, the normal security arrangements apply.

3. You are placed in front of the instrument known as the Breathalyzer and directed to blow into it.

4. You are notified of the reading.

5. You are taken to the charging room. (If the Breathalyzer test has taken place in the bus, you are taken in a police car to the police station.)

6. You are placed in the dock. All valuables plus your tie and belt are removed to be returned on your release.

7. You are offered the services of a doctor of your choice, at your own expense, should you wish to undergo a blood test to verify your BAC.

8. You are formally charged and the entry made in the charge book.

9. You are told where and when to appear in Court.

10. You are finger-printed.

11. You are released as per the new bail laws or held in gaol until your Court appearance.

12. On conviction, sentence is handed down by the Court. Even the first offender with a Prescribed Concentration of Alcohol Reading of .05 could be fined up to $500 and could be disqualified from driving for six months. Higher PCA readings or second offences attract severe penalties including minimum mandatory periods of licence disqualification, fines up to $2,000 and gaol sentences up to 12 months.

Random Breath Testing. Will you be under ·05 or under arrest?

FIGURE 4.1. An early example of the RBT print advertising campaign (reprinted by the kind permission of the NSW Traffic Authority and John Bevins Pty. Limited).

lowest period of sustained interest seems to have been May to November 1984, which is of some significance in view of NSW Traffic Authority data (summarized in the following sections) suggesting that by July–August 1984 the impact of RBT on the perceived chances of arrest and on drinking and driving behaviors was actually *higher* than in May 1983 when newspaper interest had recently been at much higher levels.

Cashmore (1985) demonstrates that prior to RBT, metropolitan newspaper comment was evenly balanced between positive and negative evaluations, but that subsequently evaluative comment was overwhelmingly positive. Nevertheless, and notwithstanding general public opinion, the vigorous enforcement of a law giving police unprecedented powers to interfere with vast numbers of ordinary people met with some spirited opposition. It is worth touching briefly on the nature of this opposition, particularly since similar problems are likely to be encountered in other jurisdictions contemplating something like RBT.

The proprietors of clubs and pubs complained of greatly reduced patronage, and concerns were frequently aired about job losses in an industry which, it was claimed, was already hard hit by the effects of a recession. That these concerns had some substance, particularly with respect to beer consumption, is suggested by Cashmore's (1985) analysis of alcohol sales. One response of the breweries has been to promote low alcohol beers ("breathe easy" is a current advertising slogan).

Opposition to the law was not restricted to the liquor industry. Idle panel beaters (body shop workers) were featured in the media, and on more than one occasion a representative of the Transport Workers' Union attacked the law as being not only an infringement of civil liberties but ineffective as well. The Council for Civil Liberties, of course, had a good deal to say about the civil liberties issue. A memorandum from the Council to all Members of Parliament in the ruling New South Wales Labor Party on November 1, 1982 (6 weeks before the introduction of RBT) reaffirmed the Council's long-standing policy of opposition to the proposed law. Both in this submission and in public statements, the Council argued that RBT could be the first step in a process leading to police powers to stop, question or search citizens without any pretext, a situation they characterized as being typical of a "police state" (NSW Council for Civil Liberties, 1982, p. 1). However, in its memo to the politicians, the Council went on to moderate this hard-line position:

Nonetheless, we recognise that in a matter of such social concern as alcohol related road deaths that a civil liberty might be set aside in the specific instance if it can be demonstrated that the practice of random breath tests achieves the aim of reducing road deaths. Consequently the issue becomes not civil liberties versus reducing the road toll, but whether the facts available on RBT justify setting aside that civil liberty (NSW Council for Civil Liberties, 1982, p. 1).

Thus the debate shifted from theoretical arguments about civil liberties to a dispute about the empirical evidence for the effectiveness of RBT.

ENFORCEMENT

Even more impressive than the official publicity was the commitment of the police to the enforcement of the law. In the first 12 months of RBT (December 17, 1982 to December 31, 1983), nearly one million (923,272) preliminary breath tests were conducted, representing approximately one test for every three licensed drivers (Cashmore, 1985). To put this figure into perspective, it should be compared with the 113,985 nonrandom preliminary breath tests conducted in 1982, the year prior to the introduction of RBT. It should also be compared with the figure of one million tests in Sweden in the first 3 years of RBT, and 335,000 tests in 18 months in France, with a population 10 times as large as New South Wales. In more recent years testing has continued at even higher levels and has been extended to the early hours of the morning to counter the avoidance behavior of motorists who were staying out late hoping to avoid RBT. The majority of tests have been conducted in Sydney (52.9% in 1983 and 1984), but country regions, where the rate of traffic crash fatalities is higher, have by no means been neglected.

One basic problem with RBT, from the police point of view, is that very few drinking drivers are actually caught. RBT operations are time consuming and boring, and in the opinion of many police officers deflect them from their real job, which is "catching crooks." Even at times of peak drink-driving, the charge rate is at most 1.5%, and the average rate is only about 0.4 or 0.5%. Research by McLean in South Australia (McLean et al., 1984) demonstrates convincingly that drink-drivers are sometimes able to avoid RBT operations so the police charge rate in New South Wales cannot be taken as a reliable index of the actual rate of drinking and driving post-RBT. Similarly, the fact that the total number of convictions for drinking and driving declined in New South Wales in 1983 (Cashmore, 1985) may indicate less drink-driving in the community, or it may simply illustrate that police who would otherwise have been employed detecting impaired drivers were now occupied with RBT.

In summary, RBT has been enforced in New South Wales in a vigorous and wholehearted manner, and has been extensively supported by high quality media publicity. Moreover, both enforcement and publicity have been maintained at high levels for several years. This level of enforcement and publicity over a long period is in marked contrast to the conditions prevailing in most other jurisdictions which have introduced sudden changes to drink-drive law or its method of enforcement (Ross, 1982). As more and more jurisdictions in various parts of the world experiment with changes to the drink-drive laws and their methods of enforcement, the

New South Wales RBT campaign (together with that in Tasmania) may emerge as being, from a scientific point of view, of particular importance. For evaluation purposes the legal intervention is reasonably "pure," well-sustained, and very specific with respect to the main variable which the legislators intended to manipulate (the perceived risk of arrest for drinking and driving).

The Effects of RBT in New South Wales

Some critics of RBT have argued that any drop in the road toll can be attributed to the effects of economic or other factors, and that in any case (echoing Ross, 1982) the effects of these laws are invariably short term. It will be useful therefore to examine the crash statistics for a number of Australian states, to control to some extent for economic factors. More-over, data for exactly 4 years following the introduction of RBT in New South Wales are examined, so that any trends concerning a wearing off in effectiveness should be discernible.

In Figure 4.2a the fatal crash statistics for New South Wales are shown, for each month from January 1971 to November 1986. The figures plotted are fatal crashes and not fatalities, since the latter statistics are affected to some extent by random fluctuations in the numbers of persons killed in a given crash. The dotted line marks the date on which RBT was introduced.

The most noticeable feature of Figure 4.2a is the marked decline in fatal crashes coinciding with the inauguration of RBT. Whereas the series can be shown to be stationary for the 6 years prior to this date, with a monthly mean of 95.7 fatal crashes, the mean for the 48 months after RBT was 76.0, a decline of 20.6%. The second noticeable feature of Figure 4.2a is the variable nature of the data. The low points are nearly always February, suggesting a sizeable seasonal effect, as well as the need for controls for length of month. The considerable amount of variation in the data under-lines the need for time series techniques to be applied in order to assess the statistical significance of the apparent decline in December 1982 (Ross & McCleary, 1983).

An interrupted time series analysis applied to these data was in fact high-ly significant, and showed that the reduction in fatalities was sustained up till 1985 (when the analysis was carried out; Arthurson, 1985). Indeed, a noteworthy feature of Figure 4.2a is the failure of the curve to return to pre-RBT levels after 4 years, suggesting that following the initial shock of RBT the expected decline in perceived risk of detection, even if it occurred (Ross, 1982), did not translate into pre-RBT levels of drinking and driving. Actually there was a steady upward movement in the fatal crash statistics from 1983, with the number of crashes in 1985 being 8.4% higher than the 1983 figure, but the 1986 figure was identical with that for 1985. This could indicate a degree of wearing off in the effects of RBT, although Figure 4.2b

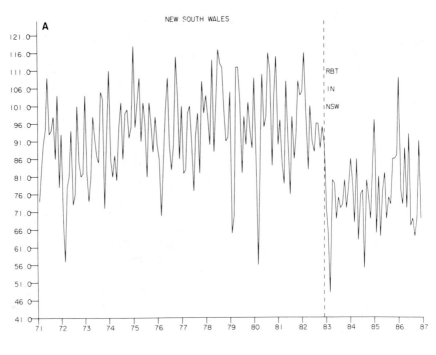

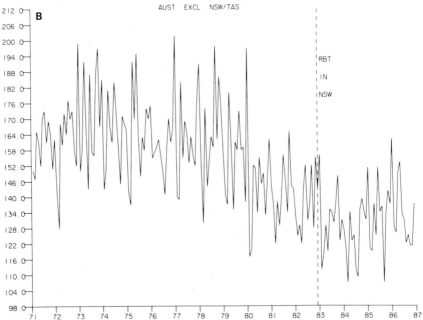

FIGURE 4.2. Fatal crashes for Australian states for each month from January 1971 to November 1986. (a) New South Wales; (b) Australia, excluding New South Wales and Tasmania; (c) Victoria; (d) Queensland.

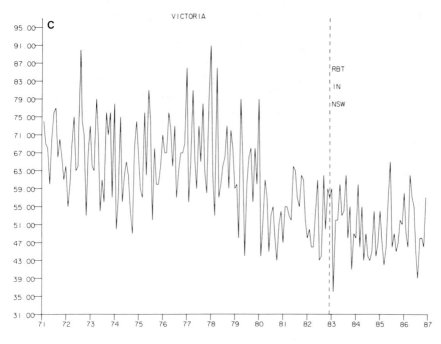

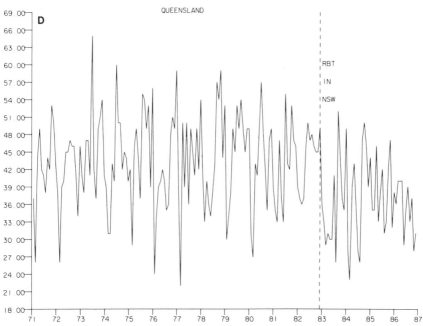

shows that there has also been an increase in states outside of New South Wales.

Another point to note from Figure 4.2b is that when the statistics for all states and territories of Australia other than New South Wales and Tasmania are combined, a downward trend in fatal crashes from 1980 to mid-1984 is evident. What needs to be emphasized, however, is that this pattern is not at all characteristic of New South Wales. In that state, as we have seen, the series was stationary from about 1977 until RBT, when there was a sudden reduction in fatal crashes which persisted for at least 4 years. This pattern is very much what would be predicted if RBT were the key causal agent. The graphs for other states suggest that economic or other forces common to the whole country are not responsible for the sudden drop in the New South Wales figures, although it is possible (even likely) that these forces have helped to keep the post-RBT figures down when an upturn might have been expected (Ross, 1982; Thomson & Mavrolefterou, 1984).

It is of interest to examine the statistics for the two most populous states outside New South Wales (Victoria and Queensland), both to discern the impact of countermeasures in those states and to use them as controls for the New South Wales experience. These statistics are presented in Figures 4.2c and 4.2d. These figures cannot of course provide a perfect control, since economic and other forces are not identical in all areas, and each state has conducted some form of drink-drive countermeasure program over the past few years. Fortunately, only one state — Queensland — introduced a major change in drink-drive law coincidental with RBT in New South Wales, when the limit was lowered from .08 to .05. Significantly only Queensland (Figure 4.2d) experienced a sudden decline in fatal crashes in December 1982, but unlike New South Wales the drop seems to have lasted for only a few months. One hypothesis, which needs more rigorous testing before it can be accepted, is that the .05 legislation caused a temporary scare. Victoria (Figure 4.2c), which has had RBT since 1976, experienced no sudden decline in fatal crashes coincident with RBT in New South Wales, but seems to have benefited from a steady decline from 1980 to 1985. The reasons for this trend are not well understood.

Figure 4.2, together with the time series analysis, establishes a prima facie case for an impact of RBT in New South Wales. Further analyses of the crash statistics strengthen the case for a deterrent effect. For example Arthurson (1985) has shown that the proportion of fatal crashes occurring late at night or on weekends (when drink-driving is at its peak) declined from 42% pre-RBT to 33% post-RBT. Consistent with this, the proportion of dead drivers with BAC levels over .05 declined markedly, from over 40% to 33%. Perhaps surprisingly, the reduction in fatalities among drivers aged 20 to 24 years was as great as for any other age group, suggesting that at the very least RBT had a marked effect on young drivers, even if they were not *more* deterred than older drivers.

SURVEY DATA

Analyses of traffic crash statistics necessarily throw little light on the mechanisms by which an intervention achieves its effects. Fortunately several government surveys have been conducted, and these in their own ways support the interpretation of a deterrent impact sustained over a period of some years. Cashmore (1985) reports the results of several surveys of attitudes, knowledge, and behavior. Compared with pre-RBT figures she found increasing acceptance of RBT and increased approval of the .05 level, especially among women; a high rate of exposure to RBT in the early months; and changes in drinking and driving behavior as a result of RBT. Many of her results are very close to those reported in Chapter 6. One point made by Cashmore that is worth emphasizing is that the same level of exposure to RBT was achieved in 12 *weeks* in New South Wales as in Victoria in 2 years.

These observations concerning exposure rates are confirmed by Carseldine (1985) in an analysis of survey data collected by the NSW Traffic Authority on three occasions: November 1982 (one month before RBT), May 1983 (6 months after the law), and July to August 1984 (20 months after the law). However, the most remarkable aspect of these surveys was that noted above in the context of publicity surrounding RBT: the percentage of motorists reporting that their chances of arrest were "much higher" now that RBT was in force rose from 26% in the second survey to 40% in the third survey, despite a decline in media interest in the issue. Parallel to this finding there was a decline from 33% to 27% between these two surveys in the proportion of motorists who claimed that RBT operations could be avoided by careful planning, and a steady decline in the proportion of men who reported drink-driving more often than once a month (the figures were 39%, 34%, and 30% in the three surveys). The main behavioral change appears to have been a shift from relying on feelings or subjective evidence of impairment to the more objective strategy of counting drinks. The results of a fourth survey conducted early in 1987 strongly suggest a *further intensification* of the deterrent effects of RBT, with all indicators pointing to increased levels of compliance with the law and higher perceptions of the chances of detection for drink-driving (Homel, Carseldine, & Kearns, in press).

Thus the official government surveys, taken together, strongly reinforce the argument that deterrence through RBT was a major factor in the decline in casualty crashes in New South Wales coincident with the new law. The finding of higher subjective arrest probabilities 4 years after the intervention, compared with levels 6 months after the law, together with the steady drop in self-reported drink-driving by men over the four Traffic Authority surveys, must surely rank as one of the most remarkable outcomes in the literature. It seems that not only did RBT achieve a deterrent effect in New South Wales, the deterrent effect was sustained for some years.

Summary

What conclusions can be drawn from this brief survey of the effects of RBT in Australia? First, it needs to be remembered that RBT is enforced differently in every state, and that because it has apparently not worked in one jurisdiction does not mean it cannot work if a different approach is adopted. Having said that, it does appear that in order for RBT to achieve a simple deterrent effect, it is necessary that it be enforced and publicized along New South Wales or Tasmanian lines—the "boots and all" approach.

There is no entirely satisfactory evidence for the deterrent effect of RBT as such in Victoria, although it is clear that periodic blitzes have had short-term simple deterrent effects. Unfortunately it is *not* clear that RBT is an essential ingredient in these intensive campaigns. The most intriguing aspect of the Victorian research is the gradual decline in the road toll and the gradual increase in the perceived risk of apprehension over the past few years. However, there is no apparent connection between specific legal interventions and the perceived risk scores, and there are no data linking changes in perceived risk with changes in drink-driving behavior. Consequently conclusions concerning deterrence are very difficult, and in the absence of evidence for changes in such things as moral attitudes and the sources of these changes, explanations in terms of the educative effects of the law must remain tentative.

The evidence from South Australia suggests that a weak intervention achieves very little, except paradoxically with motorists who have already been charged with drink-driving. Apart from this theoretically interesting finding perhaps the most valuable feature of the South Australian evaluation was the demonstrated increase in alcohol-related crashes on back roads as motorists sought to avoid RBT. However there are only limited data from South Australia on perceptions of sanctions, rendering conclusions about deterrence, or the lack of deterrence, weaker than is desirable.

Although by the standards discussed in previous chapters the case for the deterrent effectiveness of RBT in New South Wales cannot yet be said to have been proven beyond all doubt, certainly a good case has been made that in the first 4 years it operated as an effective deterrent. The initial marked decline in fatal crashes is what would be expected if RBT were the key causal factor, and the continuing low fatality rates in the 4 years since the law are consistent with arguments that the effects have been sustained. Similar results have been obtained in Tasmania, where a similar strong legal intervention was implemented. The further analysis of the accident statistics for New South Wales demonstrated that alcohol-related crashes declined in frequency more than other kinds of crashes, reinforcing arguments that RBT caused at least some of the decline in casualties.

The results of the analysis of crash data are supported quite strongly by survey data on perceptions and behavior. RBT enjoyed an increasing level of public support in the years just prior to and following the new law, and after the law was implemented a high proportion of the driving population were exposed to RBT both through publicity and through personal experience. Most remarkably, perceptions of the likelihood of apprehension intensified in the 4 years following RBT, with an increasing percentage of motorists apparently being convinced that RBT cannot be avoided and modifying their drink-driving practices accordingly.

In Chapters 5 and 6 a study based largely on the model of deterrence in Chapter 2 is described. The research design described in Chapter 5 builds on the experiences of earlier researchers, and incorporates measures of aspects of the deterrence process (such as exposure to law enforcement and group pressure to drink), which hitherto have been somewhat neglected in the literature.

5
The Random Breath Test Study: Research Questions and Method

This chapter has two objectives: to enumerate in detail the research questions for the study of random breath testing in New South Wales and to describe the methods. Methods of analysis as well as the sample design and the questions in the interview schedule are described. Particular emphasis is placed on describing the rationale for each step in the research and relating decisions about method to the methodological issues discussed in Chapter 3. The problems involved in constructing reliable and stable measures are given close attention throughout the chapter. Since the study has a longitudinal component, it is possible to determine the test-retest reliabilities of some of the key measures.

The Research Questions

The Causal Chain Reflecting Simple Deterrence

A number of research questions arise from the model depicted in Figure 2.2, and from the literature reviewed in Chapters 3 and 4. Not all of these questions could be investigated in the present study, since some variables of interest could not be measured. The most important variable for which a measure was not available was official publicity, broken down by area and by type of media. It is therefore not possible in the present analysis to test the relationship between the intensity of official (and unofficial) publicity and exposure to that publicity. An analysis of aspects of media coverage of RBT in New South Wales may be found in Cashmore (1985).

In order to establish a general deterrent effect of RBT, it is necessary to demonstrate that there is a causal chain linking police enforcement (an aspect of Lp) with drink-drive behavior (De and Dr), via perceptions of the likelihood and unpleasantness of punishment (Pp) (see Fig. 2.1). Therefore the major questions are: (a) Can exposure to police enforcement be predicted reliably from official levels of police RBT activity (Lp→ Ex)? (b) What is the relationship between the intensity of police enforcement experienced by motorists in an area and the perceived likelihood of being tested, or of being arrested for drink-driving ($Ex \rightarrow Pp$)? (c) Is exposure to publicity or exposure to police testing the primary determinant of perceptions of sanctions? (d) Which type of publicity—television, radio, or print—has the greatest influence on perceptions of sanctions and on drinking and driving behaviors? (e) Which form of exposure to policy activity— being tested personally, driving past RBT operations, or knowing other people who have been tested—has the greatest influence on perceptions of sanctions and on drinking and driving behaviors? (f) What is the relationship between perceptions of sanctions and modifications to travel and drinking behaviors ($Pp \rightarrow De$)? (g) Is fear of arrest or perception of the severity of punishment the chief influence on drinking and driving behaviors?

Correlations between elements of the hypothesized causal chain cannot of course be taken as proof of a causal relationship. In the present analysis, there are two ways in which causal inferences can be made more plausible. First, many of the variables being correlated represent changes in some quantity. For example, exposure to RBT enforcement could only take place *after* the introduction of RBT. Before RBT, its value was zero. Similarly, official radio and television publicity did not begin until after RBT, although there were many newspaper articles which preceded the law. Much of the knowledge of RBT in the present survey therefore represents the impact of publicity through the electronic media.

The second way in which causal inferences can be made more plausible is through the introduction of statistical controls for sociodemographic variables such as age and sex. The value of these controls is that if correlations between key theoretical variables (such as exposure to testing and perceptions of arrest certainty) remain significant after adjustment, the evidence for a causal relationship is strengthened. For example, a correlation between being personally tested and arrest certainty may simply reflect the fact that young men drive more often, are more likely to be tested, and are more likely to have a realistic idea of the chances of arrest. Therefore, a general research question is whether the relationships listed before can survive adjustment for the effects of sociodemographic variables.

Informal Sanctions

Among the ways in which RBT may influence drink-driving behavior is through a reduction in the pressure some people may feel to start or continue drinking in a group situation. Therefore an important research question is whether the relationship between exposure and the behavioral variables is mediated primarily through perceptions of arrest certainty and severity of punishment or through perceptions of changes in informal sanctions, such as pressure to drink.

Who Has Been Most Exposed to RBT and Most Deterred?

The sociodemographic variables are useful not only for controlling the relationships between elements of the hypothesized deterrence model, they are important as descriptors of the target population. Major questions are: (a) Which groups in the population have been most exposed to RBT enforcement, both personally and through the experiences of others? (b) Which groups in the population have been most exposed to RBT publicity (television, radio, and print)? (c) Which sociodemographic variables predict perceptions of sanctions and changes in drinking and travel behaviors? In particular, has the reaction of young men been comparable with that of the rest of the driving population?

Interaction Effects

Many hypotheses are possible concerning interactions between variables. Major questions are: (a) Do fear of arrest and perceptions of the severity of punishment interact with each other, so that neither has an influence on drinking and driving behaviors if the value of the other is very low? (b) Do exposure to police enforcement and exposure to publicity interact in their effects on perceptions of sanctions (e.g., is the effect of TV publicity greater if someone has been personally tested as well)? (c) Are there interactions between different forms of publicity (e.g., is the combined effect of television and radio greater than either alone)? (d) Does the effect of arrest certainty on modifications to drinking and driving behaviors depend on the strength of informal sanctions which encourage drinking after driving? (e) Is there an interaction between arrest certainty and the possession of a conviction for drink-driving? In particular, are the relationships between arrest certainty and changes in drinking and travel behaviors more pronounced for those with a conviction than for those without? (f) Are there interactions between arrest certainty and other sociodemographic variables, especially age, sex, alcohol consumption, and socioeconomic status?

Changes Over Time

There is another set of research questions which arises out of the hypothesis advanced by Ross (1982) that fear of arrest, and therefore the deterrent effectiveness of the law, declines after an initial peak coinciding with the introduction of measures like RBT. (a) Do perceptions of the chances of arrest decline over time? (b) Do motorists make fewer attempts over time to avoid drinking and driving? (c) Do changes in the perception of arrest certainty predict changes in drinking and travel behaviors? (d) Are such relationships affected by other factors, such as peer pressure to drink?

Drink-Drive Behavior

The longitudinal component of the design also affords an opportunity to examine actual drink-drive behavior, and its relationship with exposure to RBT and perceptions of sanctions at the beginning of the period over which drink-drive behavior is measured. Many of the research questions parallel those discussed before. Major questions are: (a) Do perceptions of arrest certainty and perceptions of penalty severity predict involvement in drink-driving? (b) Is there an interaction between the two components of sanction perceptions? (c) Does exposure to RBT influence drink-drive behavior through perceptions of sanctions? (d) Is there an inverse relationship between attempts to avoid drink-driving and the subsequent incidence of drink-driving behavior (De→ Dr)?

Method

Design of the Sample and Sampling Procedures

Two features of the sampling method are of fundamental importance. First, the study was carried out in two stages, with 185 respondents from the first stage being reinterviewed 6 weeks later. This longitudinal aspect of the study allows changes over time to be investigated, and also allows an analysis of the relationship between perceptions of sanctions at the first stage and drink-drive behavior in the 6 weeks between surveys. The second important feature of the design relates to variations in police activity. In the first stage, only Sydney residents were interviewed, but in the second stage the sampling frame was extended to include eight towns and cities outside Sydney. These regional centers were selected in such a way as to maximize variation in the intensity of police enforcement over Easter 1983. This was done to facilitate the analysis of the relationship between objective levels of enforcement on the one hand and exposure to RBT, perceptions of arrest certainty, and modifications to behavior on the other.

In planning the study it was assumed, on the basis of the international experience with drink-drive countermeasures reviewed in Chapter 3, that the effects of RBT would be reasonably short-lived, perhaps lasting only a few months or a year (Homel, 1983a). Since RBT was introduced on December 17, 1982, it was expected that by late February the initial scare would be starting to wane, but that the extensive publicity campaign planned for Easter would boost its deterrent impact. Given that in late February a lull in the effects of RBT was expected, changes in perceptions or in behavior reported by the 185 reinterviewed respondents between interviews can be interpreted in the following ways: (a) an increase or no change in arrest certainty or in attempts to avoid drinking and driving would presumably reflect the effects of the Easter campaign, and would show that a wearing off of the effects of RBT was not inevitable, at least in the short term; (b) a decrease in arrest certainty or in attempts to avoid drink-driving would be the strongest result since it would imply a wearing-off effect despite additional publicity and enforcement over Easter.

A longer time period between surveys would have had the advantage of more behavior change (and more self-reported drinking and driving) during the interval, making analysis more reliable. On the other hand, a longer interval would have entailed more attrition in the number of respondents (Anderson, 1979), and the accuracy of items relying on memory may have been reduced.

DETAILS OF FIRST STAGE SAMPLING

The first wave of interviews was conducted in the last week of February 1983, 10 weeks after the introduction of RBT. The sample consisted of 400 residents of Sydney aged 18 years and older. Households were selected by stratified area sampling, using a cluster size of two. Political subdivisions were stratified according to Liberal/Labor voting patterns, which are a good measure of socioeconomic status. Within selected subdivisions starting addresses, proportional in number to the number of voters, were selected at random from the electoral roll. Interviews were attempted at the selected addresses and at one house next door, alternating the direction from the starting address.

Since strict probability sampling procedures were employed at all stages, households at which contact could not be made were *not* immediately replaced. If no one was at home at the first call, the interviewer was instructed to call back twice before abandoning that household. When a contact was made, the interviewer listed all males 18 years and older in the dwelling, starting with the oldest, and then all females in a similar manner. One person was selected for interview using a random number grid. Interviews were completed at 69% of sampled dwellings. Most of the non-respondents were not at home at each of the three calls. Of the 400 adults interviewed 314 were licensed drivers, 255 of whom drank at least once a year (63.5%). Questions relating to knowledge of and exposure to RBT were asked of all respondents, but questions about perceptions of sanctions and drinking and driving behavior were asked only of drinking license holders.

DETAILS OF SECOND STAGE SAMPLING

The second set of interviews was conducted the week after Easter 1983 and 6 weeks after the first stage. The second survey consisted of three components. First, 185 of the 255 drinking license holders interviewed in February were reinterviewed; second, a new sample of 200 residents of Sydney was drawn, matched with the initial sample by starting point; and third, 400 residents of eight regional centers throughout New South Wales were interviewed, 50 from each center. For the second-stage interviews, the questionnaire was enlarged to probe in more detail perceptions of police enforcement, exposure to RBT, and some other issues.

The success rate for the repeat interviews was 73% (185/255). With one exception the 70 respondents not contacted a second time did not differ significantly from the 185 who were contacted again in terms of information available from the February interview. The single significant difference was total alcohol consumption on a drinking day: those not followed up drank an average of 5.1 standard drinks, while those reinterviewed drank an average of only 3.9 standard drinks (a *standard drink* will be defined later). Even here, however, the difference was only marginally significant ($p = .046$), and was not apparent when frequency of drinking was examined or when a joint index of frequency and quantity was constructed. There was also a tendency for 21 to 24-year-old respondents to be underrepresented, but again this was not statistically significant ($p = .15$). Therefore on the whole the follow-up sample is a random subsample of the full February sample, with a tendency for heavy drinkers and young people (these groups not necessarily being conterminous) to be underrepresented.

The response rate for the second-stage interviews in Sydney (additional to the 185 repeat interviews) was about the same as for the first stage (70%), but the average response rate for the interviews outside Sydney was higher, at about 80%. However, for reasons which are not immediately apparent the two Sydney samples differed rather more than expected in terms of the percentage of license holders and percentage of license holders who drank, with only 71.5% (143) of the 200 second-stage respondents being license holders and only 50.5% (101) of the total sample being license holders who drank (the latter figure for the first stage was 63.5%). On the other hand the composition of the sample of 400 respondents outside Sydney was similar to the first stage Sydney sample, with 82.0% (328) license holders and 60.3% (241) license holders who drank.

Measures

The questions used in both stages of the study can be organized under five headings, all of which are represented in Figure 2.2. These five groups of variables, together with available information on their validities and reliabilities, will be described in this section. The first group of variables, almost all of which are common to both stages of the survey, are labeled as *sociodemographic* in Figure 2.2. The second set relate to *exposure* to RBT publicity and enforcement, the third set to *perceptions of sanctions*, the fourth to *drinking and driving behaviors* (which includes drink-driving since RBT and attempts to avoid drink-driving), and the last set of variables relate to *peer pressures to drink*.

The first four of the five groups of variables were represented on the February questionnaire. In the April interviews, the February questions on exposure, perceptions of police activity, alcohol use, and drinking and driving behaviors were repeated exactly. In addition, these issues were explored in more detail by means of additional questions, and the questions on peer pressure and convictions for drink-driving were added. The questionnaires used in both stages of the survey are reproduced in the Appendix, to which reference should be made for exact wording and categories. In the following discussion, FQ refers to a February question, AQ to an April question.

License status (FQ4: current automobile or motorcycle license holder, disqualified, not licensed, and not disqualified). For purposes of analysis, disqualified drivers (of whom there were only two or three) were grouped with license holders. *Sex, Education, Age* (grouped into seven categories, from 17–20 to 65+ years) and *Occupation* (senior professional/business/academic; upper (skilled) white-collar; lower (semiskilled/unskilled) white-collar; skilled blue-collar; semiskilled or unskilled blue-collar; pensioner/retired; student; housewife/home duties; unemployed; refused). Occupation was not assessed according to any hard and fast rules, but was based on what people gave as their main occupation. Generally speaking, people working 20 hours a week or more were classified into an occupational category.

Quantity and Frequency of Alcohol Consumption

This was based on two questions: FQ7 (frequency of drinking, divided into 11 levels from 3+ times a day to never drink) and FQ8 (quantities of alcohol consumed on an average drinking day, broken down by type of drink). These questions were repeated in the second stage (AQ11 and AQ12). The responses to FQ8 were converted into the numbers of standard drinks of each type (normal strength beer, low alcohol (LA) beer, wine, port/sherry, spirits, and other) and the total number of standard drinks. A standard drink was defined as a middie (285 mL) of normal strength beer, and this was regarded as equivalent to a nip (1 ounce) of spirits, 2 ounces of port or sherry, a glass (4 oz.) of wine, and a schooner (1.5 middies) of LA beer. A bottle of wine was coded as six glasses.

There is a great deal of discussion in the literature about the validity and reliability of self-reports of alcohol consumption. Pernanen (1974) reviewed much of the survey literature and showed that, on average, estimates of consumption derived from surveys were about half the estimates based on sales statistics. Part of the reason for this is that some heavy drinkers (such as those on "skid row") are less likely to be included in conventional sampling frames than lighter drinkers, and also even when included in the sampling frame they are harder to locate and maybe more likely to refuse an interview if it is known to be related to drinking. However, Pernanen argues that the main problem is underreporting, due presumably to the stigma connected with the use of alcohol and with the behavior connected with alcohol use. Since the present study does not aim to estimate *absolute* levels of consumption, but is concerned more with an ordering of individuals into broad categories, underreporting may not be a serious problem if it occurs to about the same extent in different subgroups of the population. Unfortunately, as Pernanen points out, given the different norm sets and role definitions prevailing in the community, it would be surprising if some groups did not underreport to a greater extent than others.

In a more recent paper, Popham and Schmidt (1981) present data which suggest that the level of underreporting is much greater for heavy drinkers than for light and moderate drinkers. The degree of underreporting is nonlinear when considered in relation to an individual's true level of drinking. If sustained, their argument would imply that heavy drinkers cannot be identified with any degree of confidence using survey methods. However, a number of researchers have responded to Popham and Schmidt, arguing that the data presented do not support their strong conclusion (de Lint, 1981) and that in fact heavy drinkers can and do report their alcohol consumption to a survey interviewer with sufficient accuracy to place themselves in the appropriate consumption category (Mulford & Fitzgerald, 1981).

It seems clear that survey methods do not allow a reliable classification of people into more than a few categories. In the present study, the two alcohol questions were combined into a quantity-frequency index with six categories, following the method discussed by Caetano and Suzman (1982). The method is summarized in Figure 5.1.

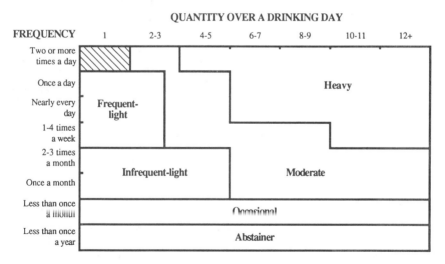

FIGURE 5.1. Quantity-frequency index of alcohol consumption.

As Caetano and Suzman point out, any attempt to reduce a phenomenon as complex as alcohol consumption to a single measurement will result in the loss of information. However, given the literature discussed above, the use of finer categories would attract criticism concerning validity. Notwithstanding the obvious virtues of a small number of categories reflecting both quantity and frequency of consumption, Caetano and Suzman present data showing that such a categorization is insensitive to changes in alcohol consumption over time in a longitudinal sample. For the purpose of detecting change, finer measures such as frequency of drinking occasions and the number of drinks per month are required. This suggests that although the quantity-frequency index should be the major measure of consumption, it should be supplemented by the use of finer measures which, although subject to validity doubts, may be more sensitive to small variations, cross-sectionally or longitudinally. In the present study, total drinks on a drinking day and total beer consumption on a drinking day have been employed in this subsidiary fashion.

The reliability of the alcohol consumption measures was assessed by examining the association between scores obtained in February and April in the sample of 185 Sydney residents who were interviewed twice. Although the marginal distribution did not change much between the two surveys, there was considerable instability in individual category membership. Only 56.2% of the 185 respondents stayed in the same categories, and some changes were quite marked. High rates of transfer between frequent-light, infrequent-light, and moderate were perhaps to be expected (indicating that we should not put too much weight on these distinctions), but more worrying was the six heavy drinkers (a third of the total) who became moderate or frequent-light in April (and the seven who went in the opposite direction), as well as the six light or moderate drinkers who became abstainers or very occasional drinkers (less often than once a year). Of course these changes in reporting could reflect real changes in behavior, but given the short period between interviews the influence of response error is probably greater. In fact an analysis of those who changed their levels of drinking up or down, in terms of their exposure to RBT in the 6 weeks between interviews, suggests that exposure to RBT, or lack of exposure, was completely unrelated to changes in reported levels of drinking.

An examination of the frequency of drinking supported the interpretation of random response errors, since 55 dropped to a lower category and 41 moved up ($p = .15$; Sign test). The most unreliable categories were the extremes (twice a day or three or more times a day) and the in-between categories (nearly every day and two to three times a month). The correlation between the two measures of total standard drinks on a drinking day was acceptable, at .80, and a paired t test indicated no shift in mean consumption levels (mean difference = .005, $s = 2.61$, $p = .98$). However, the test-retest correlations for the consumption of individual beverages were less satisfactory (normal strength beer = .59, LA beer = .20, wine = .52, port/sherry = .49 and spirits = .20).

EXPOSURE TO AND KNOWLEDGE OF RBT

Knowledge was probed in the first question (FQ1) without giving any information about the new law. The questions on *exposure* (FQ2, asked of all respondents) were preceded by a definition of RBT and a reminder of when it was introduced. The questions on exposure could be checked to some extent for validity and reliability. The first question (FQ2[a]) asked about the direct experience of being tested, and can therefore be checked against police statistics on the actual number of tests conducted. Of course the comparison is not perfect, since FQ2(a) also asked about the experience of passengers. However, the survey figure of 9.5% (out of 400 respondents) compares well with an estimate from official police figures if it is assumed that cars pulled over by RBT operators contained an average of 1.8 occupants. This is a reasonable assumption, based on government surveys (Homel, 1986).

Since the exposure questions were repeated in April, it is possible to throw some light on their test-retest reliabilities. Of the 185 drinking license holders interviewed twice, the same number (21, or 11.4%) in both interviews claimed to have been tested or to have been a passenger in the car when the driver was tested. Unfortunately, only 10 respondents gave the same answer twice! Eleven who gave an affirmative response in February changed their answer to "no" in April. What are we to make of this? It is possible that the question was misunderstood by some people, and was taken to apply in the second interview to the 6-week period since the last interview. However, nothing in the wording of the question (which was exactly the same both times) should have encouraged such an interpretation. It is much more likely that the 11 respondents simply forgot that they had been tested. Perhaps also the inclusion of passengers reduced the reliability of the question, since passengers may be less likely to remember the experience than drivers. An examination of the characteristics of the 11 errant respondents suggested that in most respects they were indistinguishable from the majority. Their only distinctive features were lower than average occupational status and, to some extent, lower levels of achievement at school.

These figures should serve as a salutary warning that even apparently simple and concrete questions in surveys, particularly addressed to less well-educated respondents, may yield responses of limited reliability. One solution is to ask a series of questions around a theme, according no individual question preeminent status. It is important, therefore, to examine the consistency of responses to the other questions on exposure to RBT. Paradoxically the picture is rather brighter for these less directly personal questions. Of the 94 respondents who in the February interview claimed to have driven past police carrying out random testing, only 18 said "no" in April. Similarly, of the 108 people who said in February that they knew someone who had been randomly tested, 21 changed their response in the second interview. Nine respondents gave inconsistent answers to both these questions, so it is not surprising that analysis of both groups suggests a similar set of characteristics associated with contradictory responses: being male, being young (21 to 24 years old), and finding it hard to resist pressure to drink.

In the April interview some additional questions were asked about exposure to RBT. Those who had driven past or who had been driven past police carrying out random testing were asked how often (AQ3[a]) and how long ago (AQ3[b]). Answers to these two questions were combined into a *recency-frequency index* with 10 categories, in line with the observed frequencies in the cells and in the light of the psychological significance of fine distinctions in the recency and frequency of observations of RBT activity.

Following the question asked in the first stage as to whether people knew someone who had been randomly tested (FQ2[c]), the *number* known was elicited in the second stage (AQ4[b]). Following the question on *publicity* asked in the first stage (FQ[d]), respondents were probed about details of recent advertising in the media (AQ6[a] and AQ6[b]). These responses were scored by summing the total number of items recalled across all media, and also by recording through which of the media the respondent had been exposed to publicity.

PERCEPTIONS OF THE CHANCES OF BEING TESTED/ARRESTED AND
PERCEPTIONS OF PENALTIES

The importance of developing a reliable measure of *perceptions of the chances of arrest* has been stressed a number of times. This is a little more than the perceived chance of being randomly tested, which was probed directly in both stages (FQ5 and AQ9), since it involves other aspects of the enforcement process as well. In the April questionnaire, these aspects were probed in a series of questions.

In order to understand the thinking behind the development of the index of subjective arrest probability, it is necessary to recall the distinction between probabilities (or subjective probabilities) and decision weights (Tversky & Kahnemann, 1981). Someone may, for example, exaggerate the personal implications of low perceived probabilities, or they may regard with equanimity a high perceived risk of being tested. Second, it is necessary to appreciate that being arrested for drinking and driving is the culmination of a process that involves several earlier steps, and that each of these steps has a certain perceived likelihood of occurring which may affect the weight attached to the perceived chances of a step earlier in the chain. Thus, for example, a motorist may regard the chances of being randomly tested in the next month as quite high, but may also believe that he stands a good chance of talking his way out of a positive breath analysis. Thus the perception of the chances of an event higher in the chain may effectively cancel the impact on decision making of the perception of the chances of an event earlier on. Bringing together the concept of arrest as a chain of events and the concept of decision weights attached to perceived probabilities for each stage creates a very complex measurement problem.

An approach was adopted in the present study which led to the development of an index of *perception of arrest certainty*. The reason for this term is that all questions used in the formation of the index deal with the process leading up to the arrest of a motorist driving with the prescribed concentration of alcohol. The index entails abandoning any attempt to develop a measure of perceptions distinct from a measure of evaluations of those perceptions. The method rather is to probe perceptions of as many stages and aspects of the arrest process as can be reasonably distinguished in an interview, create a summed score from answers to each of the questions, and interpret a high score as indicating both a high perceived probability of arrest (if one were to drive with the prescribed concentration of alcohol) and a high evaluation of this perception (in the sense that it ought to be an important factor, if deterrence theory is correct, in the decision not to drink and drive). The index can therefore be given an operational meaning even though it conflates two theoretically distinct concepts.

The eight questions asked fell into three groups. One of the questions (AQ28) directly probed the evaluative rather than the perceptual aspect of being tested by asking how *worried* people would be at being asked to take a breath test. The focus here is on the anxiety caused by the thought of being tested, rather than on the perceived chances of being tested. A second group of questions probed the general issue of the chances of apprehension if one were to drive over the limit (AQ7, AQ20, and AQ23). The third group of questions explored perceptions of various stages of the enforcement process and the extent to which respondents believed they could "fall between cracks" in the system. AQ9 asked about the perceived chances of being tested in the next months; AQ24 asked about the chances of being arrested if found by the police to be over .05; AQ29 asked how easy or hard it is to avoid police carrying out random testing; and AQ30 asked about the chances of being pulled over if one drives past police (on their side of the road).

These eight questions were designed to provide a broad base for a single measure of perceptions/evaluations of police enforcement of drink-drive law, while forming at the same time a pool of items from which selections could be made for specific analyses. In using the term "perception of arrest certainty" it should be understood that the *weights* attached to aspects of this perception are also included in a complex way in the measure, although as discussed before, analytically the weight function is distinct from the actual (subjective) probabilities. Indeed, in ordinary conversation with people it is very difficult to maintain these kinds of theoretical distinctions. In this regard, it is worth noting that despite the care with which they were selected some respondents saw the eight questions as being very similar; so similar, in fact, that they objected to answering what they saw as the same question several times over. To some extent this was the effect intended, since it was hoped that scores would be unidimensional and at least moderately correlated. Unfortunately these hopes were not fully realized, since the correlations were on the whole rather weak.

In computing the correlations, it is necessary to deal with "unsure" responses, of which there were quite a few to some questions. It is also necessary to decide whether to use all points on the scale, or simply to differentiate extreme responses from the more common. One tactic for dealing with "unsure" responses is to exclude those subjects from the analysis, but in this case that would reduce the sample size to unacceptably low levels (in excess of 100 cases would have to be discarded). In any case, it can be argued that an "unsure" response is valuable information, since it indicates that the respondent is undecided between alternatives and therefore does not perceive the risk of detection as being either very high or very low. In addition, the idea of concentrating on extreme responses is attractive, since such a procedure improves the face validity of an index constructed by summing individual item responses. For these reasons, it was decided to retain all cases and to score each question on a 3-point scale, with "unsure" and "middle range" responses forming the midscore. The questions used in construction of the index, together with the methods of grouping into extreme categories, are in Table 5.1.

Correlations between these items were nearly all positive, but the average magnitude was only .079. The summed index for the eight items had a reliability (alpha) of .41, and no item appeared to be redundant. It seems that despite the similarity of many of the questions, interviewees generally saw them as probing different aspects of police enforcement and responded accordingly. In fact the low correlations tend to confirm the value of probing separately each aspect of enforcement.

Perceptions of the severity of penalties were covered by four questions. FQ13 was asked only in the February survey, and was designed to identify respondents who believed (correctly) that penalties had increased with the introduction of RBT. AQ25 probed an important "crack" in the system by asking how much chance respondents believed they had of being let off without penalty if convicted (the actual rate is 5% in New South Wales: Homel, 1983b). The next question (AQ26) was adapted from Grasmick and Green (1980), and was designed to measure directly the subjective evaluation of penalty severity, rather than the perception of what the penalty would actually be. As these authors and Tittle (1980a) have argued, it is the degree of fear of a penalty which is the crucial quantity theoretically; AQ26: "For this question, I would like you to imagine that you had been arrested for drinking and driving, and that the court had found you guilty and imposed a punishment. *Think* about what that punishment would be for *you*. From this card (SHOWCARD 10), in general, how big a problem would that punishment be in your life?" (no problem at all, hardly any problem, a little problem, a big problem, a very

TABLE 5.1. Method of construction of index of perception of arrest certainty*

Item	Low probability category	N of cases	High probability category	N of cases	No. unsure
AQ7	Lower chance of testing since RBT	14	Higher chance of testing since RBT	381	5
AQ9	Extremely unlikely to be tested	70	Extremely likely to be tested	36	10
AQ20	1 or 1,000 times without being caught	48	Not at all without being caught	86	53
AQ23	Probably or definitely not be caught	68	Definitely would be caught	105	11
AQ24	Quite or extremely likely to be arrested	31	Certain to be arrested	242	12
AQ28	Not at all worried	40	Very worried	268	6
AQ29	Very easy to avoid police	29	Very hard to avoid police	112	96
AQ30	Quite or extremely unlikely to be pulled over	50	Extremely likely to be pulled over	74	18

*April survey, $N = 517$ drinking license holders.

big problem, unsure.) The criticisms leveled at this question by Paternoster and Iovanni (1986), particularly that it confounds formal and informal punishments, are considered in the interpretation of results in Chapters 6 and 9. The final question (AQ27) was also designed to probe the dreadfulness of punishments, but this time by contrasting the perceived harshness of imprisonment for 2 weeks and disqualification from driving for 6 months. This question was taken directly from Buikhuisen (1974), with the purpose of replicating his finding for Dutch drink-drive offenders, that about half would prefer imprisonment.

DRINKING AND DRIVING BEHAVIOR

Driving while intoxicated was probed in FQ9 ("Have you ever driven when you felt you had had *too much* to drink?") and FQ10 ("Since random breath testing was brought in just before Christmas, have you driven when you felt you had had *too much* to drink?"). FQ10 was followed by an unstructured probe designed to elicit reasons either for drinking and driving or not drinking and driving since RBT. Questions FQ9 and FQ10 were repeated in the April survey, so it is possible to examine the consistencies of responses among the 175 drinking license holders who were reinterviewed (the 10 respondents who became less than annual drinkers were not questioned again about drinking and driving behavior). A total of 25 out of 175 respondents (14.3%) gave inconsistent answers to FQ9 on the two occasions. For FQ10, a total of 20 respondents admitted in February to driving while under the influence since the advent of RBT, and 16 of these told the same story in April. In other words, four gave inconsistent responses.

The consistencies of responses to these two questions are not as high as one would hope, but they compare favorably with the consistencies of responses to the exposure questions, suggesting that the source of error is not so much the attempt to conceal the commission of illegal or socially unacceptable acts, but more the simple process of forgetting (or not being bothered to try and remember). In addition, it should be noted that both questions required the respondent to make a subjective judgment concerning his or her state of inebriation at some date in the past, and also a judgment about the effects of this level of alcohol consumption on driving performance. It is quite likely that someone could recall the same incident on two different occasions but, without dissembling, make two different decisions about whether they had really had too much to drink. In other words, without the kind of objective procedures employed (for example) by Snortum and colleagues (1986), there is a certain level of unreliability inherent in questions about drink-driving behavior.

In the April survey, the question on drink-driving since the introduction of RBT was augmented in a number of ways. Those who admitted to driving under the influence were asked (AQ14[b]) how many times they had done it, and those who claimed not to have driven under the influence since RBT were asked (AQ14[c] and AQ14[d]) to nominate from a card the statement which "best described" their reasons for not drinking and driving. The statements were: "drinking and driving is wrong, drinking and driving leads to accidents, drinking drivers stand a good chance of being caught and punished." The purpose of this question was to determine the relative importance of moral attachment (Norström, 1981) or concern about safety, as opposed to fear of punishment. The three alternative statements were derived from analysis of responses to the open-ended question asked in the first interview.

Driving when one believes one has not had too much to drink is not the same as *driving under the legal limit*. Drinking license holders in the April interviews were therefore asked (AQ18) about driving over the limit of .05 since the introduction of RBT. (This question was preceded by a check that the respondent was in fact aware of the legal limit—nearly all were.) Tabulation of responses to this question against responses to AQ14(b) (driving while impaired) revealed a surprising degree of consistency. Interestingly, 40 of the 109 motorists who admitted to driving over .05 gave a negative response to AQ14, suggesting that their personal limit was higher than .05 and thereby confirming the value of the .05 question. In order to summarize the information available from AQ14(b) and AQ18, a *combined measure of drink-drive behavior since RBT* was constructed: not driven over .05; driven over .05 but not over personal limit; driven over the personal limit once; driven over the personal limit two or more times.

Convictions for drinking and driving were probed directly, but an attempt was made to reduce the stigma associated with a conviction by pointing out in the preamble that over the years about a quarter of a million people in New South Wales have been convicted for drink-driving (AQ19). Nevertheless, the work of Locander, Sudman, and Bradburn (1976) would suggest that the obtained figure of 7.4% is at least 35% lower than the true figure.

Attempts to avoid drinking and driving: FQ12 and AQ16 were the same question (with the addition of one item in AQ16), probing the immediate behavioral impact of RBT. They were designed to operationalize as far as possible the theoretical quantity De discussed in Chapter 2. Without explicitly asking people about the reasons for their behavior, the question was intended to get at changes in behavior caused by RBT. A limitation of the question is that only *types* of responses to RBT were probed, and not the total number of occasions in the last month when the respondent took action to avoid driving after drinking. Although there are no major theoretical impediments to a measure based on drinking occasions, to get reasonably accurate answers it would probably be necessary to ask respondents to keep a diary over a period of some weeks. The wording of FQ12 and AQ16 was adopted as the most practical, given the resources available for the study.

TABLE 5.2. Items contributing to the measures of number of modifications to travel arrangements and number of modifications to drinking behavior

Modifications to travel arrangements	Modifications to amount or place of drinking
Not using the car as much	Drinking at home more often, drinking away from home less
Driving more carefully at all times	
Stopped driving to places where you will be drinking	Carefully limiting your drinking when driving
Driving more carefully after drinking	Stopped drinking altogether when driving
Using taxis more often after drinking	Drinking more soft drinks when driving
Using public transport more after drinking	Switched to low alcohol beer when driving
Staying overnight after drinking	Drinking at places closer to home than before
Having someone else drive you home after drinking	
Sleeping in car instead of driving home after drinking	
Using special buses or drive home schemes organized by clubs or pubs (April survey only)	

Nevertheless it needs to be recognized that by focusing on types of strategies rather than on occasions when drink-driving was a risk, there is a danger that a person who employs a single strategy frequently may not score as highly as someone who tries a few approaches only once or twice. One advantage of the timing of the surveys was that it is likely that in the early days of RBT many people were experimenting with alternate drinking and travel arrangements, and therefore at that time there was probably a fair correlation between the number of strategies being adopted and total occasions when driving over the limit was avoided. It should also be remembered that the method used distinguished between people doing something as a response to RBT and people not doing anything.

Two scores were derived from the behavior check list: the number of changes to travel arrangements, and the number of changes to the amount of drinking or the place of drinking. The items contributing to the construction of the travel and drinking indices are shown in Table 5.2.

SOCIAL PRESSURE TO DRINK

In addition to the questions on formal sanctions for drinking and driving, *informal sanctions* for not drinking in a group situation were explored in one question in the April survey (AQ21). This question was adapted from Sloane and Huebner (1980). A second question probed the theory that RBT had had an impact on the pressure to drink through the provision of an acceptable reason for saying "no" to offers of alcohol before driving (AQ22).

Statistical Analysis

For purposes of analysis it is convenient to divide the study into two sections. The major section contains the analysis of the relationships between variables derived from the April interviews, using Figure 2.2 as a framework. This part of the study could be called the *cross-sectional analysis*, except that as noted in Chapter 2, not all variables can be regarded as synchronic in the sense in which Gibbs (1978) used the term. A number of the variables, including exposure to RBT enforcement and modifications in behavior as a response to RBT, are interpreted in this analysis as measures of change. The focus of the April survey analysis is on modifications to drinking and travel arrangements and on the variables in the causal chain which predict these modifications.

The second stage of the analysis is focused on changes occurring between the two interviews, and might therefore be called the *longitudinal analysis*. There are two central questions in this analysis: whether there is any evidence of a decline in the deterrent effectiveness of RBT over the 6-week period, and whether there is any evidence for a relationship between changes in the perceptions of the chance of being randomly tested and driving while intoxicated between February and April. Since the data for the longitudinal analysis are restricted to a subset of the February questions, the analysis is more limited than the April survey analysis.

The major value of Figure 2.2 is to provide a framework for the analyses reported in Chapter 6, each of which is based on a variant of the linear model (regression, multivariate analysis of variance, or logistic regression). In effect, a form of path analysis has been carried out, but on one set of dependent variables at a time. Thus in the first analysis the relationship between the level of official police enforcement in an area and an individual's chances of being exposed to RBT is explored (several aspects of exposure are the dependent variables), while in the second analysis perceptions of arrest certainty are the dependent variables. However, not all groups of variables have been analyzed as dependent variables, since the focus of the study is on the factors which comprise the basic deterrence model, rather than on factors like peer pressure which are, from this limited perspective, simply covariates.

WHY PATH ANALYSIS IS INAPPROPRIATE

It was pointed out in Chapter 2 that although Figure 2.2 is an attempt to depict causal relationships between elements of the deterrence process, it is not strictly a path diagram since groups of variables rather than individual variables are represented and interaction terms are implied as well (for example, between perceived arrest certainty and penalty severity). It may be appropriate at this point to explain in more detail why path analysis was considered an inappropriate statistical technique.

First, many of the variables included within the general types depicted in Figure 2.2 cannot be ordered in any clear causal fashion. For example, attempts to avoid drinking and driving may entail modifications to travel arrangements or modifications to drinking practices. One type of response does not obviously cause the other, yet a form of analysis is required which takes into account the correlation between the two forms of behavior. Multivariate analysis achieves this objective, while path analysis leads only to unnecessary complications (like nonidentified models).

Second, traditional linear models analysis is superior to path analysis because many of the variables are measured not at the interval but at the nominal level. They should therefore be represented as dummy variables in a linear model when treated as independent variables, and analyzed using log-linear or logistic models when treated as dependent variables. At present this is very difficult to do in path analysis, although progress is being made at the theoretical level in incorporating log-linear model approaches into path analysis (Winship & Mare, 1983).

Third, path analysis typically requires that ordinal variables, such as perceived severity of penalties, be assigned arbitrary numerical values (e.g., 1 to 3 or 1 to 5) to allow the computation of correlation coefficients. Although sometimes useful for descriptive purposes, when ordinal variables are used as independent variables in a model such coding imposes an unwarranted constraint of linearity which is avoided by the use of dummy variables. When ordinal variables are used as dependent variables the threshold logistic model (Bock, 1975), which is described in the following section, is much to be preferred.

Finally, as noted previously, path analysis does not allow interaction terms to be incorporated in the model. Some interactions, such as those hypothesized between perceptions of arrest certainty and penalty severity, are of fundamental theoretical importance. These interactions are best investigated through the incorporation of conventional interaction terms in a linear model.

In summary, path analysis is not considered to be the best analytical procedure for the present data, despite the fact that a causal model is depicted in Figure 2.2. As Wolfe (1980) has pointed out, the major value of path analysis is not so much the algebraic equations and their solutions but the obligation on the researcher to express and present ideas in explicit form. This is the purpose of the theoretical model described in Chapter 2 and the analytic model shown in Figure 2.2.

LINEAR MODELS ANALYSIS

Path analysis is of course an application of the linear model. However, the linear models employed in this book are simpler in form, being variants of the *generalized general linear model* (Nelder & Wedderburn, 1972; Timm, 1975). The general linear model includes as special cases univariate and multivariate analysis of variance and multiple regression. Generalized linear models include dependent variables with distributions belonging to the univariate or multivariate exponential families, such as the binomial (logistic regression), the Poisson (log-linear models), and the multinomial (multivariate logistic models).

There are a number of practical consequences of the use of the linear model concept in preference to specific techniques like analysis of variance (ANOVA) or multiple regression. One consequence is that predictor variables can be represented in all models in a form which is appropriate to their levels of measurement. Thus a numerical variable such as the arrest index can be included as a numerical score in a model which also contains dummy variables corresponding to ordinal and nominal scale variables. Moreover, interactions between numerical and nominal or ordinal variables can be investigated (this is normally considered in the context of testing for parallelism in analysis of covariance, but the application of the concept is very much wider than this).

Ordinary least squares procedures were of course used when (as with the arrest index) the dependent variable was numerical. For binary response variables logistic models were employed (Cox, 1970). As noted above, the threshold model estimated by iterated reweighted least squares (Bock, 1975; Gilmour, 1984; Nelder & Wedderburn, 1972) was used for ordinal variables, such as the perceived probability of being randomly tested in the next month. In the threshold model there is assumed to be a process underlying the allocation of respondents to categories which is scalar valued and distributed continuously. There are assumed to be certain values on the continuum called *thresholds*, such that the response categories correspond to the intervals from $-\infty$ to $+\infty$ defined by the threshold values. This is a more satisfactory model for ordinal variables (such as Likert scales) than one based on ordinary least squares in which the responses are gratuitously assigned arbitrary numerical values. In fact the most appropriate scaling of the categories is a by-product of the analysis, since the threshold values are estimated from the model. Frequently an equal interval scale is not appropriate (Bock, 1975).

Following what has now become conventional usage (Fienberg, 1980), deviances from log-linear models (logistic, threshold, etc.) will be denoted by G^2, and the Pearson goodness-of-fit statistic by x^2. Both statistics have an asymptotic chi-square distribution under the null hypothesis.

MODEL BUILDING PROCEDURES

The emphasis in the RBT analysis is on the relationships between sets of variables in Figure 2.2, building up to a full model of predictors for the dependent variable(s) in question. The full model is then reduced to a *minimal adequate subset* (Aitkin, 1974, 1978) by fitting models in various orders and deleting variables which are not significant. The actual order of fit depended very much on the context; sometimes the variables which were most significant either as individual predictors or when adjusted for all other variables were given priority, but in most cases orderings suggested by Figure 2.2 were explored as well. Automatic procedures like backward elimination were not employed. Aitkin's criterion for a reduced model was used in order to guard against Type I errors. The method is a fairly conservative simultaneous testing procedure which involves the calculation of the error rate for the full model (i.e., the probability of at least one Type I error). The level of significance of individual terms was generally set at .025, so if there were 19 terms in the full model the family error rate would be $1 - .975^{19} = .38$.

The aim of the model reduction procedure is to produce a model with the minimum number of terms. A model is *adequate* if the sum of squares (or deviance) for omitted terms is not significantly large by the simultaneous test procedure, and a model is *minimal adequate* if no proper subset of it is adequate. Since the procedure is conservative, sometimes variables which are statistically significant below the .05 level have been retained in the model when they should have been omitted according to Aitkin's criterion. These variables are indicated in the text, and are not given the same weight in interpretation as the more highly significant variables.

6
Results of the Random Breath Test Study

In this chapter, data from the February and April surveys are analyzed. The analysis of the April data is presented first, using Figure 2.2 as the framework and focusing on the elements of the hypothesized causal chain through which respondents are influenced to modify their pre-RBT drinking and travel practices. The research questions were explained in detail in Chapter 5. In summary, the major objective of the analysis of the April data is to verify that the correlations predicted from the simple deterrence model actually occurred. In particular, the aim is to demonstrate: (a) that motorists living in areas in which RBT was intensively enforced reported a higher than average level of exposure to RBT; (b) that the higher the level of exposure to RBT (both through police activity and through publicity), the higher the subjective probability of being randomly tested and of being arrested for driving while intoxicated; and (c) that subjective test and arrest probabilities were positively correlated with the number of ways in which respondents modified their drinking and travel practices.

The major findings of the analysis of the 517 drinking license holders interviewed in April are that these correlations are all present in the data, and that the correlations survive adjustment for the influence of socio-demographic variables like age, sex, and alcohol consumption. In addition, the correlations survive adjustment for peer pressure to drink. Although the majority of respondents reported that since RBT it was easier to reduce alcohol consumption in a group situation, this change in perceived pressure acted as an additional predictor of modifications to drinking and travel behaviors, not as an alternative to perceptions of sanctions.

The analysis of the data from the 185 respondents who were interviewed twice provided strong support for the finding of a simple deterrent effect from the April data. In addition, however, there is evidence of a decline in the perceived probability of being randomly tested over the 6 weeks between interviews, although there was no decline overall in the number of attempts which respondents were making to avoid drinking and driving. The analysis of driving while intoxicated between interviews provides further support for the deterrence model, but in a surprising fashion: the perceived severity of punishments appeared to be a better predictor of such behavior than the perceived probability of being randomly tested.

Descriptive Analysis of the April Data

In all, 385 men and 400 women were interviewed during the April survey. Of the total of 785 respondents, 185 were Sydney residents who had been previously interviewed, 200 were new Sydney residents matched with the original sample of 400, and 400 were residents of eight towns and cities throughout New South Wales. There was a total of 656 license holders of whom 517 drank alcohol at least once a year.

Before reporting the results of the multivariate analyses which were used to explore the paths of the deterrence model, it will be useful to summarize some of the simpler features of the survey findings. In this preliminary section the main focus will be on the distributions and correlates of variables which in later analyses constitute the independent variables, and are therefore (in those sections) treated as "givens." Detailed correlations may be found in Homel (1986).

Knowledge of and Exposure to RBT

Awareness of RBT 3 months after its inception was very high. Only 41 respondents (5.2%) could not identify *any* new methods the government was using to deal with drinking and driving (AQ1[a]), and 653 (83.2%) mentioned RBT without prompting. The level of awareness of RBT in Sydney ($n = 286$) was 82.3%, about the same as the figure of 81.8% recorded 6 weeks earlier. However, there were some marked regional variations, with a score of 100% in the rural center of Bathurst ($n = 50$) but only 58.8% in Wollongong ($n = 50$). The high figure for Bathurst undoubtedly reflects the effects of an enormous police blitz during motorcycle races held in the city over Easter each year, but the Wollongong figure is a little harder to explain. Wollongong is an industrial city just south of Sydney with a high proportion of immigrants from non-English speaking countries, and possibly the media publicity was less effective there than elsewhere. It should also be noted that the level of police enforcement in Wollongong during the first part of April (and particularly over Easter) was rated by the police as "low," suggesting a direct correlation between awareness and intensity of enforcement. The correlation between the police figures for the first half of April (per thousand license holders) and level of awareness was in fact .53. The only other significant correlate of awareness was level of education, with the more poorly educated being slightly less aware (80% compared with 88%).

In contrast to the rate at which RBT was spontaneously mentioned, when asked directly if they had seen, heard, or read any publicity about

RBT (AQ5), 95.2% or respondents answered in the affirmative. This discrepancy is, of course, to be expected. The first question probably underestimates the percentage of those aware of RBT since the respondent must be able to remember, without prompting. On the other hand, the direct question probably yields a percentage which is too high since the respondent may feel he or she *should* have heard of the law (especially since it is important enough to run a survey about) or may confuse RBT publicity with other publicity about drinking and driving. On balance, the open-ended question is probably more useful to those wishing to know how far the new law penetrated public consciousness. After all, if the law is to have an effect on a person's behavior, it should be able to be recalled without difficulty. It is also worth noting that the impact of publicity can be quite ephemeral. Among the 185 Sydney residents who were reinterviewed, reported exposure to publicity actually declined from 97.3% to 91.9%, despite an additional quarter million dollars spent over Easter.

As would be expected, television reached the widest audience at slightly more than two out of three people (68.3%), followed by newspapers with a penetration of 44.4% and radio with 19.9%. When asked what they recalled, respondents mostly mentioned either features of the TV advertisements or they answered in terms of a generalized message about the risks involved in drinking and driving (e.g., "Don't take the risk," "Drink and drive and you are gone."). Stiff penalties and the role of alcohol in causing accidents were mentioned by a few (7.2% and 8.5% respectively). The power of television in communicating a message is illustrated by the contrast between the mean numbers of items recalled from the publicity by those exposed and those not exposed to TV advertising: 1.4 compared with 0.4 ($r = .57$). There were, as expected, variations between regions, but perhaps surprisingly Sydney recorded the lowest rates of exposure for all three media. The "working class" cities of Newcastle and Wollongong recorded quite high levels, suggesting that the low rate of awareness in Wollongong was more a matter of relative police inactivity over Easter than a deficiency in publicity.

Exposure to publicity (particularly on the radio) was correlated with knowing people who had been tested. In addition, listening to the radio was associated with alcohol consumption (particularly the consumption of beer), being a young man, and having high perceptions of the chances of arrest. It seems that through radio more than through the other media the message may have effectively reached a group of young but heavy drinkers. However, with the possible exception of television, the correlations between exposure to publicity and changes to travel and drinking arrangements were quite modest.

Turning from awareness of publicity to personal exposure, 13.9% of the population claimed to have been either randomly tested or a passenger in the car when the driver was tested. Although from the test-retest analysis reported in Chapter 5 we know these figures are not completely reliable, there seems no doubt that a higher percentage of the population in areas outside Sydney had had direct exposure to RBT, with Bathurst heading the list at 40.0%. Nearly half (48.8%) of the April sample had driven past police carrying out random testing, and of these 12.0% had driven past only a few days ago. Conversely, a substantial proportion of those who had driven past had not seen an RBT operation for a month or more (57.2%). A high proportion knew someone who had been tested, at 58.5%, and nearly one in six (15.9%) claimed to know four or more people who had been tested. One in five (20.3%) knew one person who had been tested.

Not surprisingly, the several measures of exposure were moderately correlated with each other. The strongest correlation was between recency and frequency of driving past ($r = -.42$), with those who had most recently driven past also being those who had driven past most frequently. Young people tended to be exposed to RBT more, probably because they generally drive more, particularly at high risk times (Homel, 1983c). Exposure was weakly correlated with awareness of publicity, but rather more strongly with perceptions of sanctions. In particular, the more people the respondent knew who had been randomly tested, the higher the perceived certainty of arrest for drinking and driving ($r = .21$). Consistent with this result, those exposed to RBT were more likely to modify their travel and drinking behaviors, although they were also more likely to report drinking and driving since the introduction of RBT. This is partly because certain groups, such as young men, are at greater risk of drink-driving because of their lifestyle and the amount of driving they do, and therefore have more scope for modifying their usual practices. This issue is probed in more detail in subsequent sections.

Drinking, Driving, and Drink-Driving

Some fairly clear drinking patterns emerged from the data. Of respondents classified as drinking license holders, about one in five (20.5%) drank once a day, and slightly more than a third (34.6%) drank once or twice a week. Only 2.3% admitted to drinking more often than once a day, while more than a quarter (26.9%) claimed to drink no more often than two or three times a month. By far the most frequently consumed beverage was beer, with a mean of 2.36 standard drinks on a drinking day (Table 6.1). Total standard drinks consumed on a drinking day averaged 4.0, which given the literature on self-reported alcohol consumption reviewed in Chapter 5, we can safely assume is an underestimate. As with the frequency of drinking, amounts consumed had a skewed distribution. For example, although one respondent claimed to drink 36 middies on a drinking day, more than half of all respondents stated that they drank no beer at all. The skewed nature of the distribution of stated consumption is clearly reflected in the quantity-frequency index (Table 6.1), in terms of which only 9.5% of the sample are

Table 6.1. Quantities and frequencies of alcohol consumption

Quantity-Frequency		Amounts consumed on a drinking day				
Category	% (N = 517)	Beverage	% Who consume any[a]	Mean	Standard deviation	Maximum
Occasional	6.8	Beer	47.2	2.36	3.96	36
Frequent-light	39.4	LA Beer	9.5	0.25	0.95	12
Infrequent-light	18.0	Wine	39.3	0.82	1.22	6
Medium	26.3	Port	4.3	0.09	0.51	6
Heavy	9.5	Spirits	17.2	0.48	1.39	15
All drinking license holders	100.0	All beverages		4.01	3.68	36

[a] Since drinkers may consume more than one type of beverage on a drinking day, these percentages sum to more than 100%.

heavy drinkers, but 54.2% are occasional, frequent-light, or infrequent-light.

Marked differences in drinking patterns according to age, sex, and type of beverage were evident. Wine drinkers tend to imbibe occasionally, beer drinkers heavily and frequently. Heavy but less frequent drinking (especially beer drinking) is characteristic of young men; older men drink more often, but in smaller quantities. Women drink less frequently than men, and consume smaller quantities of beer but more wine and (to some extent) more spirits. The more highly educated drink more wine and port, but less beer and less alcohol overall. Among occupational groups, the heaviest consumption levels were reported by semiskilled and unskilled blue-collar workers (7.16 standard drinks—mainly beer—on a drinking day) and by the unemployed (8.36). Housewives and pensioners reported the lowest levels of consumption (3.13 and 3.62 respectively).

Quantities of beer consumption were positively associated with group pressure to drink ($r = .38$), but the correlation of group pressure with wine consumption was weak and negative ($r = -.10$). Nearly a quarter (22.5%) of those classified as heavy drinkers on the quantity-frequency index said they find it "extremely hard" to drink less than their friends in a group situation, compared with only 2.8% of lighter drinkers. Overall, more than one drinking license holder in four (26.3%) claimed to find it at least "quite hard" to resist the blandishments of alcohol when in a group situation (AQ21), and a substantial minority of these people (26.5%) said that RBT had made it even *harder*, not easier (perhaps this involves a fear of being called "chicken?"). Overall, 8.5% of the sample claimed that RBT had made it harder to resist group pressure, but (more in line with theoretical expectations) 40% said RBT had made it easier while 51.5% claimed no change. Those who felt subject to the most pressure to drink tended to be young, male, and less well-educated, and to be unemployed, blue-collar workers, or students. The correlation between group pressure and perceptions of change in pressure since the introduction of RBT was .29 (Cramer's V), with a clear trend for those under the greatest pressure to be more likely to report a negative impact of RBT in this respect.

Both perceived pressure to drink and personal levels of consumption were correlated with drinking-driving behavior. Nearly half (49.9%) of all drinking license holders reported drink-driving at some time in the past, and 7.4% reported a conviction for drink-driving. Indeed, it was clear from the data that drink-driving is far from rare behavior. The recorded conviction rate of 7.4% is undoubtedly underestimated by at least 35% (Locander et al., 1976), but of even greater importance is the fact that more than one person in five (21.1%) in the population at risk admitted to driving over the legal limit in the 3 months since the introduction of RBT. Nearly 1 in 10 (9.1%) did it several times. Since this drinking and driving took place at a time when perceptions of the chances of arrest were much higher than before the law (Carseldine, 1985), it seems reasonable to conclude that whatever the deterrent impact of RBT, no form of police enforcement of drink-drive law is likely to even get close to eradicating drinking and driving, at least in Australia. This might seem like a banal observation, but it needs to be emphasized since the apparent success of RBT which is documented in later sections might lead some to conclude that drinking and driving is no longer a problem in New South Wales.

It should come as no surprise that heavy drinkers were more at risk. While 21.1% of the total sample admitted to drinking and driving since the introduction of RBT, the figure for heavy drinkers was 44.9%, with 22.5% claiming to have driven while impaired at least twice. The correlation between alcohol consumption on a drinking day and the frequency of drink-driving since RBT was .32, a relatively high figure. Total alcohol consumption was correlated with having a conviction for drinking and driving ($r = .29$), and those with a previous conviction were in turn twice as likely to have driven while impaired as those without a previous conviction (39.5% compared with 19.6%). Similarly, those most conscious of social pressure were more likely to have driven while impaired and have a conviction.

As indicated in Chapter 1, drinking and driving tends to be male behavior, and this fact is clearly reflected in the survey responses ($r = .32$ for having ever driven while impaired and .19 for having driven while impaired since RBT). Moreover, the survey data suggest that it is a practice more common among young people, particularly those aged 21 to 24 years, although this pattern is not as evident from available roadside survey data (Homel, 1983c). The rate of self-reported drinking and driving since RBT in this age group was 41.2%, twice as high as the average of 21.1%. These correlations reflect peer pressure and levels of alcohol consumption among young people. Drinking and driving was also more commonly reported by blue-collar workers and the unemployed, which once again is consistent with the drinking and social pressure correlations. Contrary to the earlier pattern there was a trend for the more highly educated to report *more* drink-driving since RBT ($r = .09$), but this probably reflects the relative youthfulness of the better educated. There was no correlation between need for a vehicle and the incidence of drinking and driving since RBT, nor was there any correlation between need for a vehicle and peer pressure to drink.

In summary, the various indices of drinking, peer pressure to drink and drink-drive behavior were all quite strongly correlated, in predictable ways. Group pressure seemed to be especially critical for heavy drinkers as a factor encouraging drinking and driving, and contrary to what might have been expected the introduction of RBT made it *harder* for many of these people to reduce their alcohol consumption in a group situation (at least that is what they claimed). Young men in blue-collar occupations, particularly those aged 21 to 24 years, appear to be at high risk for drinking and driving. The respondent's need for a vehicle did not seem in itself to be a very useful predictor of such behavior.

On the face of it, these statistics tend to implicate as the villain of the piece the young, beer drinking "ocker" male — the archetypal uncultivated young Australian working man. There is, as noted above, an element of the predictable about many of the correlations, and they parallel closely the findings of Berger and Snortum (1985) for the United States, particularly with respect to the central importance of a beer drinkers' subculture. Perhaps what is less predictable in the present study is the association between this cluster of variables and modifications to behavior as a response to RBT. Frequency of drink-driving since RBT was in fact *positively* correlated with the number of steps being taken to avoid drinking and driving, especially through modifications to traveling arrangements ($r = .20$). Similarly, modifications to behavior were more commonly made by the young ($r = -.19$), by men ($r = .15$), by heavy drinkers ($r = .22$), and by those most conscious of group pressure ($r = .29$). This suggests that although still drinking and driving more than others, these groups responded to RBT in quite a positive fashion. Clearly it would be useful, in evaluating the extent to which an individual has driven while impaired since the introduction of RBT, to take account of his or her frequency of drinking and driving *prior* to the new law. Unfortunately this information is not directly available in the present study, although it may be inferred from responses to other questions.

The interpretation of a deterrent impact of RBT is supported by the positive correlations between levels of exposure and perceptions of the chances of arrest, and the positive correlations between perceptions of sanctions and the numbers of modifications to travel and drinking habits. The evidence for such a deterrent effect is examined more rigorously in the following sections.

The Effects of Police Testing: An Area-Level Analysis

Much of the deterrence literature is based on an analysis of correlations between variables at the aggregate level. One good reason for beginning the formal analysis of the present data in this manner is the central importance of the objective probability of arrest or imprisonment in the deterrence model. This variable is operationalized in the present study as the number of random tests conducted by police in the period between the introduction of RBT and the completion of the survey interviews (April 16, 1983). In Figure 2.2, the level of police enforcement of RBT is proposed as being one of the major influences on an individual's chances of being exposed to RBT, and hence of his perceptions of sanctions and resulting changes in behavior. Since the only way levels of enforcement can be conceptualized and measured is as an aggregate phenomenon, an area-level analysis is clearly essential, at least to the extent that police enforcement itself is the object of analysis.

One of the many advantages of using the offense of drinking and driving as a vehicle for studying deterrence is that the intensity of police enforcement in an area can be reliably quantified through the RBT statistics. Of course there is a lot more to police enforcement than the simple number of tests conducted: time of day, location, duration of testing at a site, type of unit (special van or regular highway patrol), and a number of other factors are all aspects of police activity that could affect the amount of deterrence achieved. However, the number of tests conducted has the great advantage that it was a statistic which was readily available for the areas sampled, and is arguably the best summary measure of the level of enforcement, provided it can be related to the size of the population at risk of being tested. The only practical way of estimating the size of this population in an area is to use the number of resident license holders, so random tests per 1,000 license holders in each area was used as the index of intensity of police enforcement.

It is convenient to construct three measures of the extent to which a population has been exposed to RBT: the percentage tested, the percentage who have driven past an RBT operation, and the average number of people known to have been tested. Perceptions of arrest certainty can be measured by the mean score on the arrest index, and also by the mean score on AQ9, the perceived likelihood of being randomly tested in the next month (to conform with the direction of scoring of the arrest index, the codes for the five responses to this question have been reversed so that a high mean score indicates a high perceived chance of being tested). Similarly, behavioral responses to RBT can be measured by the mean numbers of changes to travel and drinking behaviors, and by the percentage admitting to driving over .05 since RBT. Given their potential importance as mediating variables, several measures of drinking behavior are also included: the mean number of standard drinks consumed on a drinking day

TABLE 6.2. Scores for components of the deterrence model averaged for each town or city[a]

Town or city	Tests/1,000 license holders[b]	Licensed drinkers surveyed	% Tested randomly	% Driven past RBT	Mean number known	Mean arrest score	Mean chances in next month	Mean alcohol consumed
Sydney	85	276	11.2	57.6	1.23	1.61	1.57	3.37
Newcastle	165	24	20.8	75.0	1.38	0.67	1.39	3.84
Wollongong	165	29	20.7	62.1	1.86	1.79	2.17	3.23
Bathurst	194	35	42.9	34.3	2.51	2.94	2.00	3.13
Lismore	30	28	7.1	46.4	1.68	2.11	2.18	1.73
Goulburn	93	29	24.1	44.8	2.28	2.00	2.90	2.72
Wagga Wagga	86	25	16.0	40.0	1.72	2.56	2.39	3.14
Tamworth	95	33	15.2	42.4	2.27	1.73	2.42	2.64
Dubbo	72	38	18.4	52.6	1.89	2.66	2.08	3.30
Median	93	517[c]	18.4	46.4	1.86	2.00	2.17	3.14

Town or city	% Abstainers	% Heavy/ Moderate drinkers	% Very or ext. hard to resist	% Harder since RBT	Mean mods. to travel	Mean mods. to drinking	% Driving over .05
Sydney	15.9	30.2	12.7	5.1	0.63	0.68	21.0
Newcastle	22.6	29.0	29.2	20.8	0.00	0.08	33.3
Wollongong	27.5	40.0	27.6	41.4	0.55	0.86	37.9
Bathurst	22.2	24.4	17.1	11.4	1.00	0.66	20.0
Lismore	31.7	17.1	7.1	3.6	0.54	0.68	7.1
Goulburn	32.6	18.6	13.8	3.5	0.31	0.48	17.2
Wagga Wagga	32.4	18.9	12.0	4.0	0.52	0.64	16.0
Tamworth	26.7	22.2	12.1	12.1	0.48	0.51	12.1
Dubbo	17.4	39.1	10.5	5.3	0.53	0.66	26.3
Median	26.7	24.4	12.7	5.3	0.53	0.66	20.0

[a] The percentage of people who drove past RBT and were randomly tested in each area are based on the total sample of 385 respondents in Sydney and 50 in each area outside Sydney (April survey). The remaining variables are based on the number of license holders in each area who drank alcohol at least once a year (referred to as "licensed drinkers surveyed" in column 2 of the table).

[b] Based on police statistics on the number of random breath tests conducted in each area between December 17, 1982 and April 16, 1983.

[c] Total number of license holders who drank.

in the area, the percentage of abstainers, the percentage of heavy or moderate drinkers, the percentage who find it hard or very hard to resist group pressure, and the percentage who have found it harder since RBT to resist such pressure. These data for all areas are listed in Table 6.2.

There is a fair degree of agreement between the official number of tests per 1,000 license holders and the percentage of respondents who reported being tested. Lismore attracted the lowest rate of enforcement and also recorded the lowest percentage tested, while Bathurst, which was heavily blitzed over the Easter period, recorded by far the highest percentage tested. In fact the correlation between the two sets of figures is .79 (see Table 6.3), a comforting confirmation that two types of data which *ought* to agree actually *can* agree. There are several reasons why the correlation is not higher. First, the survey figures pertain to the percentage personally tested or in the car when the driver was tested, and should therefore be somewhat higher than the official police rates. This is so for every area, although in the case of Bathurst the discrepancy is marked. Second, the official rate for an area will be a little high, since it includes people tested more than once. Third, the official police rate of testing takes no account of differential rates of exposure due to different driving patterns, which are reflected in the survey figures. Finally, there is an approximate 15% error either way in the survey percentages, due to sampling error (the sample size in each area outside Sydney was 50).

The association between levels of drinking, peer pressure, and the extent of driving over .05 is confirmed by the correlations in Table 6.3. Since only nine areas were sampled, correlation coefficients can be strongly influenced by scores for a single city, and statistical tests are not powerful. Nevertheless, provided care is taken in identifying outliers, the correlation coefficients are useful for indicating associations which are particularly strong. The strong association between the number of official tests and the proportion tested in the survey does not extend to the other measures of exposure (the correlations are .22 and .26). However, an examination of the scatterplot of the percentage of people who drove past an RBT operation versus the official police rate of testing reveals Bathurst as an outlier, with a high rate of testing but with a low percentage of motorists having driven past. Presumably the explanation for this is that testing was so intense in Bathurst that a very high proportion of passing motorists were pulled over. In any case, if Bathurst is omitted the correlation rises from .22 to .72. The low correlation with the number of people known to have been tested is probably due to the fact that this latter quantity is affected by many variables in addition to the actual level of enforcement in an area.

It is possible to carry out a more rigorous analysis of the relationships between police activity and aspects of exposure. Regressing the proportion tested against test rate using a logistic model (since the dependent variable is a proportion), the relationship is highly significant ($G^2(1) = 6.59$, $p = .010$). An increase of 100 tests per 1,000 license holders corresponds to

TABLE 6.3. Correlations between components of the deterrence model, computed at the area level ($N = 9$)

Variable	Tests/1,000 license holders	% Tested randomly	% Driven past RBT	Mean number known	Mean arrest score	Mean chances in next month	Mean alcohol consumed
% Tested randomly	.79*						
% Driven past RBT	.22	-.29					
Mean number known	.26	.66*	-.71*				
Mean arrest score	-.14	.37	-.81*	.57			
Chances next month	-.30	-.11	-.67*	.52	.60		
Mean alcohol consumed	.62	.34	.54	-.30	-.30	-.55	
% Abstainers	-.22	-.12	-.36	.30	.09	.53	-.59
% Heavy/Moderate	.35	.08	.58	-.23	-.12	-.23	.60
% Very hard to resist	.82*	.36	.69*	-.16	-.57	-.46	.65
% Harder since RBT	.66*	.19	.53	-.03	-.38	-.05	.36
Mean mods. to travel	.11	.40	-.67*	.43	.78*	.39	-.22
Mean mods. to drinking	-.19	-.06	-.42	.18	.64	.56	-.34
% Driving over .05	.66*	.27	.73*	-.25	-.36	-.44	.79*

Variable	% Abstainers	% Heavy/Moderate drinkers	% Very or ext. hard to resist	% Harder since RBT	Mean mods. to travel	Mean mods. to drinking
% Heavy/Moderate	-.66*					
% Very/Ext. hard	-.12	.48				
% Harder since RBT	-.02	.60	.84*			
Mean mods. to travel	-.19	.02	-.37	-.12		
Mean mods. to drinking	.04	.23	-.35	.10	.75*	
% Driving over .05	-.40	.83*	.86*	.77*	-.26	-.10

$* p < .05$.

a threefold increase in the odds of being tested. How often people have driven past an RBT operation is a variable (not explicitly represented in Table 6.3) which may be analyzed at the individual level as a numerical response, and regressed against the rate of testing in an individual's area of residence. That is, as indicated in Chapter 2, each individual is assigned the rate of testing which applies in his or her area of residence, and this is used as a predictor of how often he or she has been tested. Consistent with the low correlation in Table 6.3, the relationship was not significant ($p = .60$), although if Bathurst is omitted the relationship once again becomes significant ($p = .02$, $r^2 = 1.1\%$), with an increase of 100 in the rate of testing corresponding to an increase of .5 in how often people have driven past. There was no significant relationship between police testing and how *recently* people had driven past an RBT operation ($p = .21$). The number of people known to have been tested can also be treated as a numerical response, but in contrast to the correlation based on the mean values for each area the relationship was significant ($p = .004$, $r^2 = 1.7\%$). An increase of 100 in the testing rate corresponded in the model to an increase of .5 in the number known to have been tested.

It is fair to conclude that there is a strong association between the official intensity of enforcement in an area and the extent of exposure of the target population to RBT. This is hardly a surprising conclusion. However, it is necessary to verify the existence of this relationship if exposure is to be an element in a causal chain linking official police activity with perceptions of sanctions and drink-drive behavior. In the analyses reported in later sections, which are all based on individual responses rather than on average scores for areas, the measures of exposure act essentially as "proxies" for the intensity of police enforcement in the area, in the sense that the effects of enforcement on perceptions and behavior are assumed to take place through an individual's personal exposure to RBT. (The possibility of a direct link between enforcement levels and perceptions of arrest certainty is explored in the next section.)

In addition to being correlated with the exposure measures, official police testing is correlated with alcohol consumption (.62), with social pressure to drink (.82 and .66) and with driving over .05 (.66). It is not directly correlated, at the area level, with perceptions of arrest likelihood or modifications to drinking or travel behaviors. On the face of it, the positive correlation with the proportion driving over .05 is paradoxical. Is police testing actually encouraging drinking and driving? A much more plausible explanation is that police concentrated their efforts in areas with a reputation for heavy drinking, and that these areas are characterized by high rates of drinking and driving. This explanation is fully supported by the correlations. The partial correlation between police testing rate and the incidence of driving over .05, controlling for mean alcohol consumption, is only .35. Controlling for social pressure to drink (the proportion who find

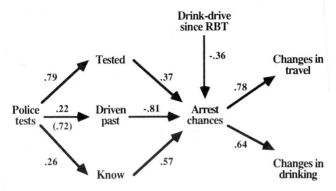

FIGURE 6.1. Ecological correlations associated with each link in the simple deterrence model.

it extremely or very hard to resist pressure) the effect is even more pronounced, with a partial correlation of −.15.

It is possible from Table 6.3 to follow the causal chain implied by the deterrence model. The correlations associated with each link in the chain are set out in Figure 6.1. By and large, these correlations are consistent with what would be expected if deterrence were actually occurring, and this fact could be discerned from ecological correlations. For example, the rate of police testing correlates well with the proportion tested in an area. This in turn correlates moderately well with the average perceived chances of arrest, which in turn correlates strongly with the mean number of attempts being made to avoid drinking and driving. The more people report drinking and driving, the lower are the mean scores for arrest certainty, which is consistent with the hypothesized experiential effect.

However, the correlation between the proportion of people who had driven past an RBT operation and the mean arrest score was not in the predicted direction (−.81), and was not unduly influenced by outliers. To reconcile this correlation with deterrence theory, we could argue that simply driving past police is actually counterproductive from a deterrence point of view, since motorists are encouraged to believe that their chances of being pulled over are small. Unfortunately for this explanation, the correlation between these two variables when calculated at the individual level was (as expected) small and positive at .08, which is nothing like −.81.

The fact that ecological and individual level correlations can be discrepant is well-known. There are thus two basic problems in deterrence research generally and in Table 6.3 in particular: correlation does not necessarily imply causation, but, more than that, ecological correlations bear no necessary relationship to correlations between the same variables calculated at the individual level. The crucial questions then become: What is the theoretically appropriate unit of analysis, and given a resolution of this problem, how do we go from correlation to causation?

Gibbs (1979) and a number of other deterrence theorists (e.g., Grasmick, 1981) insist on an aggregate-level analysis because only at the level of jurisdictions does it make sense to talk about the objective properties of legal sanctions. This point is conceded. It does *not* follow, however, that all the links in the deterrence model should therefore be traced at the aggregate level. Deterrence is in essence a psychological process; it is the sum of individual responses which constitutes the deterrent impact of a law in a jurisdiction (although of course individual responses take place within a sociological framework). In Figure 2.2, *individual exposure* to RBT is the crucial factor linking official rates of enforcement with perceptions and behaviors. Provided measures of exposure are included in the analysis, and provided it can be shown that exposure is related to official levels of enforcement, it seems that analysis at the aggregate level has little value.

In summary, the main use of Table 6.3 is in helping to establish the link between police testing and exposure to RBT, and in showing that the level of police activity may well be strongly influenced by the drinking patterns in an area. Readers who wish to draw stronger conclusions from Table 6.3 and Figure 6.1 are welcome to do so (although the small sample sizes in areas outside Sydney should be kept in mind). The further problem of establishing causal connections between elements of the deterrence model is dealt with, as far as is possible, in subsequent sections, which are all based on analyses conducted at the individual, not at the aggregate, level.

The Relationship Between Exposure to RBT and Perceptions of the Chances of Being Randomly Tested and Arrested for Drinking and Driving

Having established a link between police testing and exposure to RBT, the next question we will investigate is whether exposure has any influence on perceptions of the chances of being tested, or of being arrested for drinking and driving. This is a crucial question, since deterrence is a psychological process in which calculations of arrest chances play a central role. If it cannot be demonstrated that exposure to RBT had some influence on perceptions of arrest certainty, it is difficult to see how the deterrence model could be valid, even if a link between police testing and changes in behavior could be established. Of course there is a problem of method, as well: it may be that if perceptual measures do not play an effective mediating role that the measures are defective in some way. It should be remembered for example that the arrest index had relatively low reliability.

A further question is the role of publicity in forming perceptions of arrest certainty. Is publicity as important as personal exposure to RBT?

The Effects of Exposure to Police Enforcement of RBT

For purposes of the present analysis, we will focus on the arrest index as well as on responses to AQ9 (the perceived chances of being randomly tested in the next month). The effects of publicity will be considered below. The perceived chance of being tested in the next month, which is one element of the more general index, is of special interest, for two reasons. First, this question was asked in both surveys, and therefore it can be used to examine changes over time (this is done later in this chapter). Second, it was the express aim of the architects of RBT to convince all motorists that their chances of being tested at any time are high, and AQ9 was addressed specifically to this issue. In fact, more people thought the chances were low rather than high: nearly one in three (32.1%) said "quite unlikely" or "extremely unlikely," and fewer than a quarter (22.4%) thought they were "extremely likely" or "quite likely" to be tested. This moderate skew in the distribution is not clearly reflected in the complete index, which was close to being symmetrically distributed about a median score of 2 (minimum -4, maximum 8, mean 1.85, and standard deviation 1.88).

All three measures of exposure were significantly correlated (using a threshold model) with the perceived chances of being tested in the next month. Being personally tested (G^2 (1) = 4.78; $p = .029$) doubled the odds of an "extremely likely to be tested" response (12.7% compared with 6.1%). Recency and frequency of driving past was even more significant (G^2 (9) = 21.4; $p = .011$), with those who had driven past four or more times, most recently a few days or a week or two ago, being much more likely to record high subjective probabilities (more than half the motorists in these categories gave ratings of "extremely" or "quite likely," compared with fewer than a quarter of motorists in other categories). Conversely, those who had last driven past more than a month ago, or who had not driven past at all, generally had lower estimations of the chances of being tested. However, these figures are not presented in more detail since further analysis, reported in the following sections, suggests that neither factor is the critical element in forming perceptions.

By far the strongest association was with the number of people known to have been tested (G^2 (4) = 50.9; $p < .001$). There was a clear trend for subjective probabilities to increase with the number known, so that, for example, 15.5% of those who knew four or more tested (18.8% of the 517 drinking license holders) thought it "extremely likely" that they would be tested, compared with 3.4% of those who knew no one. The number known was also the strongest predictor of the overall arrest score ($F(4, 512) = 8.60$, $p < .001$, $r^2 = 6.3\%$), with the same strong monotonic trend. In fact, despite their association with the perceived chances of being tested in the next month, neither of the other exposure measures successfully predicted arrest certainty ($p = .19$ and .42). This suggests that these aspects of exposure are rather specific in their psychological effects and do not flow over to the more general aspects of police enforcement covered by the items from which the arrest score is formed.

The importance of the number of people known to have been tested is reinforced by linear models analysis, which incorporates all exposure measures simultaneously. The recency and frequency of driving past was not significant as a predictor of either dependent variable when adjusted for the other two measures of exposure ($p = .17$ and $.65$ for AQ9 and the arrest index respectively), and neither was the personal experience of being tested ($p = .99$ and $.53$). However, the number of people known remained highly significant ($p < .001$ for both response variables).

The Effects of Exposure to Publicity

Perhaps surprisingly, only exposure to radio advertising significantly elevated the perceived probability of being breath tested or arrested for drink-driving ($p = .001$ for the chances of being tested and $p < .001$ for the arrest index), although TV and newspaper publicity came close to achieving a significant result ($p = .075$ and $.101$ for television and $.063$ and $.074$ for newspapers). The total number of points recalled from all sources of advertising had no predictive power at all ($p = .81$ and $.83$). These results were confirmed by an analysis in which all publicity variables were fitted simultaneously. For both outcome variables, radio maintained its predictive power ($p = .008$ and $.000$ adjusted for other publicity variables) while television, papers, and recall remained nonsignificant. The effect of exposure to radio was to increase scores on the arrest index by an average of .74 (.39 standard deviations) and by .65 standard deviation units on the latent scale underlying responses to AQ9 (the perceived probability of being randomly tested in the next month). However, when variables measuring both exposure to publicity and exposure to testing were fitted simultaneously, the number of people known to have been tested retained its significance (adjusted for other variables), while the significance of radio publicity became marginal.

Influences on Arrest Certainty: Towards a Parsimonious Model

The Relationship Between Levels of Police Enforcement and the Perceived Probability of Being Tested or Arrested

According to the model of the deterrence process described in Chapter 2, police enforcement in an area should manifest itself in the exposure of individuals to RBT, which in turn should influence perceptions and behaviors. It is not clear that there should be any direct link between the intensity of police enforcement and perceptions of arrest certainty. In fact analysis of the data confirmed that there was no direct connection between police testing and perceptions of the chances of being tested or arrested, whether or not exposure was taken into account. However, as we have seen, there *was* an indirect link via the number of people known to have been tested, although the linking correlations were small ($r^2 = 1.7\%$ for the relationship between police testing and the number known to have been tested [calculated at the individual level], and $r^2 = 6.3\%$ for the number known as a predictor of arrest certainty).

Other Influences on Perceptions of the Chances of Arrest

Following Figure 2.2, there are several types of variables which could influence perceptions of arrest probabilities and could also be correlated with exposure to RBT or exposure to publicity. It is necessary, therefore, to check that the significant exposure variables remain significant when adjusted for the effects of these additional variables. However, before describing the results of these tests, it will be useful to examine which factors do correlate with arrest certainty. The main focus will be on arrest certainty, rather than on the perceived chances of being tested in the next month, since the analysis of behavior changes reported in the next section demonstrates that the index of arrest certainty is the more powerful predictor. (In these and following analyses, when a predictor consists of more than one degree of freedom and has been represented by several dummy variables, the strength of association between it and a response variable will be reported in terms of the squared multiple correlation coefficient R^2. Since the addition of degrees of freedom may spuriously inflate R^2, it should always be interpreted in the light of its significance level p.)

Of all the sociodemographic variables, only education, occupation, and area of residence had significant associations with arrest certainty. The precise patterns are graphically shown in Figure 6.2. In general, lower white-collar and blue-collar workers, with lower education levels, gave higher estimates of the chances of arrest (education level: $p = .010$, $R^2 = 3.3\%$; occupation: $p = .040$, $R^2 = 3.5\%$). The area effect was most marked ($p < .001$, $R^2 = 7.4\%$), with residents of Bathurst giving the highest estimates and those in Newcastle giving the lowest.

Both measures of social pressure correlated with arrest certainty (perceived change in pressure since RBT: $p = .003$, $R^2 = 2.3\%$; current pressure: $p = .009$, $R^2 = 3.0\%$). Those who found it harder to resist pressure to drink since RBT had arrest estimates about half a standard deviation *higher* than those who found it easier since RBT (Fig. 6.2).

Contrary to the experiential effects often found in deterrence research, the frequency of drinking and driving since RBT was not significantly associated with arrest certainty ($p = .61$, $R^2 = .3\%$). This surprising result might be attributable to the short time (3 months) that RBT had been operating, or maybe it reflects shortcomings in the measure of arrest cer-

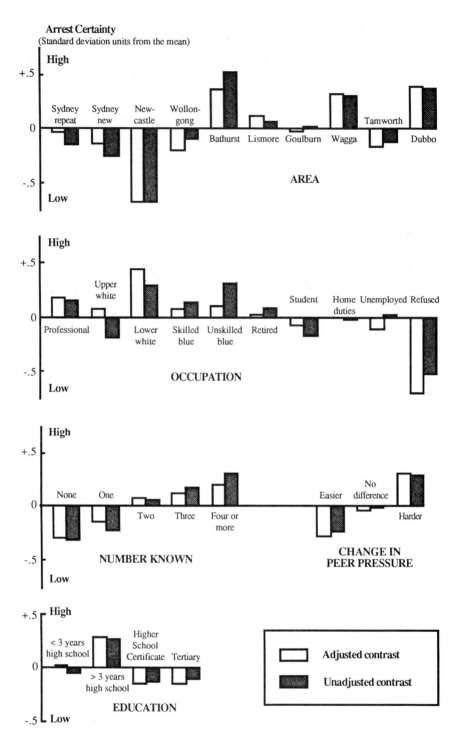

FIGURE 6.2. Reduced model of predictors for arrest certainty: adjusted and un-adjusted effects.

tainty. There was also no discernible effect of drink-driving experience on the estimated chances of being tested in the next month ($p = .10$).

The key question theoretically is whether the exposure variables remain significant as predictors of arrest certainty, adjusted for the sociodemographic, peer pressure, and experiential variables. Consistent with the results reported above, only the number of people known to have been tested was clearly significant ($p = .002$), with radio again being marginal ($p = .048$). Taking the perceived chances of being tested in the next month as dependent variable and fitting a threshold model, the number known remained significant ($p < .001$) but radio had no predictive power at all ($p = .58$). Fitting radio exposure and other variables in different orders suggests that the effects of radio publicity are partly explained by regional variations. In other words, the penetration of radio publicity in different areas is to some extent correlated with other features of those areas that influence arrest estimates.

In conclusion, it seems clear that RBT had an influence on arrest certainty (and on the perceived probability of being randomly tested) via the mechanism of people's social networks. This link does seem to reflect a real causal effect, since none of the other variables depicted in Figure 2.2 affected the significance of the relationship.

Influences on Arrest Certainty: A Parsimonious Model

The analysis so far has been concentrated on building a model from the individual components of Figure 2.2. In order to summarize the influences on arrest certainty, it will be convenient to fit all predictors in a full model and reduce to a minimal adequate subset (Aitkin, 1974). R^2 for the full model was 26.6%, with the number known to have been tested ($p = .005$), social pressure ($p = .030$), change in social pressure ($p = .005$), education ($p = .002$), and area of residence ($p = .001$) being the most significant terms, adjusted for all others.

An adequate subset consisted of the number known to have been tested ($p = .007$; $R^2 = 3.3\%$), education ($p = .001$; $R^2 = 3.6\%$), occupation ($p = .024$; $R^2 = 3.3\%$), area of residence ($p = .006$; $R^2 = 5.2\%$), and perceived change in social pressure ($p = .006$; $R^2 = 2.6\%$). This subset was not minimal adequate since occupation could have been omitted, but because this term was significant at .025 it was decided to retain it in the model. R^2 for the reduced model was 20.2%, and the R^2 value quoted before for each term represents the contribution to the total sum of squares of that term when fitted last in the reduced model. Using these R^2 values as a measure of the relative importance of each variable, one can see that area has the greatest predictive power (5.2%), with all the others making approximately equal contributions at about 3%.

The patterns of association are shown in Figure 6.2. The vertical axis, representing arrest certainty contrast scores, is marked in units of standard deviation above or below the mean. The shaded bars represent the effects of each factor unadjusted for the effects of others in the reduced model, while the unshaded bars represent the adjusted effects.

It appears that lower white-collar workers and those with minimum high school qualifications saw arrest for drink-driving as most likely. The effects of having a network of friends who have been tested is very clear, the credibility of the legal threat increasing steadily with the number tested. Although adjustment for other factors slightly diminished the impact of this variable, the difference between those who knew no one and those who knew four or more was still .49 standard deviation units. It is of great interest that those finding it harder since RBT to resist peer pressure to drink also had higher than average arrest scores. This suggests that for this group RBT achieved its objective of making the legal threat more credible, but simultaneously helped to create a situation where the chances of drink-driving may have been enhanced.

The persistence of area as a predictor of arrest certainty merits a comment, since we might have expected that area would disappear after adjustment for exposure. Although Bathurst residents did not have the highest arrest estimates after adjustment, probably because of the large number of friends and acquaintances of respondents who were known to have been tested in that region, their scores were nevertheless higher than average. Presumably this is because Bathurst was heavily blitzed over Easter. Thus it would seem that the impact of RBT in an area is not explained solely by the aspects of exposure measured in the present study, and that features of police enforcement unique to each region may have an influence. It is also possible that aspects of the social and demographic makeup of an area influence estimates of arrest certainty. An explanation along these lines seems necessary for the working class city of Newcastle, which according to the figures presented in Table 6.2 was by no means neglected by police RBT squads.

Interaction Effects

It is likely that a number of variables are important only in interaction with others, but there is little theory to guide the selection of interaction terms. Since a completely systematic investigation would greatly reduce the power of tests of main effects, the possibility of interaction effects was checked only for selected exposure variables. Interactions were fitted one at a time in an additive model containing all exposure and publicity variables. The 15 two-factor interactions investigated included the three interactions of television, radio, and newspapers; six interactions involving the three personal exposure variables and radio and TV publicity; and six interactions involving the age and sex of the respondent with the number known to have been tested, and television and radio publicity. These interactions were selected because they covered most of the potentially interesting combinations of publicity and personal exposure, and also because they allowed a test of the hypothesis that publicity and exposure had different effects for men and women and for people of different ages. This last question is of some interest in view of the discussion in Chapter 1 concerning young men as high risk drinking drivers. To protect against Type I errors each of the 15 tests should have been carried out at approximately the .003 level of significance, in which case none of them would have been significant. The following results should therefore be regarded as exploratory and tentative.

Two of the 15 interactions were significant at the 5% level: the recency and frequency of driving past an RBT operation with TV publicity ($p = .019$), and TV publicity with newspaper publicity ($p = .046$). However, when adjusted for the first interaction the second became nonsignificant, while the reverse was not true, so only the first is interpreted.

The combined effect of driving past an RBT operation four or more times, most recently only a few days ago, together with having seen TV publicity, created the highest mean arrest score of any group in the sample. This result is intuitively appealing, and demonstrates the value of investigating the combined effects of variables. Less intuitively appealing, however, was the finding that for respondents who had last driven past an RBT operation more than a month ago, the apparent effect of television was to *reduce* their mean arrest scores to a level well below average. It almost seems that in these cases there was a rejection of the official message in the light of experience, which might be seen as evidence for the evanescence of deterrent effects. For respondents who had not passed an RBT operation at all, as well as for most others, television seemed to make no difference to arrest certainty.

In summary, while there was some evidence for an interaction between two of the exposure variables, most interactions tested were not significant. In particular, there was no evidence that factors influential in the formation of perceptions of arrest certainty operated in a different manner depending on the age or sex of the respondent. Except in the negative sense of indicating a commonality of effects across subgroups, the analysis of interactions in this analysis does not greatly advance the understanding of how perceptions of arrest certainty are formed.

Modifications to Travel and Drinking Behaviors in the April Survey

Following the paths of Figure 2.2, the analysis so far has been focused on levels of police enforcement, exposure to RBT, and perceptions of arrest certainty. It has been shown that the level of police activity in an area is a major influence on the probability that an individual will be exposed to RBT in some way, and that at least one aspect of exposure (the number of friends and acquaintances who have been randomly tested) is a major influence on the perceived probability of being arrested. It is now time to examine the determinants of changes in travel and drinking practices, particularly the role of perceptions of arrest certainty. It will be shown that arrest certainty does correlate with the number of ways respondents were modifying their normal practices, confirming the predictions of the deterrence model. However, there are a number of other influences, including aspects of exposure to RBT, peer pressure, and area of residence.

We will begin the analysis with descriptive statistics of behavior change. This will lead to a multivariate analysis, first with predictors considered individually, then jointly. Two reduced models will be presented, one for travel modifications and the other for changes to drinking practices. Finally, the possibility of a number of interactions involving arrest certainty and some other variables will be examined.

The Pattern of Responses to RBT

More than half the 517 drinking license holders (58.0% to be exact) reported making some modification to their lifestyle as a direct result of RBT. These modifications were more commonly made by young beer drinking males than by other groups, but nevertheless a wide cross-section of the sample was affected. Carefully limiting drinking when driving was the single most popular strategy (23.4%), which is not surprising since of all the options considered in AQ16 it probably involves the least inconvenience and personal effort. The second most popular response was having someone else drive you home (15.3%), which for men at least is probably a more effective strategy than trying to reduce consumption. Other responses, such as drinking at home more (13.5%) or staying overnight after drinking (7.5%), represent more radical departures from accepted practices and suggest that RBT had, at least in the first 3 months, more than a superficial impact on the lives of many motorists.

On average, respondents reported 1.22 adjustments to their pre-RBT behaviors, with modifications to the amount or place of drinking being slightly more common than modifications to travel (a mean of .63 compared with .58). The majority of motorists modified their drinking and driving practices in only one or two ways, so the frequency distributions for travel and drinking modifications were both quite skewed. The correlation between the number of modifications to drinking and travel practices was moderate (.32) but significant, making necessary a multivariate analysis of the two behavior measures.

The Significances of Predictors Considered Individually

A total of 21 variables were used to construct a model of behavior change due to RBT. These included the three measures of exposure to enforcement, the four measures of exposure to publicity (including the recall of the media advertising), the measure of arrest certainty, two measures of penalty severity (the perceived probability of being let off without penalty and the Grasmick question [AQ26]), the two measures of peer pressure to drink, reported drink-drive violations since RBT, and the eight socio-demographic variables discussed previously.

Arrest certainty was highly significant ($p = .001$; $\eta^2 = 2.8\%$), although other factors, such as the quantity and frequency of drinking, explained more variance. (η^2 is a measure of variance explained in a multivariate model and is based directly on lamda, which is the test statistics for the multivariate tests [Tabachnick & Fidell, 1983; Timm, 1975].) The relationship with arrest certainty was as predicted: an increase in the arrest score corresponded to an increase in modifications to both travel and drinking behaviors. A belief that one could be arrested but escape punishment was associated with fewer than average modifications to drinking patterns ($p = .027$), but the more general Grasmick question on evaluations of penalty severity failed to reach significance ($p = .173$). However, many other factors also were significant, and it remains to be seen whether fear of arrest or beliefs about "getting off" can be argued to *cause* these behavior changes.

The single strongest predictor was level of drinking ($\eta^2 = 12.9\%$), with heavy and moderate drinkers being more likely than others to modify their driving patterns. Of even greater significance was the fact that these groups were also more likely than others to modify their *drinking* habits. Although it might be argued that these findings are to some extent artifactual, in that heavy drinkers have more opportunities to drink and drive and more scope for behavior change, the figures should be viewed in the light of a literature which suggests that heavy or high risk drinkers are essentially undeterrable (e.g., Bø, 1978). The fact that heavy drinkers reported *any* behavior change is significant.

Consistent with the association with level of drinking, respondents who confessed to drink-driving since the introduction of RBT and those conscious of heavy pressure to drink were more likely than others to be taking steps to avoid drinking and driving on future occasions ($\eta^2 = 5.1\%$ and 9.2% respectively), although these groups more often changed their travel than their drinking patterns. Similarly, young men were more responsive to RBT ($\eta^2 = 6.7\%$ for age and 2.0% for sex), although once again changes in driving were more popular than changes in drinking (especially among those aged 21 to 24 years, who scored a little below average in terms of drinking modifications). Occupation was also quite significant ($\eta^2 = 7.1\%$), but its effects were difficult to interpret. Contrary to the general effect of age, students were less likely than average to change either type of behavior, but there was no clear trend for variations in response according to status.

Personal exposure to RBT was more strongly correlated with behavior change than exposure to publicity. Of all the indices of exposure to publicity only television was significant, and that only for travel modifications ($p = .011$; $R^2 = 1.3\%$). Those personally tested were also more likely to make changes to their driving but not their drinking. The number of people known to have been tested appeared to have the greatest overall effect, since knowing a number of people was associated with changes to both travel and drinking behaviors ($\eta^2 = 5.0$).

A Parsimonious Model for Predicting the Number of Modifications to Travel and Drinking Behaviors

As with the analysis of the arrest measure, the simplest way of sorting out the relative importance of the 21 predictors is to fit a full model and then reduce it to a model or models which are minimal adequate (or parsimonious). The model with all 21 predictors included had 75 degrees of freedom and an η^2 of 47.0%. The R^2 for the number of modifications to travel was 34.9%, and 23.8% for modifications to drinking. In the full model, "significant" factors (adjusted for all other factors) were exposure to TV publicity ($p = .009$), pressure to drink ($p = .054$), change in peer pressure ($p = .002$), area ($p = .001$), and level of drinking ($p < .001$). These factors were used as a starting point for the model reduction process, but many other combinations were also considered. Given the post hoc nature of the process, Aitkin's (1974, 1978) criterion was again employed as a guide to keeping Type I errors in check. With 21 terms in the model and using a nominal error rate of .025, the error rate for the model was $1 - .975^{21} = .41$. Two slightly different minimal adequate models were uncovered. Statistics for these models are set out in Table 6.4.

The two models are identical in the first four terms: area, awareness of TV publicity, perceived change in pressure to drink, and arrest certainty. Arrest certainty is highly significant in both models, but seemed to have more influence on travel behavior than drinking. The two models differ with respect to variables which are correlated and are therefore alternatives to each other: Model 1 contains peer pressure and the quantity and frequency of drinking, Model 2 contains instead the age and sex of the respondent and whether they had driven over the limit since RBT.

The effects of all four variables common to both models were much the same in both models. An increase of one standard deviation in arrest certainty (1.88) corresponded to an increase of about .14 in the number of modifications to travel behavior, and about .09 in the number of modifications to drinking behavior. These effects could not be described as massive, but they do nevertheless constitute strong evidence for deterrence, since the correlation between arrest certainty and behavior change has been demonstrated not to be a reflection of other factors. Perceptions of the chances of arrest do seem to be an important influence on the extent of behavior change, as predicted by the deterrence model.

However, arrest certainty is by no means the only influential variable.

TABLE 6.4. Summary of reduced models for the number of modifications to travel and drinking practices[a]

Predictor	D.F.	Bivariate response		Modifications to travel		Modifications to drinking	
		P	η^2 (%)	P	R^2 (%)	P	R^2 (%)
			Model 1				
Area	9	.001	7.9	.001	4.6	.033	3.3
Television	1	.001	2.8	.001	1.8	.585	.1
Change in pressure	2	.000	5.1	.000	3.7	.014	1.5
Arrest certainty	1	.001	2.7	.001	1.7	.020	1.0
Peer pressure	5	.006	4.9	.028	2.0	.014	2.6
Drinking	4	.000	9.2	.000	6.3	.042	1.8
Full model	22	.000	29.8	.000	23.3	.000	13.0
			Model 2				
Area	9	.000	8.4	.001	5.0	.018	3.8
Television	1	.000	2.1	.003	1.5	.756	.0
Change in pressure	2	.000	4.4	.000	3.2	.025	1.4
Arrest certainty	1	.004	2.2	.005	1.3	.018	1.0
Age	6	.007	5.4	.031	2.3	.017	2.9
Sex	1	.012	1.8	.012	1.1	.030	.9
Drink-drive	3	.003	3.9	.000	3.3	.577	.4
Full model	23	.000	24.9	.000	19.5	.000	10.8

[a] The statistics for all terms represent the effects adjusted for all other terms.

Those aware of TV publicity reported on average .31 more changes to their travel behavior than those who had not seen the TV ads, an influence at least comparable with that of arrest certainty. But why did television have this effect? The most plausible explanation, given the extremely heavy emphasis in the advertisements on arrest and imprisonment, was fear. In theory therefore, the effect of television should have been via the sanctions pathway in Figure 2.2, suggesting that the measure of arrest certainty is less than completely satisfactory. In any case the fact that TV publicity was significant lends further weight to the deterrence argument.

Another important feature of both models is the role played by perceived changes in peer pressure. Those who were finding it easier since RBT to resist pressure to drink were more likely than others to be modifying both their travel and drinking behaviors (see Fig. 6.3 and 6.4). This is an example of how RBT affected *nonlegal* sanctions operating to encourage drinking and driving. As indicated in Figures 6.3 and 6.4, the effect was of the same order of magnitude as that of TV but somewhat less than that for arrest certainty.

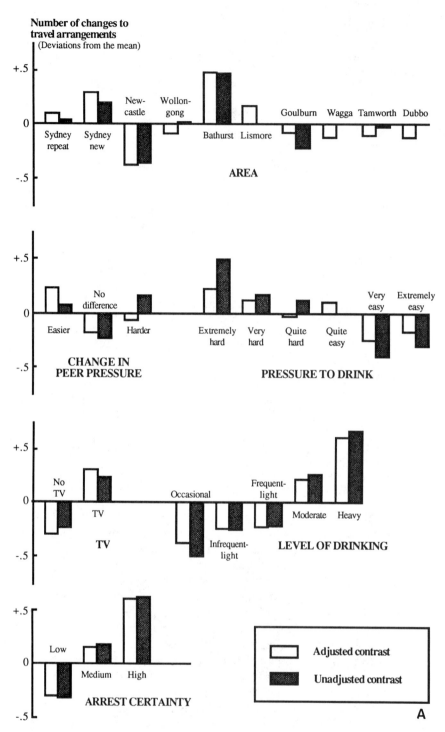

FIGURE 6.3. Reduced models of predictors for the number of changes to travel arrangements: adjusted and unadjusted effects. (a) Model 1 predictors; (b) Model 2 predictors not in Model 1.

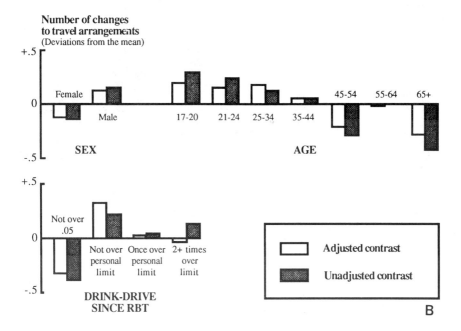

The most noticeable feature of area of residence was the large number of changes in travel methods (but not in drinking practices) in Bathurst, and the virtual absence of change in Newcastle. As discussed previously, these effects are probably attributable to features of police enforcement not captured by the exposure measures. Since these patterns conform very closely to the variations in arrest certainty depicted in Figure 6.2, the area effect further supports claims that RBT has had a deterrent impact.

The effects of the remaining variables in Table 6.4 and Figures 6.3 and 6.4 are much as described previously: adjustment for other factors in most cases makes little difference. The most important point is that RBT appears to have had its greatest impact among the most conspicuous target group, namely young men who drink lots of beer. Even the heaviest drinkers responded, although they tinkered with their driving more than their drinking.

Generally speaking, the contrast scores for drinking parallel those for transportation, but are smaller in magnitude. Although overall slightly more people were modifying their drinking than their driving, changes in travel behaviors seemed a more sensitive index of the effects of RBT inasmuch as these models had greater explanatory power. In this respect it should be recalled that the most popular response to RBT was to "carefully limit your drinking when driving," which quite possibly was a convenient answer to a question which may have put some people under pressure to report that they were doing something.

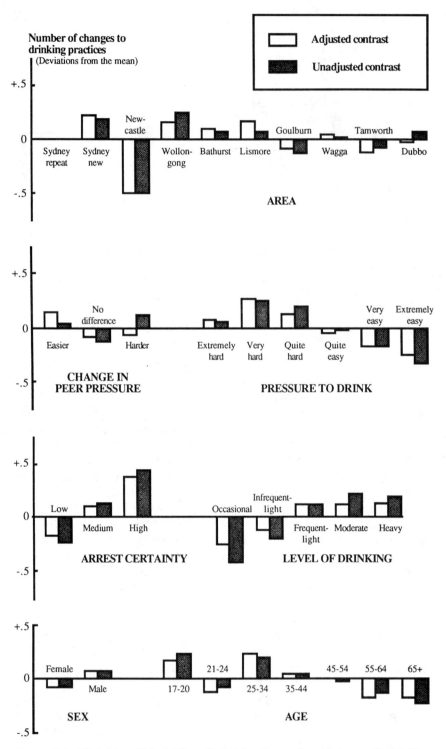

FIGURE 6.4. Model 1 and Model 2 predictors for the number of changes in drinking habits: adjusted and unadjusted effects.

Interaction Effects

In Chapter 5, a number of hypotheses concerning interaction effects were put forward. For the analysis of behavior change, perhaps the most interesting interactions are those involving arrest certainty. Other interactions investigated included exposure to TV publicity by the three measures of exposure to police enforcement, and some interactions among demographic variables, especially involving level of drinking. However, from a statistical point of view the main problem with these hypotheses is that they generate too many interactions to be handled conveniently in a single model. In the analysis, 17 interaction terms were considered, with a total of 90 degrees of freedom. Therefore a thoroughly ad hoc procedure was adopted: interactions were tested one at a time in a model with travel and drinking modifications as dependent variables, with significant interactions being tested further in the two reduced models described in the previous section.

The interactions of arrest certainty with perceptions and evaluations of penalties are of fundamental theoretical importance. In the present study, however, there was no evidence at all for such interactions, at least using the number of attempts to avoid drinking and driving as dependent variables. Nor was there any evidence for interactions between arrest certainty and the two measures of informal sanctions (pressure to drink and change in pressure), although one approached significance ($p = .085$ for arrest by pressure). The interactions of arrest certainty with age, sex, and socioeconomic status have been investigated in the literature and are of obvious interest in the present study, but once again the p values did not approach significance. Given the finding that heavy drinkers were overrepresented among those taking steps to avoid drinking and driving, the interaction of arrest certainty with level of drinking, had it been significant, also would have been of considerable interest.

In fact, the only significant interaction involving arrest certainty was with a conviction for drink-driving. Apart from this, the only other significant interaction was between exposure to television and being personally tested (multivariate $p = .018$, with .010 for travel and .052 for drinking). This interaction was in the expected direction, with the effect of being tested heightened by TV publicity. However, when added to the reduced models this interaction became rather marginal. The evidence is therefore a little unclear with respect to the combined effects of TV publicity and direct exposure to RBT.

THE INTERACTION OF ARREST CERTAINTY AND DRINK-DRIVE CONVICTIONS

Among all the interactions involving arrest certainty, the most promising was that with the possession of a conviction for drinking and driving. The multivariate p value was .023, which would not have been significant if the tests had been protected against Type I errors, but the p value for travel modifications was .009, which is sufficiently low to warrant further investigation. Adjusted for all terms in the first reduced model, the significance dropped to .048 (multivariate), with .032 for travel and .69 for drinking. Although not quite significant when added to the second reduced model, the significant result in the first model justifies interpretation, particularly since the tests are probably conservative. The unadjusted interaction pattern is illustrated in Figure 6.5 (the adjusted pattern is very similar and is therefore not shown).

The figure shows the regression line of the relationship between travel behavior and arrest score for those with a conviction and those without a conviction. Both the number of changes to travel and the arrest score are represented as deviations above or below the mean. Only 39 respondents (7.4%) had a conviction, and none had very high and low perceptions of arrest certainty, so the equation for this group is represented by a dashed line outside the observed range of arrest scores.

The correlation between arrest score and the number of modifications to travel arrangements was .42 for those with a conviction, and only .12 for those without a conviction. Clearly the effect of arrest perceptions on travel behavior was much less marked for those without a conviction, although the relationship was still highly significant among those without a conviction ($p = .008$). For the nonconvicted group, over the whole range of arrest scores the difference in number of changes to travel was .75. By contrast, over a much shorter range the variation in travel modifications for those with a conviction was 1.8. The difference between the groups was most marked for the higher arrest scores, suggesting that the experience of a previous conviction has its greatest effect on behavior when the chances of arrest are seen as high. However there was no evidence that having a conviction of itself affected perceptions of the chances of arrest.

The interaction pattern depicted in Figure 6.5 is of particular interest in view of a finding by McLean and co-workers (1984) that the effects of RBT in South Australia were much more marked among those previously charged with drink-driving. The South Australian analysis was based on large-scale roadside surveys, and so the behavior measures (percentages of motorists over the legal limit) were of high reliability. However, McLean and co-workers (1984) were not able to relate changes in drink-driving before and after RBT to perceptions of arrest likelihood, so the interaction pattern in Figure 6.5 complements rather than duplicates the South Australian analysis. In fact Figure 6.5 suggests an explanation for the roadside survey results.

THE EVIDENCE FOR ABSOLUTE SPECIFIC DETERRENCE

The interaction between arrest certainty and a conviction for drink-driving suggests that punishment may have an absolute specific deterrent effect. However, in order to establish this beyond reasonable doubt, it is neces-

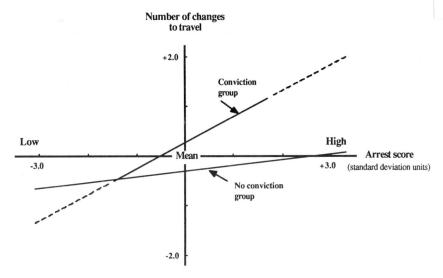

FIGURE 6.5. Number of modifications to travel arrangements: interaction between arrest certainty and a conviction for drinking and driving (unadjusted for other factors).

sary to compare behavior change among offenders who have been punished with behavior change among offenders who have never been punished. The analysis reported in the previous section does not directly address this question, since the nonconvicted group consisted of those who had never driven after drinking too much, as well as those who had but had never been caught.

Slightly more than half of all drinking license holders (52.0%) reported driving when they had had too much to drink (this included five respondents with a conviction who claimed that although they may have been over the limit, they were not impaired). Restricting analysis to this subsample of 269 respondents, the interaction of the arrest and conviction variables for the number of travel modifications was not quite significant (t (265) = 1.73; p = .086), although the pattern was very similar to that of Figure 6.5. When adjusted for all other variables except exposure to RBT publicity and enforcement the significance reduced to .17, and it dropped further to .27 if exposure variables were included. There was no evidence of any interaction for drinking modifications.

These results suggest that the experience of punishment is not sufficient to cause the convicted group to react to RBT in a way which is clearly distinguishable from the responses of never convicted drink-drivers. However, in order to conduct a completely adequate test of the absolute specific deterrence hypothesis a larger number of convicted offenders is required, preferably all convicted at the same time in the past and matched on at least recency and frequency of drink-driving with a control group of nonconvicted offenders. The fact that the interaction is close to significant, even when adjusted for a range of other factors, suggests that punishment may have a measurable, although by no means massive impact on responses of drink-drivers to legal innovations like RBT. This hypothesis is supported by the work of McLean and co-workers (1984).

Reasons for Not Drinking and Driving: Fear Versus Conscience

So far in the analysis of the data collected in the April survey, the emphasis has been on establishing the plausibility of the causal chain implicit in the theoretical model described in Chapter 2. Thus it has been demonstrated that the intensity of police random testing in an area was a major determinant of rates of exposure of the target population, and that features of such exposure predicted arrest certainty. Arrest certainty in turn predicted the extent of behavior change. Some subsidiary analyses have focused on interaction effects, with a view to exploring the nature and extent of deterrent effects in selected subgroups of the population (such as those with a conviction for drink-driving). With the exception of the measures of behavior change, which are based on assessments by respondents of alterations in practices *caused* by RBT, the analysis has been conducted within the traditional positivist framework discussed in Chapter 2. However, in the discussion of deterrence in that chapter, it was emphasized that the admission of evidence on which the respondent is the most privileged observer—namely, reasons for not drinking and driving—is essential for the determination of a verdict on whether or not deterrence has been occurring.

The importance of asking about people's reasons for drinking and driving or for not drinking and driving was recognized from the beginning of the present project. In the February survey, interviewees were asked (FQ10): "Since random breath testing was brought in just before Christmas, have you driven when you felt you had had *too much* to drink?" (Yes, no, unsure.) "Why do you say that? Any other reasons?" The analysis of responses to these questions, together with an analysis of responses to a more structured question asked in the April survey, is presented in this section. The primary objective is to throw more light on the deterrence process through a direct examination of the stated reasons for respondents' behaviors.

Of the 254 drinking license holders in the February survey, nearly 1 in 10 (9.8%) admitted to driving with too much to drink since the advent of RBT. Responses to the follow-up question fell into three main categories: "I like to go to the pub" (28.0%), "I've only done it once" (32.0%), and

"The limit's too low" (12.0%). Detailed comments indicated that convenience was frequently a major factor in the decision to drink and drive, an outcome predictable from theory.

The reasons given for their behavior by the 227 respondents who claimed not to have driven while impaired fell into four main categories. The most frequent single answer was that the respondent simply did not drink and drive (27.3%). This of course is strictly an answer to the question, but immediately raises another: Why do these respondents make a practice of not drinking and driving? A second category of response was similar in nature: 27.7% claimed to avoid the problem by not getting into situations where driving while impaired would be a possibility. Some of these (20.7% overall but 28.4% of women) said they always drank very moderately so would never (by implication) be impaired, a few (4.4%, but 9.9% of women) said they did not drive much, and a small number (2.6%) said they only drank at home. These responses seem to raise the same sort of questions about lifestyle as the previous category. A third type of reason proferred by 5.3% of the sample was that drinking and driving is unsafe (e.g., "I have two kids and don't want to see them hurt.").

Actually, it is surprising that such a small minority mentioned the chances of injury, since this is presumably why drink-driving laws exist, but it is very likely that if respondents in the first two categories had been questioned further, fear of accidents would have been mentioned more frequently. The respondents who gave the three types of answers mentioned before seem to be saying that drinking and driving is not part of their lifestyle, either because they are not much exposed to the opportunity to do it or because they consider it is wrong since it might cause crashes. Although this last point is an inference, since few respondents actually *said* that drinking and driving is wrong or causes accidents, it does seem to be at the basis of many responses.

These answers are in marked contrast to those in the fourth category, which related to *fear of apprehension and penalties*. Half of those who had not driven while impaired (50.2%, to be precise) gave as one of the reasons for their behavior fear of apprehension and/or fear of punishment. One in six (16.7%) mentioned fear of being caught (e.g., "I don't want to get arrested,"), a similar proportion (16.3%) mentioned loss of license (e.g., "I need my license for my job,"), while some (8.4%) mentioned higher fines (e.g., "I can't afford a $1,000 fine,"), and some (8.8%) simply referred to RBT (e.g., "The publicity associated with RBT makes one more aware."). Some of the comments made by people indicated the mechanisms of deterrence: some mentioned that they had been caught for drink-driving before RBT (a significant comment in view of the interaction depicted in Figure 6.5), some mentioned RBT publicity and some mentioned the operations of the police. Compared with other sociodemographic variables, the respondent's gender was by far the strongest predictor of whether fear was offered as an explanation: nearly two-thirds of the men

(65.1%) referred to fear of arrest or penalties, but fewer than a quarter (23.4%) of the women. There was also a tendency for younger drivers, higher status drivers, and heavy drinkers to be more concerned about apprehension and punishment. These patterns are interesting, since they were not clearly revealed in the analysis of perceptions of arrest certainty, but are consistent with the behavioral responses to RBT. This suggests that the open response data may have captured aspects of the subjective appraisal of RBT which escaped the more conventional measure of arrest certainty.

Building on these answers, questions were devised for the April survey which attempted to pin respondents down to a specific reason for not drinking and driving since RBT. Since in the February interview some respondents gave more than one answer, the April questions (AQ14[c] and 14[d]) asked nondrinking drivers to rank order their reasons: "From this card . . . could you choose the statement that *best describes* your reasons for not drinking and driving? What would be the *second* most important reason for your not drinking and driving?" Response categories were: drinking and driving is wrong, drinking and driving leads to accidents, and drinking drivers stand a good chance of being caught and punished. These categories were deliberately selected to force a choice between morality and/or safety on the one hand, and fear of punishment on the other. Although the earlier open-ended question had revealed that for some respondents (particularly women) drinking while impaired was not very likely because they drank or drove very little, it was felt nevertheless that since all license holders who drink are potential drink-drivers the choice should be put in this form.

In the present analysis, only the main reason for not driving while impaired is considered in detail. Of the 444 drinking license holders who claimed not to have driven while impaired since RBT, only 15 were unsure of their reasons or declined to select one of the choices offered. However, in contrast to the open-ended question fewer than a quarter (24.5%) nominated fear of punishment as their primary motive, although 24% rated it as the second most important factor. Most nominated the risk of accidents (45.5%) or morality (26.6%) as their main reason for avoiding drinking and driving. This suggests that the form of the question may have had some effect on the answers, with fear of punishment being seen as the less socially desirable response. If this is correct, then the proportion admitting to fear as their primary motive is a conservative estimate.

In considering the correlates of people's main motive for avoiding drinking and driving, we have a choice between two approaches: we could follow Meier (1979) and exclude those who did in fact drive while impaired, or we could include these malefactors in the analysis. Given that "the deterred" can be regarded as those who have refrained from drinking and driving because they said they feared punishment (Meier, 1979), the question is whether the *percentage* who have been deterred should be calculated from the total of those who said they did not drink and drive or from the total of all potential offenders. In my judgment the second approach seems most logical; that is, all potential offenders should be included, and the proportion of these who have been deterred, using the term in the sense described above, should be regarded as the quantity of interest. However, excluding self-confessed drink-drivers has the advantage that the odds that the remaining respondents will nominate punishment over safety/morality as their primary motivation can be more easily analyzed. The results of this conditional analysis are summarized later in this section.

If it is possible to identify (in the manner described) those who have been deterred, it is logical to ask whether being deterred is affected by exposure to RBT, either through publicity or through personal experience. We already know that some respondents mentioned these factors in their answers, but can their importance be documented through correlational analysis? In addition, it is of interest to ascertain whether having a conviction for drink-driving makes one more responsive than other motorists to the threat of punishment, a proposition supported by the analysis summarized in Figure 6.5 and also supported by comments made by some respondents. Finally, if the proposed method of identifying deterred motorists is valid, they should have higher arrest scores and may perceive sanctions as being more severe. (Alternatively, it is possible to regard this method of identifying deterred motorists as a way of validating the arrest measure.)

Investigation of the correlations with exposure to RBT and to RBT publicity revealed limited evidence for the hypothesized influence of these variables on the odds that a motorist would nominate fear as the main reason for not drinking and driving. The experience of being tested personally appeared to have no effect (G^2 (1) = .04), but the recency and frequency of driving past an RBT operation did seem to have some bearing: only 17.5% of those who had not driven past an RBT operation gave fear as their main reason, while twice as many (35.7%) of those who had driven past four or more times, the last time a few days ago, gave this response. However, the relationship with the recency and frequency of driving past failed to reach statistical significance (G^2 (9) = 13.2, p = .15). The only exposure variable which clearly predicted the "fear of punishment" response was newspaper publicity, with 27.5% of those exposed to newspaper publicity mentioning fear compared with 17.7% of those not so exposed (G^2 (1) = 6.6, p = .010). This variable survived adjustment for other variables in a logistic model (G^2 (1) = 5.6, p = .018), suggesting that newspaper publicity had a real impact and that the observed correlation did not simply reflect respondent characteristics.

As suggested by respondents' comments, those with a conviction for drinking and driving were much more likely to nominate fear as their primary motivation than those without a conviction (36.8% versus 19.8%, Yule's Q = .40, G^2 (1) = 5.39, p = .02). However, unlike exposure to newspaper publicity, having a conviction did not survive adjustment for other variables, weakening the evidence for the deterrent impact of an earlier contact with the law.

As predicted, those nominating fear of punishment had higher arrest scores than those nominating safety or morality (means of 2.09 and 1.75 respectively), but their scores were not much higher than those of the people who *did* drink and drive (mean of 1.92). The overall relationship was not significant (F (2,154) = 1.42, p = .25). However, there *was* a significant relationship in the expected direction between giving fear as a reason for not drinking and driving and one's rating of the likelihood of being randomly tested in the next month (X^2 (5) = 13.42, $p < .025$). Around a third of those who rated their chances of being tested as extremely or very high nominated fear as their main motive, about twice the proportion as in the lower probability categories. Similar, although weaker, relationships were observed for most of the other indices of arrest certainty, but not for perceptions of the severity of sanctions. Fear of punishment seems to be based largely on fear of apprehension.

THE CONDITIONAL ANALYSIS

As noted earlier, by excluding those who admitted to driving while impaired since RBT, it is possible to obtain a clearer idea of what factors were correlated with a concern for safety or morality as opposed to being motivated by fear. The justification for this analysis is that by examining the motivations of those who were law-abiding, we can come to a better understanding of how RBT may have influenced perceptions and behaviors (Meier, 1979). It is convenient for purposes of this analysis to group the 15 people who gave "other" or "unsure" responses with the 320 who nominated safety or moral factors.

Of the 444 law abiding motorists, three-quarters (75.5%) mentioned safety/morality. Cross-tabulations confirmed the importance of newspapers in inducing fear as a motivation, and also more clearly revealed the role of observation of RBT operations. More than half of those who had driven past an RBT operation four or more times were motivated by fear of being caught and punished, compared with only 19% of those who had not driven past any RBT operations or who had done so only once or twice some time ago (X^2 (9) = 24.6, $p < .005$). Again, having convictions for drinking and driving was significant (X^2 (1) = 9.4, $p < .001$). However, by far the most important factor was respondent gender, with men being nearly three times as likely as women to nominate fear (35.2% versus 12.2%, X^2 (1) = 31.4, $p < .001$, ϕ = .26). Age was *not* significant, suggesting that young motorists are just as likely as older ones to operate on the basis of internalized norms or beliefs about road safety.

Safety/morality was least likely to be mentioned by moderate and heavy drinkers ($p < .001$) and by those subject to the greatest peer pressure to drink ($p < .001$). Interestingly, of the 35 respondents who claimed that since RBT it was harder to resist pressures to drink, 57.1%—more than twice the average—offered fear of getting caught as their main reason for not driving while impaired ($p < .001$). This reinforces the impression gained from the analysis of the arrest certainty scores (Fig. 6.2) that for these people RBT simultaneously affected informal and formal sanctions, but in a mutually contradictory fashion. The implications for behavior of the implied psychological conflict are explored further in the analysis of the longitudinal data.

Finally, it is worth noting that the minority motivated by fear reported more attempts to avoid drinking and driving, both through modifications of travel behaviors (means of .74 versus .44; $p < .005$) and through modifications of drinking (means of .93 versus .50; $p < .001$). These correlations provide a check on the validity of the behavioral measures, and suggest that fear of arrest was one factor influencing behavior change.

SUMMARY

The analysis of the data on the stated reasons for not drinking and driving yielded results broadly consistent with predictions of the deterrence model. In particular, there appeared to be an association between aspects of exposure to RBT and the odds of nominating fear of arrest as a reason for one's behavior, and an association between being fearful and the extent of reported behavior change. Moreover, those with a conviction were more likely to nominate fear as a reason for not drinking and driving. In these respects the results of the reason analysis paralleled the formal quantitative analysis incorporating the arrest score, and might be regarded as providing some support for the validity of the arrest measure.

The analysis of reasons highlighted the importance of concerns about road safety and the immorality of drinking and driving as motivations for avoiding the offense. Although one might argue that such an exploration of motives simply invites the socially desirable response (since high-minded statements about safety present the respondent in a better light than a self-interested desire to avoid arrest), it is significant that heavy drinkers were much less likely than others to project an image of moral rectitude. In any case, it is clear that measures of moral beliefs must be incorporated in future quantitative research (Norström, 1981).

A further valuable feature of the results of the reason analysis was the pronounced tendency for men to cite RBT and the fear of arrest rather than safety/moralty as a motivation. This correlation did not emerge so clearly in the earlier analysis of the arrest measure, but is consistent with behavior change reported in the interviews. The apparent influence of newspaper publicity is another example of a possible effect of RBT not revealed in the earlier analysis.

In conclusion, the analysis of reasons provided some valuable insights into the deterrence process, and extended the understanding of the impact of RBT beyond that provided by the analysis based on the measure of arrest certainty. It seems clear that when a change in the social environment is as well-known and is as potentially influential as RBT, people are capable of providing useful information on its role as a factor actually influencing their behaviors. Such information is not simply descriptive or illustrative, but is an integral part of the total body of evidence against which the deterrence model should be tested.

The Longitudinal Study: February and April Compared

The emphasis of the analyses reported so far in this chapter has been on the interpretation of correlations arising from the second (April) survey. The analysis has, on the whole, supported the theoretical model described in Chapter 2, and operationalized in Figure 2.2. In particular, support has been found for the hypothesized causal chain linking police activity with behavior change, via the exposure of the target population to police enforcement leading to higher perceptions of the probability of arrest for drinking and driving. However, using a longitudinal design it is possible to address a number of questions which are not easily answered from the analysis of responses from a single survey.

In summary, the chief virtue of repeated interviews is that *changes* in perceptions and behaviors can be studied. It is possible to assess whether Ross' (1982) hypothesis of a decline in subjective arrest probabilities is supported, changes in reported behavior can be investigated, and correlations between changes in arrest certainty and changes in behavior can be computed. The longitudinal design has the further advantage that perceptions of arrest chances at time one can be correlated with reported drink-driving between time one and time two, thus avoiding the debates about causal order which have so plagued the perceptual research into deterrence.

One will recall that 185 of the 255 drinking license holders interviewed in Sydney in the February survey were reinterviewed 6 weeks later. Of these, 10 were not included in most analyses since they claimed at the second interview (contrary to their first report) to drink less often than once a year. Those reinterviewed appeared to be a random subsample of the original 255, with the possibility that young heavy drinking men were slightly underrepresented.

The 6-week time period was deliberately selected so that the effects of the publicity campaign over Easter 1983 could be included in the study. It was expected that by February, 10 weeks after the introduction of RBT, the initial impact would be wearing off, and that the Easter publicity would give the whole campaign a boost. Moreover, in view of the international literature on legal innovations like RBT, it was expected that the overall impact would be rather short-lived. When these considerations were added to the well-known practical difficulties entailed in locating the same people over an extended time period, a 6-week interval between surveys seemed most appropriate. The selection of such a relatively short period did, however, create some problems for the analysis. The major problem was that in 6 weeks relatively few people were exposed to RBT, and only a small minority (6.9%) admitted to driving while impaired in that period. Thus there is a rather slender data base for some of the analyses which flow from the research questions, particularly the analysis of the effects of perceptions of sanctions on the extent of drink-driving.

In analyzing the repeated interviews, the same strategy is followed as for the April data. After an analysis of the descriptive statistics and correlations, changes in perceptions of the chance of being randomly tested are investigated. This leads to an analysis of behavior change in the 6 weeks, including the testing of possible interaction effects. The analysis concludes with an investigation of the predictors of driving while intoxicated.

Summary Statistics and Correlations

A number of questions were repeated in the second survey. Other variables may be regarded as measuring constant quantities (e.g., age and sex), so that the fact that they were derived from questions asked only once is no problem. The variables available for the analysis of the repeat interviews fall into six sets: the standard sociodemographic variables previously employed; exposure to RBT, both before the February interview and between the two interviews; drink-drive behavior, both before the February interview (but since RBT) and between the interviews; perceptions of the severity of penalties; perceptions of the chances of being randomly tested at both interviews; and (at both interviews) modifications of drinking and travel behaviors occasioned by RBT. Of all these variables only the exposure, drink-drive, and one of the penalty variables were newly constructed. The distributions of these variables are in Table 6.5.

The question on impaired driving (AQ14[a]) dealt with driving when the respondent felt he or she had had *too much* to drink, not with whether they had driven over the .05 limit. The question on penalties (FQ13) dealt with changes believed to have occurred at the same time as RBT. Of the 132 respondents (out of the total 185 reinterviewed) who said changes had taken place, 118 (89.4%) believed (correctly) that the penalties had increased. In the analysis, the two questions about penalties which were asked only in the April survey were also included, on the grounds that perceptions of the severity of penalties should not vary much due to RBT publicity or enforcement. Finally, it should be noted that the exposure variables all deal with police enforcement rather than with publicity, and that each exposure item is dichotomous (yes/no). The variables were constructed in this way because that is how they appeared on the February interview schedule. Moreover in response to the one question (FQ2[d])

TABLE 6.5. Distributions of measures of exposure to RBT, drink-drive behavior, and perception of the severity of penalties (February interview) for the 175 respondents interviewed twice

	Exposure to RBT
Variable	% of 175
Tested between RBT and February interview	12.0
Driven past between RBT and February interview	52.0
Know someone tested between RBT and February interview	59.4
Tested between February and April interviews	5.7
Driven past between February and April interviews	16.0
Know someone tested between February and April	12.0
Drink-driving	
Drive impaired between RBT and February interview	11.4
Drive impaired between February and April interviews	6.9
Perceptions of penalties at the February interview	
Penalties increased with RBT	64.0
No change in penalties with RBT	14.3
Unsure/responses off the point	21.7

asked in February about publicity, 97.2% of drinking license holders (in Sydney) said they were aware of RBT publicity, so this question was not included in the analysis.

Those admitting to impaired driving prior to the February interview tended to be young ($r = .27$), male ($r. = .18$), heavy drinkers ($r = .23$), and subject to peer pressure to drink ($r = .17$). This pattern did not appear so marked for those driving while impaired *between* the interviews, since the highest correlation was .11. (Correlations less than .15 are not significant at .05; those higher than .20 are significant at less than .01.) Drink-drivers were more likely than nondrink-drivers to have friends who had been randomly tested prior to the February interview ($r = .15$ for drink-driving between RBT and February, and .22 for drink-driving between interviews). On the face of it this is contrary to the predictions of the deterrence model, and somewhat puzzling in view of the association in the April data between perceptions of arrest chances and the number of friends tested. Also contrary to what might be predicted, but consistent with previous analyses, the drink-drivers were making more attempts than others to avoid further drink-driving through modifications of their travel arrangements ($r = .18$ for behavior changes in February correlated with drink-driving prior to February, and .22 for behavior changes in April correlated with drink-driving between interviews).

A new finding of great interest is that respondents who believed in

February that penalties had increased were less likely subsequently to drive while impaired ($r = -.17$). The two measures of penalty severity from the April interview (the Grasmick question on how big a problem punishment would be and the question on the perceived chances of being let off without penalty) did not predict drink-drive behavior in the same fashion ($r < .10$ in both cases). In fact the correlations of these variables with the February item were .06 and .00, suggesting that for some reason they may not be tapping the same dimension as the February question. Surprisingly, there was no correlation between the subjective risk of being tested in February and subsequent drink-drive behavior ($r = -.01$).

Perhaps predictably, those respondents who felt that RBT had made it harder for them to resist pressure to drink were more likely between interviews to reduce the number of modifications of their driving arrangements designed to avoid drinking and driving ($r = .16$). Curiously, an increase in the number of modifications to travel arrangements between interviews corresponded to a *decline* in subjective probabilities of being tested ($r = -.15$), a phenomenon which requires further exploration. Equally strange, a negative correlation with perceived penalty severity in February ($r = -.19$) indicates that those who believed in February that penalties had increased *reduced* their number of travel modifications between February and April. More reassuringly, those tested or driving past an RBT operation between the two interviews increased their attempts to avoid drinking and driving through modifications of their travel arrangements ($r = .15$ for tested and .23 for driven past).

Changes in drinking habits were positively correlated with changes in modifications of travel ($r = .26$), but were otherwise predicted only by age (older respondents were more likely to step up modifications of their drinking habits: $r = .14$). The change in the perceived chances of being tested was also correlated with only one variable, whether the respondent had been tested between interviews ($r = -.15$). Again, however, the correlation was opposite in direction than what would have been predicted (those tested were more likely to see the chances of being tested as *lower* in April than in February).

In summary, the most interesting correlation indicates that those aware of penalty increases in February were less likely to drive while impaired in the period February to April. The most puzzling correlations are those involving changes in the perceived chances of being tested and between changes in travel behaviors and perceptions of penalties in February, all of which go in what seems to be the wrong direction.

Changes in Perceptions of the Chance of Being Randomly Tested Between February and April

The major hypothesis that we wish to test is that subjective arrest probabilities declined between February and April. A significant decline would be a strong result, since it would indicate a diminution in the deterrent effectiveness of RBT *despite* the Easter campaign. Strictly speaking, it is not possible to test this hypothesis from the longitudinal data, since only the question on the chances of being randomly tested was repeated. However, perceptions of random testing must constitute a major part of the calculation of the probability of arrest, so the restriction is not very serious. Six people were unsure of their chances either in February or in April, so the analysis was based on 169 cases. A paired t test applied to the difference scores yielded a value of t (168) = 1.73, with a two-tailed p value of .085, which is not quite significant. However, an examination of the difference scores revealed that of the 95 people who changed their ratings, 59 believed their chances had declined and only 36 that they had increased. Applying the sign test, we obtain a p value of .015. There is thus strong evidence for a decline in the perceived chances of being tested over the 6 weeks separating the two surveys. This decline occurred despite the Easter publicity campaign, but might have been greater in magnitude, of course, if the campaign had not taken place.

There was no evidence at all using ANOVA and regression that any subgroup of the population, apart from those tested between February and April, differed from any other in the rate of decline in subjective probability of being tested. As revealed by the simple correlations, for those tested in the interval between surveys the decline in the subjective probability was *greater* than for other groups ($r = -.15$, $p = .044$ from the ANOVA). However, a causal relationship between these two variables is unlikely, since controls for peer pressure to drink and the quantity and frequency of drinking are sufficient to render the test nonsignificant ($p = .075$).

In summary, there is evidence for a decline in the estimated probabilities of being randomly tested in the 6 weeks between interviews. However, there is no evidence that this decline was more pronounced among particular subgroups of the population of drinking license holders in Sydney.

Changes Between February and April in the Number of Modifications to Travel and Drinking Behaviors Due to RBT

Given the evidence for a decline in the perceived chances of being tested between February and April, it might be expected that the number of people taking steps to avoid drinking and driving, or the number of avoidance tactics employed by a given person, would also have declined. It is interesting to note therefore that without taking into account the influence of any predictors, there was no evidence of any statistically significant changes in behavior, using both the sign test and the t test. Thus, overall, the pattern of behavioral responses to RBT appeared to be stable between February and April, with about 55% of respondents in both surveys taking some steps to avoid drink-driving. However, analysis of predictors revealed a more complex pattern. Although on average there were no changes in behavior, in specific subgroups there were changes, some positive and some negative.

TRAVEL BEHAVIORS

A number of factors influenced travel behavior. The inspection of correlations revealed that increases in travel modifications were positively correlated with being tested or driving past an RBT station between interviews and with being a light drinker not subject to peer pressure. In addition, increases in modifications to travel were negatively correlated with increases in the perceived chance of being tested and with perceptions of more severe penalties in February. These same factors emerged in ANOVA, the results of which are therefore not reproduced. Following the procedures used in previous analyses, a model with all predictors was fitted and reduced to an adequate subset.

There were 22 predictors in all: the three measures of exposure to RBT between interviews and the same three measures for the period up until the February interview; two measures of change in perceptions of the chances of being tested (one's chances personally of being tested in the next month plus the question about the drink-driver who was not obviously drunk); the three measures of penalty severity discussed before; drink-drive behavior between RBT and February and between February and April; and the nine sociodemographic variables. R^2 for the model was high, at 45.7% ($p = .018$), with nearly the same set of variables which were significant in the zero order correlations emerging as significant at or near the .05 level, adjusting for all other factors. Missing from the set was the quantity and frequency of drinking ($p = .56$). Additions to the set were having a drink-drive conviction ($p = .007$) and perceptions of the chance of being let off in court without penalty ($p = .027$). Those with a conviction were more likely than those without to increase the number of modifications of their mode of travel, but those perceiving no chance at all of being let off without penalty (once caught) *reduced* their attempts to avoid drink-driving. This last effect is consistent with the effects of perceptions of a penalty increase in the February interview.

Many subsets were fitted with a view to arrive at one which was minimal adequate using a level of significance of .025. One adequate subset had an R^2 of 23.6% and consisted of six variables: driving past an RBT station between interviews (contribution to $R^2 = 7.9\%$; $p < .001$); being tested between interviews ($R^2 = 2.0\%$; $p = .041$); drink-driving between RBT and February ($R^2 = 2.9\%$; $p = .007$); peer pressure to drink ($R^2 = 7.2\%$; $p = .015$); change in pressure since RBT ($R^2 = 2.9\%$; $p = .054$); and convictions for drink-driving ($R^2 = 3.3\%$; $p = .010$). To make this set minimal adequate, being tested between interviews ($p = .041$) and change in pressure to drink ($p = .054$) should be omitted. However, since the tests of significance are probably conservative, given the discrete nature of the de-

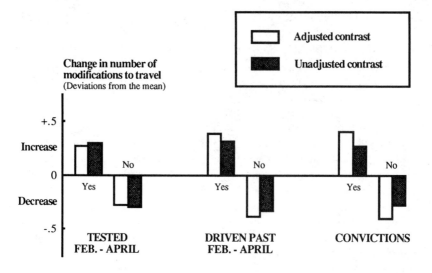

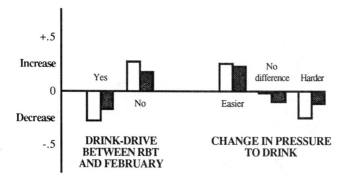

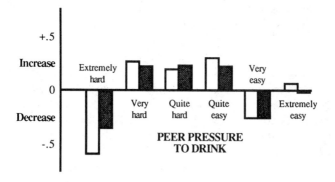

FIGURE 6.6. Reduced model of predictors for changes in the number of modifications to travel arrangements between the February and April Surveys: adjusted and unadjusted effects.

pendent variable, it was decided to retain these two variables in the model. The effects of all six variables are in Figure 6.6.

The remarkable thing about the effects depicted in Figure 6.6 is that they are so intuitively reasonable, and so consistent with the hypothesis of deterrence. Those tested between interviews and, even more strongly, those who had driven past an RBT operation were more likely than other respondents to increase their attempts to avoid drink-driving through modifications of methods of travel. Moreover, those with a conviction for drink-driving were markedly more likely than those without a conviction to increase these avoidance behaviors, a result consistent with previous analyses of travel behaviors. Consistent with the hypothesis of an experiential effect, those who had driven while impaired since RBT but before the February interview subsequently reduced their attempts to avoid drink-driving.

In an alternative reduced model, perceptions of a penalty increase in February ($R^2 = 3.7\%$; $p = .017$) replaced being tested between interviews as a predictor. As noted previously, the direction of the correlation with change in behavior was counterintuitive. The effects of all other predictors were as shown in Figure 6.6.

Interaction Effects Predicting Changes in Travel Behaviors Between Surveys

Although significant as a zero order correlation, after adjustment for the factors in the reduced model there was no evidence of a relationship between change in perceptions of the chance of being randomly tested and change in travel modifications. The failure to find a positive correlation between these quantities is an important outcome, since deterrence theory would predict such a relationship. However, according to deterrence theory a number of interactions involving arrest perceptions should be significant, so it is possible that the predicted effect can be found in certain subgroups.

In all, four interaction terms were tested: change in the perceived chance of being tested by perceptions in February of a penalty increase; change in test probability by peer pressure; change in test probability by drink-drive convictions; and drink-drive convictions by perceptions of a penalty increase. All these interactions can easily be justified on theoretical grounds. Only two interactions were close to significant at the .05 level: conviction by penalty increase ($p = .047$) and peer pressure by change in test probability ($p = .056$). Although these interactions are only marginally significant, their interpretation helps to clarify some of the puzzling correlations noted above.

Only nine respondents, or 5.3% of the sample of 169, had a conviction for drink-driving, so the conviction by penalty interaction should be interpreted carefully. Nevertheless, the six with a conviction who believed penalties had increased were much more likely than other groups to increase their attempts to avoid drink-driving. The mean increase in this group was .83, compared wth an overall average of .05. Once again, it seems that the convicted group responded more strongly to legal sanctions, but in the present case the operative dimension is penalty severity, not arrest certainty.

The peer pressure by change in test probability interaction indicated that the paradoxical correlation between change in subjective test probability and change in travel behaviors was primarily due to the responses of those who felt subject to the greatest peer pressure to drink. Among this group the counterintuitive negative correlation was very strong, but among respondents not subject to such heavy pressure there was no significant relationship between changes in subjective probability and changes in behavior. It is not clear why the relationship between these variables should be the opposite of what one would predict only among those subject to the greatest peer pressure, but an explanation in terms of the opposing forces of formal and informal sanctions seems called for. In any case, it is important to note that for no subgroup could a well-behaved positive correlation between the two sets of change scores be found.

Changes in Drinking Behaviors Between February and April

Changes in drinking behaviors were not strongly associated with any predictor. The full model with all predictors included was nonsignificant ($p = .983$). and no predictor was significant at less than .10. Thus it seems that modifications to drinking practices remained stable in all subgroups between interviews, and were not influenced by exposure to RBT activity.

Drink-Driving Between February and April

The final major question to be addressed in this chapter is the one which, in the literature, has consumed most energy. All the analyses of behavior reported so far in this study have focused on reported attempts to *avoid* drinking and driving. The question to be considered now is whether all the information we have about respondents from the February interview can be used to predict reports of actual drink-driving behavior in the following 6 weeks. Such a methodology avoids the problems involved in inferring causal relationships in a cross-sectional study, since only variables prior in time to the drink-driving behavior are included. Unfortunately, the exigencies of sampling precluded the kind of thorough analysis of drink-driving made possible in principle by the longitudinal design, since as previously noted, only 12 respondents (6.9%) could be identified unambiguously as having driven while impaired in the 6 weeks between interviews (Table

6.5). Given this small number, only limited analyses of the drinking-driving item are possible.

The item was treated as a binary (yes/no) response, and a series of logistic analyses carried out using the February variables one at a time as predictors. Only three were significant (one marginally): perceptions of penalty increases in February (G^2 (1) = 5.15; p = .023), perceptions of the chances of being let off without penalty (dichotomizing the variable as zero chance/other, G^2 (1) = 3.07; p = .080, but X^2 (1) = 3.98; p = .046), and whether the respondent knew someone before the February interview who had been randomly tested (G^2 (1) = 12.49; $p < .001$).

Respondents who believed in February that the severity of penalties had increased at the time RBT was introduced were 3.5 times less likely than the rest to report drinking and driving between February and April (3.4% of the 118 who believed penalties had increased drove while intoxicated, compared with 11.9% of the 67 who were not aware of increases). Similarly, only one of the 64 who believed they had a zero chance of being let off without penalty drove while impaired (1.6%), compared with 10 of the 108 who considered they had some chance (9.3%). All 12 who reported drinking and driving knew someone who had been randomly tested. When the two most significant variables (penalty increase and knowing someone who had been tested) were fitted together, the penalty variable became marginally significant (p = .059) but knowing someone who had been tested retained its power (p = .001). In fact, this variable retained its power when adjusted for a wide range of other variables, including age, sex, and level of drinking.

Perceptions of the likelihood of being tested did not show up at all, either as a main effect (X^2 (2) = .13) or (as deterrence theory might predict) as an interaction with perceptions of penalties (X^2 (2) = 2.70; p = .26). Moreover, there was no evidence of an interaction between drink-drive convictions and subjective probability of being tested, nor between drink-drive convictions and perceptions of a penalty increase. The failure to find significant interactions, particularly with drink-drive convictions, is probably mainly a function of the small number of cases of drink-driving available for analysis.

The Relationship Between Actions Taken to Avoid Drink-Driving and Actual Drink-Driving Behavior

In Figure 2.2 and in the formulations of the deterrence model in Chapter 2, a link is assumed between attempts to avoid drinking and driving and the actual rate at which a respondent commits the offense. That is, it is assumed, other things being equal, that the more someone modifies their drinking and travel behaviors the less likely they are to drive while impaired. The longitudinal component of the study affords an opportunity to test this assumption.

The prediction is that people making more changes to their travel and drinking behaviors in February will be less likely to drink and drive between February and April. However, the data do not support this prediction. The correlations were all in the wrong direction, although below the .05 level of significance: $-.13$ for travel modifications, $-.08$ for drinking modifications, and $-.13$ for all types of modifications to behavior. Tabular analysis did not alter the picture. Moreover, contrary to predictions of an experiential effect, the correlations between drink-driving between interviews and modifications to behavior in April were also in the wrong direction. This is consistent with what was observed in the analysis of the 517 April interviews.

What are we to make of these correlations? Three comments seem called for. First, with only 12 cases of drink-driving it is difficult to draw firm inferences. Second, it is clear from previous analyses that although many of those most at risk of drink-driving were making strenuous attempts to avoid it in future, they were still committing the offense at a higher rate than low risk groups. This suggests that the correlations between behavior modifications and drink-driving should be controlled for the effects of variables like age, sex, and level of drinking. Third, and most fundamentally, there is a need to control the correlations for baseline levels of modifications to behavior. To do this, however, three waves of interviews are required. With three interviews (say A, B, and C) it would be possible to correlate *changes* in the number of attempts to avoid drink-driving between A and B with drink-driving in the period B to C. Using this type of methodology it has already been established (from the reduced model for changes to travel modifications) that there is an experiential effect, since those who drove while impaired since RBT (A) but before the February interview (B) were more likely than other groups to have reduced the number of modifications to their travel behaviors by April (C). It seems, however, that empirical verification of the reverse phenomenon will have to await future research.

Perceptions and Evaluations of Penalty Severity

A feature of the analysis of the 175 repeat interviews is the greater than usual prominence of a measure of perceptions of penalty severity (whether or not respondents believed in February that penalties had increased with the introduction of RBT). Neither of the two questions about penalty severity in the April interview played much part in any of the analyses, but the February question seemed to tap an aspect of the December legal innovations which had some real psychological impact, independent of the effects of the fear of being tested and arrested. Given the central theoretical importance of perceptions and evaluations of penalty severity, as well as the almost complete absence in the literature of empirical evidence for their effects, it will be useful to conclude this analysis of the survey data by reporting the results of an analysis of responses to a question in which *evaluations* of penalty severity (as opposed to *perceptions*) were explicitly probed, and also by summarizing the pattern of significant correlations involving perceptions of penalty severity.

Evaluations of Penalty Severity Among Convicted Offenders

Buikhuisen (1969) asked 107 Dutch drink-drive offenders (that is, a sample of those convicted for drink-driving) whether they would find 2 weeks in prison or 6 months disqualification the harsher penalty. The purpose of Buikhuisen's survey was to demonstrate the need to qualify the frequent assertion that disqualification is regarded as the most severe penalty. An advantage of questioning convicted offenders is that all have experienced arrest and a court appearance and nearly all would have experienced license disqualification (in Holland many would also have experienced a short period of imprisonment). This means that responses to the question should accurately reflect evaluations of the severity of the two types of penalties, holding the experience of apprehension and conviction constant. About half of Buikhuisen's sample (49%) regarded prison as the harsher penalty, with offenders of higher social status and those who least needed a car preferring disqualification.

Buikhuisen's question was repeated in the present study to see whether similar results would be found in an Australian sample. Of the 38 respondents with a conviction in the April survey, 35 could state a preference and 3 regarded the penalties as being of equal severity. Of the 35 who stated a preference, 18, or 51.4%, regarded prison as the more severe penalty. This figure is almost identical with that reported by Buikhuisen. In addition, the same two variables reported by Buikhuisen, and only those two, correlated significantly with stated preferences. Out of 9 professional and white-collar workers, 8 regarded prison as the more severe penalty, compared with only 7 of the 21 blue-collar and unemployed respondents (X^2 (1) = 7.8; $p < .001$). Of the 19 respondents who claimed a car was essential for their work, more than two-thirds (68.4%) stated that disqualification for them would be more severe. This compared with a proportion of only 28.6% among the 14 for whom a car was not essential (X^2 (1) = 4.1; $p < .05$).

The identical results obtained in the two studies suggests that social factors common to industrialized countries may be operating to influence evaluations of penalty severity among convicted offenders. In the general population, the relationship between perceptions of the severity of penalties (a factor varied systematically in the Buikhuisen study) and the evaluations of such perceptions may not be purely idiosyncratic, but may vary in a systematic fashion according to an individual's social circumstances.

The Role of Perceptions of Penalty Severity in the Deterrence Process

It has been shown in the analysis of the longitudinal data that those who believed in February that penalties had increased were less likely to drink and drive in the following 6 weeks. In addition, those perceiving a penalty increase were more likely to be modifying their travel behavior at the first interview ($r = -.13$, $p = .055$). Both these correlations are consistent with an initial deterrent effect. However, with the exception of the small minority with a conviction for drink-driving, those perceiving a penalty increase were more likely than average to reduce the number of types of modifications to their travel methods (so that by April there was no significant difference between those who believed there had been a penalty increase and those who did not). A possible explanation is that (with the notable exception of the convicted group) the deterrent impact of penalty severity was beginning to wane by the time of the April interview. Alternatively, it is possible that by April some people had settled on a smaller number of methods of avoiding drink-driving, but were still as likely to take some action when there was a risk of driving after drinking.

If a real decline in avoidance tactics is indicated by the data, then it must have been bound up with the documented decline in subjective test probabilities. Unfortunately, the data on subjective test probabilities seem to reflect the operation of both formal and informal sanctions, and cannot be used to shed further light on this argument without extensive controls which are not presently possible. Nevertheless it does seem that the penalty severity analysis may provide, indirectly, another piece of evidence for an initial deterrent effect which was not completely maintained.

Summary of Main Results

The Community Context

RBT was introduced into a community in which the great majority of motorists drink. Nearly 1 drinking motorist in 10 can be classified as a heavy drinker, and many of those who consume lesser quantities frequently engage in "binge" drinking leading to drunkenness. This latter pattern of drinking is characteristic of young men, particularly those in their early 20s, for whom beer is the preferred beverage. Men of this age often feel great pressure to continue drinking when in a group situation, although such pressure can be felt by all sectors of the community.

Driving after drinking is common behavior in New South Wales. Nearly half of all drinking license holders admitted to driving while intoxicated at some time in the past, and nearly 1 in 10 had driven while intoxicated at least twice in the 4 months since the introduction of RBT. More than one in five of the heavy drinkers had driven while intoxicated at least twice, partly because they felt peer pressure very keenly. High alcohol consumption, perceived pressure to drink, and driving while intoxicated comprise a cluster of correlated attributes. However, as a response to RBT, drivers with these characteristics were adopting a wider than normal range of strategies to avoid drink-driving.

Support for the Deterrence Model

Through police enforcement and media publicity, a very high proportion of motorists were aware of RBT, and more than 1 in 10 had been tested personally within 3 months of the enactment of the law. As expected, the intensity of police random testing in an area was a major determinant of an individual's chances of being randomly tested, and was therefore a determinant of other aspects of exposure, such as the number of friends and acquaintances tested. The number of one's friends tested, rather than other aspects of exposure, was in turn a strong predictor of the perceived chances of being tested and arrested. Thus objective levels of enforcement were linked with perceptions of sanctions through this particular aspect of exposure. Finally, following the causal chain hypothesized in Figure 2.2, perceptions of the chances of arrest predicted the number of ways in which respondents were modifying both their drinking and their driving practices. The major predictions of the deterrence model might therefore be said to have been verified.

A number of other results provided support for the assertion that RBT achieved a deterrent effect in New South Wales, including the reasons offered for either drink-driving or not drink-driving and the outcome of the analysis of the longitudinal data. In the longitudinal analysis, direct exposure to RBT in the period between interviews corresponded to increased modifications to travel arrangements, and conversely experience with drink-driving corresponded to a decline in the number of such modifications. In addition, perceptions of an increase in penalty severity correlated with reduced drink-driving in the period between interviews, a surprising result in view of the literature but nevertheless in accordance with the deterrence model. The replication of Buikhuisen's (1969) study encourages the view that there is a relationship between perceptions and evaluations of penalty severity, which varies systematically with social factors.

The Relative Importance of Publicity and Exposure to Police Enforcement of RBT

Despite the intense publicity accorded RBT over Easter 1983, in the longitudinal analysis exposure to police enforcement, rather than exposure to publicity, correlated with changes to travel practices. However, at this time about 95% of the target population were aware of RBT because of the initial publicity campaign, so it is not valid to conclude that publicity did not influence perceptions or behavior. In the analysis of data from the April survey, those exposed to TV publicity (68.3% of the sample) had altered their travel arrangements to a greater extent than those not exposed to TV publicity. Nevertheless it is likely that in order to *maintain* a deterrent effect created initially by massive publicity visible police enforcement is more important than further publicity campaigns, at least in the first few months.

The Effects of RBT on Peer Pressure to Drink

A substantial minority (40%) of drinking motorists found it easier since RBT to resist pressure to drink, and this in turn appeared to be an influence on behavior independent of the effects of fear of punishment. On the other hand, 1 drinking motorist in 12 claimed to find it more difficult since RBT to cope with group pressure to drink. However, these people also had higher perceptions of the chances of arrest. In addition, among those who felt the greatest pressure to drink, an increase between interviews in the perceived chance of being tested coincided with a decline in the number of modifications to travel arrangements. These results are consistent wth the theory of Chapter 2, since they suggest that when there is a conflict between the effects of formal and informal sanctions, informal sanctions will probably emerge as the stronger force.

The Effects of Alcohol Consumption

One of the clearest findings of the study was that the greater a respondent's consumption of alcohol, and the greater the perceived pressure on him to drink, the more ways he reported modifying both his drinking habits and his travel arrangements. However, there was evidence that among heavy drinkers the contradictory pressures of peer pressure and fear of arrest produced a psychologically unstable situation, making the deterrent impact of RBT in many cases rather short-lived.

The Effects of a Conviction

One of the most interesting results was the interaction between arrest certainty and a conviction for drink-driving. Among those with a conviction, arrest certainty explained nearly 20% of the variance in the number of changes to travel practices, compared with little more than 1% among those without a conviction. However, the evidence fell short of establishing an absolute specific deterrent effect of punishment, since the interaction became nonsignificant when analysis was restricted to those who reported having driven while impaired sometime in the past. Nevertheless, those with a conviction were more likely to cite fear of arrest as a reason for avoiding drinking and driving. These results are consistent with the argument that legal threats have greater deterrent impact for those with a conviction because the threatened punishments are not merely theoretical. It is also of interest that the convicted group made more changes to their travel behaviors between interviews, an effect which was amplified if penalties were believed to have increased when RBT was introduced. This last interaction strengthens the argument that motorists with a conviction are more responsive than average to the threat of legal punishments.

The Role of the Perceived Severity of Penalty

Only one measure of perceived penalty severity — whether respondents believed penalties had increased when RBT was introduced — had any predictive power. The analyses based on this variable suggest that when the perceived chances of arrest are high, perceived penalty severity can have a deterrent impact additional to that of arrest certainty, particularly among those who have already suffered legal punishments for drinking and driving.

The Effects of Age and Sex

Neither age nor sex predicted arrest certainty on its own or after adjustment for other variables, and neither variable played any significant role in the longitudinal analysis. These results suggest that RBT had much the same impact for men and women of all ages. However, the results of the analyses of changes in behavior indicated that young men were more influenced by RBT than other groups. Moreover, men were more likely to cite fear of arrest as an explanation for their actions in avoiding drinking and driving, suggesting that the measure of arrest certainty may not be completely satisfactory. Thus men (young men in particular), were if anything more deterred by RBT than women (and older men). The only exception to this conclusion relates to men aged 21 to 24 years, who were slightly less likely than average to modify their drinking habits. Age and sex were not significant in interaction with arrest certainty, suggesting that responsiveness to RBT is not particularly characteristic of women or older drivers.

The Effects of Socioeconomic Status

The shape of the relationship between socioeconomic status (measured by occupation and education) and arrest certainty was roughly an inverted-U, with those in the middle range (lower white-collar and skilled blue collar) being most fearful of arrest. Occupation was significant as a predictor of changes in travel and drinking behaviors, but dropped out of the model when adjusted for age and other variables. It seems that RBT had roughly the same behavioral impact at all status levels.

Problems for the Deterrence Model

In a number of respects the analysis yielded findings which are not consistent with the predictions of the deterrence model. Many of the problems center on the failure of the perceptual variables to behave as predicted. The analysis of reasons for not drink-driving suggests that the measure of arrest certainty may have missed important aspects of the perceptual process. This impression is supported by the results of many of the statistical analyses. Thus the effects of exposure to RBT on behavior change should theoretically have been mediated through perceptions of the chances of arrest, but frequently exposure had a direct correlation with behavior. In addition, drink-driving between interviews should have been predicted by perceptions in February of the chances of being randomly tested. Most serious was the failure to find a positive correlation between changes in the perceived probability of being tested between interviews and changes in the number of modifications to behavior.

Additional problems relate to the negative correlation between drink-driving and the number of friends known to have been randomly tested, the failure to find evidence for an interaction between perceptions of arrest certainty and perceptions of penalty severity, and the apparent lack of relationship between the number of modifications to behavior and the probability of drink-driving.

The reasons for these apparent failures in the deterrence model are explored further in Chapter 9, after an examination of some empirical evidence for the validity of marginal specific deterrence. In Chapter 7 the method of the study is described, and the results are presented in Chapter 8.

7
The Penalties Study: Research Questions and Method

In Chapter 6 the focus was on the evidence for general deterrence through RBT. By contrast, the analysis reported in Chapter 8 is addressed to one part of the question posed by Andenaes (1974): How does the actual experience of punishment influence the deterrent effect of the legal threat—a deterrent effect that has proved, in at least one instance, insufficient to prevent the offense? According to the deterrence model, motorists who have been punished should be more responsive to the threat of punishment than offenders without a conviction (absolute specific deterrence), and those who have received severe penalties should be more responsive than those who received light penalties (marginal specific deterrence). As we saw in Chapter 6 there is some evidence for the absolute specific deterrent effect of punishment for drink-driving, since motorists with a conviction tended to be more responsive to RBT than drink-drivers without a conviction. However, the evidence was not strong, probably because the small number of respondents with a conviction reduced the power of statistical tests.

The present chapter, which parallels Chapter 5 for the RBT study, describes the research questions and the method of the penalties study. The focus is *marginal* specific deterrence. The research method departs from that of the RBT study chiefly in the use of archival data from the courts rather than survey data, and so most of this chapter is devoted to describing the indirect technique adopted for measuring the perceived severity of the penalty. The method is, in essence, to carry out an analysis of the sentencing process, thereby constructing measures of the entitlement for punishment and the severity of the penalty, which are then combined into an index of penalty severity relative to entitlement.

In addition to the material on penalty severity, in describing the research methods attention is paid to the role of environmental variables in the reconviction process and to the method used for the development of a typology of convicted drink-drive offenders.

The Research Questions

The penalties study is concerned with the marginal deterrent impact of punishment. However, it was argued in Chapter 2 that a penalty is never imposed in a vacuum, but on a human being with a certain social background and probably a general feeling as to what he deserves in the way of punishment—or at least what he can expect to get. In contrast to the assumptions upon which so much research is based, people are not just organisms that respond to stimuli; rather, they engage in a continuous process of interpretation and evaluation, acting toward things on the basis of the meanings that the things have for them (Blumer, 1969). There is an essential difference between an electric shock and a judicial penalty, since the judicial penalty is perceived in terms of an offender's "world taken for granted" (Schutz, 1970), which comprises both his previous experience and his understanding of the customs and rules operating in the society of which he is a member. In short, the offender's perception of the severity of the penalty and his evaluation of its fairness are the critical factors in his reactions to punishment.

Given the reliance in the present study on official court records, a theoretical orientation that emphasizes perceptions and evaluations clearly creates some problems for research methodology. However, it is argued in this chapter that through judicious use of archival data, some of these problems can be overcome. Thus the major research question consists of two parts: Can the perceived severity of the penalty be simulated by a measure of relative severity, constructed from data available in court records, and do penalties of high relative severity correspond to lower rates of drink-drive recidivism (or recidivism for other offense types) than penalties of low relative severity? In the absence of survey data on offenders' evaluations of the *fairness* of their punishments, hypotheses concerning the specific role of such evaluations must remain (for the present) unexplored.

A second research question, which arises from the interactionist literature discussed in Chapter 1, is whether improvements in predictions of recidivism can be obtained by considering interactions with characteristics of the environment. Gottfredson and Taylor (1986), in a study of offenders released from jail, have argued that the person, his environment and his behavior interact in a process of mutual and reciprocal influence. Using various measures of recidivism as dependent variables they were able to demonstrate statistical interactions between indices of neighborhood quality (such as percent residential versus commercial street frontages) and offender characteristics (such as criminal history). Thus, for example, poor risk offenders released to better neighborhoods failed more frequently and more seriously but were free for longer periods of time.

The hypothesis of an interaction between person and neighborhood characteristics was explored in the present study, using previous record (e.g., criminal offenses) and demographic characteristics (e.g., age) together with three indicators of the environment, the most important of which is a social problems index. However, of greater importance from the point of view of deterrence, interactions between *penalties* and neighborhood characteristics were also investigated. It could be argued, for example, that long periods of license suspension are more effective in rural communities where surveillance by the police is easier. Unfortunately, as indicated in the following discussion of the methods used to measure locality characteristics, the hypothesis of interaction effects was not supported in the analysis.

The final issue addressed in this study is the construction of an offender typology. Like all legal and administrative categories, a record for "drinking and driving" is a label that applies to people who are otherwise quite varied in characteristics and behavior. Even on the basis of the limited data available from official records, it is apparent from the literature that convicted drink-drivers are a mixed group, with some responding (it seems) to penalties and some not responding. It would assist both in understanding why people drink and drive and in understanding how penalties act as a deterrent if it were possible to abstract from the data a classification or typology of offenders that was capable of reducing the complexity of the observed correlations. It is argued in Chapter 8 that the results of the present study can usefully be summarized in terms of a typology revolving around role careers, particularly careers that are mixed in the types of offenses committed by offenders.

The Design of the Penalties Study

The study is based on an analysis of 1,000 drink-drivers convicted for driving with the prescribed concentration of alcohol (PCA) in 1972, and followed up for 3 years from the date of conviction or release from prison. The method of sampling was designed to facilitate the construction of measures of the relative severity of penalties, and hence to get closer to the key theoretical variable of perceived penalty severity than would be possible by relying on the actual penalties imposed. Of course direct measures of the perceived severity of punishments would be preferable to the indirect measure employed in the present study. However, such direct measures could only be obtained through contact with offenders, possibly using a self-complete questionnaire but preferably through face-to-face interviews at the time of their final court appearance. Unfortunately, a study of this kind was beyond the resources available for the project.

Sampling was carried out retrospectively from the 15,736 PCA (breath analysis) cases brought before magistrates' courts in New South Wales in 1972. On the basis of a simple model of the sentencing process, described below, an index of *entitlement for punishment* was constructed, together with an index of *penalty severity*. Offenders were classified as high, medium, or low in terms of entitlement and high, medium, or low in terms of penalty severity, making nine categories altogether. Offenders were then sampled from each of these nine categories. In addition, all offenders who were sentenced to prison, a bond, or probation in 1972 were sampled, to ensure that a sufficient number of the severe penalties were included in the study. For present purposes these offenders have been distributed to the nine categories described before. The result was a sample stratified with unequal sampling fractions in each stratum, so in order to obtain unbiased estimates of reconviction rates and other quantities it is necessary to apply corrections to the sample values. The methods of Cochran (1963) were employed to produce these weighted estimates.

In about 25% of cases offenders were convicted of one or more offenses in addition to the drink-drive offense. In these cases the total penalty for all offenses was recorded. Thus if an offender was fined $150 and $200 for two separate offenses, the total fine was recorded as $350. The same rule was followed for disqualification period: the total length of disqualification was computed as the period from the date of conviction or release from prison to the date the license was officially restored. In a number of cases, the disqualification included a period that carried over from previous offenses. The length of time in prison was computed to the date of actual release; it was not based on the magistrate's sentence. In a number of cases offenders were released from prison earlier than their due date.

It was intended that comparison of the cells in the 3×3 table (entitlement by severity) would allow an evaluation of the effect of punishment severity relative to entitlement. For example, an offender with low entitlement who received a high severity penalty could be assumed to have been punished more severely than an offender with high entitlement who received a high severity penalty. On the other hand an offender with high entitlement who received a low severity penalty could be expected to feel that he had got off rather lightly. Table 7.1 summarizes the idea behind the sampling scheme, and also shows the numbers sampled in each cell of the design.

Independent validation is required before relative severity can be equated with perceived severity. A convenient index for validation is the percentage in each category who appealed against the severity of the penalty. If, for example, a very high relative severity corresponds to a very high perceived severity, this group should have the highest rate of appeals. The appeal data that are presented in Table 7.4 do tend to confirm the validity of the method. However, appeal cases were excluded from the sample itself since it was considered that the psychological impact of penalties would be different for offenders who had appealed. In most cases in 1972 appeals against the sentence were successful, with higher court judges reducing the severity of the penalty imposed in the magistrate's court.

TABLE 7.1. Sample structure in relation to relative severity of penalties[a]

Severity	Entitlement		
	High	Medium	Low
High	Average (203)	Heavy (115)	Very heavy (20)
Medium	Light (129)	Average (127)	Heavy (111)
Low	Very light (94)	Light (100)	Average (101)

[a]Numbers shown in brackets are the numbers of cases sampled in each category.

Reconvictions as an Index of Penalty Effectiveness

The present study, like so many of its predecessors, uses some kind of reconviction within a certain time period as an index of the effects of penalties. Other possible criteria include accident records, self-reported infractions of the law (particularly drinking, driving, and traffic offenses), and changes in knowledge, attitudes, or lifestyle, as reported in an interview. Accident statistics have been widely used in American studies of traffic offenders (Sadler & Perrine, 1984), and are especially attractive in investigating drink-drive offenders, given the close connection between drink-driving and accidents. Unfortunately, at the time of the study it was not possible to link conviction and accident records. The use of self-reported infractions is attractive since it would allow a measure of the true rate of reoffending. However, the study carried out by Robinson (1977) indicates some of the problems associated with such research. A satisfactory response rate can only be achieved by a direct-interview technique combined with extensive field work, rather than through mail questionnaires, and there are in addition the perennial problems of exaggeration or concealment in the reporting of offenses. Such problems can be overcome, but a satisfactory methodology would be extremely expensive.

In the absence of all this information, a reconviction in 3 years remains as the sole index of penalty effectiveness in the present study. A follow-up period of 3 years was chosen since it was determined that a shorter time period would not yield a sufficient number of reconvictions for the various detailed analyses that were proposed. Moreover, 90% of drink-drivers in 1972 received a disqualification period shorter than 3 years, so a 3-year follow-up allowed sufficient time for the effects of most periods of disqualification to be monitored.

An offender was classified as being reconvicted if either police or Motor Transport Department files contain a record of a criminal, traffic, or drink-drive offense in the 3-year period following the date of original conviction in 1972 or the date of release from prison for the offenses dealt with at the time of the original conviction in 1972. In other words, the follow-up period did *not* include the time an offender may have spent in prison for the original offense. In a couple of cases offenders committed a criminal offense in jail (for example, attempting to escape). The follow-up period of these offenders was taken as 3 years from the date of conviction for the recording of criminal offenses, and 3 years from the date of release from prison for traffic and drink-drive offenses (since criminal but not traffic offenses could be committed in jail). The incidence of offenses in jail was not sufficient to make this a general rule for all offenders.

Each offender could be convicted of one or more of each of the three types of offenses: criminal, traffic, or drink-drive. Only the *categorical recidival rate* for each type of offense was recorded (Gibbs, 1975). That is, record was kept of whether a criminal, traffic, or drink-drive offense was committed in the 3-year period, but the total number of offenses in each category was not recorded. The categorical recidival rate has more meaning than any other measure of recidivism, since the aim of the research is to link penalties for the target or original offense with reoffending. Once another offense has been committed and the offender has been convicted and sentenced, the new penalties constitute a major additional variable in the analysis. Under these circumstances, it does not seem meaningful to continue to ask whether the penalties imposed for the original offense are still affecting the likelihood of reoffending. At the very least, data on the new penalties would have to be included in the analysis. Since this introduces complications beyond the scope of the study, the decision was made to use only categorical recidival rates. However, in studying categorical recidival rates for specific offenses (e.g., drink-driving) statistical controls were introduced to represent offenses of other types (e.g., a criminal offense) committed before the target offense (if it occurred in the 3-year period).

It is not possible to claim that reconviction statistics yield an estimate of the true rate of reoffending, nor is such a claim necessary for the research design. The crucial question is whether one penalty compared with another is more or less effective in preventing reoffending, and all that is required to answer this question is an unbiased indicator of reoffending. The problem then becomes: Is every offender equally likely to be caught and charged each time he commits an offense? According to the model set out diagramatically in Figure 2.3, in order to link penalties with reconviction rates it is necessary to take into account both the sentencing and apprehension processes. First, the sentencing process distributes certain kinds of offenders to certain penalty groups (for example, previous offenders are much more likely to go to jail), the different types of offenders having varying probabilities of reoffending, regardless of penalties. Second, the process of police apprehension probably makes some offenders more likely to be caught and charged than others, even if these offenders are no more likely to reoffend (Homel, 1983c).

Knowing the relative contribution of each kind of bias is not as important as ensuring that as many relevant factors as possible are included as controls. The details of the analyses incorporating these controls are not presented in this book, but may be found in Homel (1980a, 1981a). A brief description of the variables available from police and court records which were used as statistical controls is included in the following discussion of the construction of the offender typology.

Relative and Perceived Severity of Penalty

Evidence was presented in Chapter 2 showing that the overwhelming majority of drink-drive offenders have an idea of the penalty which they can expect to receive before they appear before the magistrate. Offenders will almost certainly not be aware of the latest statistics on penalties, but it would be surprising if their expectations of punishment did not, on average, have a reasonable correlation with the penalties actually imposed by magistrates. The present argument is essentially a statistical one; offenders who, for example, receive penalties markedly in excess of the norm, given their entitlement, may be expected *on average* to feel they have been dealt with severely. In other words, although it is not possible to measure directly what an offender expected, we should be able to measure to what extent he received a penalty of above or below average severity given his personal characteristics and the circumstances of his offense. Provided we do not attempt to make too many fine distinctions, this measure of relative severity should reflect, at least in part, perceived severity.

The first step is to develop a measure of the seriousness of an offense and the severity of the penalties imposed, which leads directly to a consideration of the sentencing process. For present purposes, we will assume that the sentencing process can be modeled very simply, by an extension of the tariff model (Homel, 1983b; Thomas, 1980). We will suppose that magistrates, in determining an appropriate penalty, assign weights to various features of an offender and his offense, these weights being mentally added to produce a composite score of the seriousness of an offense, or the offender's entitlement for punishment. Similarly, we will suppose that the various components of the penalty—amount of fine, period of license disqualification, period of imprisonment, and so on—can be assigned mental weights and that these weights can be summed to yield a composite severity score.

The proposed method of constructing relative severity categories does not depend for its validity on a theory of the sentencing process in which all magistrates literally assign weights to all aspects of the case. Lawrence and Browne (1981) have presented evidence that as part of a general cognitive strategy employed to process different pieces of evidence, some magistrates do think explicitly in terms of weighting various factors. For example, one magistrate multiplied the BAC by four to determine an appropriate fine. However, other magistrates use procedures best described in terms of sifting and sorting, employing an iterative process of checking and rechecking to arrive finally at a sentence or verdict.

The present argument is that the average behaviors of all magistrates can be simulated by a complex tariff model, even if they do not explicitly operate in this fashion. Dawes (1982) points out that such *paramorphic* representations of judges' psychological processes have been extremely successful in contexts in which predictor variables have conditionally monotone relationships to criterion variables, a condition which should be met in the sentencing situation.

Since we will assume that magistrates seek to match penalty severity as closely as possible with entitlement for punishment, it seems a reasonable procedure to estimate the weights on both sides of the equation by requiring the offender/offense scores and the severity scores to have maximum possible correlation over all offenders and all magistrates. An appropriate statistical technique for accomplishing this is canonical correlation analysis.

The success of this method will depend both upon the adequacy of the assumptions on which it is based and the comprehensiveness of the information included in the calculations. The data available are derived from statistical summaries of each court appearance. Perhaps the most crucial data omitted from the statistical returns from the courts relates to what lawyers call "the facts" of the case—whether an accident was caused, how dangerous the police considered the offender to be, whether there were any extenuating circumstances, and so on. Since this information is missing from the present study, we would not expect perfect correlation between the measures of seriousness and severity. Nevertheless, we should arrive at meaningful weights for the data which are available, such as an offender's age, BAC, and previous convictions.

Since much subjective data is missing from the analysis, all the data available, including factors which would not normally be considered relevant, have been included. Variables such as marital status and occupational status could well reflect aspects of the offender and his offense which the magistrate would take into account in determining an appropriate penalty, especially if he was considering letting the offender off without penalty (for which there is explicit provision in the *Crimes Act* of New South Wales in Section 556A).

The relative weights derived from the canonical correlation analysis are presented in Tables 7.2 and 7.3. The analysis was carried out on 15,054 cases completed in New South Wales during 1972 for which complete information was available, and the correlation between the composite severity and offender/offense or entitlement scores was found to be .70. This means that nearly half the variance of the severity index was explained by the entitlement index. A correlation at the level of .70 reflects a high degree of consistency between offender/offense characteristics and the penalties imposed and allows us to continue in confidence to investigate the properties of these variables.

TABLE 7.2. Weights derived from a canonical correlation analysis of 15,054 drink-drive cases (1972): Index of offense seriousness (entitlement of offender for punishment)

Variables/ Categories	No. of cases	Weight	Variables/ Categories	No. of cases	Weight
Age			Sex		
18–24	4,852	.83	Female	253	.00
25–39	5,798	.51	Male	14,801	−.02
40+	4,404	.00	Occupational status		
Marital status			A (high)		
De facto	93	.35	B	189	−.21
Separated	269	.20	C	1,010	−.14
Divorced	117	.16	D (low)	6,342	−.06
				7,513	.00
Single	4,848	.10	Blood alcohol concentration (BAC)		
Married	6,770	−.12	.080–.159	7,853	−.80
Widowed	138	−.17	.160–.229	5,715	−.46
Not known	2,819	.00	.230+	1,486	.00
Plea			Previous traffic convictions		
Guilty	14,905	.12	Yes	9,041	.19
Not guilty	149	.00	No	6,013	.00
Number of charges			Previous drink-drive convictions		
One only	13,876	.00	Yes	3,420	1.88
More than one	1,178	.52	No	11,634	.00
Defendant legally represented			Criminal record		
Yes	7,443	−.42	Children's court only		
No	7,611	.00	Indictable	136	.35
			Summary, not	443	.32
			indictable	4,040	.13
			No criminal record	10,435	.00

For the offender/offense variables (Table 7.2), the higher the weight, the greater the contribution of that factor to the seriousness of the offense (entitlement for punishment). Thus previous drink-drive convictions, with a weight of 1.88, is the single most important factor contributing to the offender/offense score. A disqualification period exceeding 2 years contributes more than anything else to a heavy penalty (Table 7.3).

Generally, the weights agree with what would be expected if the analysis were simulating a complex tariff model of sentencing. On the offender/offense side, having previous drink-drive convictions, having more than one charge, being under 25 years of age, and having a low blood alcohol concentration weigh most heavily (only the last in the offender's favor). On the penalty side, long periods of disqualification and imprisonment weigh most heavily, far more so than fines. Note that a dismissal under Section 556A of the NSW *Crimes Act* would receive a weight of zero, since it corresponds to the absence of all penalties.

TABLE 7.3. Weights derived from a canonical correlation analysis of 15,054 drink-drive cases (1972): Index of penalty severity

Variables/Categories	No. of cases	Weight	Variables/Categories	No. of cases	Weight
Fine ($)			Period of license disqualification		
1–100	3,557	-.24	Rising of court, 24–48 hours	476	.77
101–150	5,993	-.18	Over 48 hours, up to 14 days	678	.59
151–200	2,415	.31	14 days, up to 1 month	1,274	.76
201–400	1,203	.76	1 month up to 2 months	1,951	.96
No fine	1,886	.00	2 months up to 3 months	940	1.03
Period of imprisonment			3 months up to 6 months	1,912	1.19
1 month and under	45	1.49	6 months up to 12 months	1,270	1.51
2 months, under 3 months	61	.17	1 year up to 2 years	3,470	1.76
3 months, up to 6 months	143	1.39	2 years up to 5 years	1,494	2.97
6 months	34	1.42	5 years +	184	2.75
No prison	14,771	.00	No disqualification (S.556A)	1,405	.00
Bond					
Yes	989	.62			
No	14,065	.00			

There are some apparent anomalies in the table. Why, for example, does imprisonment weigh less heavily than long periods of license disqualification? The answer is that the weights reflect intercorrelations between items and should actually not be considered on their own. If we define a high severity score as a score in the top third of the total range, then 94% of those sentenced to 6 months imprisonment had such a score, compared with only 76% of those receiving a license disqualification of more than 5 years. The *total* score is the important thing, and when it is calculated, all the apparent anomalies in the table disappear.

It is possible to conclude that the canonical correlation analysis has been highly successful in isolating patterns in the statistical data, and that the patterns seem to be meaningful. Using the entitlement and severity scores for each individual, we can construct Table 7.1 and proceed to compare reconviction rates in the various cells of the table. However, it is necessary first to validate the procedure and justify, if possible, the link between relative severity and perceived severity.

Validation of Measures of Entitlement for Punishment and Penalty Severity

The method described above for constructing the severity of penalty and offender/offense indices has a considerable degree of face validity. In addition, there are several kinds of evidence which increase our confidence that these indices are related in a meaningful way to the sentencing process and to the psychological impact of penalties.

Casper (1978), in a study of 90 offenders imprisoned in three cities in the United States, demonstrated that there was a strong correlation between the perceived severity of the prison term and the relative severity of the sentence. Perceived severity was determined directly from interviews with offenders, and relative severity from a comparison of the actual sentence with the median term imposed in each city (this measure took no account of offender or offense variables). Collapsing each variable to two categories (lighter/same and heavier), the correlation was .46 using ϕ and .75 using Yule's Q. In other words, offenders had a very accurate perception of the toughness of the penalty they received. Moreover, Casper demonstrates that there was a strong negative correlation between perceived severity and the percentage saying they were treated fairly. Fewer than one in four (23%) of those who believed they received heavier penalties than others said they were treated fairly, compared with 70% who believed they had received lighter penalties than others.

Using the entitlement and severity indices from the present study, Homel (1979) has shown that a measure of *magistrate toughness* can be derived which accords closely at the extremes with independent information about magistrates. Moreover, in the same analysis it was possible to show that the variance in the severity scores increased as the offense got

TABLE 7.4. Percentages of appeals in relative severity categories[a]

Severity index	Offender/Offense index (entitlement)		
	Most serious	Average seriousness	Low seriousness
High	6.1 (485)	←——————— 15.4 (400) ———————→	
Average	7.9 (613)	7.9 (1,385)	9.5 (534)
Low	2.7 (294)	3.4 (3,185)	4.4 (8,158)

[a]The numbers in brackets are the totals in each cell and add to 15,054. The appeal rates were checked by random sampling and found to be higher than reported in the official statistics. The increased sizes of the standard errors due to the incorporation of the random sampling check have been taken into account in the statistical analysis of these data.

more serious, which is consistent with the observations of Hood (1972) for the sentencing of traffic offenders in Britain. Both of these results provide further evidence that the measures of penalty severity and entitlement for punishment are valid.

If offenders receiving penalties of high relative severity perceive their punishment as tough (and probably also unfair), they should be more likely to appeal. The appeal rates in each category are shown in Table 7.4. The categories "high severity, average seriousness" and "high severity, low seriousness" have been combined, since there were too few cases (20) in the latter category for reliable analysis.

There is a highly significant relationship between entitlement/severity and appeal rates $(G^2(7) = 39.1; p < .005)$. The appeal rate was highest among those offenders who received a heavy penalty relative to their entitlement (15.4%), and was lowest among those who received a very light penalty relative to their entitlement (2.7%). Multiple comparisons showed that the four groupings of categories depicted in Table 7.1 were internally homogeneous (i.e., appeal rates did not differ significantly within these theoretical categories). Using the groupings suggested by Table 7.1, the appeal rates are graphically illustrated in Figure 7.1. It is clear from this figure that as relative severity increases, so does the appeal rate.

Table 7.4 and Figure 7.1 suggest at least three ways of measuring perceived severity. First, the eight categories of Table 7.4 can be used, analyzing the table according to the main effects of penalty severity and entitlement, and the interaction between the two. Second, Figure 7.1 and the multiple comparisons show that we are justified in using the categories of Table 7.1; that is, very low, low, average, and high relative severity. Third, we may simply use the appeal rates themselves as a direct index of perceived severity. (The reader is reminded that in the selection of the offenders for the sample, all appeal cases were excluded. We are using appeal rates from the whole population of drink-drivers convicted in 1972 as an index of the average perceived severity of penalties in a number of categories.) For simplicity of presentation, results are presented in Chapter 8, using the last two methods.

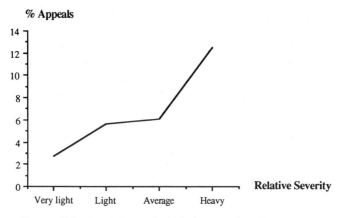

FIGURE 7.1. Appeal rates by relative severity of penalties.

Environmental Factors

Information on the offender's area of residence was available in the court records. There is strong evidence from Chapter 5 and from other sources (e.g., Vinson & Homel, 1976) indicating that levels of drinking and the extent of drink-driving vary considerably from region to region. In addition, there are good theoretical and empirical grounds for believing that local influences, such as the kinds of social groups in which drinking takes place, may affect some offenders more than others (Gottfredson & Taylor, 1986; Gusfield, 1981a). Thus close attention was paid to making the best use of the area of residence data, with a view to constructing interactions with offender characteristics and with the penalties imposed by magistrates. At the same time, it was recognized that drink-driving is rather different from traditional crimes, and that more immediate aspects of the social environment may be more pertinent (such as the type of group the offender associates with). However, data on these aspects of the offender's environment were not available in official records.

The simplest classification of area of residence was urban versus rural. Urban areas were defined as the Sydney Statistical District plus the cities of Wollongong and Newcastle. A second method of measurement was based on a "risk" index developed by Vinson and Homel (1976). This is an index of the cumulative social disadvantage of a region (a local government area), based on 25 social indicators. High risk areas are characterized by high rates of crime and other social and health problems, as well as higher than average levels of BAC for those convicted of PCA. It is likely that risk is related to the probability of apprehension for drink-driving (Zylman, 1972). In addition, risk has been shown to be strongly associated with (among other things) parents' and children's satisfactions with the neighborhood, parent and child social networks, and levels of community solidarity among families (Burns & Homel, 1986; Homel & Burns, 1985, 1987). The risk index is therefore a good surrogate measure of those aspects of neighborhood quality highlighted by Gottfredson and Taylor (1986) as likely to be important in a study of recidivism.

The most general system of classification of area of residence was based on 46 "court circuits" operating in New South Wales. Each circuit was served by one or more magistrates and represented a sociologically meaningful region, such as a rural area or a defined part of a major city.

Unfortunately, despite the use of the different measures of the quality of the environment, none of the interactions investigated was significant beyond levels predicted by chance. Indeed there was no evidence from the data that the probability of reconviction for any type of offense (drink-driving, traffic, or criminal) was influenced at all by area of residence, whether as a main effect or as an interaction with offender characteristics or penalties. The result for main effects, but not for interactions, is consistent with the findings of Gottfredson and Taylor (1986). The null result suggests that locality may not be a salient aspect of the environment for drink-drive offenders.

A Typology of Convicted Offenders

One aim of the study was to contribute to the debate on how convicted drink-drivers should be classified by suggesting a typology based both on offender characteristics and on reactions to penalties, while recognizing that much more sophisticated social and psychological data (including better measures of the social environment) would be required to confirm (or correct) the suggested groupings. The approach adopted is akin to the role career method discussed by Gibbons (1975) and by Hood and Sparks (1970). The emphasis is on mixed as well as homogeneous careers, and the distinction discussed by Hood and Sparks between occasional and persistent offenders is built into the proposed classification scheme.

The method used examined the relationship between actual penalties (not the relative severity measure described before) and reconviction rates, controlling for a range of variables, including the environmental factors described before, plus "intervening offences" (e.g., a criminal offense committed before a drink-drive offense), background characteristics (age, sex, occupational, and marital status), previous offenses (drink-drive, traffic, and criminal), details of the court case (BAC, plea, legal representation, time from arrest to sentence, and the relative severity of the magistrate), and offenses dealt with at the same time as the drink-drive offense (e.g., criminal, driving while disqualified, other traffic charges). In addition the possibility of interactions between many of these variables and the penalties was investigated, and the role of all of these variables as predictors of recidivism in their own right was carefully examined. From this a detailed picture emerged of the role of both penalties and other variables in predicting recidivism. These analyses are summarized in the next chapter, and details may be found in Homel (1980a, 1981a).

The typology is built on these results. It revolves around a distinction between "good risk" and "bad risk" offenders, with good risk offenders being defined operationally as those who will never be reconvicted for drinking and driving. Although it is based on detailed data analysis, the typology is really an exercise in "grounded theory" (Glaser & Strauss, 1979), and explicit criteria for the allocation of individuals to one of the categories cannot be given. Groups can be identified by certain predominant characteristics, but in every case there are a number of offenders who could be assigned equally well to more than one category. The typology is offered primarily as a contribution to theory rather than as a diagnostic scheme for individuals, and at all times the essential "fuzziness" of the dividing lines between groups should be kept in mind.

8
Results of the Penalties Study

The emphasis in this chapter is on the responses of individuals who have already been punished to threats of further legal sanctions. The first part of the chapter is devoted to an examination of reconviction rates over the 3 years of the study, and the relationship between reconviction rates and the relative severity of penalty measures described in the last chapter. The purpose of this analysis is to test the hypothesis of a marginal specific deterrent impact of punishment, using the relative severity measures as proxies for perceived severity. It is shown that the evidence for marginal deterrence is rather weak, with the exception of "good risk" offenders, for whom tougher penalties corresponded to lower reconviction rates for traffic offenses less serious than drinking and driving.

This analysis is followed by a description of a typology of convicted offenders. The typology serves to bring together all the information available in the study on the characteristics of offenders and their responses to penalties, thereby throwing some light both on the process of deterrence and on the failure of deterrence. As indicated in the last chapter, the hypothesis that rates of reconviction would correlate with measures of the quality of the area of residence of the offender, in interaction with penalties or offender characteristics, was not supported in the present study. Since all analyses involving area of residence yielded nonsignificant results, further details are not reported, and the typology makes no reference to the area of residence of the offender.

Marginal Specific Deterrence: Reconviction Rates and Relative Severity of Penalties

In this section, some results from the analysis of reconviction rates among the 1,000 convicted offenders are examined. Reconviction rates for drink-driving, criminal offenses, and nondrink-drive traffic offenses are considered within the framework of the measures of relative severity of penalties developed in Chapter 7. Following the method described in that chapter, penalty effects are considered in terms of combinations of severity and entitlement for punishment, using the four relative severity categories depicted in Table 7.1 and the appeal rates in the eight cells of Table 7.4. According to deterrence theory, the pattern of reconvictions should be roughly the inverse of the pattern for appeal rates shown in Figure 7.1.

Reconvictions in 3 Years

Out of 1,000 offenders in the sample, 378 were reconvicted for some offense committed within 3 years—that is, for a drink-drive, criminal, or traffic offense. The figure of 378 corresponds to an estimated 37.5% for convicted drink-drivers as a whole (this latter figure is weighted to take account of the nonproportional sampling method). It can be shown (Homel, 1980a) that about 58% of drink-drive offenders in New South Wales will be reconvicted for some offense if they are followed up indefinitely, although offenders with a record for driving while disqualified recidivate more quickly and at a slightly higher rate (63.8% for all offenses).

The great majority (83.6%) of the 378 offenders who were reconvicted committed their first offense within 2 years of the commencement of the follow-up, and nearly half (46.6%) committed their first offense within the first year. In the sample, roughly equal numbers of offenders committed drink-drive, criminal, or traffic offenses as their first offense, but when the numbers were weighted, nondrink-drive traffic offenses emerged as the single most common type (17.1%, compared with the overall figure of 37.5%).

In all, 149 offenders were reconvicted for a drink-drive offense in 3 years, which corresponds to a weighted estimate of 13.0%. The corresponding figure for criminal offenses was 13.4% and for all traffic offenses (including drink-driving) the figure was 28.9%. It can be shown (Homel, 1980a) that the long-term recidivism rate for drink-driving is 23.4%, which is close to the figure of 25% cited by Ennis (1977) for the United States and is also consistent with the figure of 22% over a 6-year period reported by van der Werff (1981) for Holland.

It is interesting to note that drink-drivers who reoffend are quite as likely to commit other kinds of offenses as drinking and driving, a finding which is consistent with our knowledge of their previous records. The frequency with which a range of traffic offenses is committed is particularly interesting. Given the emphasis on categorical recidival rates discussed in Chapter 7, in the present study only the most serious traffic offense was recorded using an ordering based on the maximum penalty provided for each offense. It turned out that drink-driving was the most serious traffic offense actually committed by offenders in the study, since no offenders were reconvicted for manslaughter, "inflict grievous bodily harm by furious and

TABLE 8.1. Reconviction rates for each offense type by relative severity of penalty

Relative severity category	Base for percentages		Offense type		
	DUI/ Criminal	Traffic	DUI %	Criminal %	Traffic %
Very light	94	70	16.0	12.8	17.1
Light	229	167	14.4	20.5	19.8
Average	431	294	17.2	20.4	12.9
High	246	211	11.0	15.1	10.0

negligent driving," or for not stopping after an accident where death or injury was caused (which were the only traffic offenses rated as more serious than drink-driving). Nevertheless, despite the restriction that only the most serious traffic offense was recorded, violations included (among many others): driving while disqualified (4.3% weighted estimate), speeding (5.9%), negligent driving (3.3%), and failing to yield (1.3%). Since 9% of offenders in the population had a disqualification period in excess of 3 years, and since many of these may have been reconvicted for a traffic offense after 3 years, the figure of 4.3% for drive-disqualified is an underestimate of the eventual rate of reconviction for that offense.

The Relationship Between Perceived Severity and Rates of Reconviction

The reconviction rates for drinking and driving, criminal offenses and for nondrink-drive traffic offenses are shown in Table 8.1. The traffic offense conviction rates are computed differently from the others for two reasons, one theoretical and one practical. In terms of the logic of the analysis, there does not seem much point in comparing those reconvicted for nondrink-drive traffic offenses with those not reconvicted for such an offense, since the nonreconvicted group would combine people who were reconvicted for drinking and driving or a criminal offense with those who recorded no offense in 3 years. That is, it would lump the best and worst offenders together. There is also the technical problem: because the principal offense method was followed, a conviction for most traffic offenses would be recorded only if it occurred before the drink-drive offense or if no drink-drive offense was committed in the 3 years.

For these reasons it seems appropriate to exclude offenders reconvicted for drinking and driving or for a criminal offense from the analysis of traffic offenses, and simply compare offenders reconvicted for a traffic offense with those not reconvicted for anything. This means that the analysis is conditional, excluding drink-drive and criminal offense recidivists. The 726 remaining offenders will be called *good risks*, which seems reasonable since all traffic offenses for which convictions were recorded in 3 years were less serious than drink-driving, and therefore were less serious than most of the criminal offenses.

DRINK-DRIVE RECONVICTIONS

Analysis of variance of the drink-drive recidivism rates in Table 8.1 (using an arcsine transformation) indicated no statistically significant relationship with relative severity ($\chi^2(3) = 5.2$; $p > .10$). There is no clear trend in the percentages, except that offenders receiving penalties of high relative severity did recidivate at a lower rate, which is consistent with deterrence theory. However, in the absence of statistical significance it is hazardous to put much weight on this result.

The analysis of drink-drive reconviction rates against the proportion of appeals in each penalty/entitlement cell provided little further support for deterrence. Fitting appeal rates as a cubic polynomial, neither the linear nor the quadratic term was significant ($G^2(1) = 2.3$ for the linear term and .03 for the quadratic), but the cubic term was significant ($G^2(1) = 5.3$; $p = .02$). The cubic model was an adequate fit ($G^2(4) = 5.3$), but the fitted values showed that only over a narrow range (appeal rates between 6% and 9%) did the hypothesized negative relationship between proportion of appeals and reconviction rates actually occur. At best, therefore, penalties had a marginal deterrent impact when they were perceived as of about average severity, as measured by the appeal rate. However, as is apparent from Table 8.1, this result is not consistent with the analysis based on relative severity categories.

CRIMINAL RECONVICTIONS

The relationship between criminal reconviction rates and relative severity was also not statistically significant ($\chi^2(3) = 6.1$; $p > .10$), although there is evidence for an inverted U-pattern, contrary to deterrence theory. The appeal rate analysis failed completely to clarify the relationship, since even a fifth-order polynomial did not fit the data ($G^2(3) = 12.7$, $p = .015$ for the residual).

TRAFFIC RECONVICTIONS

Contrary to the patterns for criminal and drink-drive reconviction rates, the reconviction rates for traffic offenses (Table 8.1) support the general impression of a deterrent impact ($\chi^2(3) = 8.1$; $p < .05$). (It should be recalled that the traffic analysis excludes offenders reconvicted of criminal or drink-drive offenses.) Moreover, the pattern is strongly linear ($\chi^2(1) = 5.2$; $p < .025$).

The appeal rate analysis also gave simple results. A model linear in the logit scale was adequate ($G^2(6) = 12.1$; $p = .06$), and the linear term was

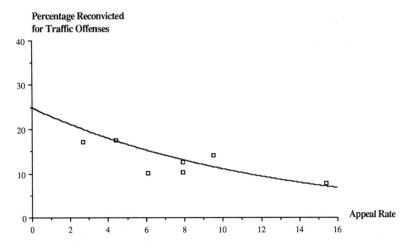

FIGURE 8.1. Traffic reconviction rates by appeal rates, excluding those reconvicted for drinking and driving or for criminal offenses.

highly significant $(G^2(1) = 12.0; p = .000)$. The correlation between fitted and observed proportions was .62. Observed and fitted values are shown in Figure 8.1.

Summary of Penalty Effects

The evidence for a marginal specific deterrent effect of penalties is at best rather weak, using drink-drive recidivism as criterion and the relative severity measure as an index of perceived penalty severity. The results using criminal reconvictions are contrary to the predictions of a deterrent effect. However, there is strong and consistent evidence from an analysis of the relative severity categories and from the analysis based on appeal rates that penalties which are perceived as heavy relative to entitlement correspond to lower rates of traffic reconvictions among low risk offenders.

It is not clear, however, which components of the penalty are most effective. In order to answer this question it is necessary to incorporate the actual penalties in the analysis. Results of these analyses are summarized below in the context of the offender typology.

A Typology of the Convicted Drinking Driver

Detailed analysis of the correlations between reconvictions and penalties, controlling for offender and offense characteristics (Homel, 1981a), generally supported the impression gained from the analysis of the relative severity measures that the hypothesis of marginal specific deterrence is not supported. Consistent with the analysis of Table 8.1, no kind of penalty appeared to be more effective than any other in deterring offenders from reoffending for criminal offenses. Moreover, with the exception of offenders who were convicted of driving while disqualified at the same time as their drink-drive conviction, neither heavy fines nor long disqualification periods were more effective than light fines or short disqualification periods in reducing the rate of reconvictions for drinking and driving. Surprisingly, for offenders with a concurrent conviction for driving while disqualified, heavy fines, and to a lesser extent long periods of disqualification, were associated with lower drink-drive recidivism rates. However it is possible that these results are due to some of these offenders being imprisoned for nonpayment of fines, so the evidence for deterrent effects in this group was equivocal.

Paralleling the relative severity analyses, the major evidence for deterrence from the analysis of actual penalties emerged for good risk offenders, defined as those not reconvicted for a drink-drive or criminal offense for 3 years. For these offenders license disqualification appeared to be the most effective deterrent, since longer periods of disqualification corresponded to lower reconviction rates, controlling for all other factors. The optimum period of disqualification was around 18 months, or 3 years for offenders with a concurrent conviction for a serious traffic offense. Serious traffic offenders, including those convicted of offenses such as driving dangerously or without stopping after an accident, were reconvicted for traffic offenses at a much higher rate than other good risk offenders. For example, reconviction rates for those disqualified for 3 months were 48% for those with a conviction for a serious traffic offense, but only 21% for other good risk offenders.

It is noteworthy that after the introduction of appropriate controls, analysis of disqualification periods of up to 18 months duration suggested that for all groups of offenders longer periods of disqualification were not associated with higher rates of driving while disqualified than shorter periods. Thus the disqualification period itself does not seem to be a major factor in determining the likelihood of driving while disqualified.

In view of the recent popularity in the United States of mandatory imprisonment for drink-drivers (Voas, 1986), it is of interest that in the present study imprisonment was no more effective than any other penalty for any group of offenders. Indeed, there was strong evidence that longer periods of imprisonment, especially beyond 6 months, encourage reoffending, especially for drinking and driving.

Good Risk Versus Bad Risk Offenders

It was convenient for purposes of analysis to distinguish good risk from bad risk offenders on the basis of their performance over the 3-year period of the follow-up. This procedure raises an obvious problem, however: How is it possible to determine at the time of sentencing which offenders are good risks with respect to criminal and drink-drive offenses? It is all very well, on the basis of offenders' actual performances over the 3 years from conviction, to identify the group for whom disqualification appears to be a deterrent. But can this identification be made on independent grounds?

The simple answer to this question is that reliable identification of good risks *on an individual basis* cannot be made using the kind of data collected in this study, since the models which can be constructed from official records do not have sufficient predictive power to label individual offenders correctly. At the very best they can be used to identify small subgroups of offenders at either extreme, most of whom either will or will not be reconvicted, leaving the majority in an "undecided" category. However, it is possible to describe in general terms which factors tend to distinguish offenders reconvicted for drink-drive or criminal offenses from the remaining offenders. This does not amount to prediction, but it does allow some light to be shed on the characteristics of the subsample of offenders for whom long disqualification periods appear to have some effect. This information is of limited value to the sentencing magistrate, but it is useful for research purposes.

Offenders reconvicted for drinking and driving or for a criminal offense (i.e., high risk offenders) were more likely than other offenders to be: (a) younger — offenders under 21 years in particular were much more likely to be reconvicted for criminal offenses; (b) widowed, separated, or living in a de facto relationship; (c) convicted at the same time as the drink-drive offense for driving while disqualified, breaching the conditions of a bond, larceny, or breaking, entering, and stealing; (d) of lower occupational status; (e) of low to average BAC (up to .15), which reflects their youth; (f) not legally represented; and (g) recidivist with respect to criminal offenses, although not with respect to traffic or drink-drive offenses. Conversely, good risk offenders (those not reconvicted for drink-drive or criminal offenses) were more likely than others to be: (a) over 35 years old; (b) married; (c) free of concurrent convictions in addition to drinking and driving; (d) high occupational status; (e) high BAC (over .23); (f) legally represented; and (g) free of previous criminal convictions.

Obviously these attributes are correlated. Linear models analysis identified age, marital status, and driving while disqualified as sufficient to discriminate between the groups. The predictive power of the model was only $R^2 = .12$, which reinforces the comments made before about the unreliability of using these data as a guide to sentencing. To the extent that the analysis provides any guide to sentencing, it suggests that the older, married, white-collar, or skilled offender with a high BAC and no criminal record should be disqualified for much longer periods than is usual at the present time, at least in Australia. He is relatively unlikely to be reconvicted for a drink-drive or criminal offense, and the longer period of disqualification may, on the evidence of the analysis presented in this section, discourage him from committing a traffic offense, at least for a period of

Table 8.2. Overview of typology of convicted drink-drivers

	Increasing range and seriousness of offenses for which offenders will be reconvicted		
Never reconvicted for drinking and driving/generally responsive to license disqualification	(A) Never convicted again driver	(B) Minor traffic offender	(C) Serious traffic offender
Eventually reconvicted for drinking and driving/generally no more responsive to heavy penalties than light penalties	(D) Dedicated (or specialist) drinking driver	(E) Criminal offender	(F) Drive-disqualified offender

time. Of course in practice this type of offender is most likely to be dealt with leniently (Homel, 1983b).

The Typology

On the basis of the detailed analyses of penalty effects, it is possible to identify six types of offenders. These types can be organized into a pattern, as depicted in Table 8.2. The simplest way of distinguishing the groups is to separate those who will eventually be reconvicted for drinking and driving from those who will not (or who probably will not). This method of classification also corresponds (more or less) to whether or not offenders are responsive to penalties, although the apparent impact of fines among the *drive-disqualified* group is an exception to this rule. Within each of these two categories there are three groups, which can be arranged in order according to the range and seriousness of offenses for which their members will probably be reconvicted. Thus those offenders who will probably never be reconvicted for drinking and driving can be ordered from the *never convicted again* to the *serious traffic offender*, while those reconvicted for drinking and driving can be ordered from the *dedicated drinking driver* to the *drive-disqualified offender*, who commits practically every kind of offense.

The Never Convicted Again Driver

A comparison with the general driving population and with those convicted of criminal offenses at magistrates' courts (Homel, 1986) suggests that drink-drivers are midway between these two groups in terms of age and criminal record. Convicted drink-drivers tend to be younger than the average motorist but older than other criminal offenders, while fewer of them have a criminal record than is usual for magistrates' court offenders. This finding is consistent with the hypothesis that some drink-drivers are "normal motorists" who, apart from their conviction for drinking and driving, are otherwise law-abiding, or perhaps more precisely, that there are more drink-drivers than offenders of other kinds who are otherwise law-abiding. It is equally consistent with the two other hypotheses that some drink-drivers are older problem drinkers or alcoholics who repeatedly drink and drive but do not commit criminal offenses, and that some drink-drivers are specialist traffic offenders.

The existence of a group of drivers who will henceforth go straight in all respects (or who at least will not get caught) is supported by the analysis of long-term reconviction rates which indicated that somewhere around 40% of offenders will never record another conviction for anything. The precise value of this figure is not important; it is sufficient for present purposes to know that there are some offenders in this category. Of course only some of those who will never be reconvicted will never reoffend, and in theory it is possible that all of the 40% will reoffend without getting caught. This is unlikely, however, especially if very minor traffic offenses are excluded.

The data analyses suggest that the *never convicted again driver* will (more likely than not) have no concurrent conviction for driving while disqualified or for serious traffic or criminal offenses, and that he will tend to be a married man in his thirties or forties. However, it is important to note that as many as a third of the offenders with a concurrent conviction for driving while disqualified will never be reconvicted for anything, and that therefore at least some of them can be numbered among those who will go straight. Nevertheless the never convicted again driver is generally similar to the good risk offender described before. He will tend to be white collar in occupation and legally represented, although again it is necessary to note that 60% of the unskilled offenders remained free of convictions for 3 years. Since he is older than average, he is quite likely to have previous convictions for drinking and driving or for traffic offenses, and may well have recorded a high BAC at his last conviction for drinking and driving. He is less likely than average to have a *criminal* record.

It is possible that the never convicted again drivers learned their lesson after one or more convictions, but it is equally possible that they matured or moved out of the social group that encouraged certain types of offenses. Whether the never convicted again drivers have been deterred by penalties is ultimately a matter for conjecture in the absence of any information on a matched group of offenders who have never been caught or punished. The analysis of traffic reconvictions would suggest that good risk offenders, some of whom are among the never convicted again group, are responsive to disqualification and that it therefore acts as a deterrent. In view of

Figure 2.3 and the argument presented by Homel (1983c), an equally likely explanation is that the drivers who will never be reconvicted, being older and of higher occupational status, may be less visible to the police than younger lower status offenders, and may therefore escape detection even if they commit traffic offenses (including drinking and driving) from time to time. In any case, the point of the present argument is that there is a group who have ceased to come to the attention of the law, regardless of the cause.

MINOR TRAFFIC OFFENDERS

A group of good risk offenders closely related to the never convicted again drivers are those who continue to commit minor traffic offenses such as drinking and driving or driving while disqualified. We might label this group *minor traffic offenders*. Since we are considering a wide of range of common offenses, such as negligent driving and speeding, the minor traffic offender is likely to be much more common than the never convicted again driver. Unlike the never convicted again driver, the minor traffic offender is indistinguishable from other offenders in terms of age, marital status, occupational status, BAC, or likelihood of being legally represented. He is, in other words, the "average drinking driver" in many respects. He is unlike the majority only in that he is less likely to have a current conviction for criminal offenses or driving while disqualified, and he is less likely to have a record of convictions for drinking and driving. He is average with respect to current or previous traffic offenses, but appears to be responsive to license disqualification.

DEDICATED DRINKING DRIVERS

Just as the data imply the existence of two good risk groups (minor traffic offenders and those never convicted again) it is even more clear that at the other end of the spectrum some offenders are *dedicated* or *specialist drinking drivers* who are no more deterred by heavy penalties than by light penalties and probably deserve the label "alcoholic." For the majority of offenders, neither type nor severity of penalty made much difference to the likelihood that an offender would be reconvicted for drinking and driving. Dedicated drinking drivers seem to be drawn from all occupational groups, and to the extent that legal representation is an indicator of income, from all income groups. Offenders who were separated, widowed, or living in a de facto relationship were more likely than others to be reconvicted for drinking and driving, indicating the importance of domestic stress or unstable personal relationships, but contrary to what we might expect BAC was not particularly useful in differentiating those who were reconvicted from those who were not.

This last finding appears to be inconsistent with the contention that dedicated drinking drivers are mostly alcoholics, if we take a high BAC reading as evidence of alcoholism. High BAC offenders were no more likely than those with a low BAC to be reconvicted for drinking and driving. However, there are a number of other indications that alcohol is a particular problem for this group:(a) offenders with two or more previous convictions for drinking and driving were nearly twice as likely as others to be convicted for the same offense again, indicating that for some offenders drinking and driving is a persistent behavior pattern; (b) those reconvicted for drinking and driving tended to record much higher BACs than average at their second offense; (c) offenders with a high BAC were more likely to be reconvicted for driving during their disqualification period, indicating that they were probably not in control of either their drinking or their driving; and (d) among those reconvicted, older men were more likely to be reconvicted for drink-driving alone, while young men were more likely to commit a variety of offenses, particularly criminal offenses.

What all this adds up to is a picture of the dedicated drinking driver as an older man with a high BAC, two or more previous drink-drive convictions, and a strong tendency to commit no offenses other than drinking and driving. This does not prove that he is what would usually be called an alcoholic or problem drinker, but it seems the most likely explanation.

Before leaving the dedicated drinking driver group it is worth noting that they are probably a minority among all convicted drink-drivers, since only about a quarter or a fifth of drink-drivers will eventually be reconvicted for the same offense. This implies that only a minority continue to offend on a regular basis, since it is necessary to repeat the offense to have a high chance of getting caught. It is also quite possible that many drink-drivers are alcoholics who do not fall into the dedicated drinking driver category. However, in order to identify these offenders it would be necessary to have finer measures than BAC and previous drink-drive convictions. The converse hypothesis seems well established; namely, that the majority, if not all, the persistent drink-drivers are problem drinkers or alcoholics.

CRIMINAL OFFENDERS

It was noted under (d) in the previous section that there is evidence for the existence of a group of young offenders who commit a variety of criminal offenses: for them, drinking and driving simply occurred along the way. This is consistent with the analysis of criminal reconvictions, which indicated that that the factors that were predictive of a reconviction for a criminal offense were generally *not* predictive of a reconviction for a drink-drive offense.

Criminal offenders share with the dedicated drinking drivers the characteristics of being unaffected by type or severity of penalty and also of being more likely than other groups to be single, separated, or living in a de facto relationship. Beyond this, however, there is a strong tendency for them to be young (under 20 years old) with a criminal record and concurrent convictions for offenses like larceny, breaking, entering, and stealing, and breaching the conditions of a bond. In addition, they tend to record *low* BACs, are mostly of low occupational status (especially unskilled), and are less likely to be legally represented than other offenders. This last characteristic probably reflects low income as well as attitudes of conflict with authority and a lack of sophistication in knowing how to negotiate situations to their best advantage. Finally, the criminal offender is likely to come into conflict with the law in a number of ways, and one has the impression that drinking and driving is often an incidental part of a much wider range of illegal or antisocial activities.

SERIOUS TRAFFIC OFFENDERS

So far we have identified the never convicted again driver, the minor traffic offender, the dedicated drinking driver, and the criminal offender. Two other groups can be identified: the *serious traffic offender* and the *drive disqualified offender*. The serious traffic offender is less likely than average to be reconvicted for drinking and driving but is much more likely than others to be reconvicted for a nondrink-drive traffic offense. He is no more likely than others to have a past or current criminal record, despite the fact that he is considerably younger than other offenders (probably under 24 years), but he is more likely to have concurrent convictions for both minor traffic offenses (speeding, etc.) and for offenses like assaulting police, resisting arrest, or offensive behavior. He is drawn from all occupational and income groups (using legal representation as an index of the latter).

In discussing the serious traffic offender it is important to note that we are describing a small minority of offenders. In the study only about 2.6% of offenders recorded a conviction for serious traffic offenses at the same time as their conviction for drinking and driving, and even allowing that a conviction for a serious traffic offense is only one manifestation of the serious traffic offender, they are probably still relatively few in number. Most of them probably occur in the good risk group, but are atypical of the majority of motorists in this group in that they are young and likely to record convictions for offenses like resisting arrest. Generally young men were no more likely than older men to be reconvicted for a nondrink-drive traffic offense.

Apart from his tendency to commit traffic offenses in preference to drinking and driving or criminal offenses, the serious traffic offender is distinguished from the criminal offender and the dedicated drinking driver by being (apparently) responsive to license disqualification. Although there are too few serious traffic offenders in the sample to establish firm conclusions, the analysis of nondrink-drive traffic offenses indicated that many offenders who did not commit drink-drive or criminal offenses were deterred or delayed in committing traffic offenses. On the other hand the serious traffic offender is like the criminal offender in being young, this being one of the major differences between both those groups and the dedicated drinking drivers.

The relative youthfulness of the serious traffic offender and the criminal offender may be a partial explanation for their tendency to be convicted for offenses such as assaulting police and resisting arrest. As Macmillan (1975) notes, "The youngest drivers are more competitive and aggressive, they drive faster, and they are more tolerant of 'moving' traffic offenses and non-traffic offenses" (p. 191). It is reasonable to suppose that these attitudes, especially an aggressive stance, spill over from their road behavior to their interaction with the police, particularly if alcohol is present as an aggravating factor. It is noteworthy that offenders reconvicted for drinking and driving, and by implication the dedicated drinking drivers, were *not* more likely to record these kinds of convictions than other groups. This is consistent with our view of these offenders as older and nondelinquent in other respects than drinking and driving.

DRIVE-DISQUALIFIED OFFENDERS

The final group that stands out in the present study is the *drive while disqualified offenders*. These offenders tended to be reconvicted at a higher rate, and were reconvicted more quickly. They were particularly at risk of being reconvicted for drinking and driving and for criminal offenses, although they were no more likely than other offenders to commit other traffic offenses. They were also more likely to repeat the offense of driving while disqualified, even allowing for the fact that they were more at risk since they were disqualified for longer periods. Consistent with Robinson's (1977) study of disqualified motorists, which used a mail questionnaire, the drive-disqualified offender in the present study strongly resembled those with a propensity to commit criminal offenses. However, they were distinguished from the criminal group by having in addition a deviant record for serious traffic offenses, including drinking and driving.

In short, drive-disqualified offenders seemed to combine the characteristics of the criminal offender and the dedicated drinking driver. They were the most deviant group to emerge in the study, although on the positive side they did not commit traffic offenses at a higher rate and it is possible they were responsive to heavy fines.

An Overview of the Typology

The detailed characteristics of each of the six groups are summarized in Table 8.3.

In interpreting Tables 8.2 and 8.3 it should be remembered that the groups are blurred at the edges, and that some offenders may be able to be assigned to more than one group. This is where there is a need for more detailed data. The groups are also based mainly on the current and future behavior of offenders, rather than on their previous records. Although the correspondence between previous record and group membership is generally what would be expected, there is considerable overlap between the groups. For example, many offenders in all groups had a record for traffic offenses or for drinking and driving, and therefore this information is of limited value in distinguishing one kind of offender from another.

Moreover, the typology revolves around reconvictions rather than reoffending. It would be possible to substitute the latter for the former term without altering the typology drastically, but it seems more sensible, in a study based on reconviction data, to be cautious in what is claimed. Obviously some modifications would be required if the typology were reformulated in terms of reoffending. For example, the never convicted again group would have to be split into the genuinely reformed or deterred and those who reoffend without being caught.

Finally, it is not possible or desirable in the present study to determine exactly how many offenders there are in each group. This is partly because of the overlap between groups, and partly because reconviction, rather than reoffending, is used as a criterion. For example, offenders convicted for driving while disqualified are relatively few in number, but surveys suggest that as many as 60% of offenders may commit the offense (Robinson, 1977). The analysis at this point is intended to be qualitative rather than quantitative.

Implications of the Penalties Study for the Deterrence Model

Although in the RBT study not all predictions flowing from the deterrence model were fulfilled, on the whole the model worked well as a description of the relationships between variables. The opposite is true for the results of the penalties study. Despite some indications that longer disqualification periods and (perhaps) heavier fines may be more effective than lighter penalties as deterrents for some offenders, on the whole the evidence is contrary to the predictions of a marginal specific deterrent effect.

The analysis which was framed in terms of relative penalty severity failed to yield evidence for marginal specific deterrence which was any stronger than that flowing from the analysis of actual penalties. The appeal rate data presented in Table 7.4 and Figure 7.1, together with other evidence cited in Chapter 7, suggest that the relative severity measure is a valid index of perceived penalty severity, and so the mostly null results obtained using this measure strengthen the argument that marginal specific deterrence is not a consequence of more severe punishments.

Nevertheless, the results which are consistent with predictions of the deterrence model do indicate that specific deterrence may occur in some

TABLE 8.3. Predominant characteristics of the hypothesized six groups of convicted drink-drivers

	(A) Never convicted again driver	(B) Minor traffic offender	(C) Serious traffic offender
Personal characteristics	Married Aged 35 and above Records a *high* BAC Tendency to be white collar and legally represented	Drawn from all age groups and in most respects the "average" convicted drink-driver	Under 24 years Drawn from all occupational and income groups
Previous and current record	Has record for drinking and driving and for traffic offenses Has no previous or current criminal record Not currently convicted of driving while disqualified Not currently convicted of traffic offenses	Less likely to have previous drink-drive conviction Not currently convicted of driving while disqualified or criminal offenses	Has current convictions for traffic offenses, some of them serious Has current convictions for offences like resisting arrest and offensive behavior Has criminal record
Response to penalties	May be deterred by disqualification	Responsive to disqualification Likely to be reconvicted for a minor traffic offense	Responsive to disqualification Unlikely to be reconvicted for drinking and driving Likely to be reconvicted for a traffic offense and for a criminal offense

	(D) Dedicated drinking driver	(E) Criminal offender	(F) Drive-disqualified offender
Personal characteristics	Possible marital disruption Older than 30 years High BAC Drawn from all income and occupational groups	Single, separated or living in a de facto relationship Under 24 years Low BAC Low income and unskilled	Single or living de facto Unskilled and low income All BAC levels
Previous and current record	History of two or more drink-drive convictions Doesn't commit criminal or traffic offenses	Previous and current criminal record "Average" record for traffic and drink-drive offenses Concurrent convictions for driving unlicensed	Two or more previous drink-drive convictions Five or more previous traffic offenses Criminal record Concurrent convictions for driving while disqualified Concurrent convictions for criminal offenses
Response to penalties	Penalty severity makes no difference Likely to be reconvicted for drinking and driving	Penalty severity makes no difference Likely to be re-reconvicted for a criminal offense Likely to be reconvicted for drinking and driving	May be responsive to heavy fines Likely to be reconvicted for *all* kinds of offenses

circumstances. The greater degree of responsiveness to arrest certainty exhibited by motorists with a drink-drive conviction in the RBT study (Fig. 6.5) suggests that for many offenders the experience of arrest and punishment has a deterrent impact, although the weaker results from the analysis that was restricted to self-reported drink-drivers should be kept in mind. In addition, the success of long disqualification periods in discouraging good risk offenders from committing traffic offenses suggests that deterrent objectives are achieved through license controls to some extent.

The typology described in the present chapter suggests the existence of several latent dimensions that, if made explicit, could advance the understanding of the causes of drink-driving, the nature of the role careers adopted by offenders, and the reasons why some forms of illegal behavior and some types of offenders are not adequately described within the framework of the deterrence model. These dimensions are discussed in the next chapter, as part of an overall appraisal of the deterrence model.

9
Implications of the Research

In this chapter the validity of the deterrence model developed in Chapter 2 is evaluated in the light of the data analyses carried out in Chapters 6 and 8, and the implications of the research for the operation of the criminal justice system are briefly considered.

The main results of each study are reviewed and considered in relation to the drink-drive and deterrence literatures. The RBT study is reviewed first, followed by the penalties study. Propositions in the deterrence model which may need to be modified are identified, as are aspects which require further research. The conclusion of the review of the evidence is that the predictions of the deterrence model are, on the whole, correct as a description of how RBT in New South Wales affected behavior (at least in the short term), but are incorrect with respect to the impact of severe punishments relative to the impact of lenient punishments imposed on convicted offenders.

Following the evaluation of the deterrence model, the implications of the study for social policy are considered briefly. The emphasis is on ways of improving both the deterrent effectiveness and the justice of the sentencing and enforcement processes.

The chapter concludes with a discussion of the behavioral impact of the criminal justice system on drink-drive behavior and the relationship between deterrence-based countermeasures and broader approaches to reducing the damage caused by road accidents.

Review of the Random Breath Test Study

It was emphasized in the description of RBT in Chapter 4 that the legislation was implemented and enforced in New South Wales with a thoroughness and rigor unprecedented in Australia and possibly anywhere else. Having made the decision to introduce RBT, the politicians committed the police to an extensive program of enforcement, and also committed millions of dollars for publicity of the police activity. In addition,

RBT was not introduced gradually, but all at once on a particular date. Thus in many ways conditions were ideal for a general deterrent effect to be realized, and for the effect to be measurable. Putting this proposition more forcefully, if in the first few months of its operation a close link between RBT enforcement and drink-drive behavior could not be demonstrated using the kind of model described in Chapter 2, it would probably be necessary to conclude that, as a goal, general deterrence of the drinking driver is a pure chimera.

The fatal crash data presented in Figure 4.2, as well as the other evidence cited in Chapter 4 (such as the reduced proportion of dead drivers with positive blood alcohol concentrations), are consistent with the argument that RBT was the cause of a sudden and apparently permanent decline in road deaths in New South Wales. If no decline in traffic crash rates had been discernible, it would have been hard to believe that RBT had had much impact. Note, however, that in the present study no great weight is being placed on the crash statistics, which, given the emphasis on the *process* of deterrence, essentially constitute a way of "setting the scene." The thrust of the present argument is that in order to demonstrate beyond a reasonable doubt that RBT was indeed the cause of the apparent drop in casualties and that the mechanism was deterrence, it is necessary to measure the key variables of exposure to RBT and perceptions of arrest probability, and to demonstrate that these are linked with drink-driving behavior in the manner depicted in Figure 2.2. The validity of the causal chain reflecting simple deterrence is therefore the central issue.

The major results of the study were summarized at the end of Chapter 6. It was concluded that the model of simple deterrence was supported, despite the partial failure of some measures, particularly perceived arrest certainty, to behave in all respects in the predicted manner. It is argued in this section that most of the puzzling aspects of the RBT analyses can be explained in terms of inadequate measures or in terms of unanticipated aspects of the operation of deterrence, rather than in terms of fundamental faults in the deterrence model. In particular, the weak (although statistically significant) nature of the relationships between many of the variables in Figure 2.2 is a result of limitations inherent in the survey method rather than a reflection of major theoretical deficiencies.

The Causal Chain Reflecting Simple Deterrence

THE OBJECTIVE LEGAL THREAT AND EXPOSURE TO THAT THREAT (Lp → Ex)

The high correlation (.79) between the intensity of police testing and the proportion tested in an area implies that both variables are reasonably reliable indicators of police RBT activity at the aggregate level. However, given the high proportion of inconsistent responses by motorists in the longitudinal analysis (discussed in Chapter 5), it appears that at the individual level the single question on the experience of being randomly tested (AQ2[a]) may have confused some respondents. Alternatively, the experience of being tested may not have made a strong enough impression to have been remembered 6 weeks later. In future research it will be necessary to clarify the question by separating the experience of the driver from that of the passenger. It may also be necessary to ask for details of the experience, perhaps by asking the respondent to "think aloud" (Loftus, Fienberg, & Tanur, 1985), in order to check that the driver was really tested by police conducting RBT.

The number of random tests conducted in an area correlated well with the proportion of motorists personally tested, but correlated less well with the number of people known to the respondent to have been tested. The number of acquaintances randomly tested was the one exposure variable which, after adjustment for other variables, correlated with arrest certainty, and it therefore constitutes a critical link between police testing and perceptions of arrest certainty. It is possible that the relatively low reliability of the personal exposure measure in the present study accounts for the fact that it did not play this mediating role, as it did for example in Åberg's (1986) study of Swedish drivers. In any case, the low positive correlation between intensity of testing and the number known to have been tested is not contrary to the predictions of the model, since many factors may influence the size of a motorist's network of friends and the speed with which information is communicated. Moreover, it seems obvious that a motorist must be tested personally before he can tell his friends of his experience, although the possibility that an encounter with the police might be misinterpreted as random breath testing cannot be discounted.

EXPOSURE TO THE LEGAL THREAT AND PERCEPTIONS OF THE PROPERTIES OF LEGAL PUNISHMENTS (Ex $\rightarrow$ Pp)

Apart from the possibility that the low reliability of the personal exposure measure is the problem, it is not clear why the experience of friends and acquaintances, rather than personal experience, should have been such an important factor in the formation of subjective arrest probabilities. In fact there was some evidence for the role of personal experience from the analysis of reasons for not drinking and driving. Those who had repeatedly or recently driven past an RBT operation were much more likely to nominate fear of arrest rather than fear of an accident as a reason for not drinking and driving. Nevertheless, the experiences of one's friends was the factor which most strongly correlated with the formal measure of arrest certainty, contrary to the results of the simulation study of Summers and Harris (1979), which pointed instead to media publicity and personal exposure.

In the present study, exposure to media publicity did not survive as a predictor of arrest certainty. Radio publicity correlated with arrest certainty, but when adjustments were made for area and for the number of friends tested, it dropped out of the model. The fact that area remained as a predictor in the model suggests that regional variations in the type or quantity of radio broadcasts concerning RBT may have influenced arrest scores. It should also be recalled that the arrest index had rather low reliability, and that some variables (such as radio publicity) may have been lost in the error variance. In addition, there was some evidence from the analysis of reasons for not drinking and driving that newspaper publicity may have caused people to be fearful of arrest. Nevertheless, the overall impression from all the analyses is that media publicity was less important as an influence on perceptions (and behaviors) than direct exposure to RBT in some form.

This conclusion is consistent with Åberg's (1986) Swedish research, but contrary to that of Mercer (1985), who evaluated the impact of a drink-driving blitz in British Columbia. However, in Mercer's study the majority of people questioned did not know a blitz was on, so the situation is not comparable with that in New South Wales or Sweden, where knowledge of the law and of enforcement activity is very widespread. It is probable that a certain level of publicity is essential so that police activity can create widespread fear, but beyond this point personal experience and that of one's friends is the important factor. If the critical expenditure on publicity (after the initial campaign) can be determined, campaigns like RBT may be able to be run successfully at a fraction of the cost of the New South Wales experiment.

A surprising result of the analysis of arrest certainty was that drink-driving since RBT did not result in lower perceptions of the likelihood of being tested or arrested. Such experiential effects have been common-ly found in previous research, and have even been advanced as the explanation for "deterrence relationships" in nonlongitudinal studies (Paternoster et al., 1982). It is possible that the short time (4 months) since the introduction of RBT was the reason for this result, or that the arrest index is faulty. A more interesting possibility is that those who drove over the limit since RBT reduced their estimates of the likelihood of arrest, as predicted, but were also more exposed to RBT than other groups and therefore their subjective arrest probabilities increased at some point. This suggests that the continuing enforcement of RBT may have countered the downward drift in arrest certainty due to experience. (This idea of deterrence as a dynamic process is pursued in more detail in the following section.)

PERCEPTIONS OF ARREST CERTAINTY AND BEHAVIOR CHANGE (Pp→ De)

Arrest certainty correlated with the number of modifications to both drinking and travel behaviors, even after adjustment for other variables.

The effect of arrest certainty was as marked as that of any other variable in the models, indicating that the fear created by RBT was a major influence on behavior. This inference is supported by the reasons which people gave for not drinking and driving, with those citing fear of arrest as a reason making more changes to their behavior than those who cited other reasons.

In addition, both area of residence and TV publicity predicted changes in travel arrangements (Fig. 6.3), while area predicted changes in drinking habits (Fig. 6.4). The regression coefficients for area indicated that behavior changes were least common in Newcastle, and most common (at least for travel) in Bathurst. The significance of these patterns is that they correspond exactly with the patterns for arrest certainty: residents of Newcastle had the lowest perceptions of the chances of arrest and Bathurst residents had the highest. This suggests that in the behavior change models the arrest index did not pick up all the variance associated with arrest certainty. The persistence of TV publicity as a predictor of changes in travel arrangements indicates the same problem, since theoretically television should have affected behavior via arrest certainty. The problem also appeared in the longitudinal analysis of travel changes, where two exposure variables predicted change but the subjective probability of being tested had no predictive power. Moreover, many of the correlations involving arrest certainty, although statistically significant, were small in magnitude and apparently subject to the effects of random error.

PERCEPTIONS OF PENALTY SEVERITY, BEHAVIOR CHANGE, AND
DRINKING AND DRIVING (Pp→ De→ Dr)

One of the most interesting results of the longitudinal analysis was finding that those who believed in February that penalties for drink-driving had increased were less likely than others to drive while intoxicated between interviews. A possible reason why this correlation was significant in the present study, when it has generally not been found in other research, is that the perceived severity of penalties only has predictive power when the perceived chances of arrest are high. It is likely that in previous research perceived arrest certainty varied within a range which is below the threshold required for penalty severity to have any influence on behavior.

Opposing this view, however, is the failure of perceived penalty severity in the present study to emerge as a significant predictor in the analyses of behavior change and the failure of the penalty severity/arrest certainty interaction to be significant. However, these results also need to be interpreted cautiously. The main question on penalty severity (AQ26) was based on the work of Grasmick and Bryjak (1980), and focused on the respondent's own subjective estimate of the perceived costs of the legal punishment (". . . how big a problem would that punishment be in your life?"). Unfortunately this measure did not correlate with many other variables, and may have had low reliability. This is a pity, since the wording of

238 9. Implications of the Research
9. Implications of the Research

the question is an intelligent attempt to get at evaluations of penalty severity, rather than at perceptions of what the penalties actually are (Tittle, 1980a; Grasmick & Green, 1980). Although Paternoster and Iovanni (1986) argue that Grasmick and Bryjak's "refined measure" confounds the threat of legal sanctions with the fear of informal penalties, such an explanation seems unlikely in the present study, since informal sanctions imposed for drink-driving are not a major factor in Australian culture. If such penalties had been an important consideration for the respondents in this study, we would have expected stronger correlations with the Grasmick/ Bryjak measure. As it is, the variable was a complete washout. Although this could be because perceptions of legal penalties simply were not important to respondents, the fact that perceptions of penalty increases with the RBT law proved to have some predictive power points instead to the failure of the Grasmick/Bryjak question to achieve the goal of capturing reactions to legal punishments.

Further evidence for the value of the "penalty increase" question comes from the longitudinal analysis, where (contrary to the pattern for the majority of respondents), motorists with a conviction who believed in February that penalties had become more severe stepped up the number of ways in which they were modifying their travel arrangements. Although not highly significant, the interaction is important since convicted drivers could be expected to be particularly responsive to the threat of further punishment. A balanced conclusion on the importance of penalty severity would be that when the perceived chances of arrest are high, perceived penalty severity can have some deterrent impact in addition to that of arrest certainty, particularly among those who have already suffered legal punishments for drinking and driving. This conclusion is consistent with the propositions of the deterrence model.

Changes in Behavior and Self-Reported Drinking and Driving (De → Dr)

This is the final link in the causal chain. The link was not confirmed empirically in the longitudinal analysis, partly because there were too few cases of drink-driving for reliable analysis, but mostly because a third wave of interviews would be required to correlate changes in the number of attempts to avoid drink-driving with subsequent drink-driving behavior.

Measurement Errors and Weak Correlations

In the light of the previous discussion, it is reasonable to conclude that the deterrence model is accurate, but that the key measures were less than completely reliable and were too limited in scope. For example, the low correlations between exposure to RBT and arrest certainty should be seen partly as a consequence of measurement errors and partly as a consequence of using measures which are too simple for the phenomenon under investigation. To illustrate this last point, there are many aspects of exposure which could influence an individual's perceptions and evaluations of the likelihood of arrest — the particular location of the RBT operation (are there obvious escape routes?), the time of day or night, the presence of particular police officers (some respondents believed that they had some chance of talking their way out of a positive breath analysis), the percentage of vehicles observed being pulled over, and so on. The link between the experiences of friends and an individual's perceptions of arrest certainty may also depend on which particular friends have been tested, how often, and how recently. Given the multitude of variables which could be critical in the deterrence process and the limited number of variables which can be derived from a short interview, it is not surprising that the overall predictive powers of the linear models were less than 50%, and that the variances explained by individual variables were much less.

Moreover, the measurement of behavior change posed a very difficult problem. The concept of deterrence (De) implies that on occasions when driving over the legal limit is a possibility, motorists will, because of the fear of legal punishment, alter their behavior to ensure compliance with the law. This suggests that a measure of De should be based on the number of times a motorist has taken steps to avoid drink-driving during (for example) the last 3 months, expressed as a proportion of all occasions when he was tempted to drive after drinking. However, the practical difficulties involved in constructing such a measure, even with the use of diary techniques, are all too apparent. The measures used in this study, which focus on the range of strategies currently being employed because of RBT to avoid drink-driving, get around the practical problems but suffer from the limitation that because they are uncontrolled for the number of *possible* drink-driving occasions, the changes in behavior of heavy drinkers may be overstated. Thus although heavy drinkers may report more strategies to avoid drinking and driving, expressed as a proportion of possible drink-drive occasions, their level of compliance with the law may not be as high as that of light drinkers who are seldom at risk but who are always careful to avoid driving over the limit.

Although there is no completely satisfactory way around this problem using the present measures, it should be noted that, in view of the literature, the fact that heavy drinkers reported *any* behavior change as a result of RBT is significant. Moreover, the behavior measures correlate in predictable ways with the exposure and perceptual variables, and these correlations are consistent with analyses based on crash data (e.g., Kearns & Goldsmith, 1984) and on roadside survey data (McLean et al., 1984). The general point which should be emphasized is that despite variables with a less than optimum level of reliability, and despite the survey researcher's inability to measure all the aspects of an individual's experiences, perceptions, and evaluations which might be argued a priori to be of importance, the statistically significant correlations between theoretically critical variables, as well as the agreement with analyses based on different types of data, point to the existence of underlying relationships which are consistent with the deterrence model. This is particularly the case when the correlations persist after the inclusion of statistical controls for "extraneous variables," such as age and sex.

Informal Sanctions

More than a quarter of drinking license holders reported difficulty in a group situation in resisting the pressure to drink. Moreover, these people were more likely than others to report that RBT had made the problem harder, not easier. The questionnaire provides few clues on why, overall, 1 drinking license holder in 12 blamed RBT for their increased difficulties. In some cases the reasons may relate to the dynamics of the group situations heavy drinkers find themselves in, with drinking and risk taking being seen as badges of manhood. However the data do not indicate that the problem was particularly restricted to men, or to young people, so care should be taken not to rely too heavily for an explanation on the culture of the pub. As Sargent (1979) notes, in the middle classes the unspoken rules of "shouting" (i.e., standing one's drinking companions a round of drinks) probably still apply, but research is badly needed to clarify the ways in which social pressure is conveyed when rules are relaxed or modified. Indeed, some of the top priorities for future research must be to extend Gusfield's (1981a) ethnographic research on the culture of bars, and to examine the processes by which societal subgroups influence their individual members (Clark & Powell, 1984; Snortum, Kremer, & Berger, 1987).

From the point of view of deterrence theory, it is noteworthy that the effects on behavior of perceived change in pressure to drink were no greater than the effects of arrest certainty. This result is important, since it is contrary to the common assumption that deterrence effects are small relative to the effects of informal sanctions like social stigma (Grasmick & Green, 1980). Another noteworthy feature of the behavior change analysis was that arrest certainty and pressure to drink appeared to act in an additive rather than an interactive fashion. In other words, the influence of arrest certainty on the number of modifications to travel and drinking behaviors did not depend on the extent to which the respondent felt subject to group pressures to drink. In this respect the results are consistent with most other studies of the perceptual elements in the deterrence process (e.g., Grasmick & Green, 1980).

There was one exception to the overall finding of no interactions between arrest certainty and peer pressure. In the longitudinal analysis, among those who reported finding it hard to resist the pressure to drink, an increase in the perceived likelihood of being randomly tested corresponded to a decline in the number of modifications to travel methods. One explanation for this result is that among these heavy drinkers, fear of ostracism by peers (a certain loss) outweighed the fear of legal punishments (a possible loss). There is evidence that because RBT simultaneously affected perceptions of formal and informal sanctions, it had contradictory effects on some people. For example, those who reported finding it harder since RBT to resist group pressure made fewer than average changes to their travel and drinking behaviors, yet these people scored more highly than average on the arrest index, even after adjustment for other variables (Fig. 6.2), and also were much more likely to cite fear of arrest as their main reason for not drinking and driving. Thus depending on the relative strengths of the two types of fears, RBT may actually have had an effect on some heavy drinkers opposite to what was intended.

These results illustrate the appropriateness of the parallelogram of forces analogy employed in the description of the deterrence process. What is needed now is research which throws light on how individuals resolve the psychological tensions created by these contradictory pressures. Such research should be focused on the decision-making process, and should be directed at those individuals who feel most sensitive to the threat of being exposed as an incompetent drinker.

Who Was Most Deterred by RBT?

Four groups of variables are of particular theoretical interest: age and sex, socioeconomic status (occupation and education), alcohol consumption and peer pressure to drink, and having a drink-drive conviction.

AGE AND SEX

In Chapter 1, it was argued that young men are the object of more intensive police surveillance and harsher punishments for drink-driving than other groups of road users (Homel, 1983c). Presumably one of the reasons for this bias is the belief that young men are a high risk group who can be deterred by harsh measures. It is therefore important to investigate whether age or sex affected the extent to which an individual was influenced by RBT.

It would appear that although RBT was not particularly directed at men or at young motorists, it had just as great an impact among young men as it did among women or older men. Indeed, the evidence suggests that as a result of RBT young men may have changed their lifestyles in more ways than average. This conclusion is consistent with the statistical analyses of accident data (Kearns & Goldsmith, 1984). More generally, the evidence from the analysis of the data on motivations pointed to the role of fear of arrest as a factor that influenced the responses of men. It does seem that, based upon the respondents' own reasons for their behavior, men were more deterred by RBT than women, an outcome which is highly desirable given that probably about 85% of drinking drivers in Australia are men.

One implication of these results is that enforcement policies aimed specifically at high risk groups may not be necessary, and indeed may not be as effective as more broadly based policies like RBT.

SOCIOECONOMIC STATUS

Socioeconomic status is of interest for many of the same reasons as age and sex. In particular, Andenaes (1978) has argued that high status motorists are underrepresented in the conviction statistics for drinking and driving because they are more deterred by the threat of legal and informal punishments than are low status motorists. He rejects the view that discrimination by those in power has anything to do with differential conviction rates for drinking and driving. His argument about the deterrability of high status motorists is contrary to the conclusions of Grasmick, Jacobs, and McCollum (1983), and his position on discrimination is contrary to data presented by Hollinger (1984).

Both education and occupation remained in the reduced model for arrest certainty (Fig. 6.2), with lower white-collar respondents and those with 3 to 5 years of high school education recording the highest arrest scores. In other words, the shape of the relationship between arrest certainty and socioeconomic status was roughly an inverted U. Occupation was significant as a predictor of changes in travel and drinking behaviors, but this factor dropped out of the model when it was adjusted for age and other variables. In addition, the interactions between arrest score and education and occupation failed to reach significance.

It is hard not to conclude that RBT had roughly the same behavioral impact at all status levels. If this result can be generalized to the effects of the regular enforcement of drink-drive law, the predominantly low status of convicted offenders must be ascribed to police bias or exposure to risk (e.g., amount and place of driving), rather than to differential deterrability, as Andenaes (1978) suggests.

ALCOHOL CONSUMPTION

Alcohol consumption and perceived pressure to drink are of obvious theoretical importance. Much of the debate about who the drinking driver is centers around the question of alcohol use and alcoholism (see Chapter 1), and it is frequently proposed that the heavier an individual's alcohol consumption, the less deterrable he will be (Cameron, 1979).

One of the most clear-cut findings of the study was that the greater a respondent's consumption of alcohol and the greater the perceived pressure on him to drink, the more ways he was modifying both his drinking habits and his travel arrangements (Fig. 6.3 and 6.4). With the exception of the small group of drinkers who reported that resisting pressure was "extremely hard," the longitudinal analysis of changes in travel modifications revealed a similar pattern (Fig. 6.6). This leads to the important conclusion that a campaign like RBT can have a greater impact on the lifestyles of heavy drinkers than moderate or light drinkers. Of course, as noted earlier, heavy drinkers have more opportunities to drink and drive than light or moderate drinkers and would therefore have more scope for changes in their habits, but this does not invalidate the conclusion that RBT had a greater than average impact on their lives.

The significance of this finding should not be underestimated. Not only did more respondents change their drinking habits rather than their travel methods, which in itself is a result one would not have predicted, the moderate and heavy drinkers changed *both* their drinking and their travel habits more than light drinkers. The enthusiasm with which heavy drinkers modified their travel methods might have been predicted, but hardly their willingness to reduce or alter the pattern of their alcohol consumption. Thus it seems that at least some individuals who might have been considered undeterrable were in fact the most responsive to the threat of legal punishments. In this connection it is noteworthy that Snortum and colleagues (1986), in a comparison of compliance with drink-drive law in Norway and the United States, found that 85% of Norwegian respondents who usually reach high blood alcohol levels when they drink claimed total abstention on the last drinking occasion when they had the responsibility of driving home. The authors comment that "this seems 'too good to be true' for it violates our assumptions about the limits of self-control among problem drinkers" (p. 161). In view of the evidence, perhaps it is time to reconsider conventional ideas about alcohol dependence and problem drinking.

However, lest we become intoxicated with the prospect of success at last with the problem drinker, we need to recall some sobering exceptions to the rosy picture of the suddenly temperate toper. The main problem was peer pressure, with heavy alcohol consumption being associated in a number of cases with feelings that RBT had made it harder, not easier, to resist the pressure to drink. As we have seen, the effects of such feelings were to create contradictory psychological pressures for at least some respondents. Consequently, although in general the social climate among moderate and heavy drinkers seemed to favor a definite positive response to RBT, these effects could have become blunted over time by increased drinking caused by fear of losing status as a competent drinker.

DRINK-DRIVE CONVICTIONS

A central prediction of deterrence theory is that motorists with a drink-drive conviction will be more responsive to the threat of legal punishments than those without a conviction (Tittle, 1980a). Convicted motorists are not predicted to be more *sensitive* to legal punishments (that is, to have higher arrest scores), since there is no reason why a conviction should make one believe that arrest is more likely (if one is an experienced drinking driver, it might even have the opposite effect).

The interaction between arrest certainty and a conviction (Fig. 6.5) is consistent with this prediction of greater responsiveness. The members of the convicted group, although few in number, appeared to make more changes in their travel arrangements when arrest certainty was high; at low arrest levels the difference between the two groups was quite small. In addition, those with a conviction cited fear of arrest more often than those without a conviction as a factor influencing their decision not to drink and drive. The greater number of changes in travel arrangements which were made by the convicted group in between interviews (Fig. 6.6), especially if they believed penalties had become more severe, was also consistent with the predictions of the deterrence model. These results strongly imply that convicted drink-drivers are more responsive to legal threats than motorists without a conviction, and that both arrest certainty *and* penalty severity are important components of that threat.

Deterrence as an Unstable Process

Ross (1982) has hypothesized that the impact of legal innovations like RBT are temporary because people realize after a while that the chances of getting caught are not as high as they thought at first. This hypothesis was supported in the longitudinal analysis, since it was shown that the perceived chances of being randomly tested declined between interviews, despite the publicity campaign and the police blitz over Easter. Nevertheless there was no change, on average, in the number of ways in which motorists were modifying their drinking habits and travel methods. Moreover, there were no significant correlations between changes in the perceived chance of being tested and changes in behavior.

It should be recalled that the interviews were only 6 weeks apart, and that therefore conclusions about the long term impact of RBT are not possible. However, the 6-week period was sufficiently long to reveal considerable variations between subgroups in modifications to travel arrangements (Fig. 6.6). Those who had been tested or had driven past an RBT operation between interviews increased the modifications to their travel methods, while those who had driven while intoxicated since RBT reduced the modifications to their travel methods. These results suggest *a dynamic and unstable situation*, with a constantly changing mix of those deterred through personal exposure to RBT and those "undeterred" through a successful drink-driving episode or through nonexposure to the operation of RBT. If RBT had not been enforced at all between February and April 1983, it is likely that the April interview would have revealed a substantial decline overall in attempts to avoid drinking and driving.

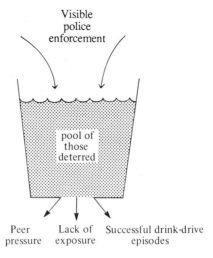

FIGURE 9.1. The "hole in the bucket model" of the deterrent impact of RBT.

The data analyses, including those focused on peer pressure and on the experiential hypothesis, suggest that RBT is always in the process of losing its effectiveness among drivers who, because they feel under pressure to drink or because they have not seen RBT in operation for some time, take the risk of driving after drinking. However, through personal exposure to RBT new groups of motorists are constantly being added to the pool of those who are deterred. This model of the deterrence process is a little less static than the picture proposed in Chapter 2, and bears an affinity to Cook's (1980) simulation model of the criminal behavior of a population of robbers. A feature of Cook's model is that there is considerable turnover among active robbers: "robbers are deterred and 'undeterred' according to their own experiences and those of their friends" (Cook, 1980, p. 225).

Thus whether a deterrent effect is maintained or not is essentially an outcome of a delicate balance, over time, between the forces maintaining and those tending to erode perceptions of arrest for drinking and driving as a likely event. This balancing process may be depicted in a diagrammatic fashion, as in Figure 9.1, which illustrates the "hole in the bucket" model of deterrence. According to this model, the long-term impact of RBT will depend on the relative sizes of the input and output effects—in other words, how full the bucket can be kept through police enforcement. If RBT is to have a sustained impact on the road toll, the number of people being reminded of the operation of RBT must exceed the number lost through the three mechanisms shown in the diagram: peer pressure, lack of exposure to RBT, or successful drink-drive episodes. Thus it is clear that visible police enforcement, in preference (if necessary) to expensive media publicity, must be maintained at a high level.

The RBT Study: An Overview

On the whole the RBT analysis supported the conclusion that RBT had a deterrent impact of considerable magnitude, and that the deterrence process can be described by the model discussed in Chapter 2. Despite problems of measurement which must be addressed in future research, the results are consistent with the proposition that police enforcement influences behavior via the exposure of the target population and via perceptions of arrest likelihood. Moreover, the predictive power of arrest certainty was comparable with the predictive power of informal sanctions, although informal pressures usually prevailed over fear of arrest when perceived group pressures to drink were very strong. This last result indicates the appropriateness of the framing of the drink-drive decision as a choice between losses, with the certain loss of one's status as a competent drinker carrying more weight than the merely possible losses entailed in getting caught.

The present study is in agreement with the majority of previous studies in suggesting that the behavioral effects of fear of legal punishments do not depend on the strength of informal pressures to break the law; in statistical terms, the effects of the two kinds of sanctions are additive. However, RBT had some unintended consequences, in that it made it harder for some heavy drinkers to resist pressure to drink, while simultaneously creating in them a high perception of the chances of arrest. A priority for future research must be to explore in depth the reasons for this unintended effect and more generally to investigate the influence of informal social controls on reactions to legal innovations like RBT.

The analysis suggests that personal exposure to RBT and the experience of one's friends and acquaintances were of greater importance than RBT publicity in shaping perceptions of arrest certainty and influencing behavior. Indeed, all aspects of exposure to RBT enforcement played some role, directly or indirectly, in influencing behavior. A continuous process whereby motorists are deterred by exposure and undeterred by lack of exposure is indicated by a number of the analyses. In addition, experience with drink-driving and heavy pressure from one's peers can lead to a diminution in the deterrent impact of enforcement. Deterrence should be seen as a dynamic process, maintained not necessarily in a single individual but in the whole target population through constant enforcement of the law. Without such constant enforcement, it seems likely that behaviors adopted as a response to the threat of punishment will eventually disappear, unless they are transformed into habits.

The RBT study is one of the few which have produced results in support of the proposition that perceived penalty severity influences behavior. The evidence from the present study is that such effects can occur when arrest certainty is high, and that motorists with a conviction are particularly responsive to the threat of more severe penalties. Indeed motorists with a conviction were generally more responsive to legal sanctions, which is consistent with the predictions of deterrence theory.

There was little evidence that any types of motorists were less deterrable than average. If anything the evidence is that high risk groups like heavy drinkers and young men were more affected by RBT than other groups. These results confirm the wisdom of not attempting to build into the deterrence model detailed predictions concerning the differential deterrability of population subgroups, apart from those with a conviction for drinking and driving. Such typologies must be developed empirically, as in the penalties study.

Review of the Penalties Study

On purely a priori grounds, finding a deterrent effect in the penalties data is less likely than in the RBT data. RBT represented a very marked and sudden change in the law, and therefore conditions were ideal for deterrence to occur and for the process to be open to scrutiny. By contrast, the routine application of penalties could not be expected to have the same dramatic impact, particularly since degrees of penalties are being compared, rather than the impact of punishment itself. In addition, there are theoretical problems entailed in the whole notion of punishment, particularly with respect to the confounding effects of perceived severity and perceived injustice. Finally, the penalties study was based on official statistics rather than on interviews, and the response measure (reconvictions) is an indirect and unreliable measure of reoffending.

Despite the theoretical and methodological problems involved in demonstrating marginal specific deterrent effects, some of the results of the analyses were consistent with predictions from the deterrence model. License disqualification, in particular, appeared to possess deterrent properties. The purpose of this section is to review the results of the penalties study, and to consider the implications for the deterrence model. In particular, attention is focused on three questions: (a) To what extent are the results (whether negative or positive) a consequence of limitations in the methods employed? (b) In what ways is the deterrence model inadequate? (c) How does the offender typology clarify the results?

Reconviction Rates

The major finding of the study is essentially negative: with one or two exceptions, neither type nor severity of penalty affected the probability that an offender would be convicted again for drinking and driving or for criminal offenses. The measures of perceived severity, based on the severity of the penalty relative to entitlement, failed to correlate in the predicted negative fashion with reconviction rates, no matter how the measures were constructed. Since the relative severity measure and the appeal rates are the most direct measures of perceived severity available, the absence of a negative correlation with drink-drive reconvictions, except possibly for penalties of moderate severity, is strong evidence against the predictions of a simple marginal deterrent effect. The implication is that if an offender is intent on repeating the offense, it does not matter whether he is fined lightly or heavily, disqualified for a short or long period, put on a bond, or even imprisoned; none of these things, by and large, appears to be more effective than any other in influencing his behavior.

The Effects of Disqualification on Good Risk Offenders

A second major finding of the study provided more positive evidence for deterrence. For offenders classified as good risk (in the sense that they were not reconvicted for drinking and driving or for a criminal offense in 3 years), penalties which were perceived as severe, as measured by the appeal rate, appeared to be more effective deterrents to committing traffic offenses than penalties perceived as lenient. The analysis suggests that license disqualification was the critical component of the penalty, and that a period of at least a year, and preferably around 18 months, was optimal in terms of reconviction rates. Moreover, there was no evidence that the probability of driving while disqualified was a function of the *period* of disqualification.

It is unlikely that these results are the product of methodological artifacts since Sadler and Perrine (1984), using a different design, came to substantially the same conclusions with respect to recidivism and accidents among drink-drivers convicted in California. These authors could not demonstrate any differences between penalty groups in terms of alcohol-related accidents or convictions, but there was clear evidence that long periods of suspension were more effective in preventing nonalcohol-related accidents and convictions than both short suspension periods and treatments involving no suspension at all.

This outcome is weaker than would be predicted from deterrence theory. Certainly long periods of disqualification appeared to deter good risk offenders, but the deterrence model made no distinction between good risk and high risk offenders. In addition, it appears both from the present study and from that of Sadler and Perrine (1984) that long periods of disqualification at best prevent traffic offenses less serious than drinking and driving. It could be argued therefore that disqualification has failed in its main aim, which is to keep the most dangerous drivers off the road, and that the deterrence model is incorrect, except possibly as a description of the behavior of the more compliant offenders.

A number of authors emphasize the serious consequences of disqualification for many offenders, and question its deterrent or reformative value. Willett (1973) notes that it tends to have only a temporary effect, and that many offenders simply resume driving when it is realized that it is based mainly on "bluff." In his earlier study, Willett (1971) documented the effects of disqualification for some individuals, pointing out that several drivers had to pay increased fares to work and some had to employ drivers or rent a room because they could not commute. Moreover, periods as long as 18 months could cost many offenders their jobs.

Willett's arguments have considerable force. It is intuitively plausible that drivers who depend on their car for work or other important activities will be highly motivated to continue driving, and indeed Buikhuisen's (1969) study and the replication reported in Chapter 6 provide some empirical support for this view. Moreover, it is commonplace in the literature to read that drivers exhibiting alcohol-related problems will be poorly motivated to comply with the law. Against this position, however, is Hagen's (1978) research, which showed that even for second offenders disqualification reduced drink-drive recidivism rates. In addition, the results of the present study for good risk offenders can be set against Willett's arguments.

There is a more fundamental argument that can be put against disqualification as a deterrent: an absence of reconvictions for traffic offenses does not necessarily imply that motorists have become safer or more law-abiding. Instead, it is possible that the behavior learned while driving under suspension is not safe driving, but proficiency at avoiding apprehension (Warren, 1982).

Several points should be noted in reply to this argument. First, Sadler and Perrine (1984) used both reconvictions and accidents as outcome measures, and demonstrated a correlation between nonalcohol-related convictions and accidents. This suggests that disqualification encourages people to drive more safely or to abstain altogether from driving, and not to develop skills in evading the police. Second, Homel (1983c) has demonstrated that crashes and speeding offenses are the reasons why the majority of motorists in New South Wales are subjected by police to a preliminary breath test. This implies that the skills required to evade police are also, at least to some extent, skills which promote safe driving. Moreover, it is likely that if an offender wished to drive without being detected, he would avoid times such as Friday and Saturday nights when the police are known to be active. Since these are the high risk times for crashes, this strategy would probably also result in greater safety. Third, there is evidence from the present study (Homel, 1980a) and from Hagen (1978) that drivers disqualified for longer periods have better driving records *after* their licenses have been restored. This implies that either safer driving habits acquired during the period of disqualification became a habit, or (consistent with the deterrence model) that drivers disqualified for long periods had a greater fear of further punishment than drivers disqualified for a short period.

On balance, the data support the argument that long periods of disqualification were more effective deterrents than short periods. However, this conclusion is restricted to good risk offenders and to nonalcohol-related traffic offenses. The model of deterrence proposed in Chapter 2 is incapable of explaining why the deterrent impact of disqualification should be restricted in this way. Nevertheless, the weight of evidence from this and other research favor the argument that when disqualification did have an effect on behavior, the reason was commonly deterrence. This does not preclude the operation of other mechanisms. For example, it is likely that both safer driving habits and skills in avoiding detection were factors contributing to lower traffic reconviction rates.

The Effects of Imprisonment

The evidence from this study is that, if anything, longer periods of imprisonment encourage reoffending, at least for drinking and driving. This finding is consistent with many previous studies in criminology. In reviewing the results of a number of studies, Hood (1971) concluded that lengthy institutional sentences are no more successful than shorter alternatives. In Australia very few drink-drivers go to jail at any one time for more than 6 months, but those who do have worse reconviction records than any other group, including those imprisoned for a short period. This worse record persists for drink-drive reconvictions even after some allowance is made for the high risk nature of this group. The implication is that prison periods longer than 2 or 3 months help to cause reoffending for drinking and driving, although caution is necessary because of the small numbers involved.

Criminologists have tended to focus on the effects of periods of imprisonment longer than a year (e.g., Banister, Smith, Heskin, & Bolton, 1973). Some researchers have concluded that few who are incarcerated for any length of time escape the dependence, the loss of self-responsibility, which are common adaptations of institutional life (Clemmer, 1971). However, not all prisoners are equally involved in the sharing of antisocial attitudes or behavior; the nature of a man's links with the outside world, the position he occupies, and the contacts he makes in prison are all important. Brody (1979) notes that:

. . . it is during the first few weeks of a prison sentence that a deterrent effect is most noticeable . . . after that time, there seems to be a hardening of attitude and an increasing feeling of resentment. If this is generally true, perhaps prison sentences could be quite drastically reduced (p. 9).

If, as seems likely, repeated convictions for drinking and driving indicate a degree of personal and social maladjustment, it is hard to see how imprisonment is likely to act as a deterrent. In fact, it is quite plausible that by contributing to the disruption of an offender's personal relationships it makes his situation worse.

One practical implication of these findings is that drink-drivers who would in the normal course of events go to prison for a few weeks or months may be dealt with more effectively and cheaply through one or two days imprisonment, or through weekend detention. Such schemes, which have been introduced recently in a number of American states but remain largely unevaluated (Voas, 1986), could hardly produce worse results than conventional periods of imprisonment. A theoretical implication is that a more phenomenological approach in research is required in order to understand the effects of imprisonment, particularly for those low income groups and ethnic minorities most likely to come into conflict with the law (Hagger & Dax, 1977). Indeed, this conclusion applies to the effects of all the punishments discussed in this section. The level of speculation can only be reduced when more is known about the *meaning* of the punishments to the offenders actually experiencing them.

The Offender Typology

The typology described in Chapter 8 was constructed from the data. It cannot be verified as a "correct" classification system in any rigorous fashion, since it frequently involved building on slender leads and on suggestions of relationships, rather than on clear-cut differences. In effect, the typology is an exercise in "grounded theory" (Glaser & Strauss, 1979)—an attempt to abstract from the quantitative data a qualitative picture of the kinds of dimensions which might underlie the demographic characteristics and criminal careers of convicted drinking drivers. Moreover, as indicated in Chapter 1, any system of classification reflects the biases and interests of the researcher, as well as the limitations of available data. One feature of the present typology which distinguishes it from many others in the literature is the incorporation of offenders' reactions to legal punishments. This features does not make it better than other classifications, just more appropriate to a study of specific deterrence, and perhaps a little more interactionist than those based on data limited to test scores and demographic characteristics.

Nevertheless, any typology reflects an attempt to make generalizations on the basis of data. It will be valuable therefore to assess the extent to which the present typology is similar to groupings of traffic offenders found in other studies. Similarities with other studies would strengthen confidence that the typology's specific objectives and idiosyncratic mode of production have not unduly limited its general application. It will also be valuable to reconsider briefly the social context of offending, with a view to suggesting ways in which future studies of drink-drive recidivism could build more on interactionist analyses.

Willett (1971) studied 653 serious traffic offenders in Britain, including 104 drink-drivers. Although he did not attempt to divide offenders into groups as systematically as in the present study, a number of parallels with his findings can be noted. For example, Willett found that the drinking drivers were noticeably older than his other offenders, consistent with the picture of the dedicated drinking driver. Since Willett's study was carried out before the introduction of the breathalyzer in England, it is likely that his drink-drivers would have repeated the offense many times to get caught, and would have been very obvious by their behavior. In other words, they were probably the more serious drunken drivers at the time and are therefore akin to the group of dedicated drinking drivers.

The drive-disqualified offenders in Willett's sample also seemed to be very similar to those in the present study. Of the 69 offenders in his study, 94% worked in manual occupations, and 54% in unskilled manual occupations. This parallels the present findings closely. Moreover, Willett found that his drive-disqualified group, just like those in the present study, were the least law-abiding of the six offense groups, being involved in criminal offenses, such as taking vehicles without consent and a range of property offenses.

There is at least one further parallel with Willett's findings. He noted the existence of a group he called "recidivist motoring offenders," whose behavior in respects other than driving was generally lawful. In addition, he found that the dangerous drivers were most likely to have previous motoring convictions. These results seem generally consistent with the pictures of the minor traffic offenders and the serious traffic offenders. Dangerous drivers were included in the present study in the category serious traffic offender, and the tendency of this group to be reconvicted for traffic offenses has already been noted.

Parsons (1978) studied a sample of 1,509 serious traffic offenders convicted in New Zealand courts between 1965 and 1969. He traced their pattern of traffic and nontraffic offending for a period of up to 15 years. Serious traffic offenders were defined as those causing death or injury, and were convicted of such offenses as reckless or dangerous driving, drink-driving, careless driving, and failure to stop after an accident. He concluded that the offenders fell naturally into three groups: a *non-offenders group*, a *traffic-violators group*, and a *criminal-offenders group*.

The non-offenders group appeared to be very similar in characteristics to the never convicted again drivers in the present study: they were older and of white-collar status, and committed fewer of the more serious traffic offenses and practically none of the criminal offenses. The traffic-violators group were almost all male, and the majority of them were young and of lower socioeconomic status. They seemed to combine the characteristics of the minor traffic offender and the dedicated drinking driver in the present study, inasmuch as they specialized in serious breaches of traffic law but tended not to commit nontraffic criminal offenses. The third group, the criminal-offenders, were the most deviant, committing a variety of traffic offenses and nontraffic criminal offenses. This group may be viewed as a combination of the serious traffic offender and the drive-disqualified offender in the present study.

Parsons noted that there was considerable common ground between the characteristics of serious traffic offenders and criminal and violent offenders generally, and he interpreted his results in terms of a subculture of violence thesis.

Shoham and colleagues (1982) carried out a study of repeat traffic offenders and a control group of drivers with "clean records' in Israel. They claimed to verify the existence of two types of drivers who have accidents: *anxious drivers* who have a high level of internalization of traffic norms but who get confused and anxious in situations requiring a decision, and *reckless drivers* who show low internalization of traffic norms, a low anxiety level, and impulsiveness, and also commit a variety of criminal offenses. The attributes of the reckless drivers were virtually indistinguishable from those of the common criminal offender. The value of the study of Shoham and co-workers is that it confirms the relationship between traffic and criminal offenses, and also suggests the existence of a group of occasional or specialist traffic offenders who seldom engage in criminal activity.

Perhaps the most thorough typological analysis specifically of driving under the influence (DUI) offenders was carried out in California by Arstein-Kerslake and Peck (1985). They used cluster analysis of 7,316 offenders to identify nine groups on the basis of psychometric data, as well as 10 groups on the basis of nonpsychometric data. Some of their groups are similar to those hypothesized from the present study. For example, their cluster 8 (from the nonpsychometric variables) consisted of offenders with an average age of 36 years who had very high alcohol problem severity scores, many multiple offenses, and low levels of satisfaction with marital relationships. This makes them very similar to the dedicated drinking drivers. However, other clusters, particularly those based on psychometric data, cannot be equated explicitly with any of those suggested from the present study. Nevertheless, a discriminant analysis of the psychometric groupings suggesting a small number of underlying dimensions which are closely related to those which can be derived from the analysis of the Australian offenders (described in the next section). Thus there is some agreement between the studies at a higher level of generalization.

DIMENSIONS UNDERLYING THE OFFENDER TYPOLOGY

The comparison with other studies suggests the validity of the offender typology developed from the present data. The present typology has the advantage that it is more detailed and explicit than some others, and also incorporates data on the likelihood of reoffending. It is of interest that three of the four studies with which the present study was compared were based on general samples of traffic offenders, not just drink-drivers, yet some of the same general groupings emerged. This suggests that the population of convicted drink-drivers may not be very different in composition from serious traffic offenders in general.

The typology can be interpreted in terms of three underlying dimensions. One dimension relates to the extent to which the offender exhibits problems associated with *alcohol abuse* (repeated drink-driving, personal and family distress, etc.). A second dimension relates to the extent to which the offender comes into *conflict with police for criminal matters*. The third dimension relates to the extent to which the offender engages in driving behavior characterized by *aggression and recklessness*. These dimensions are not statistically independent; in particular, a combination of alcohol-related problems and criminal behavior generally implies a record of traffic violence as well. The six groups of the typology can be located at various points in the three-dimensional space defined by these dimensions. For example, drive-disqualified offenders were the most deviant, and scored high on all three dimensions. Never convicted again drivers tended to score low on all dimensions, while the other four groups were at various points in-between.

As indicated in the previous section, these dimensions bear some affinity to those derived by Arstein-Kerslake and Peck (1985). They identified *consumption of alcohol* (moderate to excessive), *problem drinker predisposition* (transient to chronic), and *negligent operator characteristics* (excessive incidence of accidents and/or convictions) as the dimensions underlying their most interpretable set of clusters. These dimensions are similar to those arising in the present study, except that conflict with police for criminal matters is not distinguished from traffic delinquency in the negligent operator dimension, while the separation of alcohol consumption from problem drinker predisposition improves on the concept of alcohol abuse suggested from the present study.

The value of thinking in terms of dimensions rather than in terms of specific groups is that dimensions provide a more flexible tool for future research. It is probable that if progress is to be made in understanding the impact of penalties on convicted offenders, it will be necessary to develop a theory of differential deterrability, in the sense that the way in which offenders *evaluate* the legal threat needs to be better understood (Bennett & Wright, 1984). Since it is very difficult in practice to assign individuals to concrete categories of the type described in Chapter 9, differential deterrability will probably have to be analyzed in terms of points on the kinds of dimensions proposed in this section. For example, the typology suggests that offenders low on conflict with police for criminal matters will be more responsive to license disqualification, even if they have exhibited some alcohol related problems (the never convicted again driver). It may be, therefore, that the criminal dimension is the crucial one distinguishing deterrable from nondeterrable offenders. It is very likely, however, that the distinction is one of *degree*, rather than of kind.

THE SOCIAL CONTEXT

It is of some interest, in view of their importance in many previous studies, that indices of previous traffic, drink-drive, or criminal records were not more important in predicting reconvictions. Previous convictions did correlate with reconvictions, but they were not as important as the few variables available in the records which related to offenders' *current* social circumstances and criminal activities. This is of some theoretical importance, given the emphasis on immediate contextual factors in the sociological literature (Goode, 1978) and in the literature on alcohol use (Panel on Alternative Policies Affecting the Prevention of Alcohol Abuse and Alcoholism, 1981). Even marital status, which is a poor indicator of such contextual factors, proved more useful in predicting reconvictions for drinking and driving than did previous drink-drive convictions. Offenders who were widowed, separated, or living in a de facto relationship were more likely than others to be reconvicted for drinking and driving and for criminal offenses. This is in line with previous criminological research (Pritchard, 1979; Buikhuisen & Hoekstra, 1974), and is also consistent with the observations of Willett (1971) and Macmillan (1975).

As Gusfield (1985) has pointed out, the fact that separated or divorced men are overrepresented among various samples of drink-drivers should not divert attention from the fact that because these groups are a minority in the general population, they are also a minority (albeit a larger one) among drinking drivers. The significance of the result is that it highlights the importance of aspects of current lifestyle, rather than driver characteristics frozen in the past. In short, it suggests that a more interactionist approach be adopted by researchers, with a focus on the meaning of the drink-driving event for the drinking driver and on the social context in which the offense takes place. Gusfield suggests a focus on leisure-time uses of alcohol, driving styles, transportation patterns, and the context of the bar. We might add to this a detailed study of the nature of the peer group, particularly for young people (Clark & Powell, 1984).

Certainly there does not seem to be much mileage in studying characteristics of the drinking driver's area of residence. Although the quality of the neighborhood is clearly important in interaction with offender characteristics in predicting recidivism among traditional criminal offenders (Gottfredson & Taylor, 1986), it seems likely that the microenvironments of family, drinking companions, and the bar or pub are more critical to the performance of drink-driving offenders. The obvious importance of the peer group in the RBT study suggests that if such data could be incorporated in a study of recidivism, considerable improvements on the invariably disappointing results of predictive models would probably be obtained.

The Penalties Study: An Overview

The complexity of the analyses should not be allowed to obscure the basic finding that, in general, penalties did not appear to have a marginal specific deterrent effect. The most direct tests of the marginal specific deterrence hypothesis were those based on the relative severity measure and appeal rates. These analyses indicated that only for good risk offenders was there any clear evidence of a deterrent impact of penalties. The operative component of the penalty for good risk offenders appeared to be license disqualification, and the circumstantial evidence suggests that longer periods did have a genuine deterrent effect.

With respect to the deterrence model, two points stand out clearly. First, the impact of penalties like imprisonment will remain a mystery until the meaning of these judicial actions from the point of view of the offender becomes the primary focus of research. Secondly, it is unlikely that further progress can be made in understanding why some penalties have some deterrent effects on some people until the dimensions of alcohol-related problems, traffic recklessness, and conflict with police are incorporated into the analysis. What is required before quantitative analysis can be useful is ethnographic research which focuses on the social contexts in which these various kinds of delinquencies occur. Only when the nature of these contexts are appreciated can the impact of judicial punishments be adequately studied. One lead from the present analysis is that the dimension of conflict with the police, rather than alcohol abuse, may be the critical one distinguishing offenders responsive to legal sanctions from those who are not responsive.

The typology developed in the present study has the immediate advantage that it integrates the results of the analyses of penalty effects. Moreover, it seems to reflect dimensions which are generally found in studies of serious traffic offenders, suggesting that the results of the present study may be applicable to other jurisdictions and to other types of traffic offenses.

An Assessment of the Deterrence Model

The major positive conclusion of this book is that, despite the need for modification and development, the deterrence model fitted the RBT data reasonably well. Perhaps the major change required in the model is that more emphasis should be placed on the ways in which deterrent effects are lost as well as the ways in which they are gained. The analyses clearly suggest that deterrence is a dynamic process, with individuals constantly being undeterred through lack of exposure to police enforcement, through experience with drink-driving, or through pressures from their peer group. There is a need to study in more detail the relative importance of these

factors, as well as the psychological impact of media publicity and to quantify the duration of deterrent effects when they are not reinforced by con-
tinual exposure to police activity.

A further important outcome of the RBT data analyses was that groups
commonly regarded as high risk, such as young men and heavy drinkers,
were at least as deterrable as other motorists. This suggests that when
studying a general population sample it is not necessary to modify the model to incorporate statements about differential deterrability, a conclusion
which reinforces the argument that the changes required in the model are
not of a fundamental nature. Nevertheless, there are many unanswered
questions from the RBT study.

Apart from the need to investigate the role of the peer group in the
deterrence process (Clark & Powell, 1984), and to elaborate the social
contexts of drinking and of drink-driving (Gusfield, 1985), probably the
two major priorities for research are to probe in much greater depth the
decision-making process, and to probe the links between perceptions and
evaluations of the various aspects of law enforcement. The results of the
replication of Buikhuisen's (1969) study are especially intriguing, since
they suggest that the links between perceptions of penalties and evaluations of their severity may be strongly influenced by social factors like
occupational status. If systematic relationships between perceptions and
evaluations can be established for all aspects of law enforcement, the
predictive power of the deterrence model should be greatly enhanced.

There are many further specific questions arising from the present research. Given the framing of the drink-drive decision as a choice between
losses, we need to know more about the ways in which the costs and
benefits of driving after drinking (and not driving after drinking) are
perceived and evaluated. Why is exposure to police enforcement more of
a deterrent for some motorists than for others (i.e., how is such exposure
interpreted and given a meaning)? What is the effect of inebriation on
the perceptions and weightings of alternative modes of action? How do
the various "audiences"—one's drinking companions, one's girlfriend,
perhaps even one's mother (what would she think?)—influence evaluations of the legal threat? How do these audiences impose punishments in
their own right? In what kinds of social circles is driving after drinking
censured rather than encouraged or regarded with indifference? How influential are beliefs about the wrongness of driving after drinking?

It is likely that answers to some of these questions will be found
through ethnographic research along the lines pioneered by Gusfield and
his colleagues (Gusfield, 1981a), combined with further research on the
psychology of decision making (Pitz & Sachs, 1984). The psychological
models of decision making have gone well beyond the simple postulates
of utility theory, and it is time that some of the insights from these
models were applied to the crime decision. However, as Douglas and Wildavsky (1982) argue, not only are better psychological theories of decision

making in risky situations required, these theories need to be situated in the experiences of everyday life, with full attention being given to the social context within which the decisions are made.

The Enigma of the Penalties Study

Contrary to the RBT study, the results of the penalties study do raise some fundamental questions about the validity of the model. The major puzzle which needs to be explained is why the deterrence model worked well, on the whole, as a description of the responses of motorists to RBT, but not as a description of how convicted offenders responded to the punishments they received. The general failure of the model to describe adequately the effects of punishment is the major problem arising from the whole research program.

In this section, three ways of solving this problem are examined. First, the possibility that the deterrence model is simply wrong as a description of the behavior of many (high risk) offenders is considered. Second, the possibility that the model is valid, but that legal punishments are too weak as stimuli to have a marginal influence on behavior, is considered and evaluated in the light of the limited evidence available. The hypothesis of an absolute specific deterrent impact of punishment is also considered very briefly in this context. Third, the argument presented in Chapter 2 stating that punishment has unintended consequences (such as creating a sense of injustice), is restated. This last argument implies that the deterrence model may have partial validity.

A DISPOSITIONAL VERSUS SITUATIONAL PERSPECTIVE

The offender typology was developed partly as a response to the failure to find the predicted deterrent effects of penalties. One approach to the typology is to regard the different groups of offenders or the underlying dimensions as representative of various personality types, or at least as the manifestation of the disposition of many offenders to offend in particular ways. This seems to be the approach adopted by Shoham and colleagues (1982), given their emphasis on accident proneness as the behavioral expression of different personality types.

Within this perspective, some offenders are impelled by psychological forces beyond their control and therefore a model based on perceptions of sanctions is unlikely to have much explanatory power. It is assumed that some motorists are by nature unable to learn from experience, are so impulsive, sensation-seeking, and in general little able to behave in a rational manner that the deterrence model just does not fit as a description of their behavior. Not only are they not able to be deterred by legal punishments, all forms of sanctions, including the pangs of conscience and the disapproval of friends and relatives, have little influence.

LEGAL SANCTIONS AS A WEAK STIMULUS

An alternative approach to the typology, more consistent with an emphasis on deterrence, is to regard the typology as a classification of offenders' criminal careers (Gibbons, 1975). In this view the typology is a simple description of the combined effects over time of social circumstances, lifestyle, and opportunities to commit particular offenses at particular times. This approach, by putting more emphasis on the immediate social circumstances and on the opportunities to commit offenses, provides a framework within which the deterrence model can be applied to the behavior of the whole population of offenders and not simply to a portion of it.

It is important to note that a finding that legal punishments have no absolute or marginal specific deterrent impact will be compatible with the deterrence model, *provided* it can be demonstrated that nonlegal sanctions have high predictive power. (However, in this case the model should probably be renamed the *sanctions model*, since deterrence was specifically limited in meaning in Chapter 2 to the operation of legal punishments.) The model as formulated in Chapter 2 does not necessarily require legal punishments to be the most important type of sanction or even to be of much explanatory value at all, but simply that they be incorporated as one possible influence on behavior. The model stipulates that all individuals in the target population, provided they are exposed in some way to law enforcement, will perceive and evaluate threatened legal punishments. However, they will not act in response to these threats if they dismiss them as being of no consequence, if the certain punishments threatened by peers and others are feared more than the merely possible legal punishments, or if the attractions entailed in drinking and driving outweigh the perceived costs of not drinking and driving.

It follows from this argument that in order to salvage the deterrence model as a description of the behavior of the whole population of convicted offenders (thereby avoiding the need to rely on some kind of dispositional theory of drink-driving behavior for at least some offenders), it is necessary to demonstrate that tough legal punishments were dismissed by high risk offenders as of no more consequence than lenient penalties, or that the influence of the more severe penalties was outweighed by the effects of informal sanctions, or that the attractions of the illegal behavior (e.g., not having to make special arrangements to get home) were sufficient to tip the balance. The last two alternatives cannot be proved or disproved without research based on interviews with offenders and observations of offenders. However, some of the analyses in this book can throw light on the first argument, that the punishments imposed on offenders were not sufficiently powerful to have a marginal influence on behavior.

First, it could be argued that legal punishments differ so little in perceived severity that a marginal deterrent effect could not reasonably be expected. This is essentially the position adopted by Cook (1980), who argues that the criminal justice system overall has an absolute specific deterrent impact of considerable magnitude even if at the margins the effect is small or zero. The finding in Chapter 6 that in comparison with drink-drivers who have never been caught, drink-drivers with a conviction tended to be more responsive to the threat of arrest, suggests that the system does have such an absolute specific deterrent effect. However, this interaction was not statistically significant, especially after statistical controls were introduced, and so the evidence for absolute specific deterrence must be regarded as weak.

Against Cook's argument it is possible to set the appeal rates corresponding to penalties of varying degrees of relatively severity (Table 7.4). The implication of these figures is that the tough penalties were perceived to be quite different from light penalties in terms of severity and that therefore a marginal deterrent effect should have occurred. Moreover, the argument that the penalties did not vary sufficiently in severity to achieve a deterrent impact does not explain why disqualification possessed deterrent properties for some offenders.

A second argument for legal punishments as a weak stimulus is that in order for deterrence to occur, the probability of arrest must be seen as high. In effect, the argument is that no matter how severe the offender perceives the punishment which he has received, if he does not see further punishment as a real possibility, the experience of a severe punishment will not deter him or will not deter him any more than the experience of a light penalty. The interaction between convictions and arrest certainty in Figure 6.5 might be cited as evidence for this position. This analysis demonstrated that convicted motorists were more responsive to the threat of punishment than motorists without a conviction, but *only* if perceived probability of arrest was high. It follows from this argument that if the penalties study had been undertaken at a time when subjective arrest probabilities were very high (perhaps immediately after the introduction of something like RBT), much more pronounced marginal specific deterrent effects could have been expected.

UNINTENDED CONSEQUENCES OF PUNISHMENT

A third explanation for the general failure to find evidence for marginal specific deterrence is that offenders interpreted punishments in ways not allowed for in the deterrence model. The distinction between perceptions and evaluations is theoretically critical, yet little is known about the factors that influence evaluations of punishment. The research of Buikhuisen (1969) into the relative harshness of prison and disqualification, replicated in Chapter 6, points to the complexity of the processes involved in such evaluations.

Although a perception of the punishment as severe or lenient is probably an integral part of an offender's evaluation of his experience, it is more than likely (as argued in Chapter 2) that in addition he assesses the justice or fairness of the penalty and of the whole court process. Whether fear, resentment, or indifference is the major response of the offender is probably a complex function of many factors (Casper, 1978). Moreover, practically nothing is known about the effects of a sense of injustice on the behavior of convicted drinking drivers.

Hurst (1980) has speculated that a sense of injustice can operate to encourage driving while disqualified among convicted drinking drivers, while simultaneously *reducing* the chances of reconviction for a motoring offense. He argues that a driver chafing under the constraints of a disqualification order perceived as oppressive and unfair may, through safe driving, avoid a conviction, thereby thumbing his nose at authority. Indeed, this may be one of the psychological mechanisms underlying the deterrent impact of disqualification noted before, but research is required to test this hypothesis. Until these kinds of questions are explored in depth, it will be impossible to predict with confidence the conditions under which marginal deterrent effects can be expected.

Assessing the Deterrence Model: A Summary

The deterrence model was proposed as a general description of how the drink-drive decision may take place. Central to the model is the influence of sanctions, both legal and nonlegal. The conclusion from the research is that legal sanctions did have a major deterrent influence on the behavior of motorists in New South Wales in the first 4 months after the introduction of RBT, but that legal punishments routinely applied by the courts in 1972 had a much less certain influence, either in the sense of absolute or marginal deterrence. The offender typology was developed as a framework within which the variable impact of legal punishments could be analyzed and further researched.

One explanation for the pattern of results summarized in the typology is that some people are undeterrable, in the sense that their behavior is not dictated by perceptions of sanctions but by psychological forces beyond their control. According to this view, the deterrence model has validity for only a portion of the population.

A second explanation for the mixed results from the penalties study is that the deterrence model does indeed apply universally, but that under normal conditions of drink-drive law enforcement legal punishments have little influence on behavior. This explanation depends on the argument that punishments will not have a deterrent effect if the perceived likelihood of arrest is low, although there may be variations between population subgroups (as in the RBT study) in the extent to which low arrest estimates influence behavior. If this explanation were to be accepted, it may be necessary to refer to the *sanctions model* rather than to the deterrence model, since according to the model nonlegal sanctions would have to be the major influences on behavior (apart from the attractions of the offense itself).

Finally, it could be argued that the deterrence model has partial validity as a description of the effects of punishment, inasmuch as perceptions of penalty severity have the predicted influence on behavior, but that a sense of injustice frequently distorts or counteracts these effects.

Further research along the lines described in the previous section is required in order to determine which of these explanations is correct. In particular, there is a need to go beyond the use of reconviction rates as an index of penalty effectiveness. Research is also required to determine the exact duration of general deterrent effects, the processes whereby such effects are lost and regained, the nature of the decision-making process, and the links between perceptions and evaluations of aspects of law enforcement.

Implications for Social Policy

Random Breath Testing as a General Model for Drink-Drive Law Enforcement

Random breath testing in New South Wales had a deterrent impact of considerable magnitude, and this impact appears to have been sustained for more than 4 years. Effectively, therefore, the impact can be regarded as permanent. This raises the obvious question: Should the rest of the world copy New South Wales? Laurence Ross (1988), while conceding that ". . . drink-driving law enforcement that manages to breath-test a third of the driving population every year may exceed the threshold for long-term effectiveness" (p. 75), and conceding the cost-effectiveness of the New South Wales program, nevertheless argues that RBT is like ". . . a mass stop and frisk, which cannot clearly be distinguished from, say, stopping all passing pedestrians to be sniffed by dogs for the possession of drugs or to be patted down to see whether they are carrying weapons" (p. 75). He emphasizes, by contrast, that devices like airbags and automatic seatbelts, which provide occupant protection at no cost to civil liberties, can be effective in the three-fourths of fatal accidents where alcohol is not a cause, as well as in those caused by alcohol.

To a large extent the arguments over the intrusiveness of RBT and the cost to civil liberties can only be resolved within specific political and cultural contexts. The disadvantages of random or quasi-random enforcement methods seem obvious—drivers are subjected to a police check when they have committed no offense, and as a consequence about 99% of random tests are negative, making them largely useless as a detection technique. On the other hand, the specter of unrestrained police discretion operating through RBT is certainly incorrect. In all jurisdictions in which RBT-type programs operate, including New South Wales, police are subject to firm rules which effectively limit their discretionary powers to a much greater extent than is the case in traditional traffic law enforcement (Aizenberg,

1986; Homel, 1983c). Moreover, most people seem unwilling to accept Ross' analogy of a police frisk, since in excess of 80% of surveyed motorists in the United States and 95% in New South Wales approve the use of roadblocks or RBT (Aizenberg, 1986; Carseldine, personal communication, September 1987; Christoffel, 1984). Perhaps a better analogy is that of random (and intrusive) checks of passengers and personal baggage prior to entering an aircraft, which are widely accepted as a necessary cost in combating terrorism.

Although American police are generally enthusiastic about checkpoints and positive results are reported (Stone, 1985), in contrast to Australians they tend to see checkpoints as having a role subsidiary to traditional enforcement techniques (Smith, 1985). It seems likely that if the constitutional issues can be resolved, policy in the United States will evolve in the direction of the Victorian model, with concentrated enforcement using roadblocks in specific locations and for limited periods and being subject to firm guidelines. Thus sobriety checkpoints may not become the cornerstone of enforcement practice in the way RBT is in New South Wales. However, in other English-speaking countries, and in many European countries, the constitutional or civil liberties objections to random enforcement techniques are probably not as serious a problem. What is required in these countries is a "paradigm shift" away from an emphasis on detection and punishment to an emphasis on general deterrence. How can such a shift be brought about?

In New South Wales several factors seem to have combined to lead to the "boots and all" use of RBT. The state of Victoria was (rightly or wrongly) widely admired as having accomplished a great deal with RBT, in contrast to New South Wales, where the static road toll was blamed on ineffective drink-drive law enforcement. Thus the public in New South Wales was ready for stronger measures. Academic and traffic safety experts were almost unanimous in recommending intensive enforcement of RBT accompanied by extensive publicity (Staysafe, 1982), and citizens' groups, which might have diverted political interest into punishment/detection policies, were largely absent from the debate. Moreover it seems the Council for Civil Liberties had other fish to fry, and were not willing to invest much time and energy in opposing a generally popular measure. Added to all this was the status of traffic safety as a "motherhood issue," perhaps some latent Australian guilt feelings concerning their heavy alcohol consumption (accompanied by a search for a not-too-painful means of atonement), and a general historical willingness to obey laws perceived as having net social benefits. Whether any of these factors apply in other political contexts is for the reader to judge.

Whatever the specific reasons for the adoption of RBT in a "boots and all" fashion in New South Wales, the program can teach policy makers a number of general lessons about drink-drive law enforcement. Perhaps the most important of these lessons is that deterrence can be achieved without severe penalties such as imprisonment (even for short periods). Although the present study suggests that the increased penalties at the time RBT was introduced in New South Wales did have some deterrent impact, especially for those with a previous experience of punishment, it is not appropriate to conclude that a further increase in penalties would lead to even more deterrence.

For one thing, the evidence from the longitudinal analysis indicates that the deterrent impact of the more severe penalties may have been short-lived. Moreover, despite the significance of perceived penalty severity in one or two analyses, the major predictors of behavior change were fear of arrest and exposure to police enforcement. Without an increase in the perceived probability of arrest, penalty increases are not likely to have much deterrent impact. Finally, penalties which are too high and too inflexible may simply result in law enforcement officials (police, lawyers, judges) making more efforts to subvert the spirit of the law. If discretion is eliminated or reduced in open court, it may be exercised somewhere else, behind closed doors or on the street (Robertson, Rich, & Ross, 1973; Shover, Bankston, & Gurley, 1977; Little, 1975). Thus traditional penalties consisting of fines of a few hundred dollars and a few months of license disqualification are quite sufficient, *provided* the subjective probability of arrest is sufficiently high. A further increase in penalties, either in legislation or in practice, could create more problems than it would solve and is not necessary to achieve deterrence.

A second important lesson is that while media publicity is essential in the early stages in order to put a program like RBT "on the map" for most people, continued visible police enforcement is the crucial ingredient for continued success. Nevertheless, continued publicity of some kind is clearly desirable. How often should media campaigns be conducted and what forms should they take? A cogent argument for frequent publicity campaigns is that people forget very quickly. Among the sample of 185 Sydney motorists reinterviewed after 6 weeks in the RBT study, the rate of awareness of RBT actually *declined* from 97.3% to 91.9%, despite the $250,000 spent in media publicity over the Easter period. However, the analyses reported in Chapter 6 suggest that this decline did not have a great impact on behavior. In addition, it is simple political realism that governments will not spend massive amounts of money on media publicity indefinitely. It seems reasonable to argue therefore that large campaigns should be run, say, every 2 years, probably around Christmas, and that in the meantime less costly but continuous publicity should be funded, possibly directed at particular groups such as the young.

The major aim of the publicity should be to reinforce police activity. That is, the focus should be on the perceived probability of arrest for drink-driving. The advertisements should depict the police at work in order to remind the public that the law is still operating, and they should use whatever techniques are available to heighten awareness of the legal threat.

Although it is clear that television has the highest penetration rate and that people recall more of the TV message, in view of the results reported in Chapter 6 neither radio or newspapers should be neglected. It is possible that radio is a better medium for communicating with some groups of young people and the comments of some respondents indicated that the print media may have influenced behavior. One important target audience for the media campaigns is the police force itself. Through constant exposure to TV advertisements depicting their activities, police are encouraged to believe that RBT is valuable and it is possible that their style of enforcement will be influenced. In the absense of regular publicity, some police may come to believe that they are "on their own," and that the government does not really care about the issue.

Another lesson from the New South Wales experience is that highly visible police enforcement of RBT should be combined with enforcement practices which maximize the number of drinking drivers who are apprehended. There is a natural tendency for police to prefer "catching crooks" to the tedious routine of breath testing thousands of sober motorists, and the inevitable tendency for police to downgrade RBT in favor of strategies which increase the "hit rate" must be countered at senior levels of police and government. However, having stressed the supreme importance of continued, highly visible enforcement of RBT, there is clearly, in addition, an important place for enforcement practices designed to catch offenders. There are several reasons for this. One elementary consideration is that without some activity in the courts, it would be difficult to convince the average motorist that RBT is not a paper tiger. Beyond this, there is evidence from Chapter 6, and from the work of McLean and colleagues (1984) in South Australia, that drinking drivers with a conviction are much more responsive to the threat of further punishment than nonconvicted offenders. Moreover, McLean and his colleagues have clearly demonstrated the importance of policing back roads and apprehending at least some of those drivers who believe they are smart enough to avoid RBT operations. Thus what is needed is selective enforcement practices designed to maximize the detection rate *in parallel with but not replacing* intensive, highly visible enforcement of RBT.

There are dangers, however, in selective enforcement, since the term means different things to different people (Booth, 1980). A final important outcome of the RBT study was the demonstration that drivers perceived as high risk, including young men, were more responsive than average to the threat of arrest and punishment. What this means, in effect, is that a method of enforcement which is broadly based and not directed at any particular group of road users has been successful in deterring groups who have frequently been the target of special attention. Applying this principle more broadly, it could be argued that police enforcement of drink-drive law (apart from RBT) should be "selective" only in that high risk *times and places*, not high risk drivers, should be the center of attention (Homel,

1983c; Kirkham & Landauer, 1985). A policy of selective enforcement of this type would probably somewhat reduce the bias against young (unskilled) men, and would increase the road safety benefits of non-RBT enforcement. However, this leaves open the question of whether the effects of RBT among high risk groups could be enhanced through specially designed publicity. It was suggested before that there may be a case for radio publicity directed at young people. Moreover, a need highlighted by the present study is to find ways to reduce the pressure on some heavy drinkers who found that RBT made it harder, not easier, to refuse a drink. This is a subject which requires much more intensive research.

Sentencing the Drinking Driver

The results of the penalties study raise some serious problems for the courts. The main reason for punishing offenders, other than to demonstrate that justice has been done, is to promote road safety—yet the likelihood that an offender will continue to drink and drive is not, it seems, affected by the penalty imposed. Moreover, license disqualification is frequently ignored, even though it is the one penalty for which more seems better than less (at least for some offenders). How are convicted drinking drivers to be stopped from committing further drink-drive offenses, how can license disqualification be made more effective, and in general what criteria should be used by judges or magistrates in determining penalties?

IGNITION INTERLOCK DEVICES

Adopting a deterrence perspective, to reduce drink-drive recidivism penalties can be raised or the likelihood of apprehension can be increased. The results reported in this book suggest that only the second approach is likely to have much value, but this option is not open to the courts. Certainly there is no justification from the analyses for very severe penalties, such as long periods of imprisonment. However, deterrence does not depend entirely on increasing the fear of legal punishments. Another approach is to increase the costs of drinking and driving by making the physical act more difficult. With the move away from dispositional theories of crime causation in recent years, some criminologists have come to emphasize the role of stimulus conditions, including opportunities for action presented by the immediate environment, in providing the inducements for criminality (Bennett & Wright, 1984; Clarke, 1980; Mayhew, Clarke, Sturman, & Hough, 1976). The effects of these stimulus conditions are believed to be modified by the perceived risks involved in committing a criminal act, the anticipated consequences of doing so, and (in a complex way) the individual's past experience of the stimulus conditions and of the rewards and costs involved.

Applied to the drink-driver, the physical environment can be modified by fitting his car with a device which would prevent the car from being started if he failed a breath test. Such devices are technically feasible, and have the advantage over those based on psycho-motor-cognitive type tasks (pushing buttons and so on) that they measure blood alcohol levels directly and accurately (Homel, 1982a). It is unlikely that either the government or the public would accept the installation of these devices in all cars as a matter of course, although this could be a long-term objective (Homel, 1981b). There are likely to be far fewer political difficulties in requiring, for example, a second offender to have one installed in his car for a period as part of the penalty, and it is programs of this kind which (at the time of writing) are being investigated in several states in the United States and Australia. Of course there are obvious ways around an ignition interlock, such as getting a sober friend to blow into it. However, the RBT survey data suggest that many of the high risk offenders would not have a sober companion at the critical time. In any case, an approach based on physical prevention would not have to work perfectly to be more effective with repeat offenders than current practices. It is also probable that ignition interlocks would be seen by magistrates and by the public as a more appropriate penalty for most repeat offenders than imprisonment.

LICENSE DISQUALIFICATION

Beyond the use of ignition interlocks focused specifically on drinking and driving, there is a clear need to reduce the incidence of driving while disqualified. The U.S. National Highway Traffic Safety Administration (1979) states that although driver license suspension is the ultimate administrative sanction, as soon as it becomes necessary to actually suspend the license "we've lost the ball game" (p. 1). If extreme measures such as requiring all drivers to display a tag on the windscreen of their car indicating that they are validly licensed are unacceptable (McGuire, 1973), perhaps technological measures such as magnetic coding of the license of a disqualified driver effectively to lock the vehicle may hold more promise (Haight, 1985).

SENTENCING GUIDELINES

Ignition and license interlocks provide an additional penalty for the magistrate to use in difficult cases. They do not solve the general problem of sentencing, and they do not address the issue of bias against young unskilled offenders in the sentencing process (Homel, 1982b, 1983b). A feature of sentencing is that penalties are often individualized—they are made to fit the offender rather than the offense—on the basis of his presumed likelihood of reoffending (Hood, 1972). One implication of the penalties study is that such a policy is, on the basis of current knowledge, totally without foundation in drink-driving cases. There is no way good risk and high risk offenders can be distinguished reliably, and there is no way of assessing in any individual case the probability of reconviction for drinking and driving.

How are magistrates' decisions to be structured so that the power to exercise leniency in individual cases is retained, but factors like age and social class, as well as the individual sentencing style of the magistrate, play only a limited role? It seems clear that the basis of sentencing must become *deserving* rather than specific deterrence (Knapp, 1986; von Hirsch, 1976), but it is not clear how penalties based on desert can be implemented. Mandatory sentences based, for example, on BAC and previous convictions are unsatisfactory, because when discretion is eliminated from open court it is generally pushed behind closed doors (Little, 1975). A more satisfactory approach is to use *sentencing guidelines* (Potas, 1979; Gottfredson, Wilkins, & Hoffman, 1978).

In brief, sentencing guidelines suggest a range of penalties for an offense of given seriousness and for an offender with a given degree of blameworthiness or culpability. When the judge departs from the guidelines, he is required to give reasons (in writing) for his decision. Sufficient departures from the norm would mean that the guidelines would themselves be altered to accommodate or reduce future departures. The use of sentencing guidelines has been widely discussed in recent years and actually implemented in the United States (Knapp, 1986). One Australian judge commented (Law Reform Commission, 1980) that sentencing guidelines are an attractive and intelligent compromise between the two extremes of guesswork and mandatory penalties. However, as Tarling (1979) has commented, the guideline system as developed in the United States only states in which situations an offender should be imprisoned and for how long; there is usually little guidance on the type of noncustodial sentence to use. Nevertheless, it seems a relatively easy matter to devise a set of guidelines that would suit the drinking driver.

Following the Minnesota model (Knapp, 1986), I propose that guidelines be based on a just deserts model in which there are only two dimensions—seriousness of the offense as measured by BAC together with the perceived danger or harm to the community, and the blameworthiness of the offender as measured by previous drink-drive and driving convictions. The ranges of penalties specified for each cell in the grid should be sufficiently broad to allow for mitigating factors, such as unemployment or number of years driving experience, but much narrower than those which are customary in many jurisdictions. Depending on policies specified by the legislature, penalty ranges could refer to use and nonuse of imprisonment and period of imprisonment, together with amount of fine and period of license disqualification. It is probable that such a model would enhance any general deterrent properties of punishment (Casper, 1978) without affecting any specific deterrent effects which may occur. It would put extralegal factors (particularly age and social class) back into their place as minor and justifiable influences on the penalty, and would ensure fewer disparities in sentencing.

Conclusion

The legal threat was neglected for many years as a factor in crime control. One reason for this neglect was the dominance of the positivist school, with its emphasis on finding the root causes of crime in human biology, social organization, or "emotional disturbances" (Cressey, 1978, p. 182). Social scientists of this persuasion believed that the behavioral impact of the criminal justice system must be negligible in comparison with the influence of these fundamental forces in molding an individual's disposition to behave in a consistently criminal or law-abiding manner. There has been a resurgence of interest in the classical doctrine of deterrence in recent years, with many scholars advocating a return to deterrence principles as a major basis for penal policy (e.g., Andenaes, 1974; van den Haag, 1980). The deterrence movement is distinguished from other recent reform movements, such as diversion or just deserts, in that the emphasis is on extending and strengthening the criminal justice system, rather than on limiting its scope (Austin & Krisberg, 1981).

However, penal reformers have not always recognized that the empirical evidence for a system based on deterrence is rather weak, since the plethora of research on deterrence in the last 20 years has yielded few firm conclusions (Tittle, 1980b). The quasi-experimental research designed to evaluate the impact of drink-drive laws and their enforcement has provided some of the best evidence that deterrent effects can occur in some circumstances, but on the whole this research has failed to analyze the social and psychological process which link objective legal activities with drink-driving behavior. In particular, perceived certainty of arrest has seldom been measured and related to the intensity of enforcement and behavior change. Moreover, even if drink-drive research provides the clearest evidence that law and its enforcement can achieve deterrent effects, it also provides the clearest evidence that such effects are usually transitory (Ross, 1982). Tougher laws or enforcement policies may even be sabotaged in the very act of implementation, so that the road safety benefits of the legal innovations are nugatory or negative (Robertson et al., 1973; Shover et al., 1977).

If the research on the general deterrence of drink-driving has failed to provide a completely firm foundation for a penal philosophy based on deterrence, the research on specific deterrence is even more doubtful as a justification for deterrence-based policies. However, it is possible that the research is deficient, and that specific deterrent effects do in fact occur. Most of the research fails to deal, either at the theoretical or the empirical level, with an offender's interpretation of his experience, especially with respect to the justice of his treatment. Moreover, within the conventional paradigm, researchers have seldom paid more than lip service to the possibility that penalties will have different effects on different sorts of people (Brody, 1976).

A failure of the criminal justice system to have any appreciable road safety benefits is not surprising if the cultural perspective of Gusfield (1981b) is accepted as a valid framework for analysis. For Gusfield the activities of legislatures and courts are dramas for the consumption of an audience rather than mechanisms through which control can be achieved. The various parts of the legal process are designed as much for "the love of noise" as for "a desire to reach a target" (p. 145). While Gusfield emphasizes the role of the immediate social context and recognizes the possibility of some form of risk assessment in the drink-drive decision, he leads the analysis back to many of the issues traditionally considered by positivist criminologists: the multiple causes of drink-drive behavior and traffic crashes, the institutional settings of drinking and driving, and the nature of the informal controls which prevail within the motorist's network of friends and drinking partners (Gusfield, 1985).

The research presented in this book has been addressed to one of the major weak points in the literature on the deterrence of the drinking driver—the failure to study the process of deterrence. The results have been mixed, but have generally been more in agreement with the predictions of deterrence theory than Gusfield's (1981b) analysis might have led one to expect. Of course the RBT study was conducted only a few months after the introduction of an unusually well-publicized and energetically enforced campaign. Given the experience with similar international legal innovations (Ross, 1982), it is perhaps not surprising that the deterrence model fitted the data so well. However, the finding that license disqualification possesses deterrent properties for some offenders under conditions of routine enforcement raises important questions for further research, and encourages the belief that achieving marginal specific deterrence may not be a totally unrealistic goal.

The significance of these results is that they imply that the criminal justice system can, under certain circumstances, have a deterrent impact of considerable magnitude. For Gusfield, these effects are tangential rather than central to the operation of the system. Deterrence occurs almost as an unintended by-product of a system devoted to the moral dramatization of cultural ideals, and deterrent effects that do occur are invariably evanescent (Ross, 1982). Opposite this view is the evidence that RBT in New South Wales has achieved a permanent deterrent effect through a combination of extensive publicity and continued, visible, and intensive enforcement. Whatever the final fate of RBT in New South Wales, the available evidence suggests that, in terms of Gusfield's metaphor, the cannonball can, sometimes, hit the target. The point is that although the colorful uniforms, noise, and smoke may provide a spectacle for public consumption, the cannon need not be loaded with blanks.

Of course, the financial and human costs of achieving a reduction in road accidents through the criminal law may mean that deterrence is an inefficient, outmoded, and dangerous weapon. The costs in a democratic society of a system of enforcement and a style of publicity which rely increasingly on the creation of feelings of terror in the driving public should not be underemphasized (Ross, 1987). To continue Gusfield's metaphor, much more efficient and socially acceptable forms of artillery than the old blunderbusses of the police and the courts may be available to combat the drinking driver. It is sometimes argued, for example, that any approach which avoids trying to change individual behavior but concentrates instead on the social or physical environment is likely to have more success, and be less politically conservative (Cameron, 1979; Mosher, 1985; Quinney, 1976).

In North America, controls on the availability and advertising of liquor have a long and checkered history (Gusfield, 1963; Vingilis & De Genova, 1984; Wagenaar, 1983). Recent moves in that part of the world to deal with the effects of drinking and driving have included developing programs of bartender intervention and raising the legal drinking age (Saltz, 1985; Williams, 1986). Although these policies have been implemented partly as a response to the perceived failure of deterrence and education-based policies to have much impact on the extent of alcohol-impaired driving (Mosher, 1985), what is interesting is that many of these innovations—particularly the bartender intervention program combined with host liability—are just variations on the deterrence model. Their novelty, and possible value, lies in the shift in the target from individual drivers to the purveyors of alcohol. However, Ross (1982, 1987), in proposing the manufacture of airbags or crash-proof vehicles, has genuinely gone beyond an enforcement-based policy. Improvements in road engineering may similarly be classified as technological, rather than as deterrence-based, approaches to the problem. There is a clear need in general to extend the research agenda beyond a concern with changing individual behaviors, so that the knowledge required for the successful implementation of environmental countermeasures can be built up (Thomson, 1985).

Despite its emphasis on deterrence, nothing in this book should be taken as support for the view that it is sufficient to change individual behavior, ignoring either the social environment in which drink-driving practices are shaped and rewarded, or those aspects of the physical environment which increase the likelihood that drinking and driving will lead to death or injury (Homel & Wilson, 1987). In fact the criticism that the individual has been treated as if he existed in some kind of social vacuum is more appropriately directed at rehabilitation and some education programs than at general deterrent measures like RBT. It should be clear from the present study that RBT had an impact in New South Wales not only through the fear of legal punishments, but through a reduction in the social pressures encouraging drinkers to consume more than a safe quantity of alcohol. In addition, any long-term impact of RBT or a similar measure must entail changes in beliefs and social practices in directions which will produce quite significant alterations in the social environment, thereby posing a threat to the interests of powerful groups. It is not true therefore that policies aimed at creating general deterrent effects are necessarily individualistic and politically conservative, or that they ". . . pose the least burden on influential groups and involve the fewest risks for elected officials and bureaucrats" (Beauchamp, quoted in Mosher, 1985, p. 248). The political furor surrounding RBT in the Australian state of Queensland might be cited as a counterexample (Moller & North, 1986). Nevertheless, the social costs of a reliance on fear as a motivation for change cannot be discounted.

The potential of RBT and of similar measures as tools for bringing about social change, at least in the short term, demonstrates that the impact of the criminal justice system need not be purely symbolic. However, Gusfield (1981b) is surely correct in asserting that the utilitarian value of these kinds of legal innovations is not the main reason why they are so popular. On the contrary, it is because the *killer drunk*—that antisocial, hedonistic, uncontrolled menace—is believed to tear (or reel) around our roads, that criminal law enforcement directed at individual offenders is, and will remain, the major method for dealing with drinking and driving. In most countries, drinking and driving will continue to be construed in terms of individual moral dereliction, with vigorous police activity and severe punishments being seen as an appropriate societal response.

In this situation, the need to develop a better understanding of both the conditions under which deterrent effects occur and the processes linking legal punishments with behavior (both in the short term and in the long term), emerges as a top priority. Not only can such an understanding contribute to improvements in the effectiveness and in the fairness of drink-drive law enforcement, it can provide the basis for improvements in a theory of the behavioral impact of criminal law. The model of the deterrence process and the results of the two studies described in this book are offered as a contribution to the development of such a theory.

References

Åberg, L. (1986, September). *Routine breath testing and drivers' perceived probability of breath test*. Paper presented at the 10th International Conference on Alcohol, Drugs and Traffic Safety, Amsterdam, The Netherlands.

Aitkin, M.A. (1974). Simultaneous inference and the choice of variable subsets in multiple regression. *Technometrics, 16*, 221–227.

Aitkin, M.A. (1978). The analysis of unbalanced cross-classifications (with discussion). *Journal of the Royal Statistical Society, Series A, 141*, 195–223.

Aizenberg, R. (1986). Sobriety checkpoints as a deterrent to drinking and driving. *Journal of Traffic Safety Education, 33* (2), 6–7, 20.

Andenaes, J. (1974). *Punishment and deterrence*. Ann Arbor, MI: The University of Michigan Press.

Andenaes, J. (1977). The moral or educative influence of criminal law. In J.L. Tapp & F.J. Levine (Eds.), *Law, justice and the individual in society: Psychological and legal issues* (pp. 50–59). New York: Holt, Rinehart and Winston.

Andenaes, J. (1978). The effects of Scandinavia's drinking and driving laws: Facts and hypotheses. In R. Hauge (Ed.), *Scandanavian studies in criminology, Volume 6: Drinking and driving in Scandanavia* (pp. 35–54). Oslo, Norway: Universitetsforlaget.

Anderson, L.S. (1979). The deterrent effect of criminal sanctions: Reviewing the evidence. In P.J. Bratingham & J.M. Kress (Eds.), *Structure, law and power— Essays in the sociology of law* (pp. 120–134). Beverly Hills, CA: SAGE.

Anderson, L.S., Chiricos, T.G., & Waldo, G.P. (1977). Formal and informal sanctions: A comparison of deterrent effects. *Social Problems, 25*, 103–114.

Argeriou, M., McCarty, D., & Blacker, E. (1985). Criminality among individuals arraigned for drinking and driving in Massachusetts. *Journal of Studies on Alcohol, 46*, 525–530.

Arstein-Kerslake, G.W., & Peck, R.C. (1985). *A typological analysis of California DUI offenders and DUI recidivism correlates*. Sacramento, CA: Research and Development Office, Department of Motor Vehicles.

Arthurson, R. (1985). *Evaluation of random breath testing*. Sydney: Traffic Authority of New South Wales, Research Note RN 10/85.

Assum, T. (1986, September). *Deterrent effects of imprisonment and fines for driving while impaired*. Paper presented at the 10th International Conference on Alcohol, Drugs and Traffic Safety, Amsterdam, The Netherlands.

Austin, J., & Krisberg, B. (1981). Wider, stronger and different nets—The dialectics of criminal justice reform. *Journal of Research in Crime and Delinquency*, *18*, 165–196.

Australian Public Opinion Polls (The Gallup Method). (1974a). *The Gallup Poll: Poll No. #04/2/74*. Sydney, Australia: Field Office Survey, McNair Surveys Pty. Ltd.

Australian Public Opinion Polls (The Gallup Method). (1974b). *The Gallup Poll: Poll No. #04/4/74*. Sydney, Australia: Field Office Survey, McNair Surveys Pty. Ltd.

Australian Public Opinion Polls (The Gallup Method). (1975). *The Gallup Poll: Poll No. #07/12/75*. Sydney, Australia: Field Office Survey, McNair Surveys Pty. Ltd.

Australian Public Opinion Polls (The Gallup Method). (1979). *The Gallup Poll: Poll No. #03/3/79*. Sydney, Australia: Field Office Survey, McNair Surveys Pty. Ltd.

Banister, P.A., Smith, F.V., Heskin, K.J., & Bolton, N. (1973). Psychological correlates of long-term imprisonment. *British Journal of Criminology*, *13*, 312–330.

Barthelmess, W. (1986). *Preventive measures and behaviour changes concerning DWI offenders*. Paper presented at the 10th International Conference on Alcohol, Drugs and Traffic Safety, Amsterdam, The Netherlands.

Bennett, T., & Wright, R. (1984). *Burglars on burglary*. Aldershot, England: Gower.

Berger, D., & Snortum, J. (1985). Alcoholic beverage preferences of drinking-driving violators. *Journal of Studies on Alcohol*, *46*, 232–239.

Berger, D., & Snortum, J. (1986). A structural model of drinking and driving: Alcohol consumption, social norms, and moral commitments. *Criminology*, *24*, 139–153.

Beyleveld, D. (1978). *The effectiveness of general deterrents against crime: An annotated bibliography of evaluative research* [Microfiche]. Cambridge: University of Cambridge, Institute of Criminology.

Beyleveld, D. (1979a). Deterrence research as a basis for deterrence policies. *Howard Journal of Penology and Crime Prevention*, *18*, 135–149.

Beyleveld, D. (1979b). Identifying, explaining and predicting deterrence. *The British Journal of Criminology*, *19*, 205–224.

Blumenthal, M., & Ross, H.L. (1973). *Two experimental studies of traffic law. Volume I: The effect of legal sanctions on DUI offenders* (Report DOT HS-800825). Washington, DC: Department of Transportation.

Blumer, H. (1969). *Symbolic interactionism: Perspective and method*. Englewood Cliffs, NJ: Prentice-Hall.

Blumstein, A., Cohen, J., & Nagin, D. (1979). Deterrence and incapacitation: Estimating the effects of criminal sanctions on crime rates. *Criminology Review Yearbook*, *1*, 190–201.

Bø, O. (1978). The enigma of the present evidence on drinking-driving in Norway. *Journal of Traffic Medicine*, *6* (1), 10–12.

Bock, R.D. (1975). *Multivariate statistical methods in behavioural research*. New York: McGraw-Hill.

Booth, W.L. (1980). *Police management of traffic accident prevention programs*. Springfield, IL: Charles C. Thomas.

Bovens, R. (1986). *Special treatment of DWI-offenders in the Netherlands: The Alcohol Education Programmes*. Paper presented at the 10th International Conference on Alcohol, Drugs and Traffic Safety, Amsterdam, The Netherlands.

Braybrooke, K. (1975). The place of the traffic offender in the criminal justice system. In *Proceedings of Seminar: Road Safety and the Law, Sydney, 2–3 August, 1973* (pp. 53–57). Canberra, Australia: Australian Government Publishing Service.

Brody, S.R. (1976). *The effectiveness of sentencing—A review of the literature. Home Office Research Study No. 35*. London: Her Majesty's Stationery Office.

Brody, S.R. (1979). Research into the efficacy of deterrents. In R. Walmsley & L. Smith (Eds.), *Home Office Research Bulletin, No. 7* (pp. 9–12). London: Home Office Research Unit.

Buikhuisen, W. (1969, November). *Criminological and psychological aspects of drunken drivers*. Paper presented at the Symposium: The Human Factor in Road Traffic, Stockholm, Sweden.

Buikhuisen, W. (1974). General deterrence: Research and theory. *Abstracts on Criminology and Penology, 14*, 285–298.

Buikhuisen, W., & Hoekstra, H.A. (1974). Factors related to recidivism. *British Journal of Criminology, 14*, 63–69.

Bungey, J., & Sutton, A. (1983). *Random breath tests and the drinking driver: The South Australian experience*. Adelaide, Australia: Alcohol and Drug Addicts Treatment Board/Office of Crime Statistics.

Burgess, C.A. (1982). Recidivism of juvenile burglars: A perceptual view of specific deterrence. *Dissertation Abstracts International, 43*, 934-A.

Burns, A., & Homel, R.J. (1986, November). *Is this a good neighbourhood for children? Parental perceptions of the quality of life in the local area*. Paper presented to the 2nd Australian Family Research Conference, Melbourne, Australia.

Burns, M. (1985). Field sobriety tests: An important component of DUI enforcement. *Alcohol, Drugs and Driving Abstracts and Reviews, 1* (3), 21–26.

Caetano, R., & Suzman, R.M. (1982). A methodological note on quantity—frequency categorizations in a longitudinal study of drinking practices. *The Drinking and Drug Practices Surveyor, 18*, 7–12.

Cameron, C. (1977). *Engineering, education and enforcement: Some underlying assumptions & some constructive suggestions*. Paper presented at the Traffic Control and Road Accident Seminar, Caulfield Institute of Technology, Melbourne, Australia.

Cameron, M.H., & Sanderson, J.T. (1982). *Review of police operations for traffic law enforcement*. Melbourne, Australia: Royal Automobile Club of Victoria.

Cameron, M.H., & Strang, P.M. (1982). Effect of intensified random breath testing in Melbourne during 1978 and 1979. *Australian Road Research Board Proceedings, 11*, 1–12.

Cameron, M.H., Strang, P.M., & Vulcan, A.P. (1980, June). *Evaluation of random breath testing in Victoria, Australia*. Paper prepared for the Eighth International Conference on Alcohol, Drugs & Traffic Safety, Stockholm, Sweden.

Cameron, T.L. (1979). The impact of drinking driving countermeasures: A review and evaluation. *Contemporary Drug Problems, 8*, 495–565.

Cameron, T.L. (1982). Drinking and driving among American youth: Beliefs and behaviors. *Drug and Alcohol Dependence, 10,* 1–33.

Cannell, C.F., & Kahn, R.L. (1968). Interviewing. In G. Lindzey & E. Aronson (Eds.), *The handbook of social psychology, Volume 2* (pp. 526–595). Reading, MA: Addison-Wesley.

Carlson, W.L. (1973). Age, exposure, and alcohol involvement in night crashes. *Journal of Safety Research, 5,* 247–259.

Carlson, W.L., & Klein, D. (1970). Familial vs. institutional socialization of the young traffic offender. *Journal of Safety Research, 2,* 13–25.

Carr-Hill, R.A., & Stern, N.H. (1979). *Crime, the police and criminal statistics: An analysis of official statistics for England and Wales using econometric methods.* London: Academic Press.

Carroll, J.S. (1978). A psychological approach to deterrence: The evaluation of crime opportunities. *Journal of Personality and Social Psychology, 36,* 1512–1520.

Carroll, J., & Weaver, F. (1986). Shoplifters' perceptions of crime opportunities: A process-tracing study. In D.B. Cornish & R.V. Clarke (Eds.), *The reasoning criminal: Rational choice perspectives on offending* (pp. 19–38). New York: Springer-Verlag.

Carseldine, D. (1985). *Surveys of knowledge, attitudes, beliefs and reported behaviours of drivers—on the topic of drink-driving and random breath testing. Research Note RN 12/85.* Sydney: Traffic Authority of New South Wales.

Cashmore, J. (1985). *The impact of random breath testing in New South Wales.* Sydney: Bureau of Crime Statistics & Research.

Casper, J.D. (1978). Having their day in court: Defendant evaluations of the fairness of their treatment. *Law and Society, 12,* 237–251.

Cavender, G. (1979). Special deterrence—An operant learning evaluation. *Law and Human Behavior, 3,* 203–215.

Chambliss, W.J. (1969). *Crime and the legal process.* New York: McGraw-Hill.

Chopra, P. (1969). Punishment and the control of human behaviour. *Australian and New Zealand Journal of Criminology, 2,* 149–157.

Christoffel, T. (1984). Using roadblocks to reduce drunk driving: Public health or law and order? *American Journal of Public Health, 74,* 1028–1030.

Clark, A.W., & Powell, J.P. (1984). Changing drivers' attitudes through peer group decision. *Human Relations, 37,* 155–162.

Clark, A.W., & Prolisko, A. (1979). Social-role correlates of driving accidents. *Human Factors, 21,* 655–659.

Clarke, R.V.G. (1979). Crime prevention. In R. Walmsley & L. Smith (Eds.), *Research Bulletin No. 7, Home Office Research Unit.* London: Her Majesty's Stationery Office.

Clarke, R.V.G. (1980). "Situational" crime prevention: Theory and practice. *British Journal of Criminology, 20,* 136–147.

Clarke, R.V.G., & Sinclair, I. (1974). Towards more effective treatment evaluation. In *Methods of evaluation and planning in the field of crime: Collected studies in criminological research, XII* (pp. 53–78). Strasbourg, France: Council of Europe.

Clayton, A. (1985). Youth and traffc safety. *Alcohol, Drugs and Driving Abstracts and Reviews, 1* (1–2), 107–110.

Clemmer, D. (1971). The process of prisonization. In L. Radzinowicz & M.E. Wolfgang (Eds.), *Crime and justice, Volume III: The criminal in confinement* (pp. 92–96). New York: Basic Books.

Cochran, W.G. (1963). *Sampling techniques* (2nd. ed.). New York: Wiley.

Cohen, J. (1984). The legal control of drunken driving: A comment on the methodological concerns in assessing deterrent effectiveness. *Journal of Criminal Justice*, *12*, 149–154.

Cohen, L. (1978). Sanction threats and violation behaviour: An inquiry into perceptual variation. In C. Wellford (Ed.), *Quantitative studies in criminology* (pp. 84–99). Beverly Hills, CA: SAGE.

Cohen, S. (1973). *Folk devils and moral panics*. St. Albans, England: Paladin.

Commonwealth Department of Health. (1986). *Statistics on drug abuse in Australia*: *March 1986*. Canberra, Australia: Australian Government Publishing Service.

Compton, R.P. (1986). *A preliminary analysis of the effect of Tennessee's mandatory jail sanction on DWI recidivism*. Working paper. Washington, DC: Office of Driver and Pedestrian Research, National Highway Traffic Safety Administration.

Cook, P.J. (1977). Punishment and crime: A critique of current findings concerning the preventive effects of punishment. *Law and Contemporary Problems*, *41*, 164–204.

Cook, P.J. (1980). Research in criminal deterrence: Laying the groundwork for the second decade. *Crime and Justice*: *An Annual Review of Research*, *2*, 211–268.

Cornish, D.B., & Clarke, R.V. (1986). Introduction. In D.B. Cornish & R.V. Clarke (Eds.), *The reasoning criminal*: *Rational choice perspectives on offending* (pp. 1–16). New York: Springer-Verlag.

Cousins, L.S. (1980). The effects of public education on subjective probability of arrest for impaired driving: A field study. *Accident Analysis and Prevention*, *12*, 131–141.

Cox, D.R. (1970). *The analysis of binary data*. London: Methuen.

Cressey, D.R. (1974). Law, order and the motorist. In R. Hood (Ed.), *Crime, criminology and public policy* (pp. 213–234). London: Heinemann.

Cressey, D.R. (1978). Criminological theory, social science, and the repression of crime. *Criminology*, *16*, 171–191.

Darroch, J.N. (1981). *Comments for the Select Committee on Assessment of Random Breath Testing*, on "*Evaluation of random breath testing in Victoria, Australia, M.H. Cameron, P.M. Strang, A.P. Vulcan.*" Unpublished manuscript, School of Mathematical Sciences, Flinders University, Adelaide, South Australia.

Dawes, R.M. (1982). The robust beauty of improper linear models in decision making. In D. Kahneman, P. Slovic, & A. Tversky (Eds.), *Judgement under uncertainty*: *Heuristics and biases* (pp. 391–407). Cambridge: Cambridge University Press.

de Lint, J. (1981). "Words and deeds:" Responses to Popham and Schmidt. *Journal of Studies in Alcohol*, *42*, 359–361.

Derby, N.M., & Hurst, P.M. (1986, August). *The effects of random stopping in New Zealand*. Unpublished manuscript, Ministry of Transport, Wellington, New Zealand.

Dijksterhuis, F.P.H. (1974). The specific deterrent effect of a prison for drunken drivers. *Sociologia Needlandica*, *X*, 194–200.

Dijksterhuis, F.P.H. (1975). The specific preventive effect of penal measures on subjects convicted for drunken driving. *Blutalkohol*, *12*, 181–191.

Dix, M.C., & Layzell, A.D. (1983). *Road users and the police*. London: Croom Helm, in association with The Police Foundation.

Douglas, M., & Wildavsky, A. (1982). *Risk and culture: An essay on the selection of technical and environmental dangers*. Berkeley, CA: The University of California Press.

Douglass, R.L. (1982). Repeated cycles of concern and complacency: The public interest and political response to alcohol-related traffic accidents. *Abstracts & Reviews in Alcohol & Driving, 3* (4), 3–5.

Durkheim, E. (1964). *The division of labor in society*. New York: Wiley.

Ehrlich, I., & Mark, R. (1977). Fear of deterrence? A critical evaluation of the "Report of the panel on research on deterrent and incapacitative effects." *Journal of Legal Studies, 6,* 293–316.

Ennis, P.K. (1977). General deterrence and police enforcement: Effective countermeasures against drinking and driving? *Journal of Safety Research, 9,* 15–25.

Erickson, M.L., & Gibbs, J.P. (1978). Objective and perceptual properties of legal punishment and the deterrence doctrine. *Social Problems, 25,* 253–269.

Ericsson, K.A., & Simon, H.A. (1980). Verbal reports as data. *Psychological Review, 87,* 215–251.

Farrington, D.P. (1978). The effectiveness of sentences. *Justice of the Peace, 142,* 68–71.

Fattah, E.A. (1980). Commentary on Cook: The implications of deterrence and incapacitation research for policy evaluation. In C.H. Foust & D.R. Webster (Eds.), *An anatomy of criminal justice: A system overview* (pp. 78–90). Lexington, MA: Lexington Books.

Fattah, E.A. (1983). A critique of deterrence research with particular reference to the economic approach. *Canadian Journal of Criminology 25,* 79–90.

Federal Office of Road Safety. (1986). *Drink driving controls in Australia*. Canberra, Australia: Author.

Feeley, M.M. (1979). *The process is the punishment: Handling cases in a lower criminal court*. New York: Russell Sage Foundation.

Fienberg, S.E. (1980). *The analysis of cross-classified categorical data* (2nd ed.). Cambridge, MA: The MIT Press.

Finlay, D.G. (1979). Alcoholism is an illness. Right? Wrong! In D. Robinson (Ed.), *Alcohol problems: Reviews, research and recommendations*. London: Macmillan.

Finley, N.J., & Grasmick, H.G. (1985). Gender roles and social control. *Sociological Spectrum, 5,* 317–330.

Fischer, A.J., & Lewis, R.D. (1983). *Survey of attitudes towards random breath testing, Volume 2*. Adelaide, Australia: Economics Department, University of Adelaide.

Freedman, K., Henderson, M., & Wood, R. (1973). *Drinking and driving in Sydney: A community survey of behaviour and attitudes*. Sydney: Traffic Accident Research Unit.

Geerken, M.R., & Gove, W.R. (1975). Deterrence: Some theoretical considerations. *Law and Society Review, 9,* 497–513.

Gibbons, D.C. (1975). Offender typologies—Two decades later. *British Journal of Criminology, 15,* 140–156.

Gibbs, J.P. (1975). *Crime, punishment and deterrence*. New York: Elsevier.

Gibbs, J.P. (1978). Another rush to judgement on the deterrence question. *Crimi-*

nology 16, 22–30.

Gibbs, J.P. (1979). Assessing the deterrence doctrine—A challenge for the social and behavioral sciences. *American Behavioral Scientists, 22*, 653–677.

Gilmour, A.R. (1984). *REG—A generalized linear models programme* [Computer programme]. Sydney: Biometrical Branch, NSW Department of Agriculture.

Glaser, B.G., & Strauss, A.L. (1979). *The discovery of grounded theory: Strategies for qualitative research.* New York: Aldine.

Goode, E. (1978). *Deviant behaviour: An interactionist approach.* Englewood Cliffs, NJ: Prentice-Hall.

Gottfredson, D.M., Wilkins, L.T., & Hoffman, P.B. (1978). *Guidelines for parole and sentencing.* Lexington, MA: Lexington Books.

Gottfredson, S.D., & Taylor, R.B. (1986). Person-environment interactions in the prediction of recidivism. In J.M. Byrne & R.J. Sampson (Eds.), *The social ecology of crime* (pp. 133–155). New York: Springer-Verlag.

Gottfreidson, M.R. (1982). The social scientist and rehabilitative crime policy. *Criminology, 20*, 24–42.

Grasmick, H.G. (1981). The strategy of deterrence research: A reply to Greenberg. *The Journal of Criminal Law and Criminology, 72*, 1102–1108.

Grasmick, H.G., & Appleton, L. (1977). Legal punishment and social stigma: A comparison of two deterrence models. *Social Science Quarterly, 58*, 15–28.

Grasmick, H.G., & Bryjak, G.J. (1980). The deterrent effect of perceived severity of punishment. *Social Forces, 59*, 471–491.

Grasmick, H.G., & Green, D.E. (1980). Legal punishment, social disapproval and internalization as inhibitors of illegal behavior. *Journal of Criminal Law and Criminology, 71*, 325–335.

Grasmick, H.G., & Green, D.E. (1981). Deterrence and the morally committed. *Sociological Quarterly, 22*, 1–14.

Grasmick, H.G., Jacobs, D., & McCollom, C.B. (1983). Social class and social control: An application of deterrence theory. *Social Forces, 62*, 359–374.

Grasmick, H.G., & Milligan, H. (1976). Deterrence theory approach to socioeconomic/demographic correlates of crime. *Social Science Quarterly, 57*, 608–617.

Greenberg, D.F. (1981). Methodological issues in survey research on the inhibition of crime: Comment on Grasmick and Green. *Journal of Criminal Law and Criminology, 72*, 1014–1101.

Gusfield, J.R. (1963). *Symbolic crusade.* Urbana, IL: University of Illinois Press.

Gusfield, J.R. (1976). The literary rhetoric of science: Comedy and pathos in drinking driver research. *American Sociological Review, 41*, 16–34.

Gusfield, J.R. (1981a). Managing competence: An ethnographic study of drinking-driving and the context of bars. In T.C. Harford & L.S. Gaines (Eds.), *Social drinking contexts. Research monograph No. 7* (pp. 155–172). Washington, DC: U.S. Government Printing Office.

Gusfield, J.R. (1981b). *The culture of public problems: Drinking-driving and the symbolic order.* Chicago: The University of Chicago Press.

Gusfield, J.R. (1985). Social and cultural contexts of the drinking-driving event. *Journal of Studies on Alcohol, Supplement No. 10*, 70–77.

Hagen, R.E. (1978). The efficacy of licensing controls as a countermeasure for multiple DUI offenders. *Journal of Safety Research, 10*, 115–122.

Hagen, R.E., Williams, R.L., McConnell, E.J., & Fleming, C.W. (1978). *An evaluation of alcohol abuse treatment as an alternative to drivers' license suspension or revocation*. Sacramento, CA: Department of Motor Vehicles and Department of Alcohol and Drug Abuse.

Hagger, R., & Dax, E.C. (1977). The driving records of multiproblem families. *Social Science and Medicine, 11*, 121–127.

Haight, F.A. (1985). Impediments to effective drinking driving countermeasures with a proposal for a driver's license interlock. In S. Kaye & G.W. Meyer (Eds.), *Alcohol, drugs and traffic safety. Proceedings of the Ninth International Conference on Alcohol, Drugs and Traffic Safety, San Juan, Puerto Rico 1983* (pp. 595–608). Washington, DC: National Highway Traffic Safety Administration.

Harré, R., & Secord, P.F. (1979). *The explanation of social behaviour*. Oxford: Basil Blackwell.

Hart, R.J. (1979). Crime and punishment in the army. *Journal of Personality and Social Psychology, 36*, 1456–1471.

Hauer, E., & Cooper, P.J. (1977). Effectiveness of selective enforcement in reducing accidents in metropolitan Toronto. *Transportation Research Record, No. 643*, 18–22.

Henderson, M., & Freedman, K. (1976). Public education as a drink-drive countermeasure. *Australian Journal of Alcohol and Drug Dependence, 3*, 107–112.

Henshel, R.L., & Carey, S.H. (1975). Deviance, deterrence and knowledge of sanctions. In R.L. Henshel & R.A. Silverman (Eds.), *Perception in criminology* (pp. 54–73). New York: Columbia University Press.

Herbert, D. (1982). *Submission to NSW Standing Committee on Road Safety: Alcohol, Drugs and Traffic Safety*. Sydney: Traffic Accident Research Unit, Special Report No. SR 82/111.

Hilton, M.E. (1984). The impact of recent changes in California drinking-driving laws on fatal accident levels during the first postintervention year: An interrupted time series analysis. *Law and Society Review, 18*, 605–627.

Hindelang, M.J., Hirschi, T., & Weis, J.G. (1979). Correlates of delinquency: The illusion of discrepancy between self-report and official measures. *American Sociological Review, 44*, 995–1014.

Hingson, R., Heeren, T., Kovenock, D., Mangione, T., Meyers, A., Morelock, S., Smith, R., Lederman, R., & Scotch, N. (1986, October). *Effects of Maine's 1981 and Massachusetts' 1982 driving under the influence legislation*. Paper presented at the American Public Health Association Alcohol and Motor Vehicles Conference.

Hollinger, R.C. (1984). Race, occupational status, and pro-active police arrest for drinking and driving. *Journal of Criminal Justice, 12*, 173–183.

Hollinger, R.C., & Clark, J.P. (1983). Deterrence in the workplace: Perceived certainty, perceived severity and employee theft. *Social Forces, 62*, 398–418.

Homel, R.J. (1979). The deterrent effect of penalties on drink/drivers. In I.R. Johnston (Ed.) *Proceedings of the Seventh International Conference on Alcohol, Drugs and Traffic Safety, Melbourne, 1977* (pp. 536–546). Canberra, Australia: Australian Government Publishing Service.

Homel, R.J. (1980a). *Penalties and the drink/driver: A study of one thousand offenders. Volume 1, main report*. (Research Report 7). Sydney: Department of the Attorney General and of Justice, NSW Bureau of Crime Statistics and Research.

Homel, R.J. (1980b). Priorities for criminological research in road safety. In *Proceedings of the Road Safety Initiatives Conference, Melbourne, 1980* (pp. 531–552). Melbourne, Australia: Road Safety and Traffic Authority.

Homel, R.J. (1981a). Penalties and the drink-driver: A study of one thousand offenders. *Australian and New Zealand Journal of Criminology, 14*, 225–241.

Homel, R.J. (1981b). Motoring offences as crime: Some priorities for social and action research. *Australian Journal of Social Issues, 16*, 268–282.

Homel, R.J. (1982a). *Submission to NSW Standing Committee on Road Safety: Alcohol, Drugs and Traffic Safety.* Sydney: Macquarie University, School of Behavioural Sciences.

Homel, R.J. (1982b). *Sentencing the drinking driver: A statistical analysis of court records in New South Wales.* (Report to the Criminology Research Council under the conditions of Grant 20/75). Sydney: Macquarie University, School of Behavioural Sciences.

Homel, R.J. (1983a). The impact of random breath testing in New South Wales, December, 1982 to February, 1983. *Medical Journal of Australia, 1*, 616–619.

Homel, R.J. (1983b). Sentencing in magistrates' courts: Some lessons from a study of drinking drivers. In M. Findlay, S. Egger, & J. Sutton (Eds.), *Issues in criminal justice administration* (pp. 109–125). Sydney: Allen & Unwin.

Homel, R.J. (1983c). Young men in the arms of the law: An Australian perspective on policing and punishing the drinking driver. *Accident Analysis and Prevention, 15*, 449–512.

Homel, R.J. (1986). *Policing the drinking driver: random breath testing and the process of deterrence.* Canberra, Australia: Federal Office of Road Safety.

Homel, R.J., & Burns, A. (1985). Through a child's eyes: Quality of neighbourhood and quality of life. In I. Burnely & J. Forrest (Eds.), *Living in cities* (pp. 103–115). Sydney: Allen & Unwin.

Homel, R.J., & Burns, A. (1987). Is this a good place to grow up in? Neighbourhood quality and children's evaluations. *Landscape and Urban Planning, 14*, 101–116.

Homel, R.J., Carseldine, D., & Kearns, I.B. (in press). Drink-driving countermeasures in Australia. *Alcohol, Drugs and Driving, 4*(2).

Homel, R.J., & Wilson, P. (1987). *Death and injury on the road: Critical issues for legislative action and law enforcement.* Canberra, Australia: Australian Institute of Criminology.

Hood, R.G. (1971). Some research results and problems. In L. Radzinowicz & M. Wolfgang (Eds.), *Crime and Justice, Volume III: The criminal in confinement* (pp. 159–182). New York: Basic Books.

Hood, R.G. (1972). *Sentencing the motoring offender.* London: Heinemann.

Hood, R.G., & Sparks, R. (1970). *Key issues in criminology.* London: Weidenfeld & Nicolson.

Horne, D. (1971). *The lucky country* (3rd ed.). Blackburn, Australia: Penguin.

Hurst, P.M. (1980). Can anyone reward safe driving? *Accident Analysis and Prevention, 12*, 217–220.

Hutchinson, D. (1987). *Drink driving attitudes and behaviour, Stage II, Quantitative.* Melbourne: Road Traffic Authority.

Ihrfelt, A. (1978). Drinking and driving in Scandinavia—The legal framework: Sweden. In R. Hauge (Ed.), *Scandinavian studies in criminology, Volume 6: Drinking and driving in Scandinavia* (pp. 23–33). Oslo, Norway: Universitetsforlaget.

Jensen, G.F., Erickson, M.L., & Gibbs, J.P. (1978). Perceived risk of punishment and self-reported delinquency. *Social Forces, 57*, 57–78.

Jensen, G.F., & Stitt, B.G. (1982). Words and misdeeds. Hypothetical choices versus past behavior as measures of deviance. In J. Hagan (Ed.), *Deterrence reconsidered: Methodological innovations* (pp. 33–54). Beverly Hills, CA: SAGE.

Jessor, R. (1981). The perceived environment in psychological theory and research. In D. Magnussen (Ed.), *Toward a psychology of situations: An interactional perspective* (pp. 297–317). Hillsdale, NJ: Erlbaum.

Jiggins, S. (1985 April). *RBT in Australia*. Paper presented at the National Conference on Alcohol and Road Accidents, Wellington, New Zealand.

Job, R.F.S. (1985). Reported attitudes, practices and knowledge in relation to drink-driving: The effects of the introduction of random breath testing in New South Wales, Australia. In S. Kaye & G.W. Meyer (Eds.), *Alcohol, Drugs and Traffic Safety. Proceedings of the Ninth International Conference on Alcohol, Drugs and Traffic Safety, San Juan, Puerto Rico 1983* (pp. 707–720). Washington, DC: National Highway Traffic Safety Administration.

Johnson, E., & Payne, J. (1986). The decision to commit a crime: An information-processing analysis. In D.B. Cornish & R.V. Clarke (Eds.), *The reasoning criminal: Rational choice perspectives on offending* (pp. 170–185). New York: Springer-Verlag.

Johnston, I.R. (1982a). The role of alcohol in road crashes. *Ergonomics, 25,* 941–946.

Johnston, I.R. (1982b). *Drink-driving countermeasures—Deterrent and environmental*. (Report of a visit to Washington, November, 1982). Vermont South, Australia: Australian Road Research Board Internal Report.

Johnston, I.R. (1982c). *Deterring the drinking driver—Australia's experience*. Vermont South, Australia: Australian Road Research Board.

Jonah, B.A. (1986). Accident risk and risk-taking behavior among young drivers. *Accident Analysis and Prevention, 18,* 255–271.

Jonah, B.A., & Wilson, R.J. (1983). Improving the effectiveness of drinking-driving enforcement through increased efficiency. *Accident Analysis and Prevention, 15,* 463–481.

Jones, I.S., & Lund, A.K. (1986). Detection of alcohol-impaired drivers using a passive alcohol sensor. *Journal of Police Science and Administration, 14,* 153–160.

Kahneman, D., & Tversky, A. (1982). The psychology of preferences. *Scientific American, 246* (1), 136–142.

Kearns, I.B., & Goldsmith, H.J. (1984). The impact on traffic crashes of the introduction of random breath testing in New South Wales. *Australian Road Research Board Proceedings, 12,* 81–95.

Kelly, T.O. (1980, March). *First-year drivers—Dead, or alive and learning?* Paper presented to the First Pan Pacific Conference on Drugs and Alcohol, Canberra, Australia.

Kempthorne, O. (1978). A Biometrics invited paper: Logical, epistemological and statistical aspects of nature-nurture data interpretation. *Biometrics, 34,* 1–23.

Kirkham, R., & Landauer, A.A. (1985). Sex differences in the distribution of traffic law enforcement. *Accident Analysis and Prevention, 17,* 211–215.

Kleck, G.D. (1982). On the use of self-report data to determine the class distribution of criminal and delinquent behavior. *American Sociological Review, 47,* 427–433.

Klein, D. (1972). Adolescent driving as deviant behavior. *Journal of Safety Re-*

search, *4*, 98–105.

Klette, H. (1979). Drunken driving—The Swedish experience. In I.R. Johnson (Ed.), *Proceedings of the Seventh International Conference on Alcohol, Drugs and Traffic Safety, Melbourne, 1977* (pp. 365–372). Canberra, Australia: Australian Government Publishing Service.

Knapp, K.A. (1986). Discretion in sentencing. In I. Potas (Ed.), *Sentencing in Australia: Issues, policy and reform* (pp. 89–108). Canberra, Australia: Australian Institute of Criminology.

Knapper, C.K. (1985). Explaining young adults' involvement in road accidents: An overview of research. In D.R. Mayhew, H.M. Simpson, & A.C. Donelson (Eds.), *Young driver accidents: In search of solutions* (pp. 19–34). Ottawa, Canada: The Traffic Research Foundation.

Lambregts, E.C.F., & Soenveld, A.E. (1986). *Drink-driving—Projects inside and outside prison in the Netherlands: Content and effectiveness*. Paper presented at the 10th International Conference on Alcohol, Drugs and Traffic Safety, Amsterdam, The Netherlands.

Lattimore, P., & Witte, A. (1986). Models of decision making under uncertainty: The criminal choice. In D.B. Cornish & D.V. Clarke (Eds.), *The reasoning criminal: Rational choice perspectives on offending* (pp. 129–155). New York: Springer-Verlag.

Law Reform Commission. (1980). *Report No. 15, interim: Sentencing of federal offenders*. Canberra, Australia: Australian Government Publishing Service.

Lawrence, J.A., & Browne, M. (1981). *Magisterial decision-making: How fifteen stipendiary magistrates make court-room decisions*. Murdoch, Australia: Murdoch University, School of Education.

Lee, W. (1971). *Decision theory and human behavior*. New York: Wiley.

Lemert, E.M. (1978). Primary and secondary deviation. In E. Rubington & M.S. Weinberg (Eds.), *Deviance: The interactionist perspective* (pp. 411–413). New York: Macmillan.

Liban, C.B., Vingilis, E.R., & Blefgen, H. (1987). The Canadian drinking-driving countermeasure experience. *Accident Analysis and Prevention*, *19*, 159–181.

Lipton, D., Martinson, R., & Wilks, J. (1975). *Effectiveness of correctional treatment—A survey of treatment evaluation studies*. Springfield, MA: Praeger.

Little, J.W. (1975). *Administration of justice in drunk driving cases*. Gainesville, FL: The University Presses of Florida.

Locander, W., Sudman, S., & Bradburn, N. (1976). An investigation of interview method, threat and response distortion. *Journal of the American Statistical Association*, *71*, 269–275.

Loftus, E.F., Fienberg, S.E., & Tanur, J.M. (1985). Cognitive psychology meets the national survey. *American Psychologist*, *40*, 175–180.

MacLean, S., Hardy, J., Lane, J., & South, D. (1985). *Survey of drink-driving behaviour, knowledge and attitudes in Victoria, December 1983*. Melbourne, Australia: Road Traffic Authority.

Macmillan, J. (1975). *Deviant drivers*. Westmead, England: Saxon House/Lexington Books.

The Macquarie Dictionary. (1981). Sydney, Australia: Macquarie Library.

Madden, B. (1986). *Random breath testing (RBT) in Tasmania*. Paper presented at the Victorian Road Safety Program Initiatives Conference, Melbourne, Australia.

Magnusson, D., & Endler, N.S. (1977). Interactional psychology: Present status and future prospects. In D. Magnusson & N.S. Endler (Eds.), *Personality at the crossroads*: *Current issues in interactional psychology* (pp. 3–36). Hillsdale, NJ: Erlbaum.

Maisey, G., & Saunders, C. (1981). *An evaluation of the 1980/81 Christmas/New Year traffic enforcement blitz*. Perth, Australia: Road Traffic Authority, Research & Statistics Report No. 16.

Mann, R.E., Leigh, G., Vingilis, E.R., & De Genova, K. (1983). A critical review on the effectiveness of drink-driving rehabilitation programs. *Accident Analysis and Prevention*, *15*, 441–446.

Mann, R.E., & Vingilis, E.R. (1985). Applying the interactionist model to impaired driving: implications and new directions. *Proceedings of the Canadian Multidisciplinary Road Safety Conference IV*, 296–308.

Marsh, W.C. (1986). *Negligent-operator treatment evaluation system*: *Program effectiveness report #2*. Sacramento, CA: Research and Development Section, Department of Motor Vehicles.

Mayhew, D.R., Donelson, A.C., Beirness, D.J., & Simpson, H.M. (1986). Youth, alcohol and relative risk of crash involvement. *Accident Analysis and Prevention*, *18*, 273–287.

Mayhew, D.R., Warren, R.A., Simpson, H.M., & Haas, G.C. (1981). *Young driver accidents*: *Magnitude and characteristics of the problem*. Ontario, Canada: Traffic Injury Research Foundation of Canada.

Mayhew, P., Clarke, R.V.G., Sturman, A., & Hough, J.M. (1976). *Crime as opportunity*. *Home Office Research Study No. 34*. London: Her Majesty's Stationery Office.

McGuire, J.P. (1973). *Field research planning for driver's license law enforcement*. Washington, DC: National Highway Traffic Safety Administration.

McLean, A.J. (1984). What shall we do with the drunken driver? *Second University of Adelaide Foundation Lecture for 1984*. Adelaide, Australia: NH & MRC Road Accident Research Unit, University of Adelaide.

McLean, A., Clark, M., Dorsch, M., Holubowycz, O., & McCaul, K. (1984). *Random breath testing in South Australia*: *Effects on drink-driving, accidents and casualties*. Adelaide, Australia: NH & MRC Road Accident Research Unit, The University of Adelaide.

McLean, A.J., Holubowycz, O.T., & Sandow, B.L. (1980). *Alcohol and crashes*: *Identification of relevant factors in this association*. Adelaide, Australia: Road Accident Research Unit, University of Adelaide.

McLean, N.J., & Campbell, I.M. (1979). The drinking driver—A personality profile. In I.R. Johnston (Ed.), *Proceedings of the Seventh International Conference on Alcohol, Drugs and Traffic Safety* (pp. 145–153). Canberra, Australia: Australian Government Publishing Service.

McPherson, R.D., Perl, J., Starmer, G.A., & Homel, R.J. (1984). Self-reported drug usage and crash-incidence in Breathalyzed drivers. *Accident Analysis and Prevention*, *16*, 139–148.

Meier, R.F. (1979). Correlates of deterrence: Problems of theory & method. *Journal of Criminal Justice*, *7*, 11–20.

Meier, R.F., & Johnson, W.T. (1977). Deterrence as social control: The legal and extralegal production of conformity. *American Sociological Review*, *42*, 292–304.

Menninger, K. (1968). *The crime of punishment*. New York: The Viking Press.

Mercer, G.W. (1984 November). *Drinking driving police blitz activity, media coverage and alcohol-related traffic accident reduction.* British Columbia, Canada: Police Services Branch, Ministry of Attorney General.

Mercer, G.W. (1985). The relationships among driving while impaired charges, police drinking-driving roadcheck activity, media coverage and alcohol-related casualty traffic accidents. *Accident Analysis and Prevention, 17,* 467–474.

Michalowski, R.J. (1975). Risking death: A sociological analysis of drivers who kill. In E. Viano (Ed.), *Criminal justice research* (pp. 281–296). Lexington, MA: Lexington Books.

Middendorff, W. (1968). *The effectiveness of punishment, especially in relation to traffic offences.* London: Rothman.

Minor, W.W., & Harry, J. (1982). Deterrent and experimental effects in perceptual deterrence research: A replication and extension. *Journal of Research in Crime and Delinquency, 19,* 190–203.

Mischel, W. (1973). Toward a cognitive social learning reconceptualization of personality. *Psychological Review, 80,* 252–283.

Moller, J.E., & North, J.B. (1986, September). *Random breath testing in Queensland—Really an insidious deception.* Paper presented to The Jubilee Conference of the Australian Orthopaedic Association, Sydney.

Morris, A., & Giller, H. (1977). The juvenile court—The client's perspective. *Criminal Law Review,* 198–205.

Mosher, J.F. (1985). Alcohol policy and the Presidential Commission on Drunk Driving: The paths not taken. *Accident Analysis and Prevention, 17,* 239–250.

Mulford, H.A., & Fitzgerald, J.L. (1981). "Words and deeds." Responses to Popham and Schmidt. *Journal of Studies on Alcohol, 42,* 362–367.

National Highway Traffic Safety Administration. (1979). *Involvement of suspended/revoked drivers in traffic crashes—a statement of the problem.* Washington, DC: U.S. Government Printing Office.

Nelder, J.A., & Wedderburn, R.W.M. (1972). Generalized linear models. *Journal of the Royal Statistical Society, Series A, 135,* 370–384.

Nietzel, M.T. (1979). *Crime and its modification: A social learning perspective.* New York: Pergamon Press.

Nisbett, R., & Ross, L. (1980). *Human inference: strategies and shortcomings of social judgment.* Englewood Cliffs, NJ: Prentice-Hall.

Nisbett, R.E., & Wilson, T.D. (1977). Telling more than we know: Verbal reports on mental processes. *Psychological Review, 84,* 231–259.

Noordzij, P.C. (1983). Measuring the extent of the drinking and driving problem. *Accident Analysis and Prevention, 15,* 407–414.

Norström, T. (1978). Drunken driving: A tentative causal model. In R. Hauge (Ed.), *Scandinavian studies in criminology, Volume 6: Drinking and driving in Scandinavia* (pp. 69–78). Oslo, Norway: Universtetsforlaget.

Norström, T. (1981). *Studies in the causation and prevention of traffic crime.* Stockholm, Sweden: Almqvist & Wiksell.

Norström, T. (1983). Law enforcement and alcohol consumption policy as countermeasures against drunken driving: Possibilities and limitations. *Accident Analysis and Prevention, 15,* 513–521.

NSW Bureau of Crime Statistics and Research. (1984). *Court statistics 1982.* Sydney: Department of the Attorney-General and of Justice.

NSW Bureau of Crime Statistics and Research. (1985). *Court Statistics 1983.* Sydney: Department of the Attorney General and of Justice.

NSW Council for Civil Liberties. (1982, November). *Random breath testing and civil liberties*. Paper distributed to all members of the NSW ALP Caucus, and available from The Council for Civil Liberties, 149 St. Johns Road, Glebe, NSW, 2037, Australia.

Nusbaumer, M.R., & Zusman, M.E. (1981). Autos, alcohol and adolescence: Forgotten concerns and overlooked linkages. *Journal of Drug Education, 11,* 167–177.

Palmer, J. (1977). Economic analyses of the deterrent effect of punishment: A review. *Journal of Research in Crime and Delinquency, 14,* 4–21.

Panel on Alternative Policies Affecting the Prevention of Alcohol Abuse and Alcoholism. (1981). The nature of the alcohol problem. In M.H. Moore & D.R. Gerstein (Eds.), *Panel on alternative policies affecting the prevention of alcohol abuse and alcoholism.* Washington, DC: National Academy of Sciences.

Parker, J., & Grasmick, H.G. (1979). Linking actual and perceived certainty of punishment: An exploratory study of an untested proposition in deterrence theory. *Criminology, 17,* 366–379.

Parsons, K.R. (1978). *Violence on the road: A logical extension of the subculture of violence thesis?* Wellington, New Zealand: Department of Justice.

Paternoster, R., & Iovanni, L. (1986). The deterrent effect of perceived severity: A reexamination. *Social Forces, 64,* 751–777.

Paternoster, R., Saltzman, L.E., Waldo, G.P., & Chiricos, T.G. (1982). Perceived risk and deterrence: Methodological artifacts in perceptual deterrence research. *Journal of Criminal Law and Criminology, 73,* 1238–1258.

Paternoster, R., Saltzman, L.E., Waldo, G.P., & Chiricos, T.G. (1986). Assessments of risk and behavioral experience: An exploratory study of change. *Criminology, 23,* 417–436.

Peck, R.C. (1985). The role of youth in traffic accidents: A review of past and current California data. *Alcohol, Drugs and Driving Abstracts and Reviews, 1* (1–2), 45–68.

Peck, R.C., Sadler, D.D., & Perrine, M.W. (1985). The comparative effectiveness of alcohol rehabilitation and licensing control actions for drunk driving offenders: A review of the literature. *Alcohol, Drugs and Driving Abstracts and Reviews, 1* (4), 15–40.

Pelz, D.C., & Schuman, S.H. (1971). Are young drivers really more dangerous after controlling for exposure and experience? *Journal of Safety Research, 3,* 68–79.

Pernanen, K. (1974). Validity of survey data on alcohol use. In R.J. Gibbins, G. Israel, J. Kalant, R.E. Popham, W. Schmidt, & R.G. Smart (Eds.), *Research advances in alcohol and drug problems, Volume 1* (pp. 355–74). New York: Wiley.

Petersen, A.R. (1982). *Drink-drivers and the judicial process.* Unpublished Master's thesis, Department of Anthropology, University of Western Australia, Perth, Australia.

Petersen, A.R. (1983). Drink-drivers and the judicial process: an analysis that relates to the defendant's perspective. *Australian Journal of Social Issues, 18,* 18–32.

Phillips, L., Ray, S., & Votey, H. (1984). Forecasting highway casualties: The British Road Safety Act and a sense of déjà vu. *Journal of Criminal Justice, 12,* 101–114.

Pitz, G.F., & Sachs, N.J. (1984). Judgement and decision: theory and application. *Annual Review of Psychology, 35*, 139–163.

Plunk, B. (1984, Fall). Looking back . . . moving forward (Anniversary Editorial). *MADD National Newsletter*, p. 14.

Popham, R.E., & Schmidt, W. (1981). Words and deeds: The validity of self-report data on alcohol consumption. *Journal of Studies on Alcohol, 42*, 355–358.

Potas, I. (1979). *Limiting sentencing discretion: Strategies for reducing the incidence of unjustified disparities*. *(Research Paper No. 7, Sentencing)*. Sydney: The Law Reform Commission.

Poveda, T.G., & Schaffer, E. (1975). Positivism and interactionism: Two traditions of research in criminology. In E. Viano (Ed.), *Criminal Justice Research* (pp. 25–26). Lexington, MA: Lexington Books.

Pritchard, D.A. (1979). Stable predictors of recidivism: A summary. *Criminology, 17*, 15–21.

Queensland Transport Policy Planning Unit. (1987). *Evaluation of the Reduce Impaired Driving (RID) Campaign*. Brisbane, Australia: Queensland Department of Transport.

Quinney, R. (1976). Symposium on Wilson's *Thinking About Crime*. *Contemporary Sociology, 5*, 414–418.

RACV Consulting Services (1983). *Road safety in Victoria: Existing countermeasures and their effects*. (Report presented to the Social Development Committee of the Parliament of Victoria.) Melbourne, Australia: Author.

Radzinowicz, L., & Hood, R. (1975). Motoring offences: Their criminological significance. In *Proceedings of Seminar: Road Safety and the Law, Sydney, 2–3 August, 1973* (pp. 21–28). Canberra, Australia: Australian Government Publishing Service.

Radzinowicz, L., & King, J. (1977). *The growth of crime: The international experience*. New York: Basic Books.

Rankin, J.H., & Wells, L.G. (1981). The social context of deterrence. *Sociology and Social Research, 67*, 18–39.

Raymond, A.E. (1973). *A review of alcohol in relation to road safety*. Canberra, Australia: Australian Department of Transport/Australian Government Publishing Service.

Richards, P., & Tittle, C.R. (1981). Gender and perceived chances of arrest. *Social Forces, 59*, 1182–1199.

Richards, P., & Tittle, C.R. (1982). Socioeconomic status and perceptions of personal arrest probabilities. *Criminology, 20*, 329–346.

Riley, D. (1985). Drinking drivers: The limits to deterrence. *The Howard Journal, 24*, 241–256.

Robertson, L.S. (1981). Patterns of teenaged driver involvement in fatal motor vehicle crashes: Implications for policy choice. *Journal of Health Politics, Policy and Law, 6*, 303–314.

Robertson, L.S., Rich, R.F., & Ross, H.L. (1973). Jail sentences for driving while intoxicated: A judicial policy that failed. *Law and Society Review, 8*, 55–67.

Robinson, C.D. (1977). *The operation of driver licence disqualification as a sanction*. Melbourne, Australia: University of Melbourne, Department of Criminology.

Rochester Against Intoxicated Driving Foundation. (1986). *Are you a victim of a drinking driver? A handbook for victims, families and friends*. Rochester, NY: Author.

Room, R. (1981). A farewell to alcoholism? A commentary on the WHO Expert Committee Report. *British Journal of Addiction, 76*, 115–123.

Room, R. (1983). Sociological aspects of the disease concept of alcoholism. In R.G. Smart, F.B. Glaser, Y. Israel, H. Kalant, R.E. Popham, & W. Schmidt (Eds.), *Research advances in alcohol and drug problems, Volume 7*. New York: Plenum.

Room, R. (1984 October). *"An intoxicated society?": Alcohol issues then and now in Australia*. Paper presented at a meeting of the International Group for Comparative Alcohol Studies, Stockholm, Sweden.

Ross, H.L. (1960). Traffic law violation: A folk crime. *Social Problems, 8*, 231–241.

Ross, H.L. (1973). Law, science and accidents: The British Road Safety Act of 1967. *Journal of Legal Studies 2*, 1–78.

Ross, H.L. (1975). The Scandinavian myth: The effectiveness of drinking and driving legislation in Sweden and Norway. *Journal of Legal Studies, 4*, 285–310.

Ross, H.L. (1978). Scandinavia's drinking and driving laws: Do they work? In R. Hauge, (Ed.), *Scandinavian studies in criminology, Volume 6: Drinking and driving in Scandinavia* (pp. 55–60). Oslo, Norway: Universitetsforlaget.

Ross, H.L. (1982). *Deterring the drinking driver: Legal policy and social control*. Lexington, MA: Lexington Book.

Ross, H.L. (1984a). Social control through deterrence: drinking-and driving laws. *Annual Review of Sociology, 10*, 21–35.

Ross, H.L. (1984b). Deterring the drinking driver. In *Proceedings of the Second Provincial Conference on Traffic Safety for Community Leaders* (pp. 59–70). Vancouver, Canada: Insurance Corporation of British Columbia.

Ross, H.L. (1984c). *Deterring the drinker driver: Legal policy and social control*. (Revised and updated edition.) Lexington, MA: Lexington Books.

Ross, H.L. (1985). Deterring drunk driving: An analysis of current efforts. *Journal of Studies on Alcohol, Supplement No. 10*, 122–128.

Ross, H.L. (1986, September). *Britain's Christmas crusade against drinking and driving*. Paper delivered to the 10th International Conference on Alcohol, Drugs and Traffic Safety, Amsterdam, The Netherlands.

Ross, H.L. (1988). Deterrence-based policies in Britain, Canada and Australia. In M.D. Laurence, J.R. Snortum, & F.E. Zimring (Eds.), *The social control of drinking and driving* (pp. 64–78). Chicago: University of Chicago Press.

Ross, H.L., & Blumenthal, M. (1974). Sanctions for the drinking driver: An experimental study. *Journal of Legal Studies, 3*, 53–61.

Ross, H.L., & Blumenthal, M. (1975). Some problems in experimentation in a legal setting. *The American Sociologist, 10*, 150–155.

Ross, H.L., Klette, H., & McCleary, R. (1984). Liberalization and rationalization of drunk-driving laws in Scandinavia. *Accident Analysis and Prevention, 16*, 471–487.

Ross, H.L., & LaFree, G.D. (1986). Deterrence in criminology and social policy. In N.J. Smelser & D.R. Gerstein (Eds.), *Behavioral and social science: Fifty years of discovery* (pp. 129–152). Washington, DC: National Academy Press.

Ross, H.L., & McCleary, R. (1983). Methods for studying the impact of drunk driving laws. *Accident Analysis and Prevention, 15*, 415–428.

Ross, H.L., McCleary, R., & Epperlein, T. (1982). Deterrence of drinking and driving in France: An evaluation of the law of July 12, 1978. *Law and Society Review, 16*, 345–374.

Rothengatter, T. (1982). The effects of police surveillance and law enforcement on driver behaviour. *Current Psychological Reviews*, *2*, 349–359.

Ryan, J.P. (1981). Adjudication and sentencing in a misdemeanor court—The outcome is the punishment. *Law and Society Review*, *15*, 79–108.

Sadler, D., & Perrine, M.W. (1984). *The long-term traffic safety impact of a pilot alcohol abuse treatment program as an alternative to license suspensions. Volume 2 of an evaluation of the California Drunk Driving Countermeasure System.* Sacramento, CA: Research and Development Office, Department of Motor Vehicles.

Saltz, R.F. (1985). Server intervention: conceptual overview and current developments. *Alcohol, Drugs and Driving Abstracts and Reviews*, *1* (4), 1–13.

Salzberg, P.M., & Paulsrude, S.P. (1984). An evaluation of Washington's driving while intoxicated law: Effect on drunk driving recidivism. *Journal of Safety Research*, *15*, 117–124.

Samuels, J., & Lee, B. (1978). *The evaluation of the drink and drive advertising campaign 1976/1977.* London: Central Office of Information/Public Attitude Surveys Ltd., U.K.

Sanson-Fisher, R., Redman, S., & Osmond, C. (1986). *Rehabilitation of drink drivers in Australia and New Zealand.* Canberra, Australia: Federal Office of Road Safety.

Sargent, M. (1979). *Drinking and alcoholism in Australia: A power relations theory.* Melbourne, Australia: Longman Cheshire.

Saunders, C.M. (1977). *A study of increased intensity of traffic law enforcement as a means of reducing accidents.* Perth, Australia: Research and Statistics Division, Road Traffic Authority.

Schutz, I. (1970). *Collected papers III. Studies in phenomenological philosophy.* The Hague, The Netherlands: Martinus Nijhoff.

Selzer, M.L., & Weiss, S. (1966). Alcoholism and traffic fatalities: Study in futility. *American Journal of Psychiatry*, *122*, 762–767.

Shapiro, P., & Votey, H.L. (1984). Deterrence and subjective probabilities of arrest: Modeling individual decisions to drink and drive in Sweden. *Law and Society Review*, *18*, 583–604.

Shoham, S.G. (1974). Punishment and traffic offences. *Traffic Quarterly*, *28*, 61–73.

Shoham, S.G., Geva, N., Markowski, R., & Kaplinsky, N. (1976). Internalisation of norms, risk-perception and anxiety as related to driving offences. *The British Journal of Criminology*, *16*, 142–155.

Shoham, S.G., & Rahav, G. (1982). *The mark of Cain* (2nd ed.). St. Lucia, Australia: University of Queensland Press.

Shoham, S.G., Rahav, G., Markovsky, R., Chard, F., Ben-Haim, M., & Baruch, I. (1982). *"Anxious" and "reckless" drivers.* Tel Aviv: Tel Aviv University.

Shoup, D.C. (1973). Cost effectiveness of urban traffic law enforcement. *Journal of Transport Economics & Policy*, *7*, 37–57.

Shover, N., Bankston, W.B., & Gurley, J.W. (1977). Responses of the criminal justice system to legislation providing more severe threatened sanctions. *Criminology*, *14*, 483–500.

Simon, H.A. (1957). *Models of man.* New York: Wiley.

Sloane, H.R., & Huebner, M.L. (1980). *Drink-driving behaviour, knowledge and attitudes in Victoria: December, 1978–January, 1979.* Melbourne, Australia: Road Safety & Traffic Authority.

reply to Nisbett and Wilson. *Psychological Review*, *85*, 355–362.

Smith, J.E. (1985). California update: The battle against drinking drivers. *Police Chief*, *52* (7), 64–66.

Snortum, J.R. (1984a). Controlling the alcohol-impaired driver in Scandinavia and the United States: Simple deterrence and beyond. *Journal of Criminal Justice*, *12*, 131–148.

Snortum, J.R. (1984b). Alcohol-impaired driving in Norway and Sweden: Another look at "The Scandinavian Myth." *Law and Policy*, *6*, 5–37.

Snortum, J.R. (1988). Deterrence of alcohol-impaired driving: An effect in search of a cause. In M.D. Laurence, J.R. Snortum, & F.E. Zimring (Eds.), *The social control of drinking and driving* (pp. 189–226). Chicago: University of Chicago Press.

Snortum, J.R., Hauge, R., & Berger, D.E. (1986). Deterring alcohol-impaired driving: A comparative analysis of compliance in Norway and the United States. *Justice Quarterly*, *3*, 139–165.

Snortum, J.R., Kremer, L.K., & Berger, D.E. (1987). Alcoholic beverage preference as a public statement: Self-concept and social image of college drinkers. *Journal of Studies on Alcohol*, *48*, 243–251.

Snow, R.W., & Cunningham, O.R. (1985). Age, machismo, and the drinking locations of drunken drivers: a research note. *Deviant Behavior*, *6*, 57–66.

Sobel, R., & Underhill, R. (1976). Family disorganization and teenage accidents. *Journal of Safety Research*, *8*, 8–18.

South, D., & Johnston, I. (1984). *The zero blood alcohol law for novice and unlicensed drivers*. Unpublished manuscript, Road Traffic Authority, Melbourne, Australia.

South, D., & Stuart, G. (1983). *The effect of random breath testing on the perceived risk of detection for drink driving*. Paper presented at the Autumn School of Studies on Alcohol & Drugs, St. Vincent's Hospital, Melbourne, Australia.

Staysafe (1982). *Alcohol, others drugs and road safety*. (First report of the Joint Standing Committee on Road Safety, Parliament of New South Wales). Sydney: Parliament of New South Wales.

Steenhuis, D.W. (1983). *Drinking and driving*. The Hague, The Netherlands: Ministry of Justice.

Stone, R.F. (1985). Charlottesville intensive checkpoint program pays off. *Police Chief*, *52* (7), 60–63.

Summers, L.G., & Harris, D.H. (1978). *The general deterrence of driving while intoxicated. Volume I, system analysis and computer based simulation*. Washington, DC: U.S. Department of Transportation.

Summers, L.G., & Harris, D.H. (1979). System analysis of the general deterrence of driving while intoxicated. *Human Factors*, *21*, 205–213.

Sutton, L., Farrar, J., & Campbell, W. (1986, September). *The effectiveness of random breath testing: A comparison between the state of Tasmania, Australia and four states in the eastern United States*. Paper presented at the 10th International Conference on Alcohol, Drugs and Traffic Safety, Amsterdam, The Netherlands.

Sykes, G.W. (1984). Saturated enforcement: The efficacy of deterrence and drunk driving. *Journal of Criminal Justice*, *12*, 185–197.

Tabachnick, B.G., & Fidell, L.S. (1983). *Using multivariate statistics*. New York: Harper & Row.

Tarling, R. (1979). *Sentencing practice in magistrates' courts* (*Home Office Research Study No. 56*). London: Her Majesty's Stationery Office.

Teevan, J.J. (1976). Subjective perception of deterrence (continued). *Journal of Research in Crime and Delinquency*, *13*, 155–164.

The 0.05 line. (1982, December 28). *The Sydney Morning Herald*, p. 6.

Thomas, D.A. (1980). *Principles of sentencing* (2nd ed.). London: Heinemann.

Thomson, G.A. (1985). Drinking-driving accident countermeasures: Why not try changing the environment? *Accident Analysis and Prevention*, *17*, 207–210.

Thomson, J., & Mavrolefterou, K. (1984). Assessing the effectiveness of random breath testing. In *Proceedings of the Conference of the Australian Road Research Board*, *12*, 72–80.

Timm, N.H. (1975). *Multivariate analysis with applications in education and psychology*. Monterey, CA: Brooks/Cole.

Tittle, C.R. (1980a). *Sanctions and social deviance: The question of deterrence*. New York: Praeger.

Tittle, C.R. (1980b). Evaluating the deterrent effects of criminal sanctions. In M.W. Klein & K.S. Teilman (Eds.), *Handbook of criminal justice evaluation* (pp. 381–402). Beverly Hills, CA: SAGE.

Tittle, C.R., Villemez, W.J., & Smith, D.A. (1978). The myth of social class and criminality: An empirical assessment of the empirical evidence. *American Sociological Review*, *43*, 643–656.

Tittle, C.R., Villemez, W.J., & Smith, D.A. (1982). One step forward, two steps back: More on the class/criminality controversy. *American Sociological Review*, *47*, 435–438.

Tomasic, R. (1977). *Deterrence and the drinking driver*. Sydney: The Law Foundation of New South Wales.

Tuck, M., & Riley, D. (1986). The theory of reasoned action: A decision theory of crime. In D.B. Cornish & R.V. Clarke (Eds.), *The reasoning criminal: Rational choice perspectives on offending* (pp. 156–169). New York: Springer-Verlag.

Tversky, A., & Kahneman, D. (1981). The framing of decisions and the psychology of choice. *Science*, *211*, 453–458.

Valverius, M.R. (1985). To punish and/or to treat the driver under the influence of alcohol and/or drugs. In S. Kaye & G.W. Meyer (Eds.), *Alcohol, Drugs and Traffic Safety*. *Proceedings of the Ninth International Conference on Alcohol, Drugs and Traffic Safety, San Juan, Puerto Rico, 1983* (pp. 51–58). Washington, DC: National Highway Traffic Safety Administration.

van den Haag, E. (1980). Punitive sentences. In C.H. Foust & D.R. Webster (Eds.), *An anatomy of criminal justice: A system overview* (pp. 157–171). Lexington, MA: Lexington Books.

van der Werff, C. (1981). Recidivism and special deterrence. *British Journal of Criminology*, *21*, 136–147.

Vingilis, E.R. (1983). Drinking drivers and alcoholics: Are they from the same population? In R.G. Smart, F.G. Glaser, Y. Israel, H. Kalant, R.E. Popham, & W. Schmidt (Eds.), *Research advances in alcohol and drug problems, Volume 7* (pp. 299–342). New York: Plenum.

Vingilis, E.R. (1984, May). *Predispositional factors toward drinking and driving*. Paper presented at the National Institute on Alcohol Abuse and Alcoholism's Research Workshop on Alcohol and the Drinking Driver, Bethesda, MD.

Vingilis, E.R. (1985). Panel discussion: Session III—Evaluation of sociocultural factors in drinking and driving. *Journal of Studies on Alcohol, Supplement No. 10*, 90.

Vingilis, E.R., Adlaf, E.M., & Chung, L. (1982). Comparison of age and sex characteristics of police-suspected impaired drivers and roadside-surveyed impaired drivers. *Accident Analysis and Prevention, 14*, 425–430.

Vingilis, E.R., & De Genova, K. (1984). Youth and the forbidden fruit: Experiences with changes in legal drinking age in North America. *Journal of Criminal Justice, 12*, 161–172.

Vingilis, E.R., & Mann, R.E. (1986). *Towards an interactionist approach to drinking-driving behavior: Implications for prevention and research.* Unpublished manuscript, Addiction Research Foundation, Toronto, Canada.

Vingilis, E., & Salutin, L. (1980). A prevention programme for drinking driving. *Accident Analysis & Prevention, 12*, 267–274.

Vinson, T., & Homel, R. (1975). Crime and disadvantage: The coincidence of medical and social problems in an Australian city. *British Journal of Criminology, 15*, 21–31.

Vinson, T., & Homel, R. (1976). *Indicators of community well-being.* Canberra, Australia: Australian Government Publishing Service.

Voas, R.B. (1986). Evaluation of jail as a penalty for drunken driving. *Alcohol, Drugs and Driving Abstracts and Reviews, 2* (2), 47–70.

von Hirsch, A. (1976). *Doing justice: The choice of punishments.* New York: Hill & Wang.

Von Neumann, J., & Morgenstern, O. (1953). *Theory of games and economic behaviour* (3rd ed.). Princeton, NJ: Princeton University.

Votey, H.L. (1978). The deterrence of drunken driving in Norway and Sweden: An econometric analysis of existing policies. In R. Hauge (Ed.), *Scandinavian studies in criminology, Volume 6: Drinking-and-driving in Scandinavia* (pp. 79–99). Oslo, Norway: Universitetsforlaget.

Votey, H.L. (1982). Scandinavian drinking-driving control: Myth or intuition? *The Journal of Legal Studies, XI*, 93–116.

Votey, H.L. (1984). The deterioration of deterrence effects of driving legislation—Have we been giving wrong signals to policy makers? *Journal of Criminal Justice, 12*, 115–130.

Votey, H.L., & Shapiro, P. (1983). Highway accidents in Sweden: Modelling the process of drunken driving behavior and control. *Accident Analysis and Prevention, 15*, 523–533.

Wagenaar, A.C. (1983). *Alcohol, young drivers, and traffic accidents: Effects of minimum-age laws.* Lexington, MA: Lexington Books.

Walker, N. (1979). The efficacy and morality of deterrents. *Criminal Law Review*, March, 129–143.

Waller, J.A. (1967). Identification of problem drinking among drunken drivers. *Journal of the American Medical Association, 200*, 124–130.

Warren, R.A. (1982). Rewards for safe driving? A rejoinder to P.M. Hurst. *Accident Analysis and Prevention, 14*, 169–172.

Warren, R.A., & Simpson, H.M. (1980). Exposure and alcohol as risk factors in the fatal nighttime collisions of men and women drivers. *Journal of Safety Research, 12*, 151–156.

Webb, S.D. (1980). Deterrence theory—A reconceptualization. *Canadian Journal of Criminology, 22*, 23–35.

West, L.H.T., & Hore, T. (Eds.). (1980). *An analysis of drink driving research.* Monash University, Melbourne, Australia: Higher Education Advisory & Research Unit.

Whitehead, P.C., & Ferrence, R.G. (1976). Alcohol and other drugs related to young drivers' traffic accident involvement. *Journal of Safety Research, 8*, 65–72.

Wilkins, L.T. (1969). *Evaluation of penal measures.* New York: Random House.

Willett, T.C. (1971). *Criminal on the road* [Paperback edition]. London: Tavistock.

Willett, T.C. (1973). *Drivers after sentence.* London: Heinemann.

Williams, A.F. (1986). Raising the legal purchase age in the United States: Its effects on fatal motor vehicle crashes. *Alcohol, Drugs and Driving Abstracts and Reviews, 2* (2), 1–12.

Williams, A.F., & Lund, A.K. (1984). Deterrent effects of roadblocks on drinking and driving. *Traffic Safety Evaluation Research Review, 3*, 7–18.

Williams, R.L., Hagen, R.E., & McConnell, E.J. (1984a). A driving record analysis of suspension and revocation effects on the drinking-driving offender. *Accident Analysis and Prevention, 16*, 333–338.

Williams, R.L., Hagen, R.E., & McConnell, E.J. (1984b). A survey of suspension and revocation effects on the drinking-driving offender. *Accident Analysis and Prevention, 16*, 339–350.

Wilson, R.J., & Jonah, B.A. (1985). Identifying impaired drivers among the general driving population. *Journal of Studies on Alcohol, 46*, 531–537.

Winship, C., & Mare, R.D. (1983). Structural equations and path analysis for discrete data. *American Journal of Sociology, 89*, 54–112.

Wolfe, L.M. (1980). Strategies of path analysis. *American Educational Research Journal, 17*, 183–209.

Zimring, F.E., & Hawkins, G. (1968). Deterrence and marginal groups. *Journal of Research in Crime and Delinquency, 5*, 100–114.

Zimring, F.E., & Hawkins, G. (1973). *Deterrence: The legal threat in crime control.* Chicago: University of Chicago Press.

Zylman, R. (1972). Race and social status discrimination and police action in alcohol-affected collisions. *Journal of Safety Research, 4*, 75–84.

Appendix
Questionnaires for the RBT Study*

On the following pages are the two questionnaires used in the RBT study. The questionnaires are discussed in Chapter 5, together with the sampling procedures.

S.P. No. ....
ANOP/1802   DRINKING AND DRIVING STUDY, FEBRUARY 1983

Card (1)   Q. No. (2 - 4)

Card: 1

INTRODUCTION: *Good morning/afternoon/evening, I'm ... from ANOP the research organisation. I'd now like to ask you some questions about drinking and driving ...*

ASK ALL
Q. 1(a) Over the last three months or so, have you seen, heard or read anything about new methods the government is using to deal with drinking and driving in New South Wales?

(5)
YES...1-ASK Q.1(b)
NO..2 ⎫
Unsure......................................3 ⎬ GO TO Q.2

IF "YES" TO Q.1(a), ASK:
Q. 1(b) What new ways have you become aware of for dealing with drinking and driving? Any others? (DO NOT PROMPT)

(6)
RANDOM BREATH TESTING....................1
.05 LIMIT................................2
INCREASED PENALTIES......................3
BREATH TESTING OF DRIVERS AT ACCIDENTS....4
BLOOD TESTING OF DRIVERS ADMITTED TO HOSPITAL..................................5
RANDOM LICENCE CHECKS....................6
OTHER (Specify)..........................
....
....

ASK ALL
Q. 2 As you may know, random breath testing was introduced into New South Wales on December 17 last year. This means that the police can ask any motorist to take a breath test at any time, even if he or she has not had an accident, has not committed any offence, and has not been driving in a way which would attract police attention. Since December 17 last year:

READ OUT
(a) Have you been pulled over by the police at random and asked to take a breath test - or have you been a passenger in the car when the driver has been asked to take a random breath test?

(7)
YES...1
NO..2
Unsure......................................3

(b) Have you driven or have you been driven, past police carrying out random breath testing?

(8)
YES...1
NO..2
Unsure......................................3

(c) Has anyone you know been randomly breath tested?

(9)
YES...1
NO..2
Unsure......................................3

(d) Have you seen, heard or read any publicity about random breath testing?

(10)
YES...1
NO..2
Unsure......................................3

ASK ALL
Q. 3 I'd like you to consider the following situation. A person is driving home on a weekday after drinking in a hotel for several hours. It is about 10.30 at night and his blood alcohol level is above the legal limit. His driving is not obviously affected and he is not breaking any other traffic regulations. His trip home takes about 30 minutes over suburban main roads. Are his chances of being stopped by the police lower, about the same, or higher than they were before the introduction of random breath testing?

(11)
LOWER.......................................1
ABOUT SAME..................................2
HIGHER......................................3

ASK ALL
Q. 4 Are you a current driver or rider licence holder, are you at present disqualified from driving, or are you not a licence holder and not disqualified?

(12)
CURRENT....................................1 ⎫ ASK Q.5
DISQUALIFIED...............................2 ⎭
NOT LICENSED...............................3-GO TO Q.13

ASK ALL
Q. 5 From this card (SHOWCARD 1), how would you rate your chances of being pulled over by the police for a random breath test some time in the next month?

ASK ALL
Q. 6 If you had been asked that question the day random breath testing was introduced, how do you think you would have answered? (SHOWCARD 1)

Q.5 (13)   Q.6 (14)
EXTREMELY LIKELY..........1................1
QUITE LIKELY..............2................2
EVEN CHANCE...............3................3
QUITE UNLIKELY............4................4
EXTREMELY UNLIKELY........5................5
Unsure....................6................6

ASK ALL
Q. 7 Which of the following (SHOWCARD 2) most closely describes your drinking habits?

(15)

```
3+ TIMES A DAY...........................1  ⎫
TWICE A DAY..............................2  ⎪
ONCE A DAY...............................3  ⎪
NEARLY EVERY DAY.........................4  ⎬ ASK Q.8
3-4 TIMES A WEEK.........................5  ⎪
ONCE/TWICE A WEEK........................6  ⎪
2-3 TIMES A MONTH........................7  ⎭
ONCE A MONTH.............................8
LESS THAN ONCE A MONTH...................9
LESS THAN ONCE A YEAR....................0  ⎫ GO TO Q.13
NEVER DRINK..............................x  ⎭
```

ASK ALL DRINKERS FROM Q.7
Q. 8 On days that you do drink, how much, on average, do you have over the whole day? (PROBE EACH TYPE OF DRINK BELOW. RECORD **NUMBER** OF DRINKS AGAINST SIZE OF GLASS, BOTTLE, ETC.)

NORMAL BEER:		LOW ALCOHOL BEER:	
Middies	....	Middies....................	....
Schooners.............	....	Schooners..................	....
Large bottles.........	....	Large bottles..............	....
Small bottles.........	....	Small bottles..............	....
Cans..................	....	Cans.......................	....

TABLE WINE:		OTHER (Specify)	
Glasses (4oz).........	....	....	....

PORT/SHERRY:			
Glasses (2oz).........	....	....	....

SPIRITS:			
Glasses (1oz).........	....	....	....

OFFICE USE ONLY

	(16)	(17)
NORMAL BEER		
	(18)	(19)
L.A. BEER		
	(20)	(21)
WINE		
	(22)	(23)
PORT/SHERRY		
	(24)	(25)
SPIRITS		
	(26)	(27)
OTHER		
	(28)	(29)
TOTAL		

ASK ALL DRINKERS IN Q.7
Q. 9 Have you ever driven when you felt you had had **too much** to drink?

(30)
```
YES......................................1
NO.......................................2
Unsure...................................3
```

ASK ALL DRINKERS IN Q.7
Q.10(a) Since random breath testing was brought in just before Christmas, have you driven when you felt you had had **too much** to drink?

(31)
```
YES......................................1  ⎫ ASK Q.10(b)
NO.......................................2  ⎭
Unsure...................................3-GO TO Q.11
```

ASK ALL EXCEPT UNSURE TO Q.10(a):
Q.10(b) Why do you say that? Any other reasons? (PROBE)

....
.... (32) (33)

ASK ALL DRINKERS IN Q.7
Q.11 When they first brought in random breath testing just before Christmas, what effects did it have on you at the time. From this card (SHOWCARD 3) what if anything did you do at the time? (RECORD IN 1ST COLUMN)

Q.12 And what about **now** ... what effects is random breath testing having on you now. What (SHOWCARD 3) if anything are you doing now?

	Q.11 (34)	Q.12 (36)
. Not using the car as much...	1	1
. Driving more carefully at all times...	2	2
. Stopped driving to places where you will be drinking...............................	3	3
. Drinking at home more often, drinking away from home less..........................	4	4
. Carefully limiting your drinking when driving......................................	5	5
. Stopped drinking altogether when driving...	6	6
. Drinking more soft drinks when driving...	7	7
. Switched to low alcohol beer when driving..	8	8
. Driving more carefully after drinking..	9	9
. Using taxis more often after drinking..	0	0
. Using public transport more often after drinking..................................	x	x
. Staying overnight after drinking...	y	y

	(35)	(37)
. Having someone else drive you home after drinking..................................	1	1
. Sleeping in car instead of driving home after drinking.............................	2	2
. Drinking at places closer to home than before......................................	3	3
. Have not changed usual behaviour...	4	4

OTHER (Specify) Q.11...☐

     Q.12...☐

ASK ALL

Q.13 Did the penalties for drinking and driving change when   (38)
      random breath testing was brought in?   YES...1

      IF YES: In what ways did they change? ◄────────   NO..2
      ....   Unsure......................................3

ASK ALL

Q.14 In general, do you agree or disagree with the introduction   (39)
      of random breath testing in New South Wales?   AGREE.......................................1

                                                                    DISAGREE....................................2

                                                                    OTHER (Specify)...........................

                                                                    .... [ ]

                                                                    Unsure......................................y

ASK ALL

Q.15 From what you have seen, heard or read, what effects, if any, do you feel random breath testing has had in New South Wales?
      PROBE: Anything else it has done?

      .... (40) (41)

      .... [ ][ ]

ASK ALL

.   And now, to make sure we have a good sample, could   . What is the highest level of education you have
      you tell me your approximate age?   reached so far?   (44)

      | 17-20 | 21-24 | 25-34 | 35-44 | 45-54 | 55-54 | 65+ | Less than 3 yrs high school................1
      | 1 | 2 | 3 | 4 | 5 | 6 | 7 | (42)
                                                                       3 or more yrs high school.................2
                                                           (43)
.   SEX (BY OBSERVATION)   Male................1   Gained HSC/L.C./matric....................3

                                      Female..............2   Gained Uni degree/College diploma..........4

                                                                 . What is your occupation?
                                                                                                                (45)
                                                                    WRITE IN:
                                                                             .... [ ]

NAME OF RESPONDENT: Mr/Mrs/Miss/Ms..

ADDRESS:...

.... TELEPHONE NO................................

THIS DOCUMENT IS COPYRIGHT. REPRODUCTION IN WHOLE OR PART IF PROHIBITED WITHOUT THE WRITTEN PERMISSION OF ANOP

INTERVIEWER'S STATEMENT: *I hereby certify that this is a true and accurate record of this interview, and that I have made a
                          thorough check of all responses to questions so as to comply with the survey briefing and instructions.*

....

INTERVIEWER'S NAME AND SIGNATURE

DATE OF INTERVIEW:................................. *LENGTH OF INTERVIEW:*..................................*minutes*

S.P. No. ....

ANOP/1816   (A. NEW SAMPLE)   SECOND DRINKING AND DRIVING STUDY, APRIL 1983

Card (1)   Q. No. (2 - 4)   [1]

INTRODUCTION: *Good morning/afternoon/evening, I'm ... from ANOP the research organisation. I'd now like to ask you some questions about drinking and driving ...*

ASK ALL
Q. 1(a) Over the last four months or so, have you seen, heard or read anything about new methods the government is using to deal with drinking and driving in New South Wales?

(5)
YES..1-ASK Q.1(b)
NO...2 } GO TO Q.2
Unsure.....................................3

IF "YES" TO Q.1(a), ASK:
Q. 1(b) What new ways have you become aware of for dealing with drinking and driving? Any others? (DO NOT PROMPT)

(6)
RANDOM BREATH TESTING.....................1
.05 LIMIT.................................2
INCREASED PENALTIES......................3
BREATH TESTING OF DRIVERS AT ACCIDENTS....4
BLOOD TESTING OF DRIVERS ADMITTED TO HOSPITAL...............................5
RANDOM LICENCE CHECKS....................6
OTHER (Specify).......................... [   ]
....
....

ASK ALL
Q. 2 As you may know, random breath testing was introduced into New South Wales on December 17 last year. This means that the police can ask any motorist to take a breath test at any time, even if he or she has not had an accident, has not committed any offence, and has not been driving in a way which would attract police attention. Since December 17 last year:

READ OUT
(a) Have you been pulled over by the police at random and asked to take a breath test - or have you been a passenger in the car when the driver has been asked to take a random breath test?

(7)
YES..1
NO...2
Unsure.....................................3

(b) Have you driven or have you been driven, past police carrying out random breath testing?

(8)
YES..1-ASK Q.3(a,b)
NO...2 } GO TO Q.4(a)
Unsure.....................................3

IF YES TO Q.2(b), ASK:
Q. 3(a) About how often have you driven or have you been driven past police carrying out random breath testing?

(9)
ONCE.......................................1
TWICE......................................2
THREE TIMES................................3
FOUR OR MORE TIMES.........................4
Unsure.....................................5

Q. 3(b) How long is it since you last drove past or were driven past, police carrying out random breath testing?

(10)
A FEW DAYS AGO.............................1
ABOUT A WEEK AGO...........................2
ABOUT A FORTNIGHT AGO......................3
ABOUT A MONTH AGO..........................4
ABOUT 2 MONTHS AGO.........................5
ABOUT 3 MONTHS AGO.........................6
OVER 3 MONTHS AGO..........................7
Unsure.....................................8

ASK ALL
Q. 4(a) Has anyone you know been randomly breath tested?

(11)
YES..1-ASK Q.4(b)
NO...2 } GO TO Q.5
Unsure.....................................3

IF YES TO Q.4(a), ASK:
Q. 4(b) About how many people you know have been randomly breath tested?

(12)
ONE..1
TWO..2
THREE......................................3
FOUR OR MORE...............................4
Unsure.....................................5

ASK ALL
Q. 5 Have you seen, heard or read any publicity about random breath testing?

(13)
YES..1
NO...2
Unsure.....................................3

ASK ALL   (14)
Q. 6(a) Over the past fortnight or so, have you seen or heard
         any advertising about random breath testing?   YES, TV ADS...............................1
         IF YES: Were they TV ads, radio ads or ads in   YES, RADIO ADS............................2 } ASK Q.6(b)
         newspapers?   YES, NEWSPAPER ADS........................3 |
                                                                 NO, NOT SEEN ADS..........................4
IF YES TO Q.6(a), ASK: Unsure....................................5
Q. 6(b) What do you remember from the ads ... What did they say or show you? What was the main message they were trying to get
         across? Anything else?

         .... (15) (16)
         .... ☐   ☐

ASK ALL   (17)
Q. 7   I'd like you to consider the following situation. A person
         is driving home on a weekday after drinking in a hotel for   LOWER.....................................1
         several hours. It is about 10.30 at night and his blood   ABOUT SAME................................2
         alcohol level is above the legal limit. His driving is   HIGHER....................................3
         not obviously affected and he is not breaking any other
         traffic regulations. His trip home takes about 30 minutes
         over surburban main roads. Are his chances of being
         stopped by the police lower, about the same, or higher
         than they were before the introduction of random
         breath testing?

ASK ALL   (18)
Q. 8   Are you a current driver or rider licence holder,
         are you at present disqualified from driving, or are you   CURRENT...................................1 } ASK Q.9
         not a licence holder and not disqualified?   DISQUALIFIED..............................2 |
                                                                    NOT LICENSED..............................3-GO TO DEMOGS

ASK ALL DRIVERS   Q.9   Q.10
Q. 9   From this card (SHOWCARD 1), how would you rate your   (19)   (20)
         chances of being pulled over by the police for a random
         breath test some time in the next month?   EXTREMELY LIKELY.........................1.................1
                                                                  QUITE LIKELY.............................2.................2
ASK ALL DRIVERS   EVEN CHANCE..............................3.................3
Q.10   If you had been asked that question the day random breath
         testing was introduced, how do you think you would   QUITE UNLIKELY...........................4.................4
         have answered? (SHOWCARD 1)   EXTREMELY UNLIKELY.......................5.................5
                                                                  Unsure...................................6.................6

ASK ALL DRIVERS   (21)
Q.11   Which of the following (SHOWCARD 2) most closely   3+ TIMES A DAY............................1 ⎫
         describes your drinking habits?   TWICE A DAY..............................2 |
                                                                   ONCE A DAY...............................3 |
                                                                   NEARLY EVERY DAY.........................4 |
                                                                   3-4 TIMES A WEEK.........................5 | ASK Q.12
                                                                   ONCE/TWICE A WEEK........................6 |
                                                                   2-3 TIMES A MONTH........................7 |
                                                                   ONCE A MONTH.............................8 |
                                                                   LESS THAN ONCE A MONTH...................9 ⎭
                                                                   LESS THAN ONCE A YEAR....................0 ⎫ GO TO DEMOGS
                                                                   NEVER DRINK..............................x ⎭

ASK ALL DRINKERS FROM Q.11   OFFICE USE ONLY   (22) (23)
Q.12   On days that you do drink, how much, on average, do you   ┌──┐┌──┐
         have over the whole day? (PROBE EACH TYPE OF DRINK   NORMAL BEER   └──┘└──┘
         BELOW. RECORD NUMBER OF DRINKS AGAINST SIZE OF GLASS,   (24) (25)
         BOTTLE, ETC.)   ┌──┐┌──┐
                                                                  L.A. BEER   └──┘└──┘
| NORMAL BEER: | | LOW ALCOHOL BEER: | | (26) (27)
|---|---|---|---| ┌──┐┌──┐
| Middies | .... | Middies | .... | WINE   └──┘└──┘
| Schooners | .... | Schooners | .... | (28) (29)
| Large bottles | .... | Large bottles | .... | ┌──┐┌──┐
| Small bottles | .... | Small bottles | .... | PORT/SHERRY   └──┘└──┘
| Cans | .... | Cans | .... | (30) (31)
                                                                                       ┌──┐┌──┐
| TABLE WINE: | | OTHER (Specify) | | SPIRITS   └──┘└──┘
|---|---|---|---| (32) (33)
| Glasses (4oz) | .... | .... | .... | ┌──┐┌──┐
                                                                 OTHER   └──┘└──┘
| PORT/SHERRY: | | .... | .... | (34) (35)
|---|---|---|---| ┌──┐┌──┐
| Glasses (2oz) | .... | .... | .... | TOTAL   └──┘└──┘
| SPIRITS: | | .... | .... |
| Glasses (1oz) | .... | .... | .... |

ASK ALL DRINKERS IN Q.13   (36)
Q.13   Have you ever driven when you felt you had had   YES.......................................1
         too much to drink?   NO..2
                                                                    Unsure....................................3
                                                                    Refused/Won't say.........................4

ASK ALL DRINKERS IN Q.11
Q.14(a) Since random breath testing was brought in just before
         Christmas, has you driven when you felt you had had
         too much to drink?

(37)

YES...1-ASK Q.14(b)
NO..2-ASK Q.14(c,d)
Unsure......................................3-GO TO Q.15
Refused/Won't say...........................4-GO TO Q.15

IF YES TO Q.14(a), ASK:
Q.14(b) About how many times would that be?

(38)

ONCE..1
TWICE.......................................2
THREE TIMES.................................3   GO TO Q.15
FOUR TIMES..................................4
FIVE OR MORE TIMES..........................5
Unsure......................................6

IF NO TO Q.14(a), ASK:
Q.14(c) From this card (SHOWCARD 3), could you choose
         the statement that best describes your reasons
         for not drinking and driving?

Q.14(d) What would be the second most important
         reasons for your not drinking and
         driving?

	Q.14(c) (39)	Q.14(d) (40)
IS WRONG	1	1
LEADS TO ACCIDENTS	2	2
CAUGHT AND PUNISHED	3	3

OTHER (Specify)..........................

Q.14(c)...................................
....

Q.14(d)...................................
....

Unsure...y..........y

ASK ALL DRINKERS IN Q.11
Q.15 When they first brought in random breath testing just before Christmas, what effects did it have on you at the time. From
      this card (SHOWCARD 4) what if anything did you do at the time? (RECORD IN 1ST COLUMN)

Q.16 And what about now ... what effects are random breath testing having on you now? What (SHOWCARD 4) if anything are you
      doing now?

	Q.15 (41)	Q.16 (43)
. Not using the car as much	1	1
. Driving more carefully at all times	2	2
. Stopped driving to places where you will be drinking	3	3
. Drinking at home more often, drinking away from home less	4	4
. Carefully limiting your drinking when driving	5	5
. Stopped drinking altogether when driving	6	6
. Drinking more soft drinks when driving	7	7
. Switched to low alcohol beer when driving	8	8
. Driving more carefully after drinking	9	9
. Using taxis more often after drinking	0	0
. Using public transport more often after drinking	x	x
. Staying overnight after drinking	y	y
	(42)	(44)
. Having someone else drive you home after drinking	1	1
. Sleeping in car instead of driving home after drinking	2	2
. Drinking at places closer to home than before	3	3
. Using special buses or drive home schemes organised by clubs or pubs	4	4
. Have not changed usual behavior	5	5

OTHER (Specify) Q.15..........................

Q.16..........................

ASK ALL DRINKERS IN Q.11
Q.17 There is a legal limit to the amount of alcohol
      a driver can have in his or her blood. Can you tell
      me what that legal limit is?

(45)

LESS THAN .05.............................1
.05.......................................2
.06.......................................3
.07.......................................4
.08.......................................5
MORE THAN .08.............................6
OTHER (Specify)...........................
....
Unsure....................................y

ASK ALL DRINKERS IN Q.11   (46)
Q.18   (In fact the legal limit is .05). Since random   YES.......................................1
       breath testing was brought in just before Christmas,   NO..2
       have you driven when you felt you were over the
       legal limit of .05?   Unsure....................................3

                                                                Refuse/won't say..........................4

ASK ALL DRINKERS IN Q.11   (47)
Q.19   Over the years, about a quarter of a million   YES.......................................1
       people in New South Wales have been convicted for   NO..2
       drinking and driving. Have you ever been
       convicted for drinking and driving?   Unsure....................................3

                                                                Refuse/Won't say..........................4

ASK ALL DRINKERS IN Q.11   (48)
Q.20   Just supposing you were to drink and drive fairly   NOT AT ALL................................1
       regularly, from this card (SHOWCARD 5), about how
       often do you think you could drink and drive over   ONCE OR TWICE.............................2
       the .05 limit without being caught?   ABOUT 5 TIMES.............................3

                                                                ABOUT 10 TIMES............................4

                                                                ABOUT 50 TIMES............................5

                                                                ABOUT 100 TIMES...........................6

                                                                ABOUT 1000 TIMES..........................7

                                                                Unsure....................................8

ASK ALL DRINKERS IN Q.11   (49)
Q.21   I would like you to imagine that you are at a place   EXTREMELY HARD............................1
       with a group of friends, and that everyone at that
       place, that is, all your friends, are all drinking   VERY HARD.................................2
       alcoholic drinks. Now thinking of that situation   QUITE HARD................................3
       where everyone is drinking alcohol, I would like
       you to tell me from this card (SHOWCARD 6) how hard   QUITE EASY................................4
       or easy you personally would find it to drink less   VERY EASY.................................5
       alcohol than your friends?
                                                                EXTREMELY EASY............................6

                                                                OTHER (Specify).......................

                                                               1

                                                                Unsure....................................y

ASK ALL DRINKERS IN Q.11   (50)
Q.22   Now that we have random breath testing, is it easier   EASIER....................................1
       or harder for you to drink less alcohol than your
       friends when they are all drinking alcohol?   HARDER....................................2

                                                                NO DIFFERENCE.............................3

                                                                Unsure....................................4

ASK ALL DRINKERS IN Q.11   (51)
Q.23   From this card (SHOWCARD 7), how would you rate your   DEFINITELY NOT BE CAUGHT..................1
       chances of being caught by the police if you regularly
       drove over the .05 limit (IF WOULDN'T DRIVE OVER .05,   PROBABLY NOT BE CAUGHT....................2
       PROBE: Well, supposing you did ...)?   PROBABLY WOULD BE.........................3

                                                                DEFINITELY WOULD BE.......................4

                                                                Unsure....................................5

ASK ALL DRIVERS IN Q.11   (52)
Q.24   Supposing you were random breath tested by the police   CERTAIN...................................1
       and found to be over the legal limit of .05. How would
       you personally rate your chances of actually being   EXTREMELY LIKELY..........................2
       arrested for drinking and driving? (SHOWCARD 8)   QUITE LIKELY..............................3

                                                                EVEN CHANCE...............................4

                                                                QUITE UNLIKELY............................5

                                                                EXTREMELY UNLIKELY........................6

                                                                Unsure....................................7

       INTERVIEWER: SHOWCARD ORDER USED| 1 - 7 ...1
                     IN Q.24 AND Q.25 | 7 - 1 ...2
ASK ALL DRINKERS IN Q.11   (53)
Q.25   If you were arrested for drinking and driving,   EXTREMELY LIKELY..........................1
       how would you rate your chances personally of
       being let off by the court without any penalty?   QUITE LIKELY..............................2
       (SHOWCARD 9)   EVEN CHANCE...............................3

                                                                QUITE UNLIKELY............................4

                                                                EXTREMELY UNLIKELY........................5

                                                                ZERO......................................6

                                                                Unsure....................................7

ASK ALL DRINKERS IN Q.11   (54)
Q.26   For this question, I would like you to imagine that you
        had been arrested for drinking and driving, and   NO PROBLEM AT ALL.........................1
        that the court had found you guilty and imposed   HARDLY ANY PROBLEM.......................2
        a punishment. <u>Think</u> about what that punishment   A LITTLE PROBLEM.........................3
        would be for <u>you</u>. From this card (SHOWCARD 10), in   A BIG PROBLEM............................4
        general, how big a problem would that punishment   A VERY BIG PROBLEM......................5
        be in your life?
                                                                     Unsure..................................6

ASK ALL DRINKERS IN Q.11   (55)
Q.27   Which punishment would you personally find harsher:
        imprisonment for two weeks, or disqualification from   PRISON..................................1
        driving for six months?   DISQUALIFICATION........................2
                                                                     EQUAL...................................3
                                                                     Unsure..................................4

ASK ALL DRINKERS IN Q.11   (56)
Q.28   If you did drink and then drive, how worried would you be
        about being asked to take a random breath test ...   NOT AT ALL WORRIED......................1
        not at all worried, not very worried, quite worried, or   NOT VERY WORRIED........................2
        very worried?   QUITE WORRIED...........................3
                                                                     VERY WORRIED............................4
                                                                     Unsure..................................5

ASK ALL DRINKERS IN Q.11   (57)
Q.29   How easy or hard is it to actually avoid driving
        past where police are carrying out random breath   VERY EASY...............................1
        testing ... is it very easy, quite easy, quite   QUITE EASY..............................2
        hard or very hard to avoid them?   QUITE HARD..............................3
                                                                     VERY HARD...............................4
                                                                     Unsure..................................5

ASK ALL DRINKERS IN Q.11   (58)
Q.30   If you did drive past where police were carrying out
        random breath testing on your side of the road, how   EXTREMELY LIKELY........................1
        likely is it that you would actually be pulled over   QUITE LIKELY............................2
        and asked to take the test?   EVEN CHANCE.............................3
        (SHOWCARD 11)   QUITE UNLIKELY..........................4
                                                                     EXTREMELY UNLIKELY......................5
                                                                     Unsure..................................6

ASK ALL DRINKERS IN Q.11   (59)
Q.31   In your daily life, from this card (SHOWCARD 12), how
        essential is it for you to be able to drive a car   ESSENTIAL FOR JOB.......................1
        or other motor vehicle?   ESSENTIAL AS NO PUB.TRANS...............2
                                                                     ESSEN.IAL, BUT..........................3
                                                                     USEFUL, NOT ESSENTIAL...................4
                                                                     DON'T NEED TO DRIVE.....................5

DEMOGRAPHICS - ASK ALL
        And now, to make sure we have a good sample, could   What is the highest level of education you
        you tell me your approximate age?   have reached so far?   (63)

| 17-20 | 21-24 | 25-34 | 35-44 | 45-54 | 55-64 | 65+ | Less than 3 years at high school..........1
|-------|-------|-------|-------|-------|-------|-----| 3 or more years at high school............2
| 1 | 2 | 3 | 4 | 5 | 6 | 7 | (60) Gained HSC/L.C./Matric....................3
                                                             Gained Uni degree/College diploma........4
                                                     (61)
        SEX (BY OBSERVATION)   Male...........1   What is your occupation?   (64)
                                      Female.........2
        NO. OF 18+ IN HOUSEHOLD   (62)   WRITE IN:............................
        FROM RANDOM SELECTION GRID

LOCATION
SYDNEY	NEWCASTLE	WOLLONGONG	BATHURST	LISMORE	GOULBURN	WAGGA	TAMWORTH	PARKES/DUBBO
1	2	3	4	5	6	7	8	9	(65)

NAME OF RESPONDENT: Mr/Mrs/Miss/Ms..
ADDRESS:...
.... TELEPHONE NO............................

THIS DOCUMENT IS COPYRIGHT. REPRODUCTION IN WHOLE OR PART IS PROHIBITED WITHOUT THE WRITTEN PERMISSION OF ANOP

INTERVIEWER'S STATEMENT: *I hereby certify that this is a true and accurate record of this interview, and that I have made a
                          thorough check of all responses to questions so as to comply with the survey briefing and instructions.*

....
(INTERVIEWER'S NAME AND SIGNATURE)

DATE OF INTERVIEW:.. *LENGTH OF INTERVIEW*............................... *minutes*

Author Index

Subject Index